YOGA-SŪTRAS OF PATAÑJALI WITH THE EXPOSITION OF VYĀSA

A Translation and Commentary

Volume I—*Samādhi-pāda*

YOGA-SŪTRAS OF PATAÑJALI WITH THE EXPOSITION OF VYĀSA

A Translation and Commentary

Swami Veda Bharati

Volume I—*Samādhi-pāda*

Foreword by
H. H. Swami Rama of the Himalayas

HIMALAYAN INSTITUTE® INDIA

www.himalayaninstitute.in

Himalayan Institute India
Near Nageshwar Mandir
Chatnag, Jhunsi,
Allahabad 211019 (U.P.) India
Phone: +917408434140
Email: info@himalayaninstitute.in

www.HimalayanInstitute.in

06 05 04 03 02 01 00 99 98 6 5

Printed in India 2015

The paper used in this publication meets the minimum requirements of the American National Standard of Information Sciences—Permanence of Paper for Printed Library Materials, ANSI Z39.48-1984.

Library of Congress Cataloging in Publication Data

Patañjali.
Yoga-sutras of Patanjali with the exposition of Vyas.

Bibliography: p.
Includes index.
1. Yoga—Early works I. Vyasa. II. Arya, Usharbudh. III. Title
B132.Y6P267 1985 18 5-7570
ISBN: 0-89389-092-8

ॐ

ओ३म् नमः श्री-त्रिपुर-सुन्दर्यै सहस्रनाम्न्यै।।

हिरण्यगर्भादारब्धां शेष-व्यासादि-मध्यमाम्।
स्वामि-श्री-राम-पादान्तां वन्दे गुरु-परम्पराम्।।

Contents

Acknowledgments *ix*

Foreword *xi*

Spelling and Pronunciation of Sanskrit *xvii*

Abbreviations of Commentaries *xx*

Other Texts Cited *xxi*

General Introduction

Part 1. Prologue 3

Part 2. Overview of Sāṅkhya-yoga 23

Part 3. *Tattva-samāsa-sūtras* 41

***Yoga-sūtras*—Chapter One**
***Samādhi-pāda* [Chapter on Samādhi]**

Compendium of Sūtras and Vyāsa's *Bhāṣhya* 51

Sūtras I.1-I.51 with Vyāsa's Commentary and the Author's Discussion 59

Bibliography 431

Glossary/Index 439

Acknowledgments

My deepest appreciation, profound gratitude and sincerest thanks

to Shree
whose razor-sharp mind carefully balanced between a student's loyalty and an editor's honesty, who took the book through several stages of careful editing and typing, watching for the minutest detail;

to Michael Smith, Fran Manley, Ronald Neuhaus and several others
who read the text for precise details of language and punctuation and helped make it comprehensible;

to Rolf and Mary Gail Sovik
who served as administrators of the Center for Higher Consciousness, organized my time, fed me, washed for me, watched over my health and well-being, and remained at my disposal twenty-four hours a day;

to several patron members of the Center for Higher Consciousness
whose generosity freed me of financial concerns;

to the editors and typesetters of the Himalayan Institute
whose silent devotion and service to the Guru's mission never seeks acknowledgment; and

to Lalita, my wife,
whose silent and unrewarded sacrifices make my work possible.

Lord, make me a servant of thy servants, dāsānudāsaḥ.

Foreword

Yoga is a most ancient science, which has been taught for thousands of years. Patañjali systematized and organized it by formulating 196 aphorisms, which are called the *Yoga-sūtras.* Some scholars say Patañjali was born about 4,000 B.C. and others 400 B.C., but the exact date is unknown. Patañjali was the codifier of yoga science. He was a scientist who practiced and who gathered together the information on yoga and presented it in a concise form. The word *sūtra* actually means "string," and every aphorism is like a single flower on a garland. Patañjali made the sūtras succinct because in ancient times students learned the sayings of the great teachers by heart. This succinctness enabled the students to easily memorize these truths. In those days, there was a very close relationship between the preceptor and the student, who was taught through this oral tradition. Only the competent and accomplished yogis could impart this knowledge to their students.

Patañjali describes the entire philosophy of yoga science in the *Yoga-sūtras,* and the first four sūtras summarize the most important aspects of this science. The first aphorism says, "Now, then, and therefore, yoga science and discipline is being expounded." This means that the student of yoga should understand that without discipline, he cannot tread the path of yoga. Only discipline will help him on the path of enlightenment. The first word of the first aphorism is *atha. Atha* means "now, then, and therefore." It indicates that there is something important that needs to be understood before one practices yoga. In most of the *darśhanas* (schools of philosophy) the word *atha* has been used as the first word at the beginning of such scriptures, and most commentators think that the word is auspicious. In reality, it indicates that the student is prepared, for the preliminaries have been completed. Many students eagerly study from scriptures and they briefly try to practice, but they find it very difficult, and then give up the practice. Thus, they don't make any progress because they have not gone through the preliminary steps of training. The first sūtra means, "Now the student may attain this step." This indicates that the student has already studied philosophy, he has studied the necessary *śhāstras* (scriptures), and now the yoga discipline is being expounded and taught. So the word "now" denotes that the student has already accomplished something. The student or aspirant has already committed himself to the path and has said, "Yes, I'm committed to the path. I'm determined, and I want to follow the discipline. Discipline will assist in my growth; it will help me to attain liberation."

The word *yoga* is very ancient and is found in the Vedas, the most ancient scriptures known to man. It comes from the root *yuj,* "to unite." Yoga is the union of the individual soul with the Absolute One. The student of yoga has the capacity to unite himself with the Cosmic One. He can do it if he is fully prepared, determined, and desirous, and if his mind is made one-pointed. The modern student asks whether he has to renounce the world to attain the goal of yogic science. Yoga science says that while one does not have to renounce the world literally, there are conditions required for all *sādhana* (spiritual practice). Sādhana requires that discipline must be systematically applied. Yoga science does not lay down commandments, but it requires commitments. If one is committed to know the truth, and has the capacity and the ability, then he can attain the highest state of wisdom, *samādhi.* When no worldly fetters bind one, when nothing disturbs the mind, then one knows how to live in the world and yet remain nonattached. Yoga science recommends neither renunciation from the world nor excessive involvement in the world. Yoga requires that the student avoid these two extremes. Patañjali leads one to know the real Self, whether one is a renunciate or a householder. One simply has to act in a way so that the goal, which is contentment, can be attained. Absolute contentment means a state of equanimity, tranquility, and equilibrium.

The purpose of this science is to help students know their potential and understand the various levels of their being, so that finally they reach the highest state. The teachings of yoga science are threefold: how to live within oneself, how to live in the external world, and at the same time how to link the two and create a bridge. Then one is liberated here and now.

The second sūtra provides the definition of yoga: *Yogaśh chitta vṛtti nirodhaḥ,* "Yoga is perfect control over the mind and its modifications." That is the definition of yoga. But there is another message to the sūtra; the other meaning is the assurance that with the help of yogic practices, as explained by Patañjali, a student can definitely have such control over his mind and its modifications.

The definition given by Patañjali explains the ultimate goal of yoga science. Yoga science is related to the mind, and mental life in its totality. By practicing the method of yoga, one can attain perfect control over the mind and its modifications. Yoga psychology is the most ancient school of psychology, which describes systematically, from the very beginning, how to know, analyze, and direct the mind, so that one can attain the purpose of life. The mind is one's finest instrument. The body is the grossest instrument, and breath is another, somewhat finer, instrument. The senses are also considered instruments, but mind is the finest instrument of all. A yogi is he who has complete control over his body, senses and mind. When he has accomplished that, he has the capacity to unite himself with the Ultimate Truth.

It's not that the student has to learn something from outside himself, that he has to acquire something. Patañjali says that the student must learn *abhyāsa* and *vairāgya,* practice and nonattachment. The mind presents barriers to practice and nonattachment. It stands like a wall between the student and his goal in life. But that same mind can be made an instrument for the attainment of his goal.

First, one has to know the mind thoroughly with all its modifications. Once the mind is understood, then it does not create obstacles for the student. A yogi is one who knows the technique of uniting himself with the Ultimate Reality. Thus, the second sūtra explains yoga science; it is a definition of yoga science.

The third sūtra explains that when one has control over the mind and its modifications, he establishes himself in his essential nature. Man's essential nature is peace, happiness, and bliss. The ordinary person forgets his essential nature and identifies with his thoughts and the forms and objects of the world. Patañjali says that the essential nature of a human being is distinct from his body, breath, senses, and mind. He says that the mind and its mental processes prevent one from knowing the Absolute. When one learns not to identify himself with the thought forms or objects of the mind, he establishes himself in his essential nature. In the yogic process one must purify the unconscious mind and then go beyond the mire of delusion created by the unconscious and its *saṁskāras* to get to the fountainhead of light and life, the center of consciousness within. That is the meaning of the third sūtra.

The fourth sūtra states that if one has not attained perfect control over the mind and its modifications, then he identifies himself with the thought waves and with the objects of the world and thus remains ignorant of his true nature. All pain and misery is the result of ignorance. When one removes that ignorance, and dispels the darkness, then he attains the state of equilibrium, which brings freedom from the bondage of karma and pain. One has to learn to be free, to become master of himself. That mastery is attained by practicing the yogic techniques taught in the aphorisms. Mind and its modifications can be perfectly analyzed and controlled, and then mind can be directed according to one's aim in life.

The *Yoga-sūtras* teach not just a philosophy but, most importantly, a specific method to practice. By studying them, a student can understand that he is fully equipped to attain samādhi, the highest state of tranquility, the center of consciousness within. The student acquires self-confidence by studying Patañjali's sūtras because the sūtras say that the student can cultivate the power of concentration and use it to remove the obstacles to enlightenment, which cause all suffering.

Most people desire to enjoy the world, but for lack of inner strength and a one-pointed mind, they are not able to do so. One has to acquire the knowledge of how to control the mind and its modifications through practice. Practice and commitment to a discipline come first. When the student starts practicing, he experiences something which is supramental, and such extraordinary experiences lead him to the deeper dimensions of life. One should establish himself firmly on his meditation seat and make the body steady and still on that seat, regularly—every day at the same time. Steady posture, though a preliminary practice, is very important, for it helps the student in attaining the meditative state. Gradually one should increase the practice time, so he can remain still for a longer period. After one accomplishes this, then he will find that the breath is distracting the mind. Then one learns to breathe harmoniously. Soon one will think in a calm and serene way. In this way one can go beyond body, senses, and mind. One can go beyond the reservoir of the impressions and *saṁskāras* stored in the unconscious mind, and finally attain the center of consciousness. This is an inner journey which one can accomplish without movement. Here on this path, one has to be steady, to be regular, to be punctual, and gradually to work with the body, breath, and the conscious and unconscious mind. Then one can go beyond intellect to the center of consciousness.

This is called the path from the gross self to the subtlest Self. The moment one completely devotes himself with one-pointedness, he is at the center of consciousness. The student becomes one with the center of consciousness, as a drop of water or a river meets and becomes one with the ocean. Slowly the individual self, which is like a ripple in the vast ocean of bliss, becomes one and the same with the ocean. So the *Yoga-sūtras* of Patañjali teach the student how to attain samādhi in this lifetime if he steadily practices and works to control the mind.

Pandit Dr. Usharbudh Arya has written a commentary on the *Yoga-sūtras* in a very scholarly manner. No doubt this commentary will be beneficial to researchers and to students who are eager to study the ancient commentaries of Vyāsa, Bhoja, Vāchaspati, and other commentators. Dr. Arya is both a scholar and an accomplished meditator. I have not come across any other commentary that explains the *Yoga-sūtras* in such a clear and brilliant manner.

Swami Rama

The Spelling and Pronunciation of Sanskrit Letters and Words

Sanskrit vowels are generally the same pure vowel sounds found in Italian, Spanish, or French. The consonants are generally pronounced as in English.

a	org*a*n, s*u*m
ā	f*a*ther
ai	*ai*sle
au	s*au*erkr*au*t
b	*b*ut
bh	a*bh*or
ch	*ch*ur*ch*
chh	chur*chh*ill
ḍ	*d*ough
d	*d*ough (slightly toward the *th* sound of *th*ough)
ḍh	a*dh*ere
dh	a*dh*ere (slightly toward the *theh* sound of brea*the h*ere)
e	pr*ey*
g	*g*o
gh	do*gh*ouse
ḥ	[slight aspiration of preceding vowel]
h	*h*ot
i	*i*t
ī	pol*i*ce
j	*j*ump
jh	lod*geh*ouse
k	*k*id
kh	wor*kh*orse
ḷ	no English equivalent; a short vowel pronounced somewhat like the *lry* in revelry
l	*l*ug

ṁ	[resonant nasalization of preceding vowel]
m	*m*ud
ṅ	si*ng*
ṇ	u*n*der
ñ	pi*ñ*ata
n	*n*o
o	n*o*
p	*p*ub
ph	u*ph*ill
ṛ	no English equivalent; a simple vowel *r,* such as appears in many Slavonic languages
ṝ	the same pronunciation as ṛ, more prolonged
r	*r*um
śh	*sh*awl (pronounced with a slight whistle; German *sp*rechen)
ṣh	*sh*un
s	*s*un
ṭ	*t*omato
t	wa*t*er
ṭh	an*th*ill
th	*Th*ailand
u	p*u*sh
ū	r*u*de
v	*v*odka (midway between *w* and *v*)
y	*y*es

Vowels. Every vowel is either long or short. The dipthongs *e, ai, o,* and *au* are always long; *ḷ* is always short. Long *a, i, u,* and *ṛ* are indicated by a horizontal line over the vowel. The long form of a vowel is pronounced twice as long as the short form.

Consonants. Sanskrit has many aspirated consonants, that is, consonants pronounced with a slight *h* sound: *bh chh ḍh dh gh jh kh ph ṭh th.* These aspirated consonants should be pronounced distinctly. The retroflex consonants, *ḍ ḍh ṇ ṣh ṭ ṭh,* are pronounced with a hitting sound, as the tip of the tongue is curled back to the ridge of the hard palate. The dentals, *d dh n t th,* are pronounced with the tip of the tongue touching the upper teeth.

Accentuation. There is no strong accentuation of syllables. The general rule is to stress the next-to-last syllable of a word, if that is long. A syllable is long if (*a*) it has a long vowel or (*b*) its vowel is followed by more than one consonant. If the next-to-last syllable of a word is short, then the syllable before that receives the stress.*

*For a better understanding of Sanskrit pronunciation the student is referred to the author's basic Sanskrit cassette tape course.

Abbreviations of Commentaries

Code	Author	Title
AD	Ananta-deva Pandit	*Pada-chandrikā*
BB	Bangali Baba	*The Yogasūtra of Patañjali*
BG	Bhāvāgaṇeśha	*Pradīpikā* or *Pradīpa*
BM	Baladeva Miśhra	*Yoga-pradīpikā*
BR	Bhojarāja (Bhojadeva)	*Rāja-mārttaṇḍa* (also known as *Bhoja-vṛtti*)
HA	Hariharānanda Āraṇya	*Bhāsvatī*
HA(E)	Hariharānanda Āraṇya	*Yoga Philosophy of Patanjali* (English commentary)
MA	Mādhavāchārya	*Pātañjala-darśhanam* chapter of the *Sarva-darśhana-saṅgraha*
NB	Nāgojī Bhaṭṭa (Nāgeśha)	*Laghvī*
NBB	Nāgojī Bhaṭṭa (Nāgeśha)	*Bṛhatī*
NTB	Nārāyaṇa Tīrtha	*Sūtrārtha-bodhinī*
NTC	Nārāyaṇa Tīrtha	*Yoga-siddhānta-chandrikā*
RP	Rāma Prasāda	*The Yoga Sutras of Patanjali* (English translation)
RS	Rāghavānanda Sarasvatī	*Pātañjala-rahasya*
RY	Rāmānanda Yati	*Maṇi-prabhā*
Sh	Śhaṅkara-bhagavat-pāda	*Pātañjala-yoga-sūtra-bhāṣhya-vivaraṇa*
SS	Sadāśhivendra Sarasvatī	*Yoga-sudhākara*
VB	Vijñāna-bhikṣhu	*Yoga-vārttika* and *Yoga-sāra-saṅgraha*
VM	Vāchaspati Miśhra	*Tattva-vaiśhāradī*

Other Texts Cited

Abbreviated

BhG *Bhagavad-gītā*
TSS *Tattva-samāsa-sūtras*
YS *Yoga-sūtras of Patañjali with Vyāsa's Bhāṣhya*

Non-Abbreviated

Aitareya Upaniṣhad
Bhāgavata-purāṇa
Brahma-bindu Upaniṣhad
Brahma-sūtras
Brahma-vidyā Upaniṣhad
Bṛhadāraṇyaka Upaniṣhad
Bṛhad-yogi-yajñavalkya-smṛti
Chhāndogya Upaniṣhad
Haṁsa Upaniṣhad
Kaṭha Upaniṣhad
Kauṣhītaki Upaniṣhad
Kena Upaniṣhad
Kūrma-purāṇa
Lawbook of Manu
Mahābhārata (Mokṣha-dharma-parvan)
Mahābhāṣhya of Patañjali
Mahopaniṣhad
Maitrī Upaniṣhad
Māṇḍūkya Upaniṣhad
Muṇḍaka Upaniṣhad
Nyāya-sūtra of Gotama
Praśhna Upaniṣhad
Ṛg-veda
Sāṅkhya-kārikā
Śhvetāśhvatara Upaniṣhad
Vāyu-purāṇa
Viṣhṇu-purāṇa
Yajur-veda
Yoga-vāsiṣhṭha

General Introduction

Part 1

Prologue

If all the vast traditions of India's philosophies and literatures were to vanish and the *Yoga-sūtras* of Patañjali alone were to be saved, each of those philosophies and literatures could in time be created again. They could be created again not because their details or even basic formulas appear in the *Yoga-sūtras,* but because these sūtras form the manual of the yoga practice, the culmination of which is that process of intuitive knowledge which alone constituted the source of almost all of India's philosophies and literatures. The founders of all Indian sciences such as physics, chemistry, mathematics, astronomy, medicine, archery, polity, poetics, dance, music, dramaturgy, cosmology or metaphysics were all *ṛṣhis,* those who have entered the state of *samādhi* and thereafter brought forth a given science of their choice because of their compassion for human beings. It is made very clear in the sūtras that through the process of samādhi one may receive any or all branches of knowledge, which may then be revealed to the world. While thus serving as a conduit for such worldly knowledge one may yet dwell in a Consciousness which transcends such intuitive knowledge. The *Yoga-sūtras* teach the methods for the mastery of both; therefore one may easily conclude that they contain the seed of Indian sciences and philosophies as well as the Indian spirituality—this last forming the link between science and philosophy. If there were no more India in the geography of the world, if the highest Himalayan peak were submerged under the ocean, if every Indian language and text were to perish completely, but if there were to survive one single yogi who has reached samādhi, all the Vedas, Upaniṣhads and the *Bhagavad-gītā* would again flow from his mouth—indeed in a new form—and, to repeat, all the principles of *āyur-veda,* dance, drama, music, medicine, dramaturgy, poetics and the rest would be re-created. A whole new civilisation paralleling the experience of India's civilisation would come to exist and would nourish ever-fresh streams of spirituality in all the then-existing or future civilisations of the world. It is not that the sūtras by themselves would produce this effect, but the practical guidance given therein would bring forth in an aspirant that realization of knowledge, power and wisdom which, when well wielded, creates civilisations. This can be attested to by looking at the benevolent changes that have occurred in civilisations to which yoga practice and philosophy were introduced from time to time and in various guises and forms. There is insufficient space here for a detailed study of this history.

It is therefore essential that a translation and explanation of the *Yoga-sūtras* of Patañjali be made available, which will

- address its subject matter from within the initiatory tradition of the Himalayan masters, the founders and the continuing authoritative teachers of yoga science,
- incorporate the essentials of information and exposition given in the exegetical tradition of all past commentators whose works are available, and
- remain true to the basic tenets of the formal Sāṅkhya-yoga school of philosophy.

This task has been undertaken in the translation and commentary being presented here. Before going further with an apologia for this work, it is essential to review briefly the primary sources for the study of the *Yoga-sūtras*.

The tradition of India's philosophical lineages is lost in antiquity. According to one Tantric text (*Śhrī-vidyārṇava*) there were seventy-one teachers from Kapila, the founder of Sāṅkhya, to the greatest proponent of Vedānta, Śhankarāchārya,[1] who taught at the end of the seventh and beginning of the eighth century A.D.; and from Śhankara to the present day a lineage of up to seventy-six teachers has been enumerated. If this appears to be a long time, the reader might find interesting the fact that in approximately 1400 B.C. the *Bṛhadāraṇyaka Upaniṣhad* (VI.5.1-4) enumerated sixty-six generations of teachers up to that time. Patañjali in his work on grammar speaks of eighty-four thousand *ṛṣhis*. Within the Indian tradition it is almost impossible to assign a date to the *ṛṣhis*, for they are custodians and conduits of a perennial knowledge which is revealed repeatedly in each cycle of creation. They are self-authoritative and their work is internally self-evident (*svataḥ-pramāṇa*), requiring no other authority to approve it and not measurable by any yardstick external to divine revelation, but serving as the measure for others.

Both Patañjali and Vyāsa are regarded by the traditions as *ṛṣhis*, their words equally authentic. In the lineage of the yoga philosophy the two names have been inseparably coupled together so that in spite of the existence of later independent commentaries the word *Yoga-sūtra* calls forth the name of Vyāsa in the mind. The association is strengthened even more when some of Patañjali's words in his work on grammar, the *Mahābhāṣhya*, echo those of Vyāsa's commentary on the *Yoga-sūtras* or vice versa.

The texts in the sūtra style bear no resemblance to any other genre of writing in any tradition. The word *sūtra* is often translated as "aphorism." However, an aphorism can be read and understood on its own. A sūtra is often unintelligible by itself. It is always, like a mantra,[2] perhaps only slightly less, in need of an exposition. It is

1. This also might raise the question as to a possible confusion of Sāṅkhya and Vedānta lineages. So far as the knowledge of Ultimate Reality and Truth is concerned, the lineage is all one. One of the titles held by the Śhankarāchāryas up to this day is "Teacher and Protector of the threefold Sāṅkhya." One particular monastic seat of the Dashanami monastic order of the followers of Śhankara, the Mahānirvāni sect at Prayag, considers Kapila as the incarnate form of the deity to be worshipped at this particular seat. Kapila, it should be noted, is one of the twenty-four major incarnations of God in the traditions of India.

2. For details of the inspirational process in the revelation of a mantra see the author's work *Mantra and Meditation* (Honesdale, Pa.: Himalayan International Institute of Yoga Science and Philosophy, 1981).

an extremely succinct statement of a truth which has been realized by a *ṛṣhi* in the state of samādhi. In other words, the shortness of a sūtra is not, as is made out by many modern scholars, only a mnemonic device because it is taught in an oral tradition. It is, however, certainly both an inspired utterance and a mnemonic formula in need of much background information. Such information was imparted to close disciples within the tradition in day after day of study. The teacher sat on a little elevated seat, perhaps under a tree or in a mud hut or by the daily, ritual sacred fire. The disciple sat intent facing the teacher maintaining the same posture throughout the session. The slightest movement on his part was considered an interruption. He had no tape recorders or notebooks. Only through his immense power of concentration did he remember all that was taught. Later he recited the lesson to himself during *svādhyāya* sessions to imprint them on his memory. Furthermore there were either separate experiential sessions or sometimes the guru might flash an experience into the consciousness of a select disciple alone while enunciating the rules orally to the less prepared. This is the experience of select disciples even now. And even now it is thus that a few close disciples have learnt at the feet of a guru. Among the disciples thus taught, the most advanced ones composed a commentary, which may be either a

vṛtti: word-for-word explanation of the sūtra alone, or
bhāṣhya: including much background and experiential information, showing the connection of many sūtras to each other, refuting the views of opponents, adding many "fillers" needed to render the sūtra comprehensible.

A *bhāṣhya* composed by a realized scholar (*āchārya*) may be fairly lengthy, such as Śhankara's *Bhāṣhya* on the *Brahma-sūtras* of the Vedānta philosophy. One taught by a *ṛṣhi* is often only slightly less succinct than the sūtra itself, requiring another commentary or gloss (*ṭīkā*) by later scholars. Vyāsa's *Bhāṣhya* is in this latter category, with numerous *ṭīkās* thereupon, which may need further sub-glosses (*upa-ṭīkās*).

The *vṛttis, bhāṣhyas* and *ṭīkās* require not only that one should be taught within the tradition of the school so that the in-school information and, in the case of yoga, experience will be made available but also that the commentator will be familiar with that special branch of knowledge which was developed specifically to establish the rules of the sūtra interpretation. The rules were developed especially (*a*) in the schools of grammar, (*b*) in the Mīmāṁsā philosophy that deals with the interpretation of Vedic utterances, (*c*) in the Nyāya schools of logic, and (*d*) within each school of philosophy for its own development and later interpretation. A commentator succeeds in his work of interpretation only to the degree to which he has been immersed (*niṣhṇāta*) in these sources and methods. It is regrettable that many commentators on the *Yoga-sūtras,* whether writing in Sanskrit or in the modern languages, are sadly lacking in one or the other of these qualifications.

It may be argued that, unlike the schools of Vedānta, Mīmāṁsā and Nyāya systems of philosophy, the Sāṅkhya and Yoga systems have no continuing ancient schools where the in-school knowledge may be imparted. This may be agreed to in the case of Sāṅkhya, but Yoga is a living school—if there is any—and the masters continue to teach the *Yoga-sūtras* in the ashrams and cave monasteries in an unbroken lineage, primarily as an experiential discipline because Yoga philosophy exists only on the basis of its practices. Because the categories of Sāṅkhya philosophy are so closely allied to the Yoga system, the Sāṅkhya tradition has survived as a supportive school in association with Yoga. The Yoga school of philosophy is often referred to as Sāṅkhya-yoga, but a note of caution must be maintained in doing so. Not all the categories of Sāṅkhya are used in Yoga, as even a cursory comparison of the *Tattva-samāsa-sūtras* and the *Yoga-sūtras* will show. The categories of Sāṅkhya philosophy are employed practically by all the schools of Indian philosophy to a greater or lesser degree. They are employed more in Yoga philosophy; that is all there is to Yoga philosophy being termed Sāṅkhya-yoga. Sāṅkhya philosophy proper has its own independent existence and does not refer to much of the practical system of Yoga and cannot return the compliment by calling itself Sāṅkhya-yoga. The Yoga philosophy, both in Patañjali's work by itself and as expounded by Vyāsa, does depend on parts of the Sāṅkhya system and even gives it a new interpretation. It does not thereby lose its independent existence as a separate school of philosophy. It is thus that Vyāsa's commentary is called

> *Sāṅkhya-pravachana-bhāṣhya:* An Exposition That Enunciates Sāṅkhya.

Sāṅkhya-pravachana ("Enunciation of Sāṅkhya") is an alternative title of the *Yoga-sūtras.*

It is not, therefore, that "Vyāsa . . . often foist[s] on Yoga the philosophy of Sāṅkhya"[3] or that one needs to "combat the overpowering influence exercised by Vyāsa's scholium,"[4] but rather that Vyāsa, having fully mastered both the Yoga and Sāṅkhya systems, clarifies Patañjali's work with regard to both its Yoga and the relevant parts of its Sāṅkhya contents—but within the context of Yoga. The later *vṛttis* like that of Bhoja are excellent in that they give a word-for-word breakdown of the sūtras, but the scope of philosophical knowledge as well as experiential authenticity is often lacking in them.

It is not our purpose in this prologue to attempt even a scant discussion of the scholarly problems attendant upon the philosophy and textual composition or even dates of the authorship of the *Yoga-sūtras* and the *Sāṅkhya-pravachana-bhāṣhya,* the *Bhāṣhya,* in short. Suffice it to say that like much of the tradition in India we regard the works of Patañjali and Vyāsa as a single composite whole, a single text the two parts of which complement each other and on which alone rests the authority of all other *vṛttis* and *ṭīkās* because it is thus that the tradition of the Himalayan masters would have it.

3. J. W. Hauer, quoted by Georg Feuerstein, *The Yoga-Sūtra of Patañjali: An Exercise in the Methodology of Textual Analysis* (New Delhi: Arnold-Heinemann, 1979), p. 25.

4. Georg Feuerstein, Preface to *The Philosophy of Classical Yoga* (New York: St. Martin's Press, 1980; Manchester: Manchester University Press, 1980), p. ix.

It is also not our purpose to produce a critical edition of the texts of the *Yoga-sūtras*. Although some sūtras do have variant readings as found in manuscripts and commentaries, for our purpose we have simply accepted the renderings of Vyāsa and Vāchaspati Miśhra.

Now, let us briefly introduce the various commentaries and their authors:

1. (A) *Tattva-vaiśhāradī* (literally, "Expert Exposition of the Fundamentals"), a *ṭīkā* by Vāchaspati Miśhra, is the one most important work after the *Bhāṣhya* of Vyāsa. Vāchaspati Miśhra (VM) was born towards the end of the eighth century A.D., and in addition to *Tattva-vaiśhāradī* on Yoga, wrote commentaries on Sāṅkhya, Nyāya and the Vedānta systems. A savant of unique qualifications, he did not attempt to establish a philosophical system of his own and was content to attempt a lucid explanation of whichever text or philosophical system he was writing on. It does not appear that he was an accomplished yogi, but his commentary on Vyāsa is still the most helpful one. We have, therefore, incorporated most of his explanations in our discussions.

(B) *Pātañjala-rahasya* ("The Secret of Patañjali's System") is a sub-commentary (*upa-ṭīkā*) on VM's work by Rāghavānanda Sarasvatī (RS) of uncertain but definitely recent date. It attempts to explain arbitrarily chosen phrases from VM, especially on the points of grammar and the procedures of formal logic. Here and there it has provided helpful hints to add to our own discussions.

2. (A) *Yoga-vārttika*[5] ("Exposition on Yoga") of Vijñāna-bhikṣhu (VB), born in the sixteenth century A.D., is considered the second most important commentary (*ṭīkā*) on Vyāsa. VB is said to have authored sixteen works on widely ranging schools and topics of philosophy. One of his main contributions is his attempt to establish the points of unity between dualist Sāṅkhya and monist Vedānta, with the result that the authorities of both schools tend to disown

5. The term *vārttika* means an aphoristic statement that takes into account the stated, unstated-but-implied, and difficult-to-understand points of an original sūtra. The title of VB's work, however, uses the term very broadly.

him. In his commentary on Vyāsa he tries to read Vedānta into the *Yoga-sūtras,* and in doing so, distorts the original intent of Patañjali and Vyāsa. For example, his theory that *puruṣha* is a recipient of reflections from *prakṛti* is totally against the tenets of Sāṅkhya-yoga philosophy. In order to support his views on many issues, he quotes copiously from other texts such as the Upaniṣhads, *Bhagavad-gītā* and the Purāṇas. Only in the discussions on the first few sūtras have we examined his peculiar views; thereafter we have ignored his argumentations. But we have incorporated what he says that is supportive of the intent of Patañjali and Vyāsa.

(B) *Pradīpikā* or *Pradīpa* ("That Which Sheds Light"), the *vṛtti* by VB's disciple, Bhāvāgaṇeśha (BG), summarizes VB's commentary adding some observations of its own. We have accorded BG's views the same consideration as those of VB himself.

(C) Nāgojī Bhaṭṭa or Nāgeśha (NB) was perhaps the greatest learned man of the latter part of the sixteenth century. His works on grammar, the philosophy of grammar, Vedānta and so forth are considered definitive, and are studied not merely as commentaries but as original works. There are two commentaries (*vṛttis*) by him on Patañjali:

(i) *Laghvī* (NB), the shorter one, which seems to be a summary of VB's work with few observations of his own.

(ii) *Bṛhatī* (NBB), the longer one, which incorporates the salient points of *Laghvī* with much additional discussion.

With his own profound scholarship of Vedānta it was natural for him to follow VB's lead in trying to synthesize the dualist and the monist systems. Ignoring again this aspect of his work, our discussion takes into account his explanations of the Sāṅkhya-yoga view proper. NB begins his larger commentary (NBB) by stating that his purpose is to resolve the controversy between Vedānta and Yoga. Even though he and BG for the most part echo VB, they are pronounced Vedāntins and try throughout to reconcile the path of knowledge (*jñāna*) as taught by Vedānta with the teachings of Patañjali and Vyāsa. To this end they often quote such verses as:

> Knowledge and yoga are taught to be separate only by the foolish and not by the wise. . . . Only he sees truth who sees knowledge and yoga to be one.
>
> *Bhagavad-gītā* V.4,5

3. *Rāja-mārttaṇḍa* ("The Royal Sun"), also known as *Bhoja-vṛtti,* is by the savant king Bhojadeva, or Bhojarāja (BR), 1019-1054 A.D. He was an accomplished poet, a theoretician of poetry and an author on many sciences such as architecture. Of the royal patrons of arts, poetry, philosophy and the sciences, his name comes among the first. His *vṛtti* is on Patañjali, and is almost totally independent, although it incorporates some of Vyāsa's exposition. It is a work, as a *vṛtti* has to be, with only brief argumentation here and there, and carries the force of a personal conviction and, without exaggeration, of a personal experience of yoga.

4. Nārāyaṇa Tīrtha (fourteenth century) is a unique commentator, who does not depend on Vyāsa. He was a scholar in Vallabhāchārya's tradition, which incorporated some of the Vedānta views into the context of *bhakti* (devotion and surrender) to a divine incarnation, namely Krishna. NT has written two commentaries:

(A) *Sūtrārtha-bodhinī* ("That Which Helps the Understanding of the Meaning of Sūtras") (NTB), a *vṛtti*, is the shorter of the two, with succinct remarks on the words in the sūtra.

(B) *Yoga-siddhānta-chandrikā* ("Moonlight on the Tenets of Yoga") (NTC), a *bhāṣhya,* is the more detailed commentary.

NTC not only tries to give the *Yoga-sūtras* a perspective of *bhakti*-yoga but also fills in much information on other systems of yoga, such as details of the *kundalinī* and *chakras* as well as the various techniques of *hatha*-yoga. In other words, it shows the connections of all the systems of yoga with the *Yoga-sūtras*. The information given on these systems is not anything unfamiliar to the student of yoga; but to show which sūtras contain the seeds of which tenets and techniques of those systems is a very important contribution. In our discussion we have omitted these details from NTC, but an appendix will be added to the end of Chapter 4 to indicate the seeds of the various systems as found in the *Yoga-sūtras*.

5. (A) Rāmānanda Yati (RY) (sixteenth century) wrote *Maṇi-prabhā* ("The Lustre of Jewels"), a brief *ṭīkā* on Vyāsa.

(B) Sadāśhivendra Sarasvatī (SS) (eighteenth century) wrote *Yoga-sudhākara* ("The Moon of Yoga").

(C) Ananta-deva Pandit (AD) (nineteenth century) wrote *Pada-chandrikā* ("Moonlight on Words"), which for the most part scans the *Rāja-mārttaṇḍa* of Bhojarāja.

(D) Baladeva Miśhra (BM) (twentieth century) summarizes Vāchaspati's work in *Yoga-pradīpikā.*

All of these were aspiring *sādhakas* who have often paraphrased from the work of previous commentators. The works of SS, AD and BM are difficult to place as to whether they are *vṛttis* or *ṭīkās*. However, in places they do provide delightful, original insights; and this is especially true of RY's work, which is the most detailed of the four and shows the mark of a profound writer with some deep spiritual experience.

6. Hariharānanda Āraṇya (HA) (nineteenth and twentieth centuries) wrote *Bhāsvatī* ("The Luminous One"). He was responsible for reviving the Sāṅkhya teaching by establishing a school for that purpose. He wrote many independent works on Sāṅkhya in Sanskrit. *Bhāsvatī* is a lucid commentary meant for the layman not interested in the disputations of dogma. It adheres strictly to the original Sāṅkhya-yoga views without attempting compromises with any other schools of philosophy and totally ignores the syncretic approach of VB et al. Of course, HA's insights have been incorporated into our discussions.

7. In an entirely different category comes a very detailed commentary attributed to Śhankara (Sh). *Pātañjala-yoga-sūtra-bhāṣhya-vivaraṇa* ("An Exposition on the *Bhāṣhya*") is a work explaining Vyāsa's *Bhāṣhya* and is not so overly Vedāntic as to becloud the Sāṅkhya tenets. Because of its originality it could easily be called a *bhāṣhya* in its own right. Any efforts to prove that it is a work of the first Śhankarāchārya are feeble; obviously it was composed by one of the later Śhankarāchāryas. In spite of its complete originality

and importance we have taken no note of it in our discussions because to do so would double the size of the present book and also because Trevor Leggett's verbatim translation[6] is most accurate and reliable.

The foregoing are the commentaries in Sanskrit, some of which have been published in numerous editions with footnotes provided by Sanskrit scholars.[7] In addition there exist at least the following summaries of the philosophy of Patañjali:

1. The chapter on Patañjali's philosophy in Mādhava's *Sarva-darśhana-saṅgraha* (MA) ("Compendium of All Philosophies")

2. *Yoga-sāra-saṅgraha* ("Collection of the Essence of Yoga") of Vijñāna-bhikṣhu,[8] an independent treatise summarizing VB's interpretation of Patañjali's philosophy

3. The chapter on Patañjali's philosophy in the Jaina teacher Hari Bhadra Suri's eighth century A.D. work *Ṣhaḍ-darśhana-samucchaya* ("Compendium of Six Philosophies") and Gunaratna's commentary thereupon[9]

4. The chapter on Patañjali's philosophy in the Jaina teacher Rājaśhekhara's *Ṣhaḍ-darśhana-samucchaya* ("Compendium of Six Philosophies")[10]

6. Trevor Leggett, *Śaṅkara on the Yoga-sūtra-s: The Vivaraṇa sub-commentary to Vyāsa-bhāṣya on the Yoga-sūtra-s of Patañjali*, vol. 1, *Samādhi;* vol. 2, *Means* (London: Routledge and Kegan Paul, 1981, 1983).

7. The following minor commentaries were not available at the time of writing: (1) Balarāma Udāsīna's *Commentary on the Yoga-sutras*, ed. K. B. R. Sinha (Bankipore: 1867, 1897); (2) Krishna-vallabhāchārya's *Kiraṇa*, a sub-commentary on Bhojarāja's work, ed. Shveta-vaikuntha Shastri and Narayana Sharana Shastri (Banaras: 1939). The titles of sixteen other commentaries which are not available have been listed by Dr. Nalini Shukla in her *Pātañjali-yoga-sūtra kā vivechanātmak evaṁ tulanātmak adhyayan* (A critical and comparative study of Pātañjala-yoga-sūtra; in Hindi) (Kanpur: Shakti-yogāśhram and Nalini Shukla, 1975).

8. Readers may consult the excellent English translation of this text by Ganganatha Jha (Madras, India: Theosophical Publishing House, 1933).

9. For details of published editions see Karl H. Potter, comp., *Bibliography of Indian Philosophies*, rev. ed., vol. 1 of *The Encyclopedia of Indian Philosophies*, published for the American Institute of Indian Studies by Motilal Banarsidass (Delhi, 1979), pp. 184 and 329. The forthcoming sixth volume of the encyclopedia, entitled *Yoga Philosophy*, will contain more detailed information on yoga texts.

10. Ibid., p. 198.

5. The chapter on Patañjali's philosophy in Rāma-bhadra Dīkṣhita's "Ṣhaḍ-darśhana-siddhānta-saṅgraha" ("Collection of the Doctrines of the Six Philosophies"), never published, only a manuscript in the Tanjore Library

The first two have been taken into account in our discussions on the first few sūtras only. Mādhava's work will be used in helping to provide a final summary of Patañjali's philosophy at the end of Chapter 4. One and only one thorough study comparing the views of all these commentators on every conceivable topic of the *Yoga-sūtras* has ever been made. Unfortunately for our readers it is in Hindi.[11]

There exist a number of unpublished Sanskrit commentaries on the *Yoga-sūtras* in manuscript form, but these were not available at the time of this writing. It is also most probable that many ancient commentaries have been lost to arson by Muslim conquerors, discontinuity of a line of teachers and neglect by owners, which has always provided ancient books as a meal for termites. One example of a lost commentary is that of a versified version from which Alberuni translated into Arabic.[12]

There have been numerous translations of the *Yoga-sūtras* into English, from J. R. Ballentyne (1852) to Georg Feuerstein (1980). Most of these translations include Vyāsa's *Bhāṣhya.* Vāchaspati's commentary, *Tattva-vaiśhāradī,* was translated twice, Bhoja's *Rāja-mārttaṇḍa* once, and Yati's *Maṇi-prabhā* once. Trevor Leggett's recent translation of Śhankara's *Vivaraṇa* has been mentioned above. A complete list of these publications can be found in the indexes provided in numerous scholarly publications[13] on the *Yoga-sūtras.*

11. Vimla Karṇāṭak, *A Critical Study of the Patanjala-yoga-sutra in the Light of Its Commentators* (in Hindi), Banaras Hindu University Sanskrit Series no. 10, 1974.

12. For further information see (1) Shlomo Pines and Tuvia Gelblum, "Al-Bīrūnī's Arabic Version of Patañjali's *Yogasūtra*," *Bulletin of the School of Oriental and African Studies* 29 (1966), pp. 302-25; and vol. 40 (1977), pp. 522-49; (2)Ahmad Hasan Dani, *Alberuni's Indica* (Islamabad, Pakistan: University of Islamabad Press, 1973).

13. Those most interested in a research of this type may begin by looking at the Bibliography in Georg Feuerstein's *The Yoga-sūtra of Patañjali: An Exercise in the Methodology of Textual Analysis* (New Delhi: Arnold-Heinemann, 1979). Also see Potter, *Bibliography of Indian Philosophies.*

Of these translations the ones by J. H. Woods[14] and by I. K. Taimni[15] are the most well known in the West, the first among scholars and the second among aspirants of yoga. We have ignored both of these completely in our discussions. The translation of the *Yoga-sūtras* with the *Bhāṣhya* of Vyāsa and the commentary of Vāchaspati by Woods, though a prestigious volume first published in the Harvard Oriental Series, is a scholar's exercise to replace Sanskrit words with English ones! It shows little or no understanding of the traditions of the Yoga *school* of philosophy nor familiarity with experiential yoga practice. Taimni's work was also completely ignored because it attempts to foist theosophical doctrine on Patañjali and Vyāsa.

From time to time in our work three English translations have been consulted:

1. Translation of the *Yoga-sūtras,* with Vyāsa's *Bhāṣhya* and Vāchaspati's *Tattva-vaiśhāradī,* by Rāma Prasāda (RP).[16] The translator was not a yogi but his work at least shows the mark of a man learned in the conventions of the Sanskrit philosophical tradition. From the point of view of a practitioner of yoga this work exhibits some of the same deficiencies as those in the work of J. H. Wood.

2. Translation of the *Yoga-sūtras* and Vyāsa's *Bhāṣhya* by Hariharānanda Āraṇya [HA(E)], with an extensive commentary originally in Bangla (Bengali), rendered into English.[17] This is one of the most heartwarming works on the *Yoga-sūtras* by someone who not only revived the teaching of Sāṅkhya-yoga, but was a great Sanskrit scholar as well as a practising yogi.

14. James Haughton Woods, *The Yoga-System of Patanjali,* Harvard Oriental Series, vol. 17 (1914; reprint, Delhi: Motilal Banarsidass, 1927).

15. I. K. Taimni, *The Science of Yoga* (Madras, India, and Wheaton, Ill.: Theosophical Publishing House, 1961).

16. Rāma Prasāda, trans., *The Yoga-sūtras of Patañjali with the Commentary of Vyāsa and the Gloss of Vāchaspati Miśhra* (1912; reprint, New York: AMS Press, 1974).

17. Swami Hariharānanda Āraṇya, *Yoga Philosophy of Patañjali* (Calcutta: University of Calcutta, 1977).

3. Translation of the *Yoga-sūtras* with Vyāsa's *Bhāṣhya* by Bangali Baba[18] (BB). This translation shows a depth in and an adherence to the scholastic, philosophical, monastic and experiential traditions all at once! Especially in the copious footnotes the translator explains fine points of philosophy and exhibits his authentic learning. The choice of English words for the Sanskrit terminology is arbitrary without a clear definition of the English terms used.

If, rarely and sporadically, we have borrowed any words from any of the above translations, it has been done with due acknowledgment. Any similarities between our work and theirs, if not duly acknowledged, is quite accidental and unintentional. The works of Western scholars such as Ballentyne, Boissenain, Deussen, Eliade, Feuerstein, Frauwallner, Garbe, Hauer, Hopkins, Hultzsch, Jacobi, Janāček, Johnston, Judge, Koelman, von Mangoldt, Pensa[19] and others, as well as the westernized Eastern scholars such as Dasgupta and Takagi, were found to have no bearing on the purpose of this translation. Our present interests do not coincide with the academic discussions of those scholars, based as they are only on partial resources insofar as (*a*) the experiential tradition and (*b*) the exegetical tradition are concerned. Without a thorough grasp of these the details of the hermeneutics of the *Yoga-sūtras* remain a mystery, giving way to much academic speculation. Students and scholars whose primary interest, however, is in writing doctoral theses and such will make a grave mistake in not taking into consideration the writings of these highly trained, scholarly, well-informed, well-read, careful, academic minds. Their interest is study; our interest is the practice.

The purpose of the present translation and commentary is to open the *Yoga-sūtras* to the serious English-reading aspirant. Much of the information and explanation that was not open before is being made available in such a way, it is hoped, that it can be helpful to those who wish to embark not merely on study but on

18. Published by Motilal Banarsidass, Delhi, 1976.

19. Of all the Western scholars, Feuerstein and Pensa appear to have the most sensitivity for and respect towards the living tradition of yoga philosophy.

the long-term practice of yoga as explained in Sūtra I.14. However, the academicians will find that all the scholarly norms and rules have been carefully observed, that convictions of the tradition have not been permitted to overcloud the clarity of academically established facts, and that the translation as well as the discussion on each sūtra will serve as a useful source of information to all.

Many students used to a syllogistic construction of subject matter may find themselves somewhat at sea when they try to follow the argument from one sūtra to the next, or even the progression of argument within the explanation provided on each sūtra. Partly this may be so because of their unfamiliarity with the basics of Indian philosophy, the many tenets of which are accepted as "given" in preparing this work. Secondly, the scheme and order of the sūtras as created by the original *ṛṣhi* has its own reasons; it is not in a random sequence. The word *sūtra,* related to English "suture," means "a thread." It may be so because there runs a connecting thread of ideas from the beginning to the end of a sūtra text. Many scholars fail to comprehend the inner connections among the sūtras, as well as their relationship with the steps of a guided practice. They also often ignore the maxims of sūtra interpretation as explained on page 6 of this prologue. Their approach is criticised rightly in the following words:

> In contrast to the approach adopted by many Orientalists who *a priori* tend to deny the unity of the text under examination, fragmenting it into so many parts or heterogeneous strata until nothing remains, Feuerstein rightly asks in his methodological study whether this compulsive search for incongruencies and textual corruptions is not the expression of an ethnocentric rationalising mentality which inclines to project everywhere its own need for abstract and absolute logic, and hence is particularly prone to misinterpret paradoxical expressions so common in eastern thought, which has a *penchant* for transcending dualism and therefore in part also rational language as such.[20]

20. Corrado Pensa, Foreword to *The Philosophy of Classical Yoga* by Georg Feuerstein (New York: St. Martin's Press, 1980; Manchester: Manchester University Press, 1980).

We offer the same explanation for our approach to accepting the text on its own authority as a complete whole. One should not start studying the texts of *ṛṣhis* part by part, constructed paragraph by constructed paragraph. The entire text, with each detail in its own place, should be studied, mastered, contemplated, in that order. Slowly the hidden scheme of the entire whole will begin to emerge. This overall picture of the scheme will be provided at the end of Chapter 4. Meanwhile it should be borne in mind that the present work is not an original thesis. It is a commentary.

A commentary consists of comments on an earlier, original work and follows the scheme of the same. The subject matter in our discussions follows the scheme of Patañjali and Vyāsa. The words and ideas are explained in the order in which these occur in their work. Once again, one should read Patañjali's and Vyāsa's text, then the discussion, and again the text in the light of the discussion. This will help the reader to grasp the intent of the whole text rather than piecemeal ideas separately. Here and there, for ease of comprehension, a separate, clearer paraphrase or summary of Vyāsa's *Bhāṣhya* is provided after the same has been translated.

In translating from Sanskrit into English there always arises the problem of multilevel meanings of Sanskrit words. Most words have at least two categories of meaning:

yaugika: derivative meaning, derived from the verb root of its origin: for example, *sūtra* from the verb root *sīv* 'to sew'.
rūḍhi: conventional meaning, most often based on the derivative meaning: for example, *sūtra* 'a thread, something to sew with'.

Some words may even be derived from several different roots. Sometimes the connection between derivative and conventional meanings is not obvious, or the derivative background has been lost in antiquity.

Then there are meanings specific to a given branch of knowledge which has its own terminology. Equally important is the connotation based on mental association that the speakers of Sanskrit have with the word.[21] And most importantly, the oral tradition has preserved certain explanations, especially in the case of yoga, based on the experience of the great masters.

It is for such reasons that different translations of the same text read like different books. It is not that one translation is accurate and another false. All the meanings express different levels of the reality as expressed by a certain word. For example, again, the word *sūtra* does not mean either "something to sew with" *or* "a thread." Both ideas are conveyed together in the same word. When the word is used to express a certain genre of texts, sūtras, that idea must also be included as the top level in that case.

Since in the minds of the speakers of Western languages such a process of multilevel signification of words is now rare, it is natural for an average English-speaking reader to assume that she or he has to select from among the various translations of the same word. Such is not the case. All the meanings of different levels of the word must be seen and grasped simultaneously and as a single, comprehensive whole. In translating Patañjali and Vyāsa we have attempted to conform to this view. Let us explain this approach with an example. The first word of the *Yoga-sūtras* is *atha* 'now'. Vyāsa says:

> *Atha* 'now'—this word here has the purpose of indicating *adhikāra.*

Now, *adhikāra* means "authority," "qualification" and "commencement." We take all these different meanings of the single word and include them in one sentence as if there were several different words in the original itself. Our translation then reads:

> *Atha* 'now'—this word here has the purpose of indicating authority, qualification and commencement of the subject matter.

21. Some readers might be under the erroneously created impression that Sanskrit is a dead language. If that were so, the two thousand people who register Sanskrit as their first language in the census of India must all be ghosts! In fact, Sanskrit is still the language of traditionally learned assemblies, used to more or less a degree by hundreds of thousands of people throughout that country, and is one of the fifteen official languages of India.

All three words translating *adhikāra* will be explained in our discussion, giving their background and implications.

In some places, after giving all the meanings of a word, we have then taken those ideas together and coined a new term in English. For example, the derivative meaning of the word *asmitā* is "I-amness" and this is explained in the discussion on Sūtra I.8. But thereafter we have settled on "composite sentience" because after careful scrutiny of Sūtras I.17 and II.6 this appears to be the philosophical intent and content of the Sanskrit term. A glossary of terms is offered as an aid to the reader.

It is traditionally required of a commentator that the exposition of a text include:

- Separating the original words of the text where they are combined to form euphony (*sandhi*) and compounds
- Literal translation of words
- Parsing (explaining the grammatical and syntactical form and function) where relevant or helpful
- Rephrasing and exposition
- Answering challenges, refuting opposing opinions, eradicating doubts

An attempt was made to remain true to this system throughout without sacrificing comprehensibility to requirement. Frequently the euphonized (*sandhi*) and compound words have been hyphenated when used in our translations and discussions,[22] but this is not always the case; the hyphenated and unhyphenated forms are used interchangeably.

There are six categories of sūtras in various texts:

sañjñā: those that give a definition
paribhāṣhā: those that give rules for the application of other sūtras
vidhi: those that enjoin an act
niyama: those that restrict or give injunction against an act
atideśha: those that present an analogy

22. In Sanskrit, apposition of two sounds often produces a third one. For example, *yoga* + *anuśhāsana* = *yogānuśhāsana.* Such words have to be separated in accordance with complex rules of what is known as *sandhi.*

adhikāra or *uddeśha:* those that state the subject of a text or a portion thereof

These categories will be pointed out wherever it is relevant and helpful. For example, the first sūtra is an *adhikāra-sūtra,* stating the topic of the text.

Regarding the use of various commentaries listed above, many of them agree on some points in each sūtra; some of them disagree. Both agreements and disagreements are brought out by the discussion where possible. When the interpretation of a commentator differs from that of others without necessarily contradicting the latter, such an interpretation is incorporated. For example, take the following sentence in the discussion on Sūtra I.14:

> How is it possible that a normally infirm and weak practice, undertaken relatively recently (SS), will overpower the force of these saṁskāras (VM, VB, NB, RY) which await to waylay one (VM) and by which the practice is often blocked (VM, VB) and constricted (RY)?

The source of each segment of the above sentence is cited. Because our primary aim is lucidity, it is impossible in some places to see with absolute accuracy just which word comes from which commentator. In such doubtful places the scholar will naturally consult the text and will know the approximate place where to look: *Vidvāṁsas tatra pramāṇam.* The reader should also assume that where no source is cited, the sentences and paragraphs have originated with this author.

Finally, the work presented has been written intermittently between long periods of meditation and through the blessing, grace and guidance of Śhri-108 Swami Rama[23] of the Himalayas. Whatever is of truth here comes from the Guru lineage; whatever is erroneous is mine.

23. In the traditions of India the word *Śhri* written 108 times before a name expresses a veneration implicit in such Western terms as "His Holiness."

Part 2

Overview of Sāṅkhya-yoga

The *Yoga-sūtras* and the commentary being presented here assume that the reader is familiar with Sāṅkhya philosophy. Without such familiarity much of the terminology of the *Yoga-sūtras* will remain incomprehensible; hence this brief introduction to the extensive field of Sāṅkhya philosophy is essential and must be provided within the total framework of Indian (non-Buddhist) philosophy. One must first decide on a suitable approach to the topic of Indian philosophy since there are several ways in which it may be examined.

One way is that of a pedant bound to one of many philosophical schools who refutes the views of all others and challenges them to prove theirs right and his wrong. Most philosophers of the traditional schools fall into this category, having debated with all other schools for thousands of years. Modern Western and westernized Eastern scholars follow this trend and study each school of Indian philosophy in isolation. It is not intended here to engage in a dispute with them, because the separate schools of Indian philosophy have indeed dominated the philosophical arena for these millennia, each possessing its own closed system of internally consistent values, doctrines and logical development (*prati-tantra-siddhānta*). However, according to the *Bhagavad-gītā* XVIII.22, this approach is darkened knowledge (*tamasic jñāna*).

Another approach is the way of that savant whose primary

interest is not in logical categories only but who seeks that wisdom from which all logic begins and to which it must ultimately lead. This is the way of reconciliation and resolution of conflicts (*samādhāna*), which eventually clears the pathway to samādhi. Such a savant refuses to remain bound within a square or a cube. He must understand the internally consistent logic of the system within a given cube, no doubt, but he must also observe where the external walls of one cube touch those of another; he must then enter the other cube and understand the internally consistent logic of that cube also. Thus, when he has looked at all the interconnected cubes, he sees the whole picture which is based on one or more common principles shared by all (*sarva-tantra-siddhānta*). This is the way of active knowledge (*rajasic jñāna*) as defined in the *Bhagavad-gītā* XVIII.21.

Vastly improved on the way of that wisdom-seeking savant is the way of the wise man, a person of intuitive vision and inspiration, the yogi, who by first looking at the grand pattern sees all the squares and cubes as well as all the spirals, circles and other patterns. By understanding the grand pattern, the little geometric shapes and forms are fully and effortlessly understood. The *Bhagavad-gītā* XVIII.20 says this is the way of the pure, refined, luminous knowledge (*sattvic jñāna*).

One who understands a large square

with all its potentials (*śhaktis*) naturally understands all the smaller squares contained in it

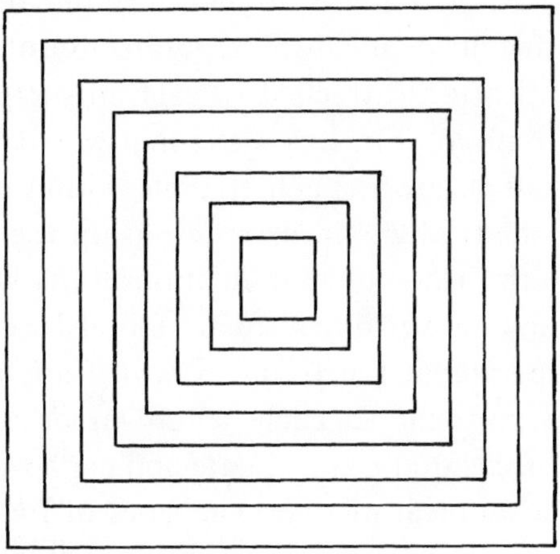

and all the triangles within it

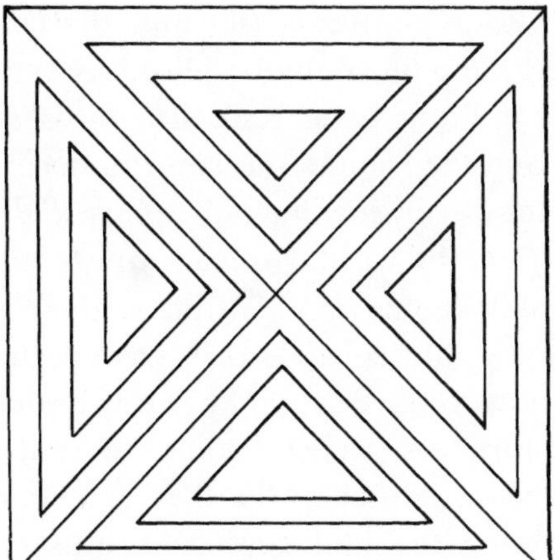

as well as the relationships among all the smaller squares and triangles and so forth.

Besides the established, narrow schools of philosophy there exist in India widely taught ways of looking at philosophy such that all the various schools may fit into a single, universal system. The question arises: If all the schools do indeed fit into a single system, why does each one have its own, separate list of categories of reality with qualifications attached to each in such a way that it cannot be compromised? The answer is that each system requires an internal logic of its own. Each triangle within a square must obey the laws of the triangle; in its relationship with the square it must also follow the rules of that relationship, while the square itself follows the laws governing a square but also permits the laws of triangles to operate in the triangles which are within it. The theoretical needs internal to each school are essential to that school, but these needs do not invalidate and cannot be invalidated by the larger philosophical picture. The rules of Euclidian mathematics are not invalidated by quantum physics *so far as* they govern the levels of reality where they are operable; in the realm of quantum physics they are inoperable.

There does exist, therefore, a single system of Indian philosophy which incorporates all the schools, assigning the categories of reality from each into a total, universal scheme. This system is often referred to as the Epic philosophy because it is expounded in that vast text of many millions of verses called the *Mahābhārata* and eighteen Purāṇas and their numerous sub-Purāṇas. These are epics of Indian cosmology, viewing human events and laws within a cosmic context. While the word *Purāṇa* simply connotes "ancient" legends, stories, philosophies and histories, these texts are often misnamed "mythological" because they have regularly employed the frame of a "myth" to give symbolic forms to that which would otherwise remain formless. Hence there developed special schools of philosophy such as Pañcharatra that are almost exclusively devoted to explaining the philosophical truths of the "mythic" forms.

The vast texts of the Epics and Purāṇas were composed by the wise men and philosophers to serve as vehicles for simplified statements of truth regarding reality for the benefit of millions of non-pedantic aspirants, to whom these are still read, sung or chanted by pandits in village temples, royal palaces and suburban homes alike. This is where the true philosophy of India lives and it is by these texts that the Indian heart—as against its intellectual mind—is really shaped.

To think that such philosophy is for millions of illiterate souls alone is to misunderstand its intent, content and context. The *Bhagavad-gītā* is an example of the philosophical portions of the Epics and Purāṇas. It is understood by many illiterate wise men and women, yet not understood by those hundreds who have gained their doctoral degrees by writing voluminous tomes about it. Great *āchāryas,* scholar-savants of many formal schools of philosophy, have written commentaries on the *Bhagavad-gītā,* each claiming it supports his own school, because it shows that universal picture within which each school of philosophy has its own internally valid place.

Because yoga transcends all castes, belief systems, laws and philosophies, the yogis—including those who cannot sign their names as well as those who know the works of Śhankarāchārya by heart—adhere more to this universal philosophy. Even if they are especially learned in the doctrines of a single school of philosophy, they teach their disciples an approach through synthesis (*samanvaya*) because that alone, as we said earlier, leads to resolution of conflicts (*samādhāna*) as both prerequisite to and conducive to samādhi. The various schools are rungs (*sopānas*) of the selfsame ladder which rises to the pinnacle of higher realization.

The Epics and the Purāṇas do not depict the universal, cosmological philosophy in a uniform way. There are various nuances, preferences, subtle and not-so-subtle variations of schemes and sequences of categories, depending on the predispositions of different teachers whose words are recorded in these texts. Here we plan to provide that general picture which seems to be basically agreed upon in most versions, especially selecting one in which the Sāṅkhya part of the scheme is closest to Sāṅkhya-yoga as propounded by Patañjali and Vyāsa. In the scheme set forth by this Epic philosophy, it will be seen that the categories accepted by various schools are not only assigned their given places but that a bridge is provided at transition points between one level of reality and the next lower one. It is thus that the schools are connected to one another. The following discussion illustrates the Epic philosophy technique.

Vedānta School

There is a single Transcendental Reality (Brahman) whose nature is Existence (*sat*), Consciousness (*chit*) and Bliss (*ānanda*). This is the Self (*parama-ātman*) of all that is. Its inherent potency (*śhakti*), which makes It omnipotent, is called *māyā,* with the twofold power to veil and to unveil. It is Brahman's very nature (*Prakṛti*) dwelling eternally in It, containing all possible aspects.

Transition

The relationship of this One Principle with the dualities and multiplicities of the universe is discussed by many *āchāryas,* each qualifying this relationship according to his own understanding and view.

In the syncretic philosophy of the Epics and Purāṇas, *māyā,* which is the very nature (*Prakṛti*) of Brahman, now projects its power of unveiling all the uncountable, unmanifest, formerly veiled aspects or *śhaktis* of Brahman.[1] It then divides into two. In this division the Bliss principle, which can be associated with undivided One Perfection only, is eclipsed.

- The Consciousness Principle coupled with Existence becomes *puruṣha,* and
- The Existence Principle, without consciousness, becomes *prakṛti* (*not* to be confused with Brahman's Perfect Nature, called Its *Prakṛti,* with a capital *P*).

1. This matter of creativity stemming from Brahman has been discussed in some detail in the author's work *God* (Honesdale, Pa.: Himalayan International Institute of Yoga Science and Philosophy, 1979).

Sāṅkhya School

There are two eternally coexistent principles:

purușha: the conscious spiritual-energy principle
prakṛti: the unconscious material-energy principle

Purușha, again, may be a God of the universe (in theistic Sāṅkhya, which is the normally accepted philosophy of the Epics and Purāṇas as well as the *Yoga-sūtras*), who may again subdivide into the Holy Trinity of Brahmā (the Creator), Vișhṇu (the Preserver) and Śhiva (the Dissolver) and, further, into their various aspects and sparks that may incarnate, become flesh, to give knowledge to and confer saving grace upon

purușhas, the numerous entities of consciousness,
who become
jīvas, souls, when they assume a connection with prakṛti.

The purușha principle is ever-pure, ever-wise, ever-free. It is that self (*ātman*) which never comes into the trap of ignorance and bondage. It is only prakṛti, activated like a magnet, that comes into association with purușha and receives his rays.

Prakṛti is the unmanifest, intangible, subtlest origin of what later becomes tangible matter. Prakṛti consists of the equilibrium of three *guṇas* (attributes):

sattva: luminosity, purity, lightness, harmony, producing pleasure
rajas: activity, energy, movement, producing pain
tamas: dullness, inertia, darkness, stasis, producing stupor

So long as the three guṇas remain in perfect equilibrium, there is no universe. Only as disequilibrium occurs are the various phenomena called *vikāras* or *vikṛtis,* modifications or evolutes, produced.

Sāṅkhya believes in a theory of causation called *sat-kārya-vāda* whereby objects are not something new produced from any quanta other than those inherent in their causes. Nothing new is created; only the energies change form. Nothing is destroyed, either. Every clay pot exists within clay, every sculpture in marble, every ice cube in water. The special attributes of a cause become manifest and tangible, given certain innate propensities of nature. Thus what lay unmanifest within prakṛti becomes manifest in its product (*vikṛti*), the phenomenal universe, with all the evolutes or products within it.

All evolutes carry within themselves all three guṇas; nothing exists that does not include all the three guṇas together. Variances in the nature of all phenomena, entities, attributes, self-identifications, tendencies and inclinations, choices, personalities, relationships and acts depend on the dominance and preponderance of guṇas. For example, where sattva dominates and is served by rajas and tamas, the manifestation appears predominantly sattvic. In that manifestation

sattva: provides refined, pure, luminous qualities;
rajas: energizes, impels, overcoming stagnation; and
tamas: stabilises.

But where tamas dominates,

tamas: causes stagnation and dullness;
rajas: struggles to change the status quo;
sattva: remains dormant, waiting to be energized with the help of rajas.

This explanation is by no means exhaustive, but provides examples of an interdependence among guṇas. Rajas provides constant oscillation and sattva and tamas produce a pull, each in its own direction, seeking to be dominant. The natures and acts of objects, phenomena and entities change as the equilibrium or balance of forces among the inherent guṇas undergoes any alteration. The most dynamic can become static and the most static may become dynamic. Rocks may release gases; gases may become caught in rocks. Hydrogen may gather more particles and ultimately become uranium, which may radiate out its particles and eventually return to hydrogen. Food may provide sattvic energy or may sit as tamasic heaviness in the stomach and may then need the rajas of digestive spices, herbs or potions to impel it in some direction. A marriage may be pleasant (sattvic) and stable (served by tamas) or volatile (rajasic) or so stagnant (tamasic) that not even a quarrel occurs. For a more detailed understanding of the natures of the three guṇas it is strongly recommended that the reader study Chapters XIV, XVII and XVIII of the *Bhagavad-gītā*.

Now, back to prakṛti. The first unmanifest prakṛti is, of course, the origin of all phenomena. It is not in itself a change in anything prior. But its evolutes or products are its

vikṛti: modifications, products, evolutes,
and yet also
prakṛti: origins of further evolutes.

Milk (like prakṛti) undergoes a change and produces cream (a *vikṛti*), which is in turn transformed into butter. These intermediate phenomena, like cream, which are both (*a*) products or effects of an earlier cause, and (*b*) producers or origins of a future effect are called

prakṛti-vikṛti: modifications that may be modified further

Only the final products which cannot be modified further are strictly called *vikṛti,* the ultimate modifications or transformations. However, the term *vikṛti* 'modification' is also quite frequently used for *prakṛti-vikṛtis,* which are the modifiable modifications. There are a total of twenty-three such *vikṛtis* produced from the original prakṛti or material-energy principle. Thus there are

1. prakṛti
2-24. *vikṛtis,* twenty-three evolutes
25. puruṣha, numerous conscious entities which become *jīvas* (souls)
26. puruṣha, the God

making a total of twenty-six principles or categories in the Epic Sāṅkhya, also accepted in the *Yoga-sūtras.* Our concern here, however, is not with God but with the permutation (*saṅkhyāna,* because of which this system is called Sāṅkhya) of the other twenty-five so that

> the self (puruṣha) and
> the non-self (prakṛti together with its 23 evolutes)

may be known as separate. This discrimination (*pra-saṅkhyāna,* because of which also this system is called Sāṅkhya) alone between the spiritual energy-self (puruṣha) and the non-spiritual material energy (prakṛti) together with its evolutes eliminates pain. Otherwise pain remains a fact for all entities as a principle inhered through the rajas component.

In order to develop discrimination (*pra-saṅkhyāna*) (*a*) as a pursuit to eliminate all pain permanently and totally, and (*b*) to attain self-realization, it is essential that all the components constituting the non-self, material, parts of the sentient (that is, living and conscious) entity must be enumerated and understood. But the material adjuncts of a sentient entity do not exist in isolation from their counterparts in the universe. The two have to be understood as a single phenomenon. Hence, one studies the chains of universal causations.

Since puruṣha is ever-pure, ever-wise, ever-free, he is unmodifiable; no change or transformation occurs in him; he is never ignorant, never in pain or bondage and therefore there is no question of his enlightenment or release. Any observation or discussion of changes pertains to prakṛti alone. Let us, therefore, look further at the modifications of prakṛti. Only a small part of prakṛti is at any time undergoing the phenomenalization. The rest remains in unmanifest nature. The first evolute of prakṛti is

> *mahat:* the Great, the *Magnum*

Mahat is the most sattvic, finest and purest product of prakṛti. On one hand it is that first disequilibrium of guṇas in which no other form or shape yet emerges. It is simply a presence, the subtle energy which will produce objects. It is also the universal *buddhi,* the faculty of discrimination which serves as a vehicle of puruṣha's consciousness. Because it is the most sattvic modification, it is fit to serve as a medium between puruṣha and the grosser material phenomena. A small spark of the universal mahat is also the individual buddhi, the faculty of discrimination, intelligence and intellection in a sentient entity.

From mahat, the next evolute to appear is

ahaṁkāra: ego, the I-maker

It is not to be confused with ego as pride. It is the state in which any self-identification begins; names and forms appear. It is here that intelligence begins to identify itself as differentiated, "this but not that." Here the process of creation begins to diversify into subjective and objective branches. The sattvic ahaṁkāra produces the subjective branch, namely

- mind
- five cognitive senses (to cognize sound, touch, form, taste, smell)
- five active senses (to speak, act, move, procreate and eliminate)

The tamasic ahaṁkāra produces the objective branch, namely

- five *tan-mātrās* (subtle elements of or potentials for audibility, tangibility, visibility, flavour and odour)

which in turn "solidify" and produce

- five *bhūtas* or *tattvas* (the physical states of matter: earth or solid, water or liquid, fire or light that is combustive and illuminative, air or gaseous, and space, which is not a vacuum but a state of matter)

Let us see these as a chart (p. 34).

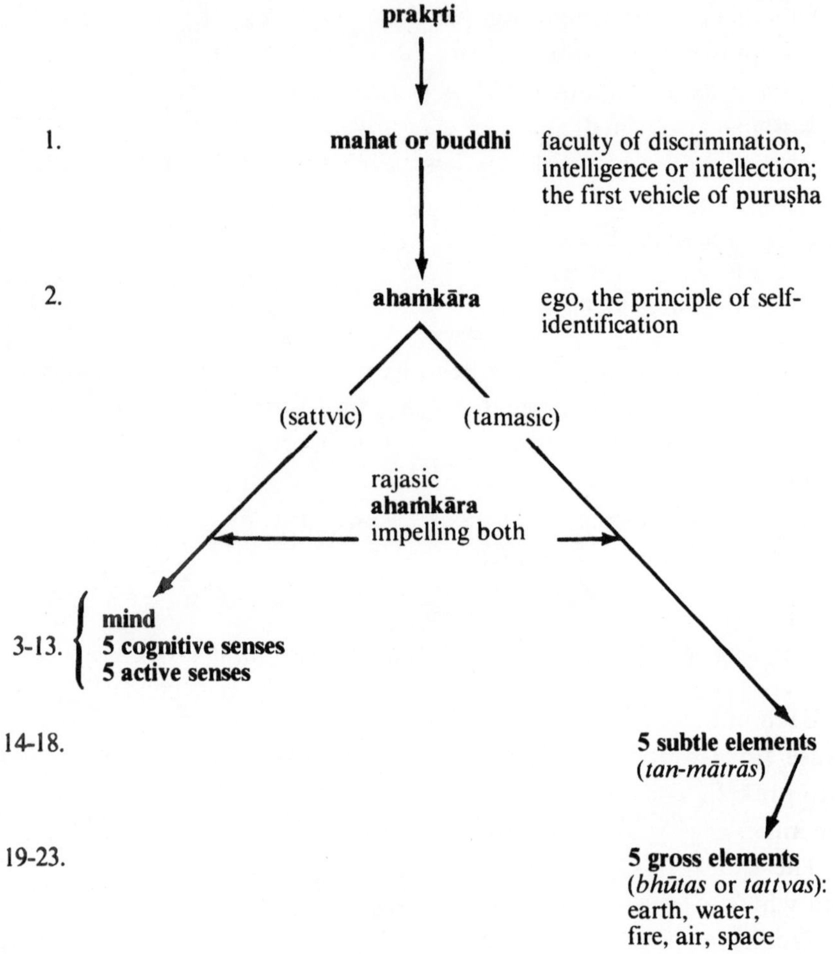
prakṛti
1.
mahat or buddhi
faculty of discrimination, intelligence or intellection; the first vehicle of puruṣha
2.
ahaṁkāra
ego, the principle of self-identification
(sattvic)
(tamasic)
rajasic
ahaṁkāra
impelling both
3-13.
mind
5 cognitive senses
5 active senses
14-18.
5 subtle elements
(tan-mātrās)
19-23.
5 gross elements
(bhūtas or tattvas):
earth, water,
fire, air, space

Yoga-sūtra II.19 gives alternative explanatory titles as follows:

prakṛti	*a-liṅga,* without a distinguishing mark
	↓
1. mahat	*liṅga-mātra,* merely a mark but with no distinguishing features
	↓
2-7. ahaṁkāra and 5 *tan-mātrās* (subtle elements)	6 *a-viśheṣhas;* general, non-specific, intermediate links between mahat and the final 16 products
	↓
8-23. mind and 5 cognitive senses 5 active senses 5 *bhūtas* (gross elements)	*viśheṣhas,* specific, final 16 products

Each of these evolutes submerges into the immediately preceding cause from which it has emerged; finally all phenomena dissolve into prakṛti. These cycles of creations and dissolutions, because of the inherent nature of prakṛti, are endless.

The twenty-three evolutes, of which the universe is constituted and which also form our personalities, are all non-self. Intelligence or faculty of discrimination, through ego and mind and all their attendant cognitions, volitions, inclinations, emotions and so forth, all the senses as well as what they sense, the components as well as the states of the physical body too—they are all non-self. Only puruṣha, the spiritual-energy principle, is the self. This realization alone eradicates all pain permanently and totally. This alone is final freedom.

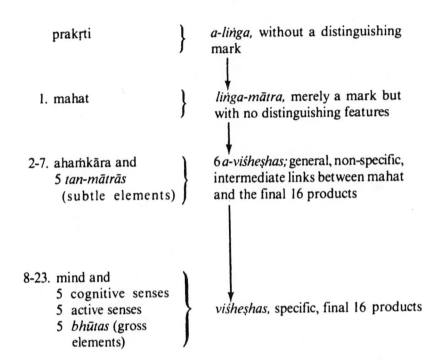

Nyāya-Vaiśheṣhika School

At the point where Sāṅkhya leaves off, the Vaiśheṣhika system picks up. It concerns itself with five of the *viśheṣhas,* namely the five gross elements or states of matter. At this point creation becomes atomic. The earliest masters defined this finest particle as having no mass but being merely a point in space. Conjunctions of these points later produce mass. The Vaiśheṣhika system, together with Nyāya, is thus atomistic. It is from Vaiśheṣhika that all physical sciences in India, such as alchemy, chemistry, pharmaceutics, branched off.

The Vaiśheṣhika system is concerned with the physical properties of matter and how the self and mind use those properties. Hence it takes into account only nine substances (*dravyas*):

1-5. five gross elements (listed as the final *vikṛtis* in Sāṅkhya; 5 of the *viśheṣhas* in the *Yoga-sūtras*)
6. time (*kāla*)
7. dimension (*dik*)
8. mind (*manas*)
9. self (ātman)

The Vaiśheṣhika system's definition of ātman is based on how its attributes manifest themselves while it is "bound" to the physical universe. In association with an atomic universe, it is seen as an *aṇu,* minute like an atom, featuring certain symptoms of its presence in the physical body. These symptoms are desire, aversion, effort, pleasure, pain and knowledge. When "freedom" from physical phenomena occurs, these symptoms cease. Vaiśheṣhika is inhibited from going any further. The later Nyāya interpreters misunderstood ātman in freedom as without action or knowledge!

How is it possible for the body-bound ātman to liberate itself? It must practise that which enhances its betterment in this life (*abhyudaya*) and in the next (*niḥ-śhreyasa*). This is to be arrived at by following the teachings of the inspired scriptures (in Vaiśheṣhika) and in addition by using the mind clearly, that is, by reasoning correctly according to the system of logic (Nyāya). This is all that is within the capacity of a delimited being, until the final yoga is reached, which is agreed to but beyond the realm of the boundaries demarcated for this school.

Later Nyāya-Vaiśheṣhika philosophers were the chief proponents of the existence of God in centuries-long debates against the Buddhists. Their arguments are remarkably similar to those of Christian theologians who revived Aristotelian logic in the West.

Mīmāṁsā School

While the Vaiśheṣhikas experimented with physical properties of matter and Nyāya philosophers established the principles of logic and correct reasoning as ramparts to safeguard against ignorance, the Mīmāṁsā philosophers developed two areas which were also agreed to as important in Nyāya-Vaiśheṣhika. These are (*a*) the nature of revealed knowledge (Veda); and (*b*) the principles governing correct action. Complex theories and debates thereupon developed within the Mīmāṁsā school and gave much impetus to the evolution of Indian ethics and laws and rules of social interaction. These rules must remain in force for the people in whom the presence of a pure self can only be surmised while mainly the impure mental and physical instrumentation exhibits desires, aversions, and so forth, which lead to an accumulation of karmas, an attempt to understand which is another primary occupation of the *mīmāṁsakas*.

Sāṅkhya-yoga School

The system of Patañjali takes into account all the concerns of Sāṅkhya, Nyāya, Vaiśheṣhika and Mīmāṁsā. All twenty-six Sāṅkhya categories are employed in this philosophy. *Pramāṇa,* or valid proof, is defined much as in Nyāya. The scriptural authority is accepted as valid. *Viśheṣhas* of the Vaiśheṣhika school are considered the end-product of an evolution of reality. Time is discussed and clearly defined in *YS* IV, although its status is at best obscure in much of Sāṅkhya. The codes of conduct are especially important in the *Yoga-sūtras* as the first two of the eight *aṅgas* 'limbs', namely the *yamas* and *niyamas.*

However, granting validity to all the schemes of Sāṅkhya and so forth, the only question that is of interest to Patañjali is: So what? What are the practical implications of all the experimenting (Vaiśheṣhika), reasoning (Nyāya), categorizing (Sāṅkhya) or studying inspired scriptures (Mīmāṁsā)? How may one finally *see* and *experience* that self and non-self are indeed ever-separate and that the self is ever-pure, ever-wise and ever-free? To this end Sāṅkhya-yoga (*a*) borrows from other systems what needs to be borrowed, and (*b*) adds an original theory wherever one needs to be added. Primarily it takes the Sāṅkhya theory of causation and applies it to understanding the states of mind. The modifications (*vikṛtis*) of mind are its *vṛttis,* all the mental fluctuations. These must be dissolved into their origin. What is *laya* or *prati-sañchara* (dissolution of the universe and its phenomena) in Sāṅkhya becomes in the *Yoga-sūtras* respectively *nirodha* or *prati-prasava* (dissolution of the vṛttis and guṇas manifest therein). This can happen only in the practice of samādhi.

An average reader of Sāṅkhya sees the evolutes or *vikṛtis* of prakṛti in the context of cosmogony, the cycles of creations and dissolutions of universes. In Sāṅkhya-yoga, that is, in the *Yoga-sūtras,* these evolutes are of interest only with regard to the material accretions around the individual puruṣha. They are his personal matter (pun intended). Everything from buddhi (mahat) and ego (ahaṁkāra) to mind, senses and the body are this personal matter. The yogi needs to know their origin and creation only so as to dissolve them, that is, dissolve puruṣha's association with them in the process of samādhi.

To facilitate an understanding of the practical processes leading to samādhi, the *Yoga-sūtras* have to employ a terminology and definitions of the evolutes a little differently from that of Sāṅkhya. For example, Sāṅkhya discusses mahat but not *asmitā.* In the *Yoga-sūtras,* it is in *asmitā* that the impression of a union between puruṣha and prakṛti, between self and non-self, between the conscious and the unconscious, first occurs.

asmitā: that process in which mahat or buddhi, being the purest and most sattvic evolute of prakṛti, becomes a recipient of a reflection of the conscious light of puruṣha.

It is the union of a crystal mirror with a reflection of the sun. Puruṣha, like the distant sun in the sky, remains unaffected by the union of its reflection with the mirror, but all the processes of the composite personality begin. Consciousness and life in us flows through this *asmitā,* which lends to ego and to mind a semblance of awareness.

All through the practical processes of yoga, the reverse begins to occur, a withdrawal, a dissolution of vṛttis, a burning of past *saṁskāras,* the final sundering between the two components of *asmitā.* Then prakṛti is prakṛti. Puruṣha is puruṣha. And the twain shall never meet even as they have never met before.

Where does prakṛti go thereafter? What are its connections with *māyā* again? In what consciousness does puruṣha dwell then? The *Yoga-sūtras* take one to the verge, and from there let the experience itself answer. The Epic philosophers say with Vedānta that puruṣha merges into Brahman—but that is another school. The final goal of the *Yoga-sūtras* is *kaivalya,* isolation of puruṣha. Perhaps it is a transition to the same state as *kūṭastham:* the unmodifiable, immutable, unchangeable Brahman. The Epic philosophers agree. The *Yoga-sūtras,* having done the work of providing practical guidance that leads to *kaivalya,* remain mute.

The Vedāntins identify Kapila, the first founder of Sāṅkhya, with Hiraṇya-garbha (as seen in Śhankarāchārya's *Bhāṣhya* on *Śhvetāśhvatara Upaniṣhad* V.2). Śhankarāchāryas up to this day bear the title *Sāṅkhya-trayī-pratipālaka* 'Guardian of the Threefold Sāṅkhya'.

GLORY TO ALL SAINTS.
HOMAGE TO ALL GURUS.

Part 3

Tattva-samāsa-sūtras (Paraphrased)

The Tattva-saṁāsa-sūtras comprise an ancient text said to have been taught by Kapila, the founder of Sāṅkhya philosophy, to his immediate disciple, Āsuri. In other words, TSS forms the very first text of the formal Sāṅkhya system of philosophy, stating all its categories and tenets.

Tattva-samāsa-sūtras

TSS 1. *atha atas tattva-samāsaḥ*

Now the summary of the categories of reality according to the Sāṅkhya philosophy.

TSS 2. *aṣhṭau prakṛtayaḥ*

prakṛtis, eight origins of evolutes:

8 prakṛtis:
- *prakṛti;* the equilibrium of three guṇas, itself not evolved from any other origin, but the primordial source of all other evolutes
- *buddhi;* faculty of discrimination, intelligence
- *ahaṁkāra;* ego, identifying principle
- *tan-mātrās;* five subtle elements of sound, touch, form, flavour and smell

(Buddhi, ahaṁkāra and the *tan-mātrās* are evolved from prakṛti and are origins of other evolutes as well.)

TSS 3. *ṣhoḍaśha vikārāḥ*

vikāras or *vikṛtis,* sixteen evolutes:

indriyas; eleven senses, as follows: mind, five cognitive senses, five active senses

bhūtas or *tattvas;* five gross elements: space, air, fire, water, earth (evolved in that order)

(Buddhi, ahaṁkāra, the five *tan-mātrās,* the eleven *indriyas,* and the five *bhūtas* or *tattvas* constitute twenty-three evolutes of prakṛti.)

TSS 4. *puruṣhaḥ*

puruṣha: The conscious principle, ever-pure, ever-wise, ever-free:

- Souls in non-theistic Sāṅkhya
- Souls and God in theistic Sāṅkhya

TSS 5. *traiguṇyam*

Three guṇas: sattva, rajas, tamas. (For an explanation see *BhG* chaps. XIV, XVII, XVIII.) Three attributes of prakṛti, which are in equilibrium before the creation of evolutes. The three attributes represent the principles of illumination, activity and stasis. Their disequilibrium in various proportions produces the evolutes.

TSS 6. *sañcharaḥ*

There is a chain of transitions from non-evolute prakṛti towards the evolutes, ending at the grossest evolute, the solids (earth).

TSS 7. *prati-sañcharaḥ*

There is also a chain of reverse transition from evolutes towards dissolution into prakṛti.

TSS 8. *adhyātmam-adhibhūtam-adhidaivam*

adhyātma: the categories under direct control of the spiritual self (puruṣha or ātman):

- Mental:
  - mahat or buddhi, intelligence
  - ahaṁkāra, ego
  - *manas,* mind
- Physical:
  - Five cognitive senses
  - Five active senses

adhibhūta: attributes of the objects of experience, such as
the intelligible,
the identifiable,
the thinkable,
the sounds heard, etc.

Corresponding to the *adhyātma* categories, but dwelling in the objects of experience.

adhidaiva: relating to the celestial and subtle worlds, conscious powers of nature, angelic beings, planetary deities, etc.

TSS 9. *pañcha abhi-buddhayaḥ*

Five activities of intelligence:

abhibuddhi: "I must do this"
abhimāna: "*I* do this"
ichchhā: desire, want
kartavyatā: indulgence of the cognitive senses
kriyā: operations of the active senses

(There are also alternative explanations in various commentaries.)

TSS 10. *pañcha karma-yonayaḥ*

Five causes and results of action:

dhṛti: resolution of mind, speech and action

śhraddhā: inclinations of faith: generosity of mind, celibacy, charity, acts of prayer

sukha: acts undertaken with prayer or expectation of a comforting or pleasant result

a-vividhiṣhā: the tendency that blocks the desire for knowledge

vividiṣhā: desire to know matters relating to spirituality, especially the conscious principle

TSS 11. *pañcha vāyavaḥ*

Five *prāṇas: prāṇa, apāna, samāna, udāna, vyāna*

The five fields of vital energy in the person.

TSS 12. *pañcha karmātmānaḥ*

Five types of living beings with regard to their actions:

vaikārika: with sattvic ego, naturally inclined to perform good deeds
taijasa: with rajasic ego, naturally inclined to perform evil acts
bhūtādi: with tamasic ego, performing acts of stupefaction; these are of two types:
- *sānumāna:* performing good acts of stupefaction
- *niranumāna:* performing evil acts of stupefaction

(The four sūtras which follow [*TSS* 13-16] enumerate fifty modifications of intelligence.)

TSS 13. *pañcha-parvā avidyā*

Five kinds of ignorance (*viparyayas* or *kleśhas* in the *Yoga-sūtras*), also known as the five major hells:

avidyā: ignorance
- mistaking the eternal for the non-eternal, mistaking the non-eternal for the eternal;
- mistaking the pure for the impure, mistaking the impure for the pure;
- mistaking pleasure for pain, mistaking pain for pleasure;
- mistaking the self for the non-self, mistaking the non-self for the self.

asmitā: I-am-ness
rāga: attraction
dveṣha: aversion
abhiniveśha: fear of death, that "May I not cease to be"

(These five kinds of ignorance have a total of sixty-two subdivisions.)

TSS 14. *aṣhṭāviṁśhatidhā aśhaktiḥ*

aśhakti, twenty-eight kinds of incapacity:

		N
• Incapacities		
of mind		1
of five cognitive senses		5
of five active senses		5
	Subtotal *N*	11
• Incapacities of intelligence		17
	Total *N*	28

The incapacities of intelligence are explained as various possible false views held concerning the nature of the categories of reality. These are the opposites of the nine *tushṭis* and eight *siddhis* of *TSS* 15-16.

TSS 15. *navadhā tushṭiḥ*

tushṭis, nine complacencies (four spiritual and five external):

- Four spiritual complacencies:
  - Matter will give me realization.
  - Renunciation will give me realization.
  - Time will bring forth realization.
  - Destiny and luck will give me realization.
- Five external complacencies, based on five steps of dispassion (*vairāgya*):
  - The ways of earning wealth are violent, exploitative and painful.
  - Guarding wealth and the sources of pleasure is painful.
  - Wealth, luxury and pleasure, even well-guarded, are temporary; there is no permanency of feeling of security about them.
  - No matter how many objects of senses one enjoys, there is no satisfaction, and the desires blaze evermore.
  - It is not possible to enjoy oneself without hurting other beings.

TSS 16. *ashṭadhā siddhiḥ*

siddhis, eight accomplishments (not to be confused with the *siddhis* of yoga):

- Three primary *siddhis:*
  - Removal of the three kinds of suffering (see *TSS* 23)
- Five secondary *siddhis* (the means to the three primary ones):
  - Contemplation with a logical mental process
  - Knowledge gained from words and from authoritative scriptures
  - Study
  - Gaining (noble) friends, that is, guru, disciples, co-seekers, with whom one may discuss spiritual matters
  - Self-purification

TSS 17. *daśha mūlika-arthāḥ*

mūlika-arthas, ten fundamental tenets of Sāṅkhya philosophy:

- There *is* a conscious self; there *is* an original, unmanifest nature, prakṛti.
- There is a *single,* unmanifest cause of all material objects, namely, prakṛti.
- The conscious self exists *for no other* one.
- Matter exists for *serving* the conscious self.
- The conscious self is *separate* and *different* from the unconscious prakṛti and its evolutes.
- The conscious self is *not an agent* of actions.
- *Union* of matter with spiritual self occurs.
- *Separation* of matter from spiritual self occurs.
- There are *many* puruṣhas, conscious selves.
- After total self-realization the body may continue by the *momentum* of its own laws.

(The fifty modifications of intelligence [*TSS* 13-16] and the ten fundamentals [*TSS* 17] constitute the sixty factors discussed in the ancient *Ṣhaṣhṭi-tantra,* 'The Book of Sixty'.)

TSS 18. *anugraha-sargaḥ*

Fivefold compassionate creation:

- The five subtle elements (*tan-mātrās*) (see *TSS* 2).
- Also, the appearance of divine, incarnate sages is considered compassionate creation.

TSS 19. *chaturdaśhavidho bhūta-sargaḥ*

Fourteen kinds of living species of this and subtler or celestial worlds (the list is irrelevant and not exhaustive).

TSS 20. *trividho bandhaḥ*

Three kinds of bondage:

prākṛtika bandha: identifying the self with the eight prakṛtis (enumerated in *TSS* 2)

vaikṛtika bandha: renunciates becoming attracted to objects of pleasure

dākṣhiṇa bandha: (1) common worldly people's involvement with ordinary desires and needs of life; (2) an ascetic's dependence on the offerings of laymen

TSS 21. *trividho mokṣhaḥ*

mokṣha, three kinds of liberation:

- Arising from the full expansion of knowledge
- Arising from the elimination of attachments
- Arising above good and evil, when the self has abandoned all prakṛtic identifications

TSS 22. *trividhaṁ pramāṇam*

pramāṇas, three valid proofs:

- Direct perception
- Inference
- Authority of realized ones and their revealed scriptures

TSS 23. *trividhaṁ duḥkham*

duḥkha, three kinds of pain:

ādhyātmika: intrapersonal; to be cured by internal means:

- *mental,* such as desire, passion, jealousy, greed, fear, depression, etc.; of these,
  - the antidote to passion is control
  - the antidote to anger is compassion
  - the antidote to attachment is self-analysis
  - the antidote to fear is wisdom about the true nature of categories (evolutes)
  - the antidote to jealousy is generosity and magnanimity
  - the antidote to depression is non-attachment
- *physical,* the imbalance of humours

ādhibhautika: caused through the agency of other beings

ādhidaivika: caused through the agency of natural forces and the conscious powers of the subtler worlds

TSS 24. *etat paramparayā yāthātathyam*

This is the order as it is taught in the Tradition.

TSS 25. *etat sarvaṁ jñātvā kṛta-kṛtyaḥ syāt na punas trividhena duḥkhena abhi-bhūyate.*

Knowing it all, one fulfils himself;

Then one is not overcome by the three kinds of pain.

Yoga-sūtras
Chapter One

Samādhi-pāda
(Chapter on Samādhi)

Compendium of Sūtras and Vyāsa's *Bhāṣhya*

Chapter One

Sūtra **Page**

STATEMENT *(UDDEŚHA)*

1. Commencing the Teaching of Yoga 57
   *Yoga is samādhi
   Five states of mind
   Effects of samādhi
   Two levels of samādhi

DEFINITIONS *(NIRDEŚHA)*

2. Definition of Yoga 93
   Samprajñāta also is yoga
   Three natures of mind: three guṇas
   Natures and inclinations of personalities according to their guṇa compositions
   Nature of consciousness
   Discriminating wisdom is the lesser goal; seedless samādhi is the final goal

3. Definition of Yoga Continued; Consciousness in *Asamprajñāta* 114
   Consciousness in worldly involvements only an appearance

* The indented portions of this compendium indicate the contents of Vyāsa's *Bhāṣhya.*

4. Consciousness in Worldly Involvements 122
Relationship between chitta and puruṣha

CHITTA-VṚTTI AND *NIRODHA*

5. Fivefold Vṛttis, Afflicted and Unafflicted 135
Cycle of vṛttis and saṁskāras
Final dissolution of chitta

6. Vṛttis Enumerated 148

7. Three Valid Proofs (*Pramāṇas*) 149
Direct perception (*pratyakṣha*) determines the specific
Inference (*anumāna*) determines the general and homogeneous
Nature of revealed authority (*āgama*)

8. Perversive Cognition (*Viparyaya*) 162
Why perversive cognition is not valid
It is identical to the five afflictions (*kleśhas*)

9. Imaginary Cognition (*Vikalpa*) 171
Philosophical errors
Examples of such errors

10. Sleep (*Nidrā*) 178
Why sleep is a vṛtti
Three kinds of sleep
Why it must be controlled

11. Memory (*Smṛti*) 185
What does the chitta remember?
Relationship of buddhi and memory
Two kinds of memory
Why vṛttis must be brought to *nirodha*

THE TWO MEANS

12. *Nirodha* by Practice (*Abhyāsa*) and Dispassion (*Vairāgya*) 193
The flow of mind-stream in two directions
Abhyāsa and *vairāgya* channelising in both

13. Definition of Practice (*Abhyāsa*) 198
Zeal in practice

14. How Practice Becomes Firm of Ground 202
By asceticism, celibacy, knowledge and faith

15. Dispassion (*Vairāgya*) Defined 205
Craving must be conquered
Stages of *vairāgya*

16. Transcendent *Vairāgya* 212
Lower *vairāgya* and higher *vairāgya*
Effects of the transcendent *vairāgya:*
first, freedom from cycles of birth and death
second, ultimate knowledge and *kaivalya*

PRIMARY AND SECONDARY YOGA

17. Four Levels of *Samprajñāta* Samādhi (Secondary Yoga) 218
Explained; these samādhis need objects of concentration

18. *Asamprajñāta* Samādhi (Primary Yoga) 248
Free of all vṛttis
Achieved through transcendent *vairāgya*
Without objects of concentration
Seedless

19. *Bhava-pratyaya* Samādhi (Secondary Yoga) 256
Videhas enjoying the subtle world of saṁskāras
Prakṛti-layas enjoying prakṛti in equilibrium
Both mistaking their state to be *kaivalya*

***UPĀYAS:* METHODS**

20. Five Methods 264
Faith is like a loving mother
Sequence in achieving success in the methods

21-22. How Quickly Yogis of What Strength Gain Their Goal 271

AN EASY METHOD

23. Practising the Presence of God 277
The easy way of grace, simply by turning one's awareness to God

24. Who Is God? 282
Afflictions, actions, fruitions erroneously attributed to God
How God is unique, different from those who have achieved liberation
Relationship of God and the Scriptures
Only one God

25. Seed of the Omniscient 295
Knowledge in the lesser beings is seed of the omniscient
Where knowledge reaches unexcelled perfection, that is God
God's purpose in imparting knowledge is to confer grace eternally in all creations

26. Guru of the Most Ancient Ones 305
He is not delimited by past or future

27. *OM* Signifies God 309
Relationship of *OM* with God, not only the signifier and the signified but an eternal relationship

28. Recitation (*Japa*) of *OM* 315
Contemplating God with *japa*
Japa helps accomplish the "sitting"
Then the Supreme Self shines forth

29. Then Inward Consciousness Develops and Obstacles Are Annulled 320
This is the result of the practice of the presence of God
Self-realization also accrues

OBSTACLES AND THEIR CORRELATES

30. Nine Obstacles (*Antarāyas*) or Distractions (*Vikṣhepas*) 324
Defining the nine obstacles

31. Five Correlates of *Antarāyas* 329
Defining the five correlates
They do not occur in a mind that has reached samādhi

OVERCOMING OBSTACLES: METHODS FOR PURIFYING AND STABILISING THE MIND

32. Practice of One Reality to Overcome *Antarāyas* 333
    Refuting the view that mind is only momentary
    Establishing that one continuous mind has many objects

33. Four Purificatories for the Mind 340
    Explaining the four
    Then the mind becomes clear, pleasant, stabilised

34. Controlled, Slow, Smooth Breathing 346
    Stabilising the mind through awareness of controlled breath

35. Experience of Subtle Celestial Elements 350
    What concentrations lead to which experiences
    Stabilising the mind through these
    Purpose of these experiences: to strengthen faith and to increase mind's capacities, leading to perfection of five methods

36. Light of Buddhi (*Jyotiṣhmatī*) 355
    Concentration in heart lotus
    Experience of lights of various kinds
    Experience of brilliant vast space
    I-am-ness as oceanic consciousness
    Jyotiṣhmatī of two kinds: *viśhokā* and *asmitā-mātrā*
    Stabilises the mind

37. Mind-field Attuned to Sages 359
    Becomes stabilised

38. Knowledge of Dream and Sleep States 361
    Stabilises the mind

39. Freedom in Choosing the Objects of Concentration 365
    The mind concentrated on any object of one's inclination will form the habit of becoming stabilised

40. Highest Control (*Vaśhīkāra*) over the Subtlest and the Vastest 368
Then the mind needs no further purificatories

SAMĀPATTIS: COALESCENCES AND SAMĀDHIS

41. Defining Coalescence (*Samāpatti*) 371
Analogy of objects reflecting in crystal is like mind's coalescence with:
the objects apprehended (*grāhya*)
the instrument of apprehension (*grahaṇa*)
the apprehender (*grahītṛ*)

42. *Vitarka*-accompanied Coalescence 380
Confusions of word, object and knowledge
They alternate in this lower coalescence

43. *Nir-vitarka* Coalescence 387
Devoid of former confusion and alternations
Mind-field totally coalescing with objects of apprehension
Unitary knowledge, not dwelling on parts, even atomic ones
How objects gain a self-nature
Refuting the view that there is no "whole" consisting of parts

44. *Sa-vichāra* and *Nir-vichāra* Coalescences 399
Respectively, accompanied with and not accompanied with the delimitations of time, space, causation
Dwelling on subtle aspects of elements and subtle objects; unitary experience
Realization as though mind devoid of its own nature

45. The "Subtle" Extends up to Prakṛti, Which Has No Marks 404
The degrees of the "subtle"; finally the subtlest is prakṛti.
Is not puruṣha the subtlest?

46. Samādhis with Seed 409
Lower coalescences have objects of concentration as seeds of saṁskāras

47. Proficiency in *Nir-vichāra* 411
Total purification leads to spiritual clarity
Then the yogi no longer suffers but is compassionate towards suffering beings

48. Truth-bearing Wisdom 414
Three ways to wisdom

49. Truth-bearing Wisdom Is Unique 416
Knowledge from scriptures or logic gives no realization of the specifics
The higher knowledge is not gained from worldly direct perception
That no external proof can test it is no refutation of higher knowledge

50. Saṁskāras of Samādhi-wisdom Counteract Other Saṁskāras 419
Reversing the cycle of vṛttis and worldly saṁskāras
Cycle of samādhi-wisdom, its saṁskāras and samādhi-wisdom again
Would these saṁskāras not empower the mind?
When realization is reached, the mind has no more function

51. Seedless Samādhi 424
It occurs when even the saṁskāras of samādhi-wisdom are countered
State of *nirodha* in *asamprajñāta* is inferred only afterwards by seeing the time elapsed
Nirodha-saṁskāras do not nurture the mind's power, which is then dissolved, together with all saṁskāras
When the mind is withdrawn, puruṣha then dwells in his own nature

Introduction to Sūtra I.1

योगेन चित्तस्य पदेन वाचां मलं शरीरस्य च वैद्यकेन।
योऽपाकरोत् तं प्रवरं मुनीनां पतञ्जलिं प्राञ्जलिरानतोऽस्मि।।

yogena chittasya padena vāchāṁ,
malaṁ śharīrasya cha vaidyakena;
yo'pākarot taṁ pravaraṁ munīnāṁ,
patañjaliṁ prāñjalir ānato'smi

He who removed the impurities
of the mind by (the teaching of) yoga,
of speech by (his exposition of) grammar, and
of the body by (composing his treatise on) the science of medicine,
unto that doyen of sages
I bow with joined hands.*

Our homage to Śheṣha,
the snake of eternal *kundalinī,*
the residue that remains
after the great dissolution,
the one who incarnates again and again
to teach the science of yoga.

* This verse is often cited by authors on yoga, although its original source is uncertain.

In the mythologies of India, which are mostly parables for explaining deeper philosophical truths, it is believed that Viṣhṇu, God as Preserver, gathers the universe unto Himself at the end of an aeon and sleeps on the ocean of cosmic milk—an idea comparable to the poetic notion of the Milky Way—on the curled-up snake of eternity known as Śheṣha, the Residue. A legend says that Patañjali was an incarnation of Śheṣha, and that at the end of his life he was seen being swallowed by a python. We believe that the greatest teacher of yoga, indeed, can be no other than a master of the snake called *kundalinī,* which is, in fact, the snake of eternity, the residue that remains after the material consciousness is dissolved. Although it is uncertain whether the verse is authentically Vyāsa's own composition, we have paraphrased the homage paid in the beginning of some manuscripts of Vyāsa's commentary. Other commentators, following the Indian tradition, all begin their commentaries with prayer verses which are neither translated nor paraphrased here.

According to the Indian tradition of textual criticism, the subject matter of a text must include:

lakṣhaṇa: definition
bheda: various divisions or categories of the science
upāya: means, instruments or methods of obtaining the desired ends of the science
phala: end results obtained

In the *Yoga-sūtras* the definition is stated in Sūtra I.2: Yoga is the control of the fluctuations of the mind-field. The divisions are *samprajñāta* and *asamprajñāta* samādhis. The method is the eight limbs of yoga. The end result is *kaivalya,* absoluteness of consciousness, as explained in the fourth chapter.

It is requisite that the author should also state in the beginning of his text the four binding reasons (*anubandhas*):

viṣhaya: the subject matter of the text
prayojana: its purpose
adhikāra: the qualification of the student
sambandha: the relationship of these three with the text

The subject of the *Yoga-sūtras* is, of course, yoga with its various categories and subdivisions, methods, and the end result. The purpose is self-realization (*kaivalya*) and release or liberation (*mokṣha*). The student is qualified whenever he has the *jijñāsā,* desire for knowledge, and *mumukṣhā,* determination for liberation. One who has the desire for knowledge is called a *jijñāsu* and one who has the determination for liberation is termed a *mumukṣhu.* These are the qualified students of yoga.

The relationship between yoga and the *Yoga-sūtras* is that of an expositor and exposition; the relationship between yoga and the student is that of a practice and its practitioner; and the relationship between the student and liberation is that of an achiever and his goal.

Sūtra I.1 is an *adhikāra-sūtra* or *uddeśha-sūtra* (see Prologue, pp. 20-21) stating the topic of the text.

Sūtra I.1 अथ योगानुशासनम्।

atha yogānuśhāsanam

atha: now, at an auspicious moment of transition
yoga-: (of) yoga
anu-: within or following (a tradition)
śhāsanam: instruction, discipline, teaching

Now, at this auspicious moment of transition begins the instruction in the discipline of yoga following the past tradition.

Vyāsa's Commentary

Atha 'now'—this word here has the purpose of indicating authority, qualification and commencement of the subject matter, so that the science called the Discipline of Yoga be known as the subject matter, the instruction of which commences by those authorized to those qualified.

Yoga is samādhi. And that samādhi is a universal attribute of the mind-field (chitta), common to all levels. The five grounds, levels, of the mind-field are:

kṣhipta: disturbed
mūḍha: somnolent, stupefied
vikṣhipta: distracted
ekāgra: one-pointed
niruddha: controlled

Among these, that samādhi subordinated and eclipsed by distraction in a distracted mind-field is not fit to be included within the category of yoga.

That, however is called samādhi of wisdom (*samprajñāta* yoga), which in a one-pointed mind-field

- fully illuminates an actual state or object (*artha*) that has become real, has been realized,
- diminishes the afflictions and impurities (*kleśhas*),

- loosens the bonds of karma, and
- brings about the possibility of control (*nirodha*) face to face, as it were.

As we shall explain later, that state of *samprajñāta* samādhi is of four types:

- accompanied by discursive thought
- accompanied by subtle thought
- accompanied by ecstasy
- accompanied by I-am-ness

However, when all the modifications (vṛttis) have come under control (*nirodha*), then it is called the acognitive (*asamprajñāta*) samādhi.

Discussion

The exposition on this sūtra will be divided into three sections, one for each of the three words *atha, yoga* and *anuśhāsana.*

I. *ATHA*

Certain words in the tradition are considered auspicious; that is, their occurrence in the beginning of a text imparts a blessing. Even though the translation of the word is not a blessing, its pronunciation in itself invokes a blessing. All the commentators quote:

> The words *OM* and *atha* came from the Creator's throat
> in the beginning of the creation;
> hence both these words are auspicious.

It is a norm in all theistic traditions to begin any undertaking with the invocation of a blessing; here no special words are used for that purpose alone; rather the word *atha* is bifunctional: May the study undertaken, the guidance given and received, and the disciplines observed come to bear their desired results without impediments. The *Brahma-sūtras,* the major text of the Vedānta philosophy, also begins with the word *atha*. Śhankarāchārya's commentary on this passage (*Brahma-sūtra* I.1) says:

> The word *atha*, used in an entirely different sense, yet invokes a blessing merely by its pronunciation.

Now we come to the literal sense of the word and its function as part of the teaching itself. *Atha* is a word of the particle (*avyaya*) category. Such words remain unchangeable in all grammatical and syntactical situations, and express states that are themselves immutable. *Atha* denotes a transition. How can a transition be immutable, when any transition always occurs only as part of a mutability? How can one conceive of a transition without a change?

The answer to this question is that it is human nature to observe transitions. People throughout the world celebrate the transitions of sun and moon from season to season and year to year. Major festivals are designed for the celebration of these transitions. The transitions of a life cycle are also observed with great joy or solemnity. Baptisms, weddings, bar mitzvahs, confirmations, as well as graduations and anniversaries, come within this category. The yoga tradition celebrates sixteen sacraments, starting from before conception and continuing through initiations, marriage, renunciation, up to the last rites. It is not possible, however, for one to celebrate every transition of life. Most people are not even aware of their subtle transitions, such as, for example, the change in breath rhythms that occurs about every ninety minutes, varying somewhat among different individuals.

In the methods that great yogis employ to teach their disciples, only the fewest words are used. A disciple must understand many levels of meaning from a single sound. The word *atha* expresses the "now" of a transition. The student is advised by use of the word *atha* that he must learn to observe the now of a transition. He must learn to notice, for instance, the exact moment when the breath rhythm shifts from one nostril to the other. The yogis know that no transition occurs without first touching the "eternal now." When this is understood, an instantaneous illumination may take place in the disciple's consciousness.

Transitions are discussed here with a view to understanding the yoga philosophy of time, space and causation. For most observers all time and space pass through a series of causes and effects—one thing seems to lead to another, each cause producing an effect, one object becoming another from one moment in time to another, moving from one space to another. While this is so at a superficial level at which those uninitiated into advanced yogic disciplines perceive the relative reality of worldly phenomena, yoga masters experience things at a deeper level. They say that it is not that a prior cause produces a subsequent effect, a former moment gives birth to a following moment, one particle causes momentum in another. Rather, all of these moments, particles and spaces are united in a common field (*kṣhetra*). No particle or moment passes from one state to another without first touching that common field on which the former and the latter are united. In other words, all transitions among pluralities occur only through the touch of a common singularity. There is no abrupt jump. All the fields are united in the supreme field of infinity. In this field there is no past, present or future—no prior or posterior. When the breath rhythm shifts from one nostril to the other—or more accurately, the energy flow moves from *iḍā* to *piṅgalā* or vice versa—for a micromoment the consciousness passes through the central stream called the *suṣhumnā.*[1] An initiate is advised to get hold of that moment, dwell in it, and enter the infinite consciousness through it.

1. In yoga teachings all movement and configurations of the physical body are considered to be gross manifestations of much subtler currents and fields, called the *nāḍīs*. Within the human personality flow 72,000 of these subtle energy channels, around which such things as the nerves and organs group themselves. The central *nāḍī,* metaphorically said to be one ten-thousandth of a hair's breadth in diameter, flows through the spinal column and is known as *suṣhumnā.* On the right side of *suṣhumnā* is *piṅgalā nāḍī,* which controls the sympathetic branch of the autonomic nervous system and governs "active" (masculine, solar) functions. On the left side of *suṣhumnā* is *iḍā nāḍī,* which controls the parasympathetic branch of the autonomic nervous system and governs "intuitive" (feminine, lunar) functions. By certain systematic yoga disciplines the *iḍā* and *piṅgalā nāḍīs* are balanced so that the *suṣhumnā* channel opens and samādhi is possible. For more complete information see Swami Rama, Rudolph Ballentine, M.D., and Swami Ajaya, Ph.D., *Yoga and Psychotherapy* (Honesdale, Pa.: Himalayan International Institute of Yoga Science and Philosophy, 1976), pp. 42-43, 45, 53-55, 58-59, 266. See also "The Awakening of Kundalini" and "Energy of Consciousness in the Human Personality" in *Inspired Thoughts of Swami Rama* (Honesdale, Pa.: Himalayan International Institute, 1983), pp. 197-230, and "Laya Yoga" and "Kundalini Yoga" in Swami Rama, *Choosing a Path* (Himalayan International Institute, 1982), pp. 147-94.

To go further: We experience our world in terms of moment-particle coordinates. Each particle has a movement within a moment, and many particles together make an object, a phenomenon; many moments following one upon another make a certain length of time. The yogi says that it is not true to say that a prior moment's cause produces the subsequent moment's effect, although it certainly does appear to be so in a world of transience. But when the many transiences are transcended, the actual reality is very different.

> Each moment arises directly from infinity.
> Each moment dissolves into infinity.
> The next moment also arises directly from infinity.
> Concentration on what is between the dissolution of the prior moment and the arising of the subsequent moment opens the gateway to infinity.

The word *atha* reminds the initiated disciple to concentrate on such immutability as is perceived in transitions as explained above. Let him dwell in the now. As the concentration is refined, the now covers only a micromoment. Soon the disciple learns to step aside from the procession in which he was previously a participant. The procession of particle-moment coordinates may continue for other participants, but not for the disciple who has stepped aside. While he may continue to watch it from outside as a spectator, as it were, he is not moved by its motion or momentum. The karma process ceases here; he dwells in the eternal now.

This *now* is the beginning and the end of the Discipline of Yoga.

There is a controversy among commentators concerning the real purpose of the word *atha*. As has already been mentioned, the word expresses:

> *ānantarya:* transition in a sequence
> *adhikāra:* a teacher's authority, a student's fulfilment of a qualification, and simply the statement of commencement

Commentators have said nothing about transition or the awareness of now within the oral tradition. They have taken into consideration other purposes of the word and agree that the word simply expresses (*a*) commencement of the topic, and (*b*) Patañjali's authority to undertake the same. In their view it does not express any kind of sequence in which there might be any implication of a student fulfilling a qualification. They say

> the word *atha* expresses here *adhikāra* and not *ānantarya.*

It is interesting to contrast this with the first sūtra of the *Brahma-sūtras* by the same Vyāsa:

> Now, from here on the desire to know Brahman.

Śhankarāchārya[2] says of that sūtra:

> The word *atha* expresses here *ānantarya* and not *adhikāra.*

Although metaphysical texts, especially those of the Vedānta philosophy, state that a student is qualified when he has practised the "six treasures" (*ṣhaṭ-sampat*):

> *śhama:* quietude
> *dama:* restraint
> *uparati:* withdrawal from worldly interests
> *titakṣhā:* forbearance
> *śhraddhā:* faith, humility, surrender
> *samādhāna:* freedom from conflicts

and although the *Bṛhadāraṇyaka Upaniṣhad* (IV.4.23) says,

2. The eighth century sage Śhankara is considered to be the greatest of the Indian philosophers. Following in the footsteps of Gauḍapāda, the guru of his guru (Govinda), who wrote the *Māṇḍūkya-kārikās,* the most complete ancient statement on Vedānta philosophy, Śhankara wrote definitive commentaries on the Upaniṣhads, the *Bhagavad-gītā* and the *Brahma-* or *Vedānta-sūtras* as well as such philosophical works as *Viveka-chūḍāmaṇi* (*The Crest Jewel of Discrimination*). Although his brief life of thirty-two years was accompanied by many miraculous events, his greatest accomplishment was the literal transformation of India by his restoration of the ancient Wisdom of the Vedas in the light of his *advaita* (non-dual) school of Vedānta and his establishment of many monastic schools to carry on the spiritual tradition. He established four seats of supreme religious and philosophical authority in India which have been occupied by an unbroken succession of saints, titled Śhankarāchāryas, from his day to the present.

> then, pacified, controlled, having withdrawn, forbearing,
> harmonized, one should see the self in the self,

none of these qualifications is implied in the *Yoga-sūtras.* This is not to say that any unqualified student may be admitted to the study and practice of yoga. The commentators are simply discussing Patañjali's actual intent in using the word *atha.* Patañjali only wished to express his desire to convey the knowledge. A desire to know (*jijñāsā*) on the part of the student is implied and that Patañjali has this knowledge (*jñāna*). There exist in the tradition preparations prerequisite to imparting a teaching, such as (*a*) a student's application and raising of questions, (*b*) his ascetic observances and purifications, (*c*) preparing the body through *rasāyanas,*[3] etc. Even though there is no question that Patañjali, himself probably an author on medical science, is aware of these and other preparations, his use of the word *atha*—in the opinions expressed by commentators—does not imply any of these preparations. He only expresses the fact that he knows, and wishes the knowledge to be conveyed.

All the other schools of philosophy, such as Vedānta, state that liberation is attained through knowledge, but they also prescribe various spiritual preparations. It is agreed among them that the means to attain that knowledge is yoga. *That* yoga is taught here. Patañjali asserts by the word *atha* that he is the authoritative teacher and wishes this knowledge of yoga to be conveyed. Hence he commences the teaching.

3. The science of *rasāyana* is not well known and requires some explanation. The word is derived from the multilevel word *rasa,* which refers to fluid essences of any kind. In alchemy it means mercury; in herbal medicine it means a juice; in the human body all fluids are called rasas. In the ancient medical science of *āyur-veda* an alchemy of the human body was practised whereby all the body's base and corrupting factors were cleansed and converted into strength, thereby rejuvenating the body. These highly complex practises required application of

- internal purifications and disciplines,
- dietary prescriptions,
- herbal juices and potions, and
- compounds of mercury, sulphur, gold, etc., administered in carefully prepared doses.

Sometimes such an alteration of body chemistry was necessary when it was intended that the person remain in samādhi for a prolonged period of time, or when it was necessary to strengthen the body for especially strenuous practices.

Mādhavāchārya clarifies that since discipline (*anuśhāsana*) includes the practices of pacification (*śhama*), etc., there is no point in also trying to make them as prerequisites under the word *atha.*

The word *atha* has these purposes here: (*a*) an auspicious invocation, (*b*) a statement of Patañjali's authority, and (*c*) a declaration of the commencement of Patañjali's teaching. This is the view of the commentators. The oral tradition, however, concurs with *YS* I.1:

> *Now,* this is the discipline of yoga.

That is to say, if one could observe his transitions and the way the states between moments serve as gateways to infinity, all the stages of yoga would be at his command. The student's qualifications are not denied but simply not stated until the word "discipline" (*anuśhāsana*) is encountered.

According to the commentators, selectiveness as to the meanings of *atha* is applicable here only and not universally. That is why Vyāsa says,

> *Atha*—this word here.

Previous traditions within which yoga is taught by Patañjali also are important to these matters. The name of Yogi Yājñavalkya occurs repeatedly in the Upaniṣhads as one of the greatest metaphysicians of his time. His statement affirms the entire yoga tradition:

> Hiraṇya-garbha alone is the teacher of yoga, and no other.
>
> *Bṛhad-yogi-yājñavalkya-smṛti* XII.5

The word *Hiraṇya-garbha* means "the Golden Womb." The word occurs in the ancient Vedas:

> In the beginning was the Golden Womb.
>
> *Ṛg-veda* X.121.1

All the yogis insist that no individual person is a teacher, master, or guru, but that the Golden Womb alone is the guru. In that womb the minds of all beings are like fetuses. As a fetus receives nourishment from the mother through the umbilical cord, so all minds in meditation receive knowledge from the Golden Womb, the Teaching Spirit of the Universe. This is similar to the Christian notion of the Holy Spirit, who is the teacher of all teachers. When one frees himself from all ego, all the knowledge of the Golden Womb flows into him effortlessly and naturally. Just as a fetus, receiving nourishment from its mother, does not know itself separate from her, so those in meditation do not know themselves separate from the Golden Womb. All revelation is of the grace that flows from the Golden Womb into the minds of those in meditation. Some traditions assert that the Golden Womb reveals itself in the beginning of creation in the minds of the first human beings. Others go so far as to say that the first human being is a Master, who is an incarnation of the Golden Womb, the Teaching Spirit that has become flesh and from whom all spiritual knowledge begins and is handed down through the lineage of the yogis. He is also known as the Progenitor (*Prajāpati*) or Brahmā (a masculine word not to be confused with the neuter word Brahman), the founder and first teacher of the Vedas. All the yogis trace their lineage, through their masters, ultimately to Hiraṇya-garbha or Prajāpati or Brahmā, whose own teacher is no other but Svayam-bhū, the Self-Existent Being.

The *Bṛhadāraṇyaka Upaniṣhad,* considered to be the oldest of the Upaniṣhads and dating back to approximately the thirteenth century B.C., states the spiritual genealogy of teachers up to that time. *Bṛhadāraṇyaka Upaniṣhad* IV.6.1-3 lists fifty-nine generations of teachers, and VI.5.1-4 lists sixty-six generations up to that time and going back to Brahmā, who is the same as the Golden Womb. Other texts such as the Purāṇas give much longer lists.

It is called a golden womb because when a master initiates a disciple into its mysteries, the disciple experiences within himself the presence of a golden light. Unlike the foggy light of the dream state, which is unclear consciousness, this golden light of the higher state of consciousness imparts a luminosity to the seeker's mind, in the presence of which intuitive knowledge often dawns (*Kena*

Upaniṣhad II.25). Often the visage of such a person shines with a golden light.

The word "womb," in addition to the explanation above, also suggests that an enlightened being, who has chosen to incarnate for the benefit of the world, often receives reminiscences of this supreme knowledge while still within the mother's womb and is then born a teacher.

The question arises that if Hiraṇya-garbha is the teacher of yoga, why is such importance given to Patañjali? Why does Patañjali present himself as such a figure of authority? The question may be answered in two ways:

1. The authenticity of the opening verse of Vyāsa's commentary is controversial because some manuscripts include it and others do not. However, the verse says that Patañjali is the same who incarnates again and again to teach the knowledge of yoga, even through he may bear different names from incarnation to incarnation.
2. The other way lies in the word *anuśhāsana,* which we have translated as "discipline."

II. *ANUŚHĀSANA*

The word *anuśhāsana* is derived from the prefix *anu* and the verb root *śhās*. The prefix *anu* denotes that something is subsequent, a follow-up to something else that formerly occurred or existed. The verb *śhās* means "to impart a discipline or a teaching" or "to teach with a definite discipline." The English word "discipline," meaning a field of study, is similar. A teaching without an attendant discipline will not be expressed with the verb *śhās.* From the same verb is derived the word for a disciple (*śhiṣhya*), one who is to be taught with and within a discipline. In the ancient education systems of India the teaching of every subject was imparted within the context of an *āśhrama* discipline with definite rules of life. There were three types of graduates:

vidyā-snātaka: one who has mastered a science
vrata-snātaka: one who has demonstrated the mastery of personal discipline
vidyā-vrata-snātaka: one who has proficiency in a field of learning and has demonstrated the mastery of personal disciplines

It was the third type of graduate who was most cherished as a disciple. Knowledge in the ancient *āśhramas* was not imparted indiscriminately.

> Knowledge came to the philosopher (*brāhmaṇa*) and said,
> "I am your treasure; do guard me.
> Do not give me away to someone malicious—
> so that I may grow in strength.
> Only whom you know to be pure, controlled,
> a master of passions, a celibate—
> give me to him, a wise man who guards his treasure
> without negligence."
>
> *Lawbook of Manu* II.114-15

Similar injunctions are given in the tradition elsewhere and repeatedly.

The prefix *anu* has these two connotations in the word *anuśhāsana:*

1. The discipline of yoga is being imparted only after the student has demonstrated his purity in observances of self-discipline and has prepared the ground in which the seed is to be sown. Because this idea was inherent in the word *anuśhāsana,* it need not be expressed in the word *atha.*
2. The commentators say, "*Śhiṣhṭasya śhāsanam-anuśhāsanam":* "*Anuśhāsana* means 'to teach that which has been taught before, to teach within an existing tradition, not claiming that anything new has been created by the author.' "

Patañjali by using the prefix *anu* issues a disclaimer to his own authorship of the science even though by the word *atha* he has stated his authority to teach it.

The word *anuśhāsana* also means "that (text) by which the science (of samādhi, in this case) is taught, together with the means of its attainment and fruits, so that it fructifies and succeeds." This knowledge is open to anyone who seeks absoluteness and liberation (*kaivalya*). Such a text taught within a tradition and with a discipline is called a *śhāstra;* hence the entire science is known as *yoga-śhāstra.*

In this context Vyāsa's sentence is again presented:

> *Atha* 'now'—this word here has the purpose of indicating authority, qualification and commencement of the subject matter, so that the science called the Discipline of Yoga be known as the subject matter, the instruction of which commences by those authorized to those qualified.[4]

III. *YOGA*

As to the word "yoga," Vyāsa simply says,

> Yoga is samādhi.

The word can be derived from the Sanskrit verb *yuj,* which occurs in Pāṇini's list of verbs (*dhātu-pāṭha*) in several forms as follows:

> *yuj* of the fourth conjugation (*yujyate*), meaning "samādhi";
> *yujir* of the sixth conjugation (*yunakti*), meaning "samādhi"; and
> *yuj* of the tenth conjugation (*yojayati*), meaning "to join" or "to restrain" or "to keep under control, as in yoking."

The English word "yoke" is acknowledged by the Oxford English Dictionary to be cognate to *yuj,* and so is the word "join." "Yoke"

4. It is interesting to note that Patañjali's *Mahābhāṣhya,* his vast exposition on Pāṇini's grammar, begins with words almost identical to *YS* I.1. The first sentences of Vyāsa's commentary on the *Mahābhāṣhya* read as follows:

> *Now,* the instruction in the discipline of words. The word *atha* 'now' has the purpose of indicating authority, qualification and commencement of the subject matter, so that the science called the Discipline of Words may be known as the subject matter, the instruction of which commences by those authorized to those qualified.

Other similarities between the Yoga-sūtras and Vyāsa, on the one hand, and the grammatical texts, on the other, have been studied by numerous scholars. The relationship of the science of yoga and the science of speech has been explained to a certain extent in the author's book *Mantra and Meditation* (Honesdale, Pa.: Himalayan International Institute of Yoga Science and Philosophy, 1981).

is derived from the third *yuj* in the above list; "join" is from the second but its meaning is from the third. Ancient Vedic texts use the former two as meaning "to experience samādhi." According to Vyāsa, the word "yoga" in this sūtra is derived not from the *yuj* of yoking or joining but from the verbs meaning "samādhi." However, one is then left with the question of why the oral tradition often states that the word may be derived from the verb meaning "joining" or "yoking." This may be explained by the fact that the ancient sages of the period of the Vedas and early Upaniṣhads experienced samādhi as a union of the individual and the universal self, thereby lending a secondary meaning to the same verb. The primary meaning was probably "samādhi," as seen in the most ancient hymns (for example, *Ṛg-veda* V.81.1), but elsewhere the Vedic and Upaniṣhadic literature is replete with usage of the verbs from the fourth and sixth conjugations in the sense of "uniting," "joining," as well as "restraining" and "yoking." Examples of this usage include *Ṛg-veda* I.82.6 and X.101.3; *Kauṣhītaki Upaniṣhad* II.6; *Kena Upaniṣhad* I.1; *Bṛhadāraṇyaka Upaniṣhad* II.5.19 and V.13.2; and numerous other places. A study of the ancient texts shows, therefore, that the forms are used interchangeably.[5]

The oral tradition has scant regard for the artificial rules of grammar, but the grammarians themselves admit, as does Patañjali (not in the *Yoga-sūtras* but in the *Mahābhāṣhya,* his work on grammar), that grammarians only acknowledge the usage of words as found in the Vedas and among the people. Therefore one need not concern himself unduly if there appears to be a conflict between grammarians and philosophers. Furthermore, since philosophy is being studied here, one needs to accept Vyāsa's statement that the word "yoga" in the *Yoga-sūtras* means "samādhi." This is also the view held by MA. The oral tradition goes on to explain that the process leading to samādhi begins with restraining the senses, and yoking the mind to the inner self, and that the experience of samādhi itself is joining the lower self and the higher self. All of these layers

5. Why Pāṇini, considered to be history's foremost grammarian, chose to differentiate them so substantially can only be answered by the guess that perhaps by his time the conjugational forms of the verbs had settled into fixed meanings as recorded by him.

and levels of the endeavour and experience are included in the word "yoga." And since "restraining," "yoking," or "joining" used separately would have been incomplete, Vyāsa chose to derive the word from the verb meaning "samādhi." This falls within the convention of Indian logic known as *aṅgāṅgi-bhāva:* that is to say, when a statement is made concerning a complete entity (*aṅgin* 'one who owns *aṅgas,* or parts'), each one of its parts (*aṅgas*) is already included. MA says that the endeavour and experience of samādhi is inclusive of restraining, yoking and joining, since these fall within the eight *aṅgas* of yoga. BR says that not only a joining or union but even a separation (*vi-yoga*) may be included among the parts that constitute the complete endeavour of samādhi. The separation, according to BR, is between the conscious self and its attachment to matter: *pum-prakṛtyor viyogo'pi yogaḥ.*

AD also says that yoga as union means the merging together of mind and self (ātman) like that of water and salt. No further explanation of this theory is given. How this merging of mind and self in a yogi differs from the personality of one still in ignorance and bondage is not explained. He goes on to say that the word "samādhi" may be explained in two ways:

- that by which the mind is brought to concentration. In this instrumental sense it is the eighth limb (*aṅga*) of yoga.
- that state in which the operations such as *prāṇa* are brought under control. In this locative sense it is synonymous with yoga proper.

The question arises that if samādhi, too, is enumerated among the eight *aṅgas,* limbs, of yoga, then how can it be regarded as that whole, the *aṅgin,* of which the others are limbs, parts, or the means thereto? This difficulty is resolved by different commentators in different ways. AD, for instance, implies that by the word "samādhi" Vyāsa does not mean the eighth limb of yoga but simply *yoga nāma samādhānam:* that "samādhi" means *samādhāna* 'harmonizing', 'a resolving of conflicts within and without', in the same sense in which the word *samādhāna* is used among the "six treasures" prerequisite to liberation (p. 67, above). Both RY and SS explain that yoga, meaning "samādhi," has two levels as explained in *YS* I.17,18. The reader is referred to those two sūtras, which explain the samādhi of wisdom (*samprajñāta* samādhi) and the acognitive (*asamprajñāta*) samādhi. Of these two the cognitive, yet alloyed, is only a step toward the final goal of the acognitive. RY and SS hold that the former is a limb and a means (*aṅga*) while the latter is the true yoga in its entirety and perfection. RY further states that when Vyāsa says that

> samādhi is a universal attribute of the mind-field (chitta), common to all levels,

Vyāsa's view is that samādhi is an attribute of the mind-field: because the modifications (vṛttis) of the mind-field are attributes of the mind-field, samādhi being only their control or cessation (as defined in the present sūtra), samādhi is an attribute of the mind-field! This seems to be totally untenable and does not fit any of the yoga traditions.

An alternative explanation is that yoga is being taught to the students of Patañjali on two different levels: (1) an experiential level, which cannot be put into formal wording; and (2) a formal system of philosophy with its own terminology. Sometimes the two do not coincide. The formal systematization of the philosophy states that yoga is the control of the modifications of the mind-field and samādhi is the eighth of its limbs (*aṅgas*) and means. Vyāsa, the commentator par excellence, does not wish the student to forget that a true follower of yoga must see even beyond these definitions; otherwise why would he venture a definition of yoga in his commentary on *YS* I.1 when Patañjali, from whose work Vyāsa could not mean to detract, has already defined yoga in *YS* I.2? When Vyāsa says

> *Yogaḥ samādhiḥ* 'yoga is samādhi',

he is referring neither to yoga as defined in *YS* I.2, nor to samādhi as defined in *YS* I.17,18, nor as it is included among the eight *aṅgas* in *YS* II.29 and III.3.

The problem is solved only by reading Vyāsa's next sentence:

> And that samādhi is a universal attribute of the mind-field (chitta), common to all levels.

The word "universal" (*sārva-bhauma*) needs an explanation. Literally it means "that which remains in all *bhūmis,*" that is, grounds, levels or plateaus that are attained and subsequently passed on the way to the highest samādhi. What exactly are these *bhūmis* at which the yogi arrives and then leaves behind as he proceeds to his goal? There are many definitions of this term in the *Yoga-sūtras* and the commentaries. These should be studied in detail as the reader refers to the pertinent sūtras: *YS* I.30, II.27, III.6. In commenting on *YS* II.27, Vyāsa defines the seven levels of attainment as follows:

1. One has recognized what he must renounce (pain); it no more needs to be known.
2. One has eliminated the causes of pain; they no longer need to be diminished.
3. One has realized the vanquishing of pain through attainment of the samādhi of total control (*nirodha*-samādhi).
4. One has cultivated the means of the removal of pain; that is, discrimination between self and non-self has been perfected.
5. The faculty of discrimination (buddhi) has now completed its work.
6. The attributes (guṇas) of nature are dissolved into their material cause and no longer bind the self.
7. The self no longer has any relationships with material nature or the non-self and is now pure light, absolute, alone.

In his commentary on *YS* III.51 Vyāsa describes the yogis at four different levels of attainment:

1. Those who have just begun the experience of light; these are called beginners (*prāthama-kalpika*).
2. Those whose intuitive wisdom (*ṛtambharā prajñā*) has begun to blossom; they are being tempted by the powerful beings of the subtle worlds to enjoy the powers recently gained; these are at the honeyed ground (*madhu-bhūmi*).

3. Those who have conquered the senses and their attractions and have mastered the elements; they have become firmly protective toward all that needs to be cultivated and firm in all the duties they need to perform; they are *prajñā-jyotis,* for wisdom is their light.
4. Those who have transcended all processes and no longer have anything remaining yet to be cultivated (*atikrānta-bhāvanīya*).

VM, however, enumerates four *bhūmis,* as follows:

1. *madhumatī:* honeyed, filled with sweetness
2. *madhu-pratīkā:* where the honey of the first ground has become as though it had been only symbolic of this second level to come
3. *vi-śhokā:* beyond grief
4. *saṁskāra-śheṣhā:* where only the impressions of past karmas and experiences remain as deposits, but no fresh karma is formed[6]

The question remains as to which one of these groups Vyāsa refers when he says that samādhi is an attribute common to all the grounds of a yogi's development. The answer is that even though VM says that the four, *madhumatī* and so forth, are meant, that does not seem to be Vyāsa's intent, since he goes on to enumerate five states of the mind-field:

kṣhipta: disturbed
mūḍha: somnolent, stupefied
vikṣhipta: distracted from meditation
ekāgra: one-pointed
niruddha: controlled

Before these five are discussed in detail, it is still necessary to understand what is meant by the statement that

6. Of these four *bhūmis* the first is the same as no. 2 of *YS* III.51. The second, *madhu-pratīkā,* is defined in Vyāsa's commentary on *YS* III.48. The third, *vi-śhokā,* is defined in *YS* I.36. The fourth, *saṁskāra-śheṣhā,* occurs in *YS* I.18. The reader should compare these references to the list.

samādhi is a universal attribute of the mind-field (chitta), common to all levels.

How can samādhi be an attribute in an agitated, somnolent or distracted mind?

As MA explains it, the nature of the spiritual self is defined throughout the Sāṅkhya and yoga philosophies to be pure, absolute, immutable. This nature never changes no matter what kind of mind serves as a mantle to the pure, spiritual self. Thus the transcendent being never loses its transcendence. Its immutability always remains unimpaired. This force, called consciousness, is never altered (*YS* II.20,21; IV.34). Only the mind-field goes through the three altered states of consciousness called wakeful awareness of objects, dream and sleep. Since transcendence remains unaffected, it equally permeates all functions, operations, experiences and states that are dependent on this consciousness. Since mind is regarded as a modification of matter and is not spiritual, it is also dependent on the consciousness of the spiritual self, whom it has no power to corrupt in any way. According to *YS* IV.18, all the vṛttis of the mind-field are always known to the spiritual self. The natural state of this self is samādhi, which always remains so even though the mind-field goes through various alterations.

This being the case, no question arises regarding Vyāsa's statement that samādhi is a state that remains throughout the various levels of attainment. A human being is a compound of the power of pure consciousness and the corruptible, alterable, mutable material (including mental) components. When a person rediscovers the separation of the spiritual component from the material one, that is called isolation of the self from matter (*kaivalya*). It is not that the spiritual self itself had ever mingled with lowly matter, but that it had lent its own power to matter so that the latter could function as the mind. Its own samādhi remains unbroken. It is the universal (*sārvabhauma*) common ground of all other operations of the compound personality.

The total and permanent incorruptibility and immutability of the spiritual self is the fundamental tenet of yoga philosophy. If any of the attributes of this self were to increase or decrease even in an immeasurably minute degree, the entire tenet would have to be rejected. In that case transcendence would be no transcendence at all because it would be subject to alteration. There would simply be no point in pursuing yoga because it would only lead to a temporary state (*pariṇāma*), which is the cause of our pains. So it must be reiterated that samādhi is the permanent and natural state of the spiritual self.

VM explains that the definition of yoga as control of the operations of the mind-field (*YS* I.2) is effective only with regard to the practical aspects of yoga. Lest one come away with the impression that the vṛttis are apprehensions or cognitions residing in the self, Vyāsa specifies that they are attributes of the mind-field. The transcendent illumination of the self imparts its luminosity to the mind-field, whereby the mind-field functions and even undergoes all of its operations and alterations. It is in this sense that Vyāsa says,

> Samādhi is a universal attribute of the mind-field (chitta), common to all levels.

VB says that a little meditative concentration shows through even in the agitation, somnolence or distraction of the mind; hence, too, samādhi may be considered as the universal ground of all these alterations.

In any case mind-field (*chitta*) is not to be confused with the pure consciousness (*chiti*).

Here a question arises: If samādhi (in the sense of transcendence) is the permanent nature of the spiritual self and mind is regarded as a mode of matter, how can Vyāsa say that

> samādhi is a universal attribute of the mind-field (chitta), common to all levels.

VM has tried to resolve the apparent conflict by saying that it is not the entire mind-field that is meant. According to Sāṅkhya-yoga philosophy, one of the four aspects of the inner sense is in closest touch with the self. That aspect is called the faculty of discrimination (buddhi). This faculty has two faces: an outward face, looking toward the conscious mind and the senses, that may be called "the faculty of intelligence"; and an inward face, looking toward the spiritual self, that may be called "the faculty of intuition."

The buddhi's faculty of discrimination serves as the channel between the spiritual self and the rest of the personality. Buddhi partakes of that finest, purest-possible aspect of nature (prakṛti) known as sattva, whose attribute is illumination. The light of the self by itself is immutable, and the self is untouched by any qualities of matter. However, the face of the self reflects in the buddhi like a ray of sun into a crystal mirror, from which it is deflected onto, or passes through to, other aspects of mind, and from there to the brain, the senses and the rest of the personality. It is this reflected or deflected light alone that operates the whole personality, while the spiritual self, the soul, remains aloof, immutable.

Without the presence of this reflected illumination the human personality is nothing but dead matter. The presence of this reflected light gives to the buddhi, and thereby to the rest of the mind-field, the power which enables the whole mind to perform all of its functions and to go through all of its stages of development. Because this light of samādhi is ever-present in the back of the mind, in the inward face of the buddhi, it is in this sense that samādhi is the permanent and universal attribute of the mind even during its lower states of awareness.

The presence of this state of samādhi, even in the lower, disturbed states, is demonstrated by the fact that no matter how agitated the mind may be at any given time it still concentrates on only one thing or another, one thought or another, one emotion or another. If it dwells on any thought for even a fleeting micromoment, it is still a level of concentration. Without this faculty of concentration, the mind could not even be agitated. The yogis dwell on and in the concentration, ignoring the surface agitation. Thus, once again, samādhi is a universal and permanent attribute of the mind.

Of the many levels of the mind's operations, one has to cease before another can be introduced. This is not possible unless buddhi and the mind-field establish control over each level. That the mind is able to shift from one level to another, one state to another, shows that it has mastery, control (*nirodha*)—the primary definition of samādhi (see pp. 86ff. and *YS* I.2)—at all times. Thus also is samādhi a permanent and universal attribute of the mind-field.

Manifestation of the degree of samādhi, however, is another matter. The mind, a modification of matter, is constituted of its three guṇas. The disturbed states of the mind reflect the simple disequilibrium of the three guṇas which is the common nature of all creation; the mind, being part of that creation, partakes of that disequilibrium. It is the varying degrees of disequilibrium in the proportion and predominance of the guṇas that cause varying states of mind. Vyāsa's concern here is not with other *bhūmis* but only with the five states of the mind-field (*kṣhipta,* etc.). Of these, the agitated (*kṣhipta*) state is dominated by rajas, totally unsteady, always flung about from one object to another. This is the wakeful state of a "normal" person in the world.

The somnolent (*mūḍha*) state is dominated by tamas, which represents the state of sleep and other forms of stupor such as being comatose, inebriated, drug-afflicted, or otherwise generally not alert. In other words, there is not a definite boundary line between *kṣhipta* and *mūḍha.* Often a wakeful person considers himself to be quite alert but, under the influence of tamas, makes a stupid mistake.

There are other examples of the alternation between *kṣhipta* and *mūḍha,* or between the dominance of rajas and tamas. For instance, says VB, rajas draws us toward the objects of attraction, causing a mood called *rāga* in which the mind is coloured by the object of attraction. When the wish to enjoy or possess the object of that *rāga* is thwarted, a negation ensues. The mind becomes clouded with tamas, and consequently depression (*viṣhāda*) begins. One can similarly analyse the alterations of moods and other emotional states by observing the alternating dominance of rajas and tamas.

Vyāsa has included *kṣhipta* and *mūḍha* in his enumeration of the five states but then throughout the rest of the text has nothing much to say about them except where it is absolutely necessary, as in the case of the vṛtti for sleep (*nidrā*), which is discussed in *YS*

I.12. The two states of *kṣhipta* and *mūḍha* are of no interest to Patañjali and Vyāsa. They have been generally ignored by Indian sages, whereas they are a major preoccupation of contemporary Western psychologists.

Our concern begins with *vi-kṣhipta,* a modification of, and some improvement on, the agitated *kṣhipta.* On the way to samādhi, sattva begins to assert its illuminative power. The mind begins here to find some concentration, but its former habits keep dragging it away from sattva. Rajas and tamas do not want to let go, but sattva has begun to make its presence felt. When the mind is still distracted from concentration, which experience has already begun, that state is called distraction (*vikṣhepa*). *Vikṣhepas* are the nine impediments (*YS* I.30) and their five companions (*YS* I.31). A mind afflicted by *vikṣhepas* is *vikṣhipta.*

There arises the possibility that those experiencing meditation with such a distraction might claim themselves to be yogis. To eliminate such a misunderstanding about the nature of yoga, Vyāsa says:

> Samādhi subordinated and eclipsed by distraction in a distracted [*vikṣhipta*] mind-field is not fit to be included within the category of yoga [that is, samādhi, since he has defined yoga to mean samādhi].

In a *vikṣhipta* mind samādhi occurs intermittently, in short bursts. It is not conducive to elimination of *kleśhas* (defined in *YS* II.3ff.). When someone is overcome by an enemy, he is powerless and ineffective; in fact, he loses his very face, his very nature. When concentration is overcome by rajas and tamas in the *vikṣhipta* state, its sattva is nowhere to be found. To give another analogy, when a seed has fallen into a fire and remains there even for three or four seconds, it is thereafter unable to sprout. Likewise, when concentration has fallen into the fire of rajas even for three or four seconds, it has no power to lead a personality toward samādhi.

Having dismissed the first three states as unworthy of a detailed definition (*a-lakṣhya*), Vyāsa introduces the fourth state of mind, *ekāgra,* or *samprajñāta* samādhi. He states that this is called *samprajñāta* yoga, samādhi of wisdom,

> which in a one-pointed (*ekāgra*) mind-field
>
> - fully illuminates an actual state or object (*artha*) that has become real, has been realized,
> - diminishes the afflictions and impurities (*kleśhas*),
> - loosens the bonds of karma, and
> - brings about the possibility of control (*nirodha*) face to face, as it were.

Here we need to refer to the original Sanskrit words to explain their purport.

Artha is a purpose, an aim, as well as an object of pursuit or of concentration. In meditation reaching *samprajñāta* samādhi (defined in *YS* I.17ff.) the concentration is so deep that the object itself develops a mental reality as the flow of concentration remains uninterrupted. The true nature of the object is then realized, and consequently the very essence of that object, wherever it may be in the universe, is completely mastered. This will be explained in greater detail in Chapter 3.

An object of concentration has to be real (*sad-bhūtam*). VM says that this eliminates a state like sleep, where there is intense concentration, but on its own tamas with no illumination of anything real.

Vyāsa could have simply said *dyotayati* 'illuminates', but he adds the prefix *pra,* resulting in *pra-dyotayati* 'fully illuminates'. This has a special significance. Objects are often illuminated in our intelligence in the ordinary state of wakefulness; but that illumination is not complete. The mind is disturbed by rajas and sees the objects in a distorted form. When a person with a diseased eye sees the moon, the mind is pseudo-illuminated by that experience and might be completely convinced that it is seeing two moons. All of our senses are at all times unreliable. Any reality we perceive is thus unreliable and not presented to us in its full form.

Similarly, the knowledge gained from inferential logic is an impaired one. It depends on data presented by unreliable, impaired, imperfect, incomplete senses. How can arguments developed on the basis of such indirect perception be reliable? What the logicians call direct perception through the senses is an indirect perception in the view of the yogis simply because (*a*) the multicoloured senses intervene between the mind and the external objects; (*b*) the imperfect mind intercepts and reinterprets to the buddhi what has been presented to it by the unreliable senses; and (*c*) the senses, mind and buddhi all together conspire to present to the inner, reflecting self a picture that is incomplete, incorrect, impaired and distorted.

In yoga epistemology, therefore, reality (*sad* or *sat*) is accurately seen only by the inner self directly in concentration without the intervention of the senses, mind and buddhi. It is this which the yogis call direct perception (*pratyakṣha*), and all schools of Indian philosophy refer to it as *yogi-pratyakṣha.* It is in *samprajñāta* samādhi that such a direct perception (*pratyakṣha*) occurs. This alone is the full illumination expressed by *pra-dyotayati.*

Such a realization of the nature of reality vanquishes the five afflictions (*kleśhas*) (*YS* II.3ff.). As these causes of bondage are eliminated, that which binds the spiritual self with buddhi automatically loses its glutinous strength. The causes of bondage are loosened. They are no longer capable of producing the future effects of any possible karma because the yogi has now risen above virtue and vice (*dharma* and *adharma*). Through this process final freedom from attachments (*para-vairāgya*) (*YS* I.16) develops and one finally sees the possibility of reaching *asamprajñāta* samādhi, that for which all this was a preparation, that which is *aṅgin,* the whole, for which all these are *aṅgas,* supports, parts and means thereto.

The question arises that since *samprajñāta* samādhi has been described as fourfold (*YS* I.17ff.), accompanied with discursive thought and so forth, does this indicate that the affliction (*kleśha*) called ignorance (*avidyā*) is still present? How can such a state be called full illumination or realization? VB answers that the first three stages of *samprajñāta* lead to the fourth and may be considered incorporated in it. In that fourth state arises the Truth-bearing intuitive wisdom (*ṛtambharā prajñā*) (*YS* I.48), and the objection is thus overruled.

But beyond the realization of cosmic realities through intense concentration is *asamprajñāta* yoga, acognitive samādhi. Vyāsa says,

> When all the modifications (vṛttis) have come under control (*nirodha*), then it is called acognitive (*asamprajñāta*) samādhi.

VB states that even the vṛtti of the mind that is present in *samprajñāta* samādhi needs to be brought to *nirodha,* rendered inoperative, through the attainment of *para-vairāgya* (*YS* I.6,18), and then *asamprajñāta* samādhi is reached. *Nirodha* is defined as that state wherein

- any fresh impressions of the external world, its experiences, relationships and memories no longer arise,
- the state of samādhi creates its own impressions on the soul's mental mantle, but
- the impressions left in the mind-field from past experiences still remain.

It is the force of these past impressions that continues to create for the yogi a physical reality, including the illness or health of the body and its regular operations, until the continuously strengthened samādhi-saṁskāras, the impressions of the samādhi being created on the mind, finally burn out even the past saṁskāras. Then the yogi is called a *jīvan-mukta,* one who is liberated while yet in a body, using the body out of benevolence for the benefit of others.

In other words, *nirodha* is not an absence of vṛttis, says VB. It is not a cessation or suppression, as many contemporary translators mistakenly assert. If this were so, yoga would have to be defined as a particular condition of the substratum of those vṛttis, the substratum being the mind-field. Samādhi is not such a state of the mind. In the actual experience of samādhi, the mind, being under the control of the spiritual self, is not made blank. The mind may continue to function according to its own nature. The yogi is not a mindless being. His mind has become, however, an instrument under his control. The modifications of the mind continue, but under his direction. Past saṁskāras remain operative at first until only the *nirodha*-saṁskāras remain (*YS* III.9,10; IV.26).

> As someone with a torch in hand finds the object he looked for, and then abandons the torch, so, attaining knowledge through spiritual awakening, one should leave the awakening behind.

(This passage has been quoted by VB from an unknown source and a somewhat similar passage is to be found in *Brahma-vidyā Upaniṣhad,* 36.) The word *bodha* is translated as "spiritual awakening," from the verb root *budh* 'to awaken', 'to get to know'. From the same verb is derived *bodhi* 'a Buddha's enlightenment'. *Bodha* can also mean "a teaching or direction given." This teaching may be given by the guru or simply be the direction one finds from one state to the next in the internal journey toward enlightenment. Finally one abandons these means to enlightenment because transcendental knowledge has dawned. Verse 5 of the *Brahma-bindu Upaniṣhad* reads:

> One should attempt restraint (*nirodha*) only until it vanishes in the heart. This is the extent of knowledge and liberation; the rest is all useless expanse of texts!

At this point VB takes up a challenge presumably presented by followers of Vedānta and Buddhist philosophies. Before we go further, let it be understood that Vedānta and Buddhism, like yoga, can also be understood at two levels:

1. The experiential level, in which there can be no disagreement with the yogis
2. The formal systems of philosophy

The discussion here centers around the formalities of the system.

Vedānta is regarded as the path of knowledge (*jñāna*). It is *jñāna*-yoga, the yoga of knowledge proper. Vedāntic texts say that liberation occurs through knowledge. Similarly, Buddhists regard samādhi as a step towards wisdom or knowledge (*paññā*) among the "three jewels" consisting of

sīla: conduct
samādhi: concentration
paññā: wisdom, knowledge

NBB starts by presenting the controversy concerning the path of *jñāna* and yoga. He then attempts to reconcile the two by stating that liberation (*mokṣha*) does occur through *jñāna,* but that yoga is the means to *jñāna.* In both commentaries, NB and NBB, Nāgeśha takes a solid Vedānta position with respect to the nature of Brahman and believes that yoga is the means of eliminating ignorance about that nature. The arguments of VB, BG, NB, and NBB as to the difference or identity between the Sāṅkhya puruṣha and the Vedānta Brahman will not be presented in our discussions. The commentators' attempts to reconcile *jñāna* and yoga throughout their works are important and are summarized here from VB's commentary.

He asks why one needs all this emphasis on *nirodha* of the vṛttis, when knowledge alone would suffice.

> Through the observance of the *aṅgas* of yoga, as impurities diminish, knowledge is kindled till discrimination produces correct wisdom.
>
> *YS* II.28

Obviously, knowledge and wisdom are the goals; and the *aṅgas*—the eight limbs of yoga that include *samprajñāta* and *asamprajñāta* samādhis—are the means thereto. It is impossible for the same state or entity to be the cause (of knowledge) and the effect (as final wisdom) simultaneously.

So, assuming at least that *samprajñāta* samādhi is the means of knowledge and that *asamprajñāta* samādhi is the effect as knowledge, one could also postulate another possibility: that *samprajñāta* samādhi is the cause of knowledge by removing impediments in the way of knowledge. This postulation is supported by *YS* I.41, which states that when the vṛttis of the mind-field have diminished as though the mind is pure like a crystal, then the mind becomes one with (*a*) that which grasps (I-am-ness, the reflection of the pure self in the buddhi), (*b*) the instruments of grasping (the ahaṁkāra and senses, including mind), and (*c*) the objects grasped (the gross and subtle elements, etc.); dwelling in them, the mind becomes as of one colour with them. But *asamprajñāta* yoga will not be regarded as a means of knowledge because it is produced by the former, *samprajñāta* samādhi. Furthermore, continues the argument, no additional means for liberation are needed once knowledge has been produced.

> To him (it appears), "I have delay only as long as I am not yet liberated. Thereafter I shall prosper."
>
> *Chhāndogya Upaniṣhad* VI.14.2

It is obvious from these scriptural words that knowledge which is totally independent of any other means or consideration is the means for liberation. When ignorance, desires, acts and so forth have ceased through the instrumentality of that knowledge, there is no further cause for transmigration (*saṁsāra*), which finally ceases. In other words, suggests the opponent, let us interpret the *Yoga-sūtras* in conformity with the demands of the Vedānta and Buddhist philosophies and consider knowledge to be the goal. Let us consider *asamprajñāta* samādhi to be that goal synonymous with knowledge which Vedānta and Buddhist philosophies propose as the final goal—the ultimate step to liberation. Many sūtras of Patañjali, examples of which are quoted in this argument, can be interpreted to support this view.

A proponent of the traditional interpretation of the *Yoga-sūtras* opposes such an interpretation and wishes to remain true to the formalities of the system. He responds to his opponent by saying that this, too, is the result of the two levels of samādhi: that pain, which remains necessary because of past karmas and continues in succeeding reincarnations, should cease when knowledge is attained. As Vyāsa says in his commentary on *YS* I.11, all these vṛttis consist of pleasure, pain and delusion; therefore all of them should be brought under control (*nirodha*). Knowledge alone is not the means to diminishing the power of karma. Yoga, which is samādhi, is that means:

> The yogi who has accomplished samādhi attains liberation in that very life, his heap of karmas immediately burnt in the fire of yoga.
>
> *Vishṇu-purāṇa* VI.7.35

Numerous other texts support this view.

Like knowledge, *asamprajñāta* samādhi is a means of liberation by elimination of karma. While samādhi has this in common with knowledge, samādhi goes further. *Asamprajñāta* samādhi burns out all past impressions (saṁskāras) and thereby eliminates the effectiveness even of those karmas accumulated in previous lifetimes which would otherwise have begun fruition, involving (*a*) the current incarnation in a particular species, (*b*) the life span destined for that incarnation, and (*c*) the pain and pleasure ordained for the life span. This, called *prārabdha,* even though it may already have begun, is all cancelled once *asamprajñāta* samādhi has burned the seeds of that *prārabdha,* whereas in the case of knowledge alone one must wait for final liberation until all the past karmas have fructified. Through yoga, as quoted above, the heap of karmas is immediately burnt, whereas in the case of knowledge a waiting period is implied by the quotation, "I have delay only as long as I am not yet liberated." Immediate liberation is the efficaciousness of yoga. Its efficacy extends to the fact that *prārabdha* karma, from previous lives, is rendered ineffective.

> There is no knowledge like that of Sāṅkhya. There is no strength like that of yoga.
>
> *Mahābhārata* (*Mokṣha-dharma-parvan*) 316.2

Here strength means the power to overcome the karma of former lives.

Pain appears in the conscious principle, the spiritual self, only through proximity of the chitta-vṛttis. It is a condition by reason of proximity (*aupādhika*) and not an innate quality. Obviously, then, yoga, consisting of the control of these vṛttis, is the best means for that liberation defined as the cessation of pain. A condition ceases when the entity from which the condition proceeds ceases to be in proximity.

So, knowledge is not opposed to yoga. Knowledge (*jñāna*), renunciation (*vairāgya*), and the diminution of karmic force (*karmāśhaya*) are efficacious in total permanent eradication of pain only through that ultimate means defined as the *nirodha* of vṛttis. The total and permanent *nirodha* of vṛttis occurs only in *asamprajñāta* samādhi, in which saṁskāras are totally eliminated and the mind-field is dissolved into the original equilibrium of prakṛti, whereupon final liberation (*mokṣha*) ensues.

Samprajñāta samādhi, being simply the foundation for *asamprajñāta* samādhi, may be called a means to liberation; but the direct means thereto is *asamprajñāta* samādhi itself, as indicated by Vyāsa in his commentary on *YS* I.3 and as substantiated in other scriptures, such as:

> Liberation means to abandon the state as though one were some other, and to dwell in the identity of one's own nature.
>
> *Bhāgavata-purāṇa* II.10.6

Liberation, then, is simply the spiritual self dwelling in its own nature.

Taking a slightly different approach, which is accepted by all others later in the work, NTC reiterates the well-known tradition of Vedānta that knowledge is gained through learning (*śhravaṇa*), contemplating (*manana*) and meditating (*nididhyāsana*). This *nididhyāsana* is the same as samādhi. Nārāyaṇa Tīrtha (NT) is a devout theist whose personal path is that of *bhakti* within the teachings of Vallabhāchārya. Devotion and surrender (*bhakti*) to a personal God according to Vallabha's version of Vedānta is NT's basic approach throughout the *Yoga-sūtras*. Though declaring his adherence to theistic Vedānta, he begins his commentary (NTC) by paying homage to the sages of all traditions. He does not try to reconcile contradictions of philosophies but asserts that all the various yogas, such as

advaita-yoga: yoga of non-duality
bhakti-yoga: yoga of devotion and surrender to a personal God
brahma-yoga: yoga of Brahman
charyā-yoga: yoga of denominational ritual devotions

dhyāna-yoga: yoga of meditation
haṭha-yoga: physical yoga within the context of interior, subtle forces
jñāna-yoga: yoga of knowledge
karma-yoga: yoga of action
kriyā-yoga: yoga of ascetic practices (*YS* II.1)
lakṣhya-yoga: yoga of practising concentration on a target
laya-yoga: yoga of dissolution
mantra-yoga: yoga of the practice of mantras
prema-bhakti-yoga: yoga of love and devotion
śhiva-yoga: yoga of Śhiva
siddhi-yoga: yoga of *siddhis* (accomplishments of powers)
vāsanā-yoga: yoga of directing hidden propensities

are included in the eight limbs (*aṅgas*) of yoga. Throughout his larger commentary, *Yoga-siddhānta-chandrikā,* he attempts to prove this view.

Sūtra I.2 योगश्चित्तवृत्तिनिरोधः।

yogaśh chitta-vṛtti-nirodhaḥ

yogaḥ: yoga (is)
chitta-: (of) mind-field
vṛtti-: (of) operations, activities, fluctuations, modifications
nirodhaḥ: control, dissolution

Yoga is the control of the modifications of the mind-field.

Vyāsa's Commentary

This sūtra was enunciated with the intent to state the definition of that (yoga).

[*Sūtra:*] Yoga is the control of the modifications of the mind-field.

Because the word "all" is not included to suggest "all operations of the mind-field," it implies that *samprajñāta* also is included in yoga. The mind-field has three dispositions: illumination (*pra-khyā* from sattva), endeavour (*pra-vṛtti* from rajas) and stasis (*sthiti* from tamas); which leads to the inference that the mind-field is constituted of the three attributes (guṇas).

The nature of the sattva of the mind-field (chitta-sattva) is illumination; in contact with rajas and tamas it loves sovereignty (*aiśhvarya*) and sensuous objects. The same mind-field, when pierced by tamas alone, comes to unrighteousness (*a-dharma*), ignorance (*a-jñāna*), lack of dispassion (*a-vairāgya*) and loss of sovereignty (*an-aiśhvarya*).

Again, when the obscuration by delusion has diminished from the mind-field, it shines in its fulness and in all directions; when this is pierced by a measure of rajas, it turns towards virtue (*dharma*), knowledge (*jñāna*), dispassion (*vairāgya*) and sovereignty (*aiśhvarya*).

When the impurity of the last vestige of rajas has been eliminated, the mind-field becomes established in its own nature. This state comprises only the discernment of the separateness of the sattva of the mind-field, the faculty of discrimination (buddhi) on the one hand and the consciousness principle (puruṣha) on the other, thus reaching up to *dharma-megha,* the samādhi of the raincloud of virtue and of the knowledge of the nature of all things.

The consciousness-potentia (*chiti-śhakti*) is immutable, unmoving, not transferable. The objects are shown to her, while she herself is pure as well as endless. The state of discernment between buddhi and the consciousness-potentia is of the nature of sattva, and is a product of sattva. This illumination of discernment is opposite to the consciousness-potentia. Consequently, the mind-field, which has become dispassionate towards this discernment, brings even that discernment under control. The mind in that state is absorbed in saṁskāras alone. That is the seedless (*nir-bīja*) samādhi. Nothing more is cognized there; hence it is called acognitive (*asamprajñāta*).

That yoga, the control of the modifications of the mind-field, is thus twofold.

Discussion

This is a *lakṣhaṇa*-sūtra or *nirdeśha*-sūtra, an aphorism defining yoga. Vyāsa's commentary also states the *bheda,* the two divisions of that yoga.

In the yoga system of psychology there is a term *antaḥ-karaṇa,* meaning "the inner instrument," which is the eleventh sense, in addition to the five active and the five cognitive senses. This *antaḥ-karaṇa,* or the psyche, is divided into four faculties according to function:

manas: the active mind that receives sensations from the senses and sends forth reactions to them

buddhi: the twofold faculty of discrimination, with its
- outward face, the intellect, and
- inward face, the intuitive wisdom

ahaṁkāra: ego, the faculty by which the personality establishes its identity, such as "I am this body"

chitta: the entire mind-field, including the universal and individual unconscious, as well as *manas, buddhi* and *ahaṁkāra*

The sūtra states:

> Yoga is the control of the modifications of the mind-field.

VB explains that the word *chitta* in this sūtra does not signify only one of the above four faculties but the entire *antaḥ-karaṇa.* It is the substratum of its vṛttis, that in which the functions take place, that in which the waves arise. It is also that very substratum into which the vṛttis dissolve, that is, go into dissolution (*laya*).

Yoga is the *nirodha* of the operations (vṛttis) of the mind-field. The mind-field is a mutation (*pariṇāma*) of sattva, which is the purest aspect of prakṛti. The waves of fluctuations (vṛttis) that arise in this field are part of that very mutation.

This sūtra may also be translated as follows:

> Yoga is the dissolution of vṛttis into their origin in the mind-field.

In some well-known translations the word *nirodha* has been rendered as "suppression" (Woods, Taimni) or "restriction" (Feuerstein). Nothing can be further from the intent of Patañjali and Vyāsa. *Nirodha* is neither suppression nor restriction, nor even absence. Here we refer the reader to the discussion on pp. 86ff. To understand the word *nirodha,* one needs to comprehend the entire Sāṅkhya scheme of evolution and involution, particularly the latter, which will be explained in the discussion on Sūtra II.19. The last sūtra of the *Yoga-sūtras* (IV.34) defines isolation or liberation (*kaivalya*) as

> *guṇānāṁ prati-prasavaḥ* 'the return of the guṇas into their causes',

which means that (RY on *YS* IV.34)

> the saṁskāras dissolve into the mind, mind into *asmitā, asmitā* into mahat or buddhi, and buddhi into guṇas.

BG also on *YS* IV.34 explains this to mean

> the dissolution of guṇas into their cause, the prakṛiti, when they have been brought to the state of *liṅga*-body.

YS IV.32 also supports this view that the ultimate state of guṇas arrives when all of the evolutes have already served their purpose insofar as the spiritual self is concerned and are of no further use. They cease to evolve or cease to continue in the state of disequilibrium. They then dissolve into prakṛiti, never again to show their faces to the spiritual self, who has reached isolation. What has been stated as the final goal in the sūtra explaining the fruit, goal, end result, of yoga (*phala*-sūtra) (IV.34) is also supported by this sūtra of definition (*lakṣhaṇa*-sūtra) (I.2). According to VB on this sūtra,

> *nirodha* of the vṛttis of the fourfold inner sense (*antaḥ-karaṇa*) means their dissolution (*laya*), which is a particular state of their substratum, the mind. Such *laya* is yoga. It is not the absence of vṛttis, because that does not fit the idea of a state of the substratum.

BR comments:

> The vṛttis are the parts (*aṅga*) of the whole (*aṅgin*), which is the mind-field (chitta). Yoga means *nirodha,* that is, their dissolution (*laya*) into their original cause when their outward transmutation ceases and the process of mutation is reversed.

Thus the effects of the guṇas are dissolved back into their respective causes until the process of gradual *nirodha* leads the guṇas to dissolve finally into the original prakṛti, at which point the isolation of the spiritual self occurs.

NB concurs:

> Yoga is the *nirodha,* turning back, of the vṛttis. This turning back is a particular endeavour which is supersensual, like the endeavor [of the mind to serve] as a source of the continuity of life-processes. This endeavour consists of conscious control (*nigraha*) of the mind-field, and causes the dissolving (*vi-laya*) of the vṛttis.

Lest the reader confuse this concept of dissolving with the idea of rendering the vṛttis non-existent, he needs to grasp the Sāṅkhya theory of causation known as *sat-kārya-vada*. This theory is succinctly presented in the *Bhagavad-gītā* (II.16):

> That which is not, does not come into being; that which is, never ceases to be.

The entities are transformed according to the attributes present within themselves, but there is never one speck of energy or entity more or less than there ever was or will be. This theory, stated by the founders of the Sāṅkhya system nearly three thousand years before the modern laws of thermodynamics, is the foundation of the Sāṅkhya view of causation. Nothing that ever exists goes into non-existence; it simply becomes unmanifest, the form returning to dwell as an attribute hidden in its cause, whence it originally arose and from which it may emerge again.

This definition of *nirodha* as dissolution of vṛttis into their source in the mind-field is confirmed by the intent implicit in many statements throughout the sūtras and explicit in their commentaries. For example, *YS* II.27 lists the seven grounds which the yogi attains and then leaves behind. Just before the seventh ground, isolation (*mokṣha*) or liberation (*kaivalya*), we read in Vyāsa's commentary the description of the sixth:

> The guṇas, like rocks falling from the peak of a mountain, (crumbling and) finding no more resting place, are facing dissolution into their cause. Together with that cause (prakṛti), they are no longer produced into effects again, because they are of no further purpose to the spiritual self.

By this Vyāsa means that they are of no further purpose insofar as the individual self who is reaching isolation or liberation is concerned (*YS* II.22).

In this context, the reader is advised to study the *Yoga-sūtra* discussions in the following sequence: II.19, I.2, I.19, I.45, II.22, II.26-27, IV.32 and IV.34.

Vyāsa's second sentence clarifies the definition of yoga:

> Because the word "all" is not included to suggest "all modifications of the mind-field," it implies that *samprajñāta* also is included in yoga.

The external vṛttis are the valid proof, etc. enumerated in *YS* I.6. But how can their control be the definition of yoga as samādhi, when sattvic vṛttis of the objects of concentration still remain in *samprajñāta* samādhi? The answer is that the sūtra does not say the control of *all* vṛttis. In *samprajñāta* the rajasic and tamasic vṛttis are under control, and so the wider definition applies. If the sūtra had said *all* vṛttis, then the definition would have been limited to *asamprajñāta.* In the earlier stages of *samprajñāta* there remain objects of concentration, and its final stage is marked as the discernment of the difference between the mental personality and the spiritual self. In *asamprajñāta* there is not even the awareness of this discernment or difference.

The concept of *nirodha* is explained in various ways by the different commentators. BR and AD say that *nirodha*, control of vṛttis, occurs when the mind's constant alteration through its involvement with external experiences ceases; the mind is then turned inwards and consequently the waves (vṛttis), as part of that very mutation or alteration, are dissolved into their origin.

NTC explains the traditional Sāṅkhya-yoga classifications and states that the mind-field (chitta) divided into the faculty of discrimination (mahat or buddhi), ego (ahaṁkāra) and mind (*manas*) constitutes the inner sense (*antaḥ-karaṇa*). The vṛttis are mutations of condition (*avasthā-pariṇāma*), like a flame from a candle, and are of two kinds, internal (*ābhyantara*) and external (*bāhya*). NTC does not define these, but presumably the internal ones are those that arise from the saṁskāras and those which guide the awareness inwards. The external ones, then, are those that are produced from sense experiences as well as those which lead the awareness outwards. Pacification or blowing out (*upa-śhama*) of vṛttis is *nirodha,* which means merger or dissolution (*laya*) into their cause. *Nirodha* may be defined, then, as that state in which all the vṛttis of the mind-field are restrained. When the mind is free from disturbance of the vṛttis, it may be held in the Supreme Self (*parama*-ātman) and be made one with Him. A yogi who has attained this state is therefore called "joined in yoga" (*yoga-yukta*) (NTC).

NB also states that *nirodha* means to return the vṛttis into their origin. This is a supernatural (*atīndriya*) endeavour, like the maintenance of the life functions, which does not occur through the efforts of the conscious mind or the senses. *Nirodha* means that the residual impressions (*YS* I.18) of the vṛttis cease to wax and wane; they no longer cause highs and lows but are rendered inoperative and ineffective; the tides of constant alterations and mutations no longer arise. *Nirodha* cannot be translated as suppression, cessation or absence of vṛttis, says NB, on two grounds:

1. In *samprajñāta* samādhi vṛttis remain as explained above.
2. An absence is inoperative. It can produce nothing; it can leave no impressions (saṁskāras). In *YS* I.50 and III.9 it is stated or implied that samādhi creates its saṁskāras on the mind. Without the constant and continuous increase in the strength of such saṁskāras, the momentum of mind's inclination and progress towards the higher ground would be unlikely.

Therefore, briefly, in the following order of development, *nirodha* is

- turning the mind away from external involvements to the inward pursuit.
- dissolving the rajasic and tamasic vṛttis into their guṇa origination within the mind-field, so that
  - the tide of saṁskāras no longer waxes and wanes; consequently
  - discernment of the distinction between the spiritual self and buddhi occurs, and
  - samādhi leaves its own saṁskāras on the mind-field.
- finally, in *asamprajñāta,* having the self dwell in the self (*YS* I.3). When an accomplished meditator who has reached *asamprajñāta* opens his eyes to the world, all the vṛttis, all the operations and modifications of the mind-field, are under the control of his volition.

Now to explain Vyāsa's statement:

> The mind-field has three dispositions: illumination, endeavour and stasis; which leads to the inference that it is constituted of three attributes (guṇas).

The commentators, studying Vyāsa's statement regarding the various mental dispositions produced by the three guṇas, have included in their discussions the five levels (*bhūmis*) named in the exposition of Sūtra 1. We follow the same traditional scheme even at the risk of repeating some of what was already explained in the last sūtra.

VM asks: How is it possible that a single entity, the mind-field, has all these different levels of agitation? The answer lies in the fact that it is a compound entity constituted of the three guṇas. This one single mind-field goes through many conditions because it is composed of the three guṇas whose disequilibrium produces conflict among them and results in one subduing the others and vice versa, so that the alternations and mutations of the mental states (*pariṇāmas*) occur. More about the *pariṇāmas* will be discussed in the commentaries on *YS* III.9-15.

Why did Vyāsa begin enumerating the five states under Sūtra 1 with rajas of the agitated (*kṣhipta*) state, whereas the normal order in the texts is sattva, rajas, tamas? BR answers that unless you first show initiative and activity, you cannot state anything about its stupefaction through tamas or its pacification in sattva. Sattva is shown last because through it one rises to the final, higher grounds of the "concentrated" in *samprajñāta* and "controlled" in *asamprajñāta*. In the "concentrated," the externalized waves cease. In the "controlled," all the waves, as well as the residual impressions of past waves, are also dissolved.

Again, Vyāsa says,

> The nature of the sattva of the mind-field (chitta-sattva) is illumination; in contact with rajas and tamas it loves sovereignty and sensuous objects. The same mind-field, when pierced by tamas alone, comes to unrighteousness, ignorance, lack of dispassion and loss of sovereignty.

> Again, when the obscuration by delusion has diminished from the mind-field, it shines in its fulness and in all directions; when this is pierced by a measure of rajas, it turns towards virtue, knowledge, dispassion and sovereignty.

The word *chitta-sattva* means sattva that has taken the form of the mind-field. The presence of sattva, the purest aspect, inclines one towards

dharma: righteousness, virtues such as non-violence
jñāna: wisdom that arises from yoga
vairāgya: dispassion and control over desires for worldly or otherworldly pleasures (*YS* I.15)
aiśhvarya: sovereignty and spiritual freedom

These four, according to *Sāṅkhya-kārikā* 23, are the natural attributes of sattvic buddhi. Of these, the term *aiśhvarya* 'sovereignty' has been given special attention by the commentators. Sovereignty is defined as "the will not being thwarted in any area"; the loss of sovereignty implies that one's will is thwarted by many impediments. The word *aiśhvarya* is an abstract noun formed from *īśhvara* 'the lord', here not in the sense of God, but rather in a human sense of power, a lordship, a commanding presence, the ability to be effective, to be in control of things. Of course, according to the yoga philosophy, one cannot be in control of things without first being in control of all one's faculties and abilities and states. The word *īśhvara* is derived from the verb root *īśh,* meaning "to have power over," "to have control over," "to be able to (create, control, direct)." The presence of sattva gives one the clearsightedness so as to enjoy such lordship and effectiveness.

The absence of sattva and the dominance of tamas robs the mind-field of such clarity, and consequently effectiveness in wielding power is lost. This does not mean that one who wields power unrighteously is also endowed with sattva. Unrighteousness is a symptom of tamas, and it is only righteous effectiveness in wielding power which marks the presence of sattva. When sattva is weakened, one becomes dependent, no longer a sovereign.

In the statement that the mind-field has illumination, initiative and stability as a result of the presence of the three guṇas, it must be understood that the list is not exhaustive. Illumination entails all kinds of knowledge, but it is only symbolic, an example (*upa-lakṣhaṇa*) of the qualities that are symptomatic of the presence of sattva. Others, such as a pleasant state of mind resulting in pleasantness of character (*prasāda-guṇa*), lightness, love, lovingness, etc. are to be understood as included. (See also the discussion on Sūtras I.16, I.33ff.). In the case of rajasic qualities, not only will (volition leading to action) but also anguish, grief and such others are to be understood. The word "stasis" (*sthiti*) to express the attribute of tamas means both "stability" and "stagnation." It signifies also the veiling of the force of saṁskāras, which would normally produce action from rajas. By *sthiti* are exemplified other qualities, like heaviness, obscuration, dejection or feebleness.

VB explains illumination, initiative and stability as follows: Illumination (*khyāti* or *pra-khyā*) is the knowledge of reality (*tattva-jñāna*), and this is meant to include all sattvic qualities attendant thereupon. Worldly inclination or initiative (*pra-vṛtti*) means action (karma), and is meant to include all rajasic qualities. Stability or stagnation (*sthiti*) means the cessation of the activities such as the vṛttis in a state like sleep. This is meant to include all tamasic qualities. Even though this explanation may appear plausible at first glance, it later proves to be untenable, for if illumination means the realization of reality, that would limit the sattvic functions of the mind-field to *dharma-megha* samādhi. If sleep is the cessation of all vṛttis, how can sleep itself be included among the vṛttis, as it has been in Patañjali's scheme? MA and VB say, however, that in any case the cessation of vṛttis in the sleep state[7] should not

7. The student is advised here to note that in Sanskrit there are two different words for sleep:

suṣhupti: the sleep state as different from or contrasted with wakefulness and dream

nidrā: the vṛtti itself, that modification of mind which causes the sleep state to ensue or to continue

The philosophical and psychological distinction between the two should be remembered in any further references to sleep, and the student should check to determine whether *suṣhupti* as a state or *nidrā* as a vṛtti is being referred to.

be confused with *samprajñāta* samādhi, because it does not lead to the elimination of afflictions (*kleśhas*).

VM says that in the mind-field when rajas and tamas are a little less powerful than sattva but are of mutually equal strength, the person loves sovereignty—that is, independence, power, success and effectiveness—and obtains these. He is also drawn to the aesthetic enjoyments of various sensuous pleasures.

NB expresses it differently: When rajas and tamas are equal in strength and dominated by and serving sattva, it is then that a person is attracted to yogic accomplishments or so-called miraculous powers (*siddhis*) as well as to sensual objects; this is the agitated, *kṣhipta,* state. When tamas is eliminated and sattva is mingled with a little rajas, then the mind turns to virtue, knowledge, dispassion and sovereignty; this is the distracted, *vikṣhipta,* state. *Vikṣhipta* is so called because it is somewhat *kṣhipta* but sometimes manages to attain stability. It is also the mind of celestial beings as well as of seekers (*jijñāsu*) who are being thwarted by the obstacles (*vikṣhepas*) which are explained in *YS* I.30 (AD).

VM says that when sattva is powerful, the person is inclined towards concentration on true reality (*tattva*). But a little obscuration of sattva by tamas causes him to think that the eight *siddhis* (*YS* III.45), yogic accomplishments, such as the power to become minute, are the true aim, the reality, which one had started out to pursue. When rajas now begins to affect the mind in that state, one is unable to maintain a hold even of the means to the attainment of *siddhis;* the mind merely loves them but is unable to accomplish them. It remains attracted only to the sensuous experiences, such as beautiful sounds, etc., which are its natural objects. These are the distractions of the sattvic mind by tamas and rajas (*vikṣhepas*).

As we have seen, the very interesting observation is made by VM, VB and NB that the state of agitation (*kṣhipta*) is that in which one thinks of the yogic accomplishments (*siddhis*) as the desirable goals and is drawn towards them. This seems to contradict the intent of Patañjali and Vyāsa, who said that the *kṣhipta* state is not at all a part of yoga, whereas the *siddhis* are a result of the practice of the threefold internal limbs of yoga (*saṁyama*). An attraction towards *siddhis*, etc. may be considered a distraction (*vikṣhepa*), the third ground, but not *kṣhipta* or a simple agitation of an ordinarily worldly mind.

BR explains: The agitated, disturbed state develops because of the predominance of rajas. When the mind is impelled by rajas, it becomes unsteady, outward rather than inward, drawn towards near or distant, alternating objects of pain and pleasure. Such a mind is of the demonic beings called *daityas* and *dānavas*. When tamas waxes, the mind becomes somnolent (*mūḍha*), unable to distinguish between right or wrong acts, fixated on conflicts through anger and the like. Such is the mind of the demonic beings called *rākṣhasas* and *piśhāchas*. AD says also that the agitated (*kṣhipta*) mind resulting from overpowering rajas belongs to demonic beings and to those who are frenzied with the pride of wealth. The tamasic mind belongs to ghoul-like beings and to those who are inebriated (AD). When sattva is on the rise, then the mind prevents and avoids the causes of pain and is inclined towards the means of pleasure, of sensuousness, such as lovely sounds. Such is the distracted (*vikṣhipta*) mind of the celestial beings called the *devas*.

The mind undertakes an initiative because of rajas. Through tamas it is drawn to malevolence towards others. Sattva brings it pleasantness and pleasure. What impels the mind to move in the direction of righteousness (*dharma*), etc.? It is the presence of a little rajas. The mind, being a composition of three guṇas, can never be without rajas or tamas. It is not, then, that rajas and tamas are to be eliminated, but rather that they are essential and their measure (*mātrā*) is ideally just sufficient to fulfil the purpose of sattva. When present within the limit of this measure, rajas initiates virtue, etc., and tamas imparts stability.

Vyāsa says:

> Again, when the obscuration by delusion has diminished from the mind-field, it shines in its fulness and in all directions; when this is pierced by a measure of rajas, it turns towards virtue, knowledge, dispassion and sovereignty.

As VM explains, all movement, energy and initiative is of rajas. It is not intended that mind become devoid of rajas. It is not possible to achieve this. All material entities, the mind being no exception, are composites of the three guṇas. The absence of any one of the three is impossible in any object, entity or experience. What is intended by the discipline of yoga is simply purification of mind so that tamas and rajas may be brought under the power of sattva. AD says that at first, one who is in the *vikṣhipta* state of mind can practise control (*nirodha*) of rajasic and tamasic vṛttis alone by replacing them with sattvic ones. When the veils of tamas, which delude the mind, are withdrawn from the face of sattva, and rajas, being in lesser proportion than sattva, serves the sattva in turn, the mind is impelled to go towards righteousness, knowledge and dispassion (*vairāgya*) (*YS* I.12,15,16), and through these to sovereignty. Such a person, according to Vyāsa, shines in fulness and in all directions. What is meant by "fulness in all directions" is that all the states of matter (prakṛti), the various divisions or segments of the twenty-three evolutes of matter, are illuminated *to* such a mind.

VB explains the same "illumination all around" to mean that the mind-field becomes filled with vṛttis concerning all the objects of experience—especially of concentration—by taking their form, thus comprehending them fully with no aspect left in concealment. A mental experience simply means that the mind-field has taken the form of the object being experienced. This applies not only to the minds of individual human beings but also to those universal beings who work with the universal mind to control and direct their bodies that are the universes. It is thus that the mind of beings such as Hiraṇya-garbha, touched by the residue of the universal rajas, impels them to direct the world towards virtue, etc.

According to VM, when tamas is stronger than rajas, it vanquishes rajas, whereupon the initiative of rajas fails to remove the veil of tamas from the mind-field. Then the mind turns towards vice, unrighteousness and such other inclinations. Ignorance (*a-jñāna*) in this context means not the absence of knowledge but rather (*a*) perversive cognition (*viparyaya*) as defined in *YS* I.8, and (*b*) sleep, that is, resorting to the concept of negation as defined in *YS* I.10. This is the stupefied state. In this context AD says that even though *kṣhipta* and *mūḍha* in a sense annul each other, it is not conducive to transcendental attainment; their mutual cancelling is not a form of *nirodha.*

Returning to Vyāsa:

> When the impurity of the last vestige of rajas has been eliminated, the mind-field becomes established in its own nature.

The word *chitta* (mind-field) should not be confused with *chiti,* which is the absolute and eternal power called consciousness (*chiti-śhakti*). The latter, being immutable, cognizes nothing external; only the faculty of discrimination (buddhi) in which vṛttis arise ever does so. NB further explains: It is established under *YS* IV.16 and 17 that there is no such thing as an individual mind. The mind-field is one and all-pervading. It appears individuated when operative within a single personality. Thus the all-pervading mind is capable of apprehending all objects at all times. It is only when veiled by the presence of tamas that it fails to do so. When the tamasic impulses that lead the mind astray to objects other than those of concentration are purged, the mind automatically and effortlessly becomes centered on the object of concentration. This is *samprajñāta.*

Vyāsa says:

> This state comprises only the discernment of the separateness of the sattva of the mind-field, the faculty of discrimination (buddhi) on the one hand and the conscious principle (puruṣha) on the other.

To reach this stage the personality needs to burn in the dual fire of practice and dispassion (*abhyāsa* and *vairāgya*) (*YS* I.12). Thereby the impurities of rajas and tamas are cleansed. Here the buddhi, which is the pure sattva of mind-field, becomes as purified as gold, dwelling in its own nature. This is not to be confused with the spiritual self dwelling in its own nature, as enunciated in *YS* I.3. When the buddhi faculty dwells in its own nature, it is no longer being fed on the experiences of senses and their objects. It acts independently of them, separated from them through the process of withdrawal of the senses (*pratyāhāra*) (*YS* II.54). Yet all of buddhi's functions are not yet completed. It has one final service still to perform for the spiritual self (puruṣha). In the buddhi awakens *viveka-khyāti,* the discernment of the distinction between itself and the spiritual self. The mental personality here recognizes the source of its illumination as being the spiritual self and ceases to identify sentience merely with body, senses and mind.

VB explains further the relationship of *samprajñāta* samādhi and the experience of *viveka-khyāti* by saying that discernment does not occur in the first two stages of *samprajñāta,* which are accompanied by the discursive and the subtle thought respectively, and where mind and buddhi still have some "other" as the objects. Only from the third stage onwards, when the mind-field and buddhi are centered upon themselves, does the discernment begin. When one speaks of *samprajñāta* as the state in which the discernment of *viveka-khyāti* occurs it should be understood that the first two stages of *samprajñāta* are included *only* as supportive to the final two, *only* as the means to the latter two, and are not by themselves experiences of such discernment.

According to VB, this *viveka-khyāti,* illuminative of all the virtues and of the knowledge of the nature of all things, is not a spiritual entity but rather a *quality* of buddhi, or it even embraces the totality of buddhi, which is an unconscious principle made of matter or prakṛti and filled with the impurities of pain and pleasure. Like a candle flame illuminating objects, it illuminates experiences. *Viveka-khyāti* is the separation of buddhi from puruṣha, and Vyāsa says:

> thus reaching up to *dharma-megha,* the samādhi of the raincloud of virtue and of the knowledge of the nature of all things.

Naturally, then, the meditation moves on to the *dharma-megha* state. It is not yet self-realization. It is only the buddhi's recognition of the difference. In *dharma-megha* samādhi all the virtues dawn, and the nature of all things in the universe becomes known; yet it is still not the self dwelling in the self.

Although *viveka-khyāti* is the highest state expounded on so far, it is so only in comparison with the false identifications formerly established. Vyāsa then proceeds from this ground and says that *viveka-khyāti* is just as undesirable as all the former grounds, which have been left behind, and that one must go further to *chiti-śhakti* because when a person has slept enough, he wakes; when one has tasted refined sugar, he considers the unrefined to be coarse. So the yogi ceases to be interested in this *viveka-khyāti* and reaches for the higher dispassion (*para-vairāgya*).

VM says that this so far explains the character of the *madhu-bhūmika* and *prajñā-jyotis,* the yogis at the middle ground, the second and third category of yogis described on pp. 77-78.

Then Vyāsa continues further to explain the mental state of the fourth category of yogis, *atikrānta-bhāvanīya,* described on p. 78, which is related to the acognitive samādhi (*asamprajñāta*), to understand which one needs to grasp the nature of the consciousness-potentia (*chiti-śhakti*). In *asamprajñāta* one becomes aware of the causes from which the bondage of transmigration (*saṁsāra*) begins. Seeing the pain of these transmigrations, one develops distaste towards worldly attractions. However, when discernment at the buddhi level has occurred, the wise meditator finds that even this does not suffice to sunder the hold of the three-stranded guṇas of prakṛti. (Vyāsa's sentence defining *chiti-śhakti* seems to be a paraphrase of a sentence of Āchārya Pañchaśhikha, one of the early founders of the Sāṅkhya philosophy, which is given in the discussion of *YS* II.20.) But here the student is advised to reread Vyāsa's passage:

> The consciousness-potentia (*chiti-śhakti*) is immutable, unmoving, not transferable. The objects are shown to her, while she herself is pure as well as endless. The state of discernment between buddhi and the consciousness-potentia is of the nature of sattva, and is a product of sattva. This illumination of discernment is opposite to the consciousness-potentia.

VB explains mutation or alteration to mean the cessation of one quality and the rise of another in the same substratum. Such mutation is not possible in *chiti-śhakti,* which, free of such mutation, remains absolute, the transcendental reality (*paramārtha-satya*). This consciousness (*chiti*) must not be mistaken as a quality, but is rather an entity whose very form or nature is light (*prakāśha*).

According to the tradition, this potentia (*śhakti*) is that very potent one (puruṣha). Consciousness is that very consciousness principle, the spiritual self. The *chiti-śhakti* is not apart from puruṣha. The spiritual self is a being of pure energy (*śhakti*). (Refer to pp. 119-20 for information concerning the genders of these terms.)

To understand the nature of the purity of *śhakti* it is well to see how VM explains the meaning of impurity. Pleasure, pain and delusion that arise respectively from sattva, rajas and tamas are the impurity. Even pleasure and delusion cause pain to the discerning sage and are to be avoided as being painful in their essence (*YS* II.15). Even the most beautiful object causes pain when one thinks of its finiteness in time, that it will cease to be. This impurity and finiteness are not attributes of puruṣha. Vyāsa says,

> She herself is pure as well as endless.

A question arises: How can she be pure when she apprehends the objects of senses, such as sounds, which are pleasant, painful or delusionary? Apprehension means taking on their nature, being coloured by them, being transformed somewhat into their being; this certainly could not be regarded as purity. Furthermore, if she goes through these alterations of taking on their form and abandoning them, going through such transience, how could she be called endless and infinite? The answer is, as the student may read again in Vyāsa:

> The objects are shown to her.

It is not that *chiti-śhakti* is transformed into transient forms and experiences, but rather that the buddhi takes on their forms and presents this transformed face to the spiritual self—the self whose power of consciousness, being reflected onto the mirror surface of the buddhi, has enabled the buddhi to develop a semblance of awareness.

Chiti-śhakti does not reach out to buddhi, is not transmitted on to something else, is not a part of the scheme of evolution, is not one of the evolutes of prakṛti. When the buddhi presents the transient transformations of itself to the view of puruṣha, the latter is not affected by the view, because this principle is immutable. The possible mutations that occur in other entities are described in *YS* III.9-15. Puruṣha's freedom from mutation in spite of what is presented by the buddhi is explained in *YS* IV.18, but here Vyāsa says:

> Consequently, the mind-field, which has become dispassionate towards this discernment, brings even that discernment under control. The mind in that state is absorbed in saṁskāras alone. That is the seedless samādhi. Nothing more is cognized there; hence it is called acognitive (*asamprajñāta*).

As one reaches self-realization, there develops a higher dispassion (*para-vairāgya*) (*YS* I.16), because of which one becomes disinterested even in *viveka-khyāti,* the earlier discernment that leads to *dharma-megha* samādhi. Now one reaches the final *nirodha,* where seedless (*nir-bīja*) samādhi occurs. In this *nirodha,* the mind-field flows quietly (*YS* III.10). Here the saṁskāras that would give birth to a future chitta in a karmic process are burnt to ashes. Only when *nirodha* leads to such burning does it become an instrument of blocking any future afflictions (*kleśhas*) and the resultant storage of karma (*karmāśhaya*) that develops into assuming the incarnation in a species, life span during the incarnation, and pain and pleasure during the life span. These now cease, because their very seed is burnt out; no more karmas and their saṁskāras are to be gathered. This is the seedless samādhi, as well as the goal that is explained in Sūtra I.3.

It would appear that some of the commentators (*āchāryas*) on the *Yoga-sūtras* did not fully understand either Patañjali or Vyāsa. Here we take issue with VB and others who paraphrase his words (e.g., NG, NBB) concerning their statements, which are basically as follows: "Some of our contemporaries claiming to be Vedāntins believe that even in *asamprajñāta* there continues to be self-knowledge, which is non-discursive (*nir-vikalpa*) awareness in the form of a vṛtti of buddhi fixed on the self's own nature (*sva-rūpa*). This is completely unauthentic, for we read in *Mārkaṇḍeya purāṇa* III.45 and other texts:

> The yogi should conquer the three guṇas, and join himself to the Supreme Self; making the self absorbed in That, he should abandon even the vṛtti of consciousness.

It is known that in the union with the Lord there is an absence of vṛttis. The non-discursive (*nir-vikalpa*) self-knowledge exists only during *samprajñāta,* when that samādhi reaches the absence of the discursive thought of word, meaning and signification."

In other words, says VB, *asamprajñāta* (acognitive) samādhi is called so because there is no cognition of any kind in that state. Obviously, here VB has missed the following points:

1. Vyāsa's commentary on this sūtra says that the mind-field becomes established in its own nature. This statement should not be confused with the purport of *YS* I.3. The statement here explains the state of the mind-field in *asamprajñāta,* whereas *YS* I.3 explains the spiritual self becoming established in its own nature in *asamprajñāta.*
2. The awareness in the mind is a vṛtti, a mutation, but the self-awareness of the consciousness principle is an immutable constant. It is not at all in the same category as the mental fluctuations. The whole point of *asamprajñāta* is to dwell in the self-nature, which is nothing if not self-aware.
3. The Sāṅkhya philosophy on which the edifice of the yoga system is built regards puruṣha to be a conscious principle (*Sāṇkhya-karika* 11). If VB is right, then what would happen to the consciousness of the very *chiti-śhakti?* The seer is the very power, the entity, the energy of seeing, the very consciousness whom VB wants to proclaim unconscious in *asamprajñāta* samādhi!

In short, VB's statement and argument contradict the intent and the content of *YS* I.3, I.51 and IV.34 and should be ignored.

Vyāsa closes his commentary on this sūtra by reiterating briefly what he had already stated on *YS* I.1.

> That yoga, the control of the operations of the mind-field, is thus twofold.

In *samprajñāta* the control is established over the vṛttis of rajas and tamas; *viveka-khyāti* is the result. When sattva also is brought under control and all guṇas are dissolved into prakṛti, the *asamprajñāta* samādhi ensues.

Summary of Discussion

Had this sūtra said that yoga means control of *all* the operations of the mind-field, only *asamprajñāta* samādhi would have constituted yoga, but since the word "all" was not used, *samprajñāta* samādhi is also included.

Because the mind is an evolute of matter (prakṛti), the three guṇas of prakṛti are clearly manifest in the mind, namely, sattva as illumination of knowledge, rajas as activity and endeavour and tamas as both stability and stagnation. That the mind exhibits these three dispositions proves that it is material and partakes of the three guṇas.

When sattva predominates, supported by rajas and tamas, it leads one to enjoyment of success, effective power and finer sensuous pleasures. When tamas predominates, one is drawn to unrighteousness and ignorance, is averse to the neutrality of dispassion (*vairāgya*) and is unsuccessful or ineffective in the world.

When sattva is purified of tamas, it sees its way clear in all areas and in all directions. In this state a slight touch of rajas gives it the initiative towards knowledge, dispassion and sovereignty.

When the last vestiges of rajas have been eliminated, the mind-field's most sattvic, purest aspect, buddhi, becomes the instrument of that discernment, which distinguishes the material personality from the consciousness principle. This is the samādhi of wisdom (*samprajñāta*), the final state of which is *dharma-megha* samādhi, the raincloud of virtue and of the knowledge of the nature of all things. This samādhi is defined in *YS* IV.29.

The conscious principle is called *chiti-śhakti,* the potentia of consciousness. Because of its ray, the faculty of discrimination (buddhi) becomes operative. This *śhakti* is immutable; it undergoes no change; unlike the evolutes of matter, it does not undergo transference from one form or state to another. It does not move from one locus to another and therefore does not reach out to objects. The objects are presented to her view by buddhi, which gathers the impressions through the mind and senses.

The process of *nirodha* is that of dissolving the guṇa evolutes into their origins until the mind reaches a state of equilibrium. In *samprajñāta* samādhi only rajas and tamas are brought under control; but before reaching *asamprajñāta,* all three guṇas are dissolved; the vṛttis then rest in their origin in the mind-field, from which they can arise only at the command of puruṣha, the spiritual self, who is now in isolation, free.

At the climax of the *samprajñāta* samādhi occurs the discernment of the distinction between the mental personality and consciousness; however, this is yet an experience within buddhi. Beyond this it is controlled by the conscious will to appear or disappear, but the attachment to it ceases. In *asamprajñāta* there is no concern for the "other," for the knowledge of separation, but only for what will be described in the next sūtra as the self residing in the self.

Sūtra I.3 तदा द्रष्टुः स्वरूपेऽवस्थानम्।

tadā drașhțuḥ sva-rūpe'vasthānam

tadā: then
drașhțuḥ: seer's
sva-rūpe: in own nature
ava-sthānam: stability, settling, remaining, being in a state

Then (upon the dissolution of vṛttis) the seer rests in his own true nature.

Even though the word *drașhțṛ* 'seer' is in the masculine gender, Vyāsa explains this word to mean *chiti-śhakti,* the consciousness-potentia. The seer, the spiritual self, is the same as the *śhakti* called consciousness. The words *chiti* and *śhakti* are both feminine; hence one could also translate the sūtra to read:

Then the seer rests in her own true nature.

Vyāsa's Commentary

When the mind-field is in that state, there being no objects, what is the nature of the spiritual self who is ordinarily identified with the apprehensions of buddhi?

[*Sūtra:*] Then the seer rests in his own true nature.

Then the consciousness-potentia is established in her own nature, as (it is described to be) in isolation (*kaivalya*). When the mind-field is involved with the external world (*vyutthāna*-chitta),[8] then she does not appear to be so, even though she is so.

8. When the mind-field is involved in the ordinary world, or in the thoughts thereof, it is called *vyutthāna-chitta.* The word *vyutthāna* means "to get up (that is, from meditation) and to be wandering about."

The mind-field in the state of samādhi is called *nirodha*-chitta or samādhi-chitta. Compared to *asamprajñāta,* the mind-field in *samprajñāta* also is considered *vyutthāna*-chitta, whereas compared to the relatively lower grounds, it is regarded as *nirodha*-chitta or samādhi-chitta. In *asamprajñāta,* the mind-field is completely *nirodha*-chitta or samādhi-chitta.

Paraphrase of Vyāsa's Commentary

In the ordinary life, the spiritual self is identified with the cognitions, apprehensions, awarenesses, of the buddhi into whom his light reflects. When the mind-field has reached the state of *nirodha,* control through the dissolution of the guṇas, the mind-field has no objects. What is then the nature of the spiritual self? The sūtra answers the question: Then the seer, the spiritual self, rests in his own true nature. This spiritual self, which is the same as *chiti-śhakti* (feminine), consciousness-potentia, then dwells in her own nature.

When the mind of an accomplished yogi is interacting with the ordinary world, the *chiti-śhakti* still remains established in her own nature, although outwardly she does not appear to be so.

Discussion

This sūtra has several aims (*ākāṅkṣhās*) (VB). The first one is to complete the definition of yoga as started in the previous sūtra. In the previous sūtra, only the state of the mind-field and its vṛttis was explained, but nothing was said about the state or condition of the spiritual self, which is the main concern of the *Yoga-sūtras.* That is accomplished in this sūtra by way of fulfilling the second aim, which is to explain what is the purpose of the spiritual self that is being served through *nirodha.* This second purpose is served by fulfilling the third aim, which is to draw attention to the absolute nature of the spiritual self, here, immediately after the definition sūtra, so that in the student's mind it may become connected to the *phala*-sūtra (*YS* IV.34), which states the ultimate goal of yoga, asserting the true nature of the spiritual self. The present sūtra, then, establishes direct connection with the final sūtra of the text; and its enunciation here points to the fact that, linking all the various subject matters discussed in the text, there runs a unifying thread (sūtra) from here to the end of Chapter 4.

We begin with the discussion of Vyāsa's clause qualifying the spiritual self (puruṣha),

> who is ordinarily identified with the apprehensions of buddhi.

This clause is the translation of a single compound word, *buddhi-bodha-ātmā,* and needs to be understood in some detail (VM and VB).

The living entities normally bound to the identity of the physical body and the mental states do not experience the pure spiritual self. Nor do others observing a living entity see such a puruṣha. Our total apprehension of a conscious self is only by way of observing and recognizing the vṛttis that arise in the mind. In other words, the existence of consciousness without an object in the mind is not suspected. However, according to the Sāṅkhya-yoga system, the buddhi, which is an evolute of matter, is not capable of functioning by itself; it derives its semblance of awareness only through the proximity of puruṣha, from whom it receives its light, in a manner similar to that in which objects are illuminated by the light of the sun. Even the analogy of the sun is imperfect (RS) because the sun is perishable, whereas the self is eternal; yet the analogy suffices for our limited purpose here.

As the sun shines on objects, so the puruṣha shines its ray upon the buddhi and thereby knows all that passes in the buddhi, and observes everything as a witness. But this is not known to the living entities bound to the identity of body, mind-field, buddhi and its vṛttis. Therefore, it is easy for one to assume that there is no other self besides the apprehension of vṛttis in the buddhi. Fire ceases to burn when the fuel is all consumed (NB and BG). The question, therefore, arises as to the condition of the spiritual self when the vṛttis have been dissolved. Would not the puruṣha, whom we ordinarily experience only as identified with the operations of buddhi, simply cease (BG)?

The question continues (VM, AD). In *asamprajñāta,* all that remains in buddhi are the past saṁskāras, which are no longer active, and even those may be burnt out. Then of what can the spiritual self be conscious? If it were suggested that puruṣha would still be conscious of the buddhi itself, in which there are no more vṛttis and only saṁskāras remain, this suggestion would go against the entire foundation of the Sāṅkhya-yoga philosophy, which believes that all material entities from the five gross elements to buddhi, the subtlest, exist only to serve the puruṣha. The service that buddhi performs for puruṣha is to present to him (her?) the view of all the experiences, of which he, puruṣha, remains an unparticipating and neutral witness. Besides performing such a service, the buddhi has no other purpose. When there are no vṛttis, no view is being presented to puruṣha; puruṣha has no interest in buddhi for its own sake. Then what purpose do *nirodha* and the mind-field, and buddhi in the *nirodha* state, serve in regard to puruṣha? As explained in the discussion of the two previous sūtras, the twofold purpose of buddhi—the experience of external objects, and the discernment of the separation between buddhi and the self—have both ended with *asamprajñāta* samādhi. Vyāsa's question follows:

> When the mind-field is in that state, there being no objects, what is the nature of the spiritual self who is ordinarily identified with the apprehensions of buddhi?

VM asks: Does puruṣha continue to illuminate the buddhi and the external objects much as was happening in the *vyutthāna* situation, except that, because there are no vṛttis, he no longer sees the objects? Or is it as the Nyāya philosophers have hypothesized, that he becomes inactive, unconscious, like a piece of wood, only to go through the necessary transmutations to become object-conscious because of certain conditions present in *vyutthāna*? Or is it, as the Buddhist philosophers believe, that he vanishes like a flame when the conditions for the continuity of the flame have ceased? These are the questions answered by the sūtra:

> Then the seer rests in his own true nature.

Insofar as the actual experience of samādhi is concerned, NTC states that the seer, which had become delimited by ahaṁkāra and who is the meaning of the word *I,* dwells in the self which is exclusive (*kevala*) consciousness. When the yogi comes into ordinary life (*vyutthāna*) and sees the time that has elapsed (compare with Sūtra I.51), he infers that he was in the state of samādhi.

It is explained throughout the Sāṅkhya-yoga literature that the self is ever-pure, ever-wise, ever-free, completely unblemished, untouched, unaltered, without regard to time, space, condition or association with matter. It is buddhi alone that undergoes transformations in association with guṇas (VM).

- In association with sattva it takes on the *śhānta,* pacific, attribute
- In association with rajas it takes on the *ghora,* fierce, attribute
- In association with tamas it takes on the *mūḍha,* stupefied or somnolent, attribute

These three—*śhānta, ghora,* and *mūḍha*—are the major personality dispositions, depending on the inclinations, thoughts, words and acts of each. It is not puruṣha, the spiritual self, who becomes pacific, fierce or stupefied. Any appearance of *śhānta, ghora* or *mūḍha* attributes in puruṣha is a temporary condition of appearance (*aupādhika*) arising from a superimposed condition (*upādhi*). It is interesting to note that the terms *upādhi* and *aupādhika* are not strictly from the early Sāṅkhya-yoga philosophical system. They have been borrowed by the commentators without reserve from the Vedānta doctrinal system, thus creating a syncretic terminology. This by no means changes the Sāṅkhya doctrine itself, but only emphasizes grounds that are shared by both Vedānta and Sāṅkhya, leaving the other areas open to discussion.

In both Sāṅkhya and Vedānta, the analogy of the clear crystal is used freely (VB, VM, NB, BG, RY). A red flower placed near a clear crystal reflects in the crystal, giving it a reddish hue, which vanishes immediately when the flower is removed. The apparent reddishness in the crystal is not innate or real. It is from the *upādhi,* the temporary condition simply attributed to it; it is *aupādhika.* Similarly any appearance of *śhānta, ghora* or *mūḍha* personality characteristics do not belong to the soul, the spiritual self, just as nothing really happens to the crystal in the presence of the red flower. The control of vṛttis through the dissolution of the guṇas is analogous to the removal of the red flower from the vicinity of the crystal. The crystal then remains in its own nature; the spiritual self then remains in his own nature. When a condition is removed, the object that was conditioned thereby does not vanish (VM) but reverts to its own nature. So, in the light analogy, the argument about puruṣha vanishing when no vṛttis are being presented to it by buddhi is untenable.

All analogies are imperfect. The analogy of the crystal and the red flower still suggests some kind of a change taking place in the supposedly unalterable puruṣha. The commentator VM therefore tries to improve on this analogy by borrowing another analogy from Vedānta. As one walks on the beach, he sees a silver-like glint and thinks he has found a silver object. As he approaches closer, the object turns out to be a mother-of-pearl seashell. But when the observer thought he saw silver, the mother-of-pearl did not actually turn into silver. Similarly, all the appearances of *śhānta, ghora,* and *mūḍha* attributed to puruṣha cannot cause or imply any internal change in him.

Prior to *asamprajñāta,* puruṣha's self-luminosity illuminated the buddhi; now when the "other" object thus illuminated has fulfilled its purposes and its service is no longer needed, its master continues to be self-luminous. The assumption that he had been an agent of actions (cf. *Bhagavad-gītā* III.27) is eradicated (BR). This completes the definition of yoga (NB): *nirodha* that leads to the seer's remaining in his own nature totally and permanently (*ātyantika*) (cf. *Sāṅkhya-kārikā* I.1 and *Sāṅkhya-pravachana-sūtra* I.2) is the definition of yoga. The word *ātyantika* 'total and permanent' implies that (*a*) momentary experiences of stillness are not to be included; (*b*) *samprajñāta* samādhi is not included except as a step and a means to the *asamprajñāta;* (*c*) sleep is not included; and (*d*) the dissolution of individual minds that is incidental to the cosmic dissolutions is not included. So, we may conclude in Vyāsa's words:

> Then the consciousness-potentia is established in her own nature, as (it is described to be) in isolation (*kaivalya*).

The *Yoga-sūtras* consider the gender of "puruṣha" merely a linguistic or grammatical convenience. This masculine word, equated with spiritual self, soul, and so forth, is used interchangeably with the feminine words

śhakti: energy, force, power
chiti: consciousness
chiti-śhakti: consciousness-potentia, consciousness power, consciousness principle
dṛśhi: sight, seeing
dṛśhi-śhakti or *dṛk-śhakti:* seeing-potentia, seeing power

This approach is based on the ancient dictum that *śhakti-śhakti-mator abhedah,* "there is no distinction between *śhakti* and the possessor of *śhakti;* the power and the power-possessor are one." Hence puruṣha and his power are one and the same. The feminine words are used in *YS* II.16,20,25; IV.34. As we have stated, *YS* IV.34 more or less reiterates the purpose of this Sūtra I.3. Vyāsa quotes a part of *YS* IV.34—*sva-rūpa-pratiṣhṭhā-chiti-śhaktiḥ*—as a commentary on I.3. The last sentence of Vyāsa's commentary is:

> When the mind-field is involved with the external world (*vyut-thāna*-chitta), then she (*chiti-śhakti*) does not appear to be so, even though she is so.

(The compound word *vyutthāna*-chitta has been explained in the footnote on p. 114.) Even though in outward appearances the consciousness-potentia, the spiritual self, seems corruptible, it is not so. "Even though she is so" (that is, pure and self-luminous, dwelling in her own nature), the appearances of corruptibility are misleading—much like the appearance of silver in a seashell.

"It is by the elimination (*nirodha*) of all other vṛttis that one gains the yoga of one-mindedness with Me," says the Lord (Śhiva) in the *Kūrma-purāṇa* and similar texts. By quoting this, NTC implies that the meaning of yoga is the union with Deity. It also means, as the *Bhagavad-gītā* states, that in this state "the self, seeing the self, is contented with the self" (VI.20).

NTC goes on to say that the great yoga (*mahā*-yoga) is that in which there are no objects of concentration as supports (*ālambana*) and there remains only the manifestation (*abhi-vyakti*) of one's own nature. He means that *mahā*-yoga is the yoga of absence or negation of all transient feelings and states (*abhāva*-yoga). This *abhāva*-yoga is yoga in which all is contemplated as Void or Empty (*śhūnya*), whereby one then begins to see the self. In *mahā*-yoga one sees the ever-blissful (*nitya-ānanda*), unanointed (*nir-añjana*) self (ātman).

Sūtra I.4 वृत्तिसारूप्यमितरत्र।

vṛtti-sārūpyam itaratra

vṛtti: (with) operations, activities, fluctuations, modifications
sārūpyam: similarity, assimilation, appearance of, identification of form or nature
itaratra: elsewhere

Elsewhere, identification with the form and nature of vṛttis.

In states other than asamprajñāta *samādhi, the spiritual self appears identified with the vṛttis.*

Vyāsa's Commentary

How then? Because then the objects are being presented to (puruṣha's) view,

> [*Sūtra:*] Elsewhere, identification with the form and nature of vṛttis.

Puruṣha appears as having no mode (vṛtti) as distinguished from that of the vṛttis of the mind-field which (arise) in the *vyutthāna* situation. The mind-field is like a magnet. It renders benefits and service by its mere presence in the proximity. Being an object of (puruṣha's) view, it becomes the property and possession (*svam*) of puruṣha, who is its master and proprietor (*svāmin*). Therefore, the cause of puruṣha's cognition of the vṛttis of the mind-field is his beginningless connection (therewith). As the sūtra (of Pañchaśhikha) says:

> There is only one perception; reflective cognition (*khyāti*) alone is the perception.

Paraphrase of Vyāsa's Commentary

Vyāsa continues from the last sentence of the commentary on *YS* I.3, which was:

> When the mind-field is involved with the external world (*vyut-thāna*-chitta), then she [the consciousness-potentia, dwelling in her own nature] does not appear to be so, even though she is so.

Then how does she appear to be? When buddhi is presenting objects in the form of vṛttis to her view, it appears as though *chiti-śhakti's* (puruṣha's) existence or mode of being in the *vyutthāna* situation is no other than that of the vṛttis, being completely undistinguished from them. As Pañchaśhikha, one of the ancient founders of Sāṅ-khya, said:

> Both the buddhi and puruṣha then appear to have only one perception, which is their single reflective cognition, as though both were one.

The mind-field is like a magnet. It does not need to make an effort. Like a magnet, simply by its presence it serves the purpose of puruṣha, presenting to his view whatever vṛttis arise from its experience of external objects. It is the property of the master, who is puruṣha himself. Puruṣha has always been its master and it has always been his possession. This relationship of theirs is beginningless and natural. No other relationship between them is possible because of their respective natures.

Discussion

A number of controversial points need clarification in order to fully understand this sūtra. The most important of these is the question as to what constitutes the actual personality. Even though this discussion is most relevant to *YS* II.6, where *asmitā* is dealt with, one could not follow the argument on the current sūtra and other subsequent sūtras without some introduction here.

The commentators, great *āchāryas* of the past, all agree that the spiritual self is incorruptible and immutable. But if this is so, why does it appear to be corruptible, mutable, impure, ignorant and consequently bound? Here the *āchāryas* present two hypotheses to try to explain this. The first of these can be summarized as follows:

The composite mental personality is created by puruṣha's illumination reflecting in the buddhi, and the vṛttis arising in the buddhi and mind that are thus illuminated.

- The subjective, composite personality experiences objects being presented to the senses, and sensations being conveyed to the mind-field.
- The current experiences as well as the impressions (saṁskāras) produce vṛttis in the mind-field, especially in the buddhi.
- The innermost aspect of the mind-field is buddhi, which is illuminated by the rays of puruṣha reflecting in it, like the sun's rays in a mirror.
- Whatever processions of vṛttis occur in the mirror of buddhi, puruṣha remains untouched by them, a neutral witness.

To summarize the argument, the body serves as the vessel to contain this composite mental personality, and this entire complex is thus ruled by the presence, proximity, of the neutral, conscious spiritual self. In this scheme the predominantly sattvic composition of the mirror of buddhi causes it to receive puruṣha's illumination, enabling it, in turn, to illuminate external objects, experience them and create the wave-like vṛttis within itself. Here puruṣha remains completely untouched. The assumption of a personality is created only in the buddhi and chitta, while puruṣha remains immutable and ever-free. The analogy of a flower's colours reflecting in the clear crystal, then, is inappropriate with regard to puruṣha because nothing is reflected therein. The buddhi illuminated by puruṣha is alone responsible for all the fluctuations and modifications. The analogy of the seashell appearing as glinting silver, however, is more applicable. An observer sees the silver, but the seashell *sui ipse* remains unchanged. It is buddhi that says, "I am happy, unhappy," etc., but puruṣha himself is a neutral witness.

The second hypothesis (especially VB, BG, NB) is the same as the first except that the vṛttis arising in the chitta-buddhi complex are reflected back into puruṣha. In this hypothesis puruṣha mistakes himself as thinking, "I am happy, unhappy," etc., and it is here that the analogy of the coloured flower reflecting in the crystal is relevant. The imperfections of this analogy, however, are obvious. How the sun-like puruṣha, the very source of the illumination reflected in the sattvic buddhi, can then become a crystal, receiving the reflection of buddhi's vṛttis into itself and actually falling into the semblance of a bondage, is difficult to understand. This hypothesis makes puruṣha changeable, mutable, subject to *pariṇāma* (alteration) through the proximity or influence of a factor outside himself, which goes against the central tenets of Sāṅkhya-yoga philosophy and destroys the very foundation of the doctrine of the eternal purity of puruṣha. Possibly the *āchāryas* postulating this hypothesis hoped to avert its adverse effects on the doctrine by citing the analogy of the crystal and using phrases like "*semblance* of mutability" and "*as if* puruṣha were undergoing a change, but *in reality* remaining unchanged like the crystal." In fact, however, the reflection of a red *japā* flower in the crystal does imply a temporary change in the crystal. If the states of buddhi were to reflect in puruṣha, one would have to admit puruṣha as being subject to colouration (*rāga*).

Most commentators have not succeeded in resolving this difficulty. In fact, they cannot make up their minds as to which of these two possibilities is upheld by Patañjali and Vyāsa. Consequently they have tied themselves into polemical knots of contradictions. In one paragraph the puruṣha is immutable; in the next the colours reflect in him; and in the third he thinks, "I am happy, unhappy," and so forth. Only BR and HA have held fast to the first hypothesis, which follows the true tenet of Sāṅkhya-yoga. The other *āchāryas,* revered as they are, have erred, as we shall see again further on.

Vyāsa establishes the ever-pure nature of the spiritual self as follows:

Because then the objects are being presented to (puruṣha's) view,

[*Sūtra:*] Elsewhere, identification with the form and nature of vṛttis.

"Elsewhere" means the state other than the *asamprajñāta* samādhi referred to in the last sūtra. The antonym of *samādhi* is *vyutthāna,* literally, "getting up, being away from (meditation)." Compared to *asamprajñāta,* even *samprajñāta* is considered *vyutthāna.* "Getting up" does not imply merely moving the body away from one's meditation seat, but rather implies the absence of stillness of the mind in which the vṛttis continue to arise.

In this *vyutthāna* state, incorporating everything lower than *asamprajñāta,* the vṛttis are shown to the spiritual self. The question naturally arises as to whether puruṣha's state undergoes an alteration, whether he is one thing in samādhi and something else in *vyutthāna* and therefore not immutable (*a-pariṇāmin*). VM says that in *vyutthāna* the mind's vṛttis of *śhānta* (peace, calm), *ghora* (ferocity) and *mūḍha* (somnolence, stupefaction) may merely appear to become the vṛttis of puruṣha. VB insists, however, that in *vyutthāna* there occurs *sārūpya*—identity or similarity of the form or nature of the seer with that of the mind-field in the vṛtti—and that this similarity or identity consists of the reflection and counter-reflection becoming one. VB's idea is that puruṣha's light illuminates the buddhi and the vṛttis of the buddhi reflect in puruṣha, becoming the latter's vṛttis; these vṛttis reflecting back into buddhi's mirror assume identity with the original vṛttis.

The vṛttis are said to be like a candle flame (VM, NB). A candle flame exists for a moment only but appears continuous because as soon as one set of particles is consumed, another set takes its place. These are, thus, mutations of state and not merely of attributes and distinguishing marks (*YS* III.13). These vṛttis are like molten copper poured into a crucible taking the latter's form. Because they are a product of the three guṇas and, therefore, seats of pleasure, pain and delusion, they become pacific (*śhānta*), ferocious (*ghora*) or stupefied (*mūḍha*). The vṛttis of puruṣha in this view become inseparable from these because the objects in the form of vṛttis are presented, shown, to puruṣha, and reflected in him. The "vṛtti" is not a mere quality, as we read in the *Sāṅkhya-pravachana-sūtra* (V.107):

> The vṛtti is a principle different from a fragment or quality. It serves the purpose of causing a connection and glides forth (among objects, senses and the mind).

Unlike a spark of fire, the vṛttis in this view are not a fragment of objects, senses or the mind but a modification that simply glides along, establishing connections.

VM says that any alteration occurs in the buddhi alone and that vṛttis can be attributed only to the reflection of puruṣha present to the buddhi. As someone who seeing his clean face in an unclean mirror might go away thinking his own face to be unclean, so puruṣha's uncleanness is a mere appearance. VB says that since the reflections of the vṛttis cast upon puruṣha are insubstantial (*a-vastu*), not a real object, puruṣha's immutability remains unhampered in spite of them, again, like that of a crystal in which a colour is being reflected. As we read in the *Sāṅkhya-pravachana-sūtra* (VI.28):

> As the *japā* flower does not really cause a colouring of the crystal, but merely an assumption

of identity, so it is in the case with the vṛttis reflecting in puruṣha. VM says: *As though* buddhi takes on the role of puruṣha, it appears *as if* puruṣha has vṛttis. But, these vṛttis, having no substance like that of objects, cannot really affect the puruṣha. All that happens is a false assumption (*abhimāna*). A superimposition (*samāropa*) occurs, which is an idea similar to Vedānta's superimposition (*adhyāropa*). Because of this, puruṣha (*a*) who has no perversive perception (*viparyaya*), may be considered as having perceived falsely; (*b*) who has no cause to experience the fruits of karma, may be considered an experiencer; (*c*) who has no discernment (*viveka-khyāti*), may be attributed to possess the discernment of the separation of self and prakṛti. *Chiti-śhakti* has no suffering and so forth so far as commentators such as VM are concerned. However, in the view of VB, NB and BG, she considers herself in *vyutthāna, as though* in suffering and so forth, but these false assumptions are, again, insubstantial (*a-vastu*). One might well ask these commentators that if the evolutes of prakṛti are all substantial, how can the modifications in the mind-field, which is an evolute, be insubstantial?

The analogy of the crystal used in this way is inapplicable also because, we repeat, the appearance of a colour is indeed an alteration. The fact is that absolutely nothing reflects on puruṣha. The commentators have failed to grasp the actual locus of the appearance of similarity and identity (*sārūpya*) of buddhi and puruṣha. This *sārūpya* can be understood only as follows: It is not as though puruṣha mimics the vṛttis of the buddhi and cries out, "I am unclean!" Puruṣha's luminosity remains constant and unaffected. It is the buddhi, an unconscious evolute of matter having been touched by the luminous presence of puruṣha, which masquerades as puruṣha, saying, "I am a spirit. Though I am pure, I appear as impure. Though not subject to suffering, I appear to suffer. It is all my play." In other words, the locus of *sārūpya* is buddhi, the innermost aspect of the mind-field. Other observers see this person and think, "He suffers" "Puruṣha within him must suffer." The buddhi also says, "I, puruṣha, suffer!" It is as though a slave at the palace gate wearing velvet and gold given by the king were to declare, "I the king am a king no more!"—yet the true king sits on his throne resplendent in all his glory.

All the repetitions of the particle word *iva* ("as though," "as if") and similar words and phrases employed by the commentators simply do not apply to puruṣha. They apply to the false I-ness (*asmitā*), which is the true explanation of *sārūpya.* It is in the sūtra defining *asmitā* (*YS* II.6) that Patañjali uses the word *iva:* "as if," "as though" the power of the seer (spiritual self) and of the seen (mind-field, an evolute of prakṛti) had assumed an identity. Any superimposition (*samāropa*) goes only this far and does not extend to puruṣha. Any assumption of false identity (*abhimāna*) is an act of the ego (ahaṁkāra), and to attribute it to puruṣha is totally contrary to Sāṅkhya philosophy.

However, to support his view that the vṛttis reflect into puruṣha, VB quotes *Viṣhṇu-purāṇa* I.14.35:

> Homage to Him, the universal self, Who has assumed the form of the inner instrument and Who presents to ātman, the self, the experiences grasped with the senses.

This may be a view presented in the *Vishṇu-purāṇa,* but it is definitely not the tenet held by Patañjali and Vyāsa.

On the other hand, VB is more coherent when he challenges the views of others who hold that "I am happy, unhappy," etc. are innate attributes of ātman, the self. He argues that if pleasure, pain, etc. were mutative modes (*pariṇāmas*) of the self, then there would be no possibility of averting the vṛttis without cutting the ātman piece by piece! There would simply be no sense in pursuing liberation. If one were to propose that the innate pleasure and pain and so forth of the self were brought into activity through the union of the mind with the self, then why not suppose that mind alone is sufficient to produce the effects such as pleasure and pain. Mind is efficacious enough. To assume the mind, self and their union, all three, to be the cause where one would suffice is logically cumbersome (*gauravam*).

A possible assumption that buddhi alone, without purusha, might be the experiencer of its own being as the self, is contradicted throughout the Sāṅkhya-yoga philosophy and will be discussed under Sūtra IV.19ff.

The viewpoint of Patañjali and Vyāsa is upheld in texts like the *Bhagavad-gītā* (XIII.29):

> Who sees the acts as being performed through prakṛti alone, he thereby sees ātman as not acting at all.

It is well here to mention Pañchaśhikha, who, after Kapila and Āsuri, was third in line among the founders of Sāṅkhya. His vast work, *Ṣhaṣhṭi-tantra,* was lost in antiquity, and from it only a handful of quotations have filtered down to the present. We read Vyāsa's quotation from him:

> There is only one perception; reflective cognition (*khyāti*) alone is the perception.

Khyāti here is not to be confused with discernment of the separateness of buddhi and puruṣha (*viveka-khyāti*), which occurs in the final stages of *samprajñāta* samādhi and leads to *asamprajñāta.* The *khyāti* here is the opposite of this discernment; it is rather an appearance of the identity of buddhi and puruṣha, whose reflective cognition in the *vyutthāna* situation appears single.

The term *khyāti* then technically combines within its meaning the entire process described on p. 124, and the reader is advised to study that description again. The locus of this perception is *asmitā,* which occurs in buddhi. Here the light of self mingles with the sattva-luminosity of matter (prakṛti). This perception (*darśhana*) is defined by VM to include only externalized perception, the mechanical process leading to the arousal of vṛttis in the mind. It is not to be confused with consciousness (*chaitanya*), which is an attribute of the spiritual self alone. It is the worldly perception that waxes and wanes, while consciousness of the self remains constant. Also what other observers perceive as a composite personality (see p. 124) is a process that occurs at this level.

We have translated *khyāti* as "reflective cognition." Even though the term *khyāti* occurs in other Sanskrit philosophical systems in a different sense (that of cognition in logic), here it has a narrowed meaning limited to the definitions within our system. We have translated the word as "reflective cognition" to include three levels of the process of *khyāti:*

1. The light of self reflecting in buddhi, thereby enabling the latter to cognize objects and to experience sensations;
2. the buddhi thereby cognizing these objects as they also reflect into the buddhi; and
3. the reflection of the self and that of the objects mingling in buddhi, producing vṛttis, and buddhi again reflecting upon them, contemplating them.

Our process of perception consists solely of this. As Pañchaśhikha has stated, there is no other perception but this process.

Because of this reflective process (HA) puruṣha and buddhi appear as if unified. They appear one (RY), like water and milk mixed, even though they are two entirely separate entities; one is not converted into the other, but their closeness causes them to seem as one. Again it must be remembered that this commingling occurs not in puruṣha but in the buddhi alone. Consciousness (VM) is the nature of puruṣha and not of the *khyāti* process.

How is it possible then that the formless puruṣha reflects in the buddhi, which, though material, is so subtle as to appear formless? The answer is that (VB) the analogy of reflection needs to be analysed. It does not mean an actual reflection like that of the sun into a jar or pool of water. The "reflection" is twofold:

1. Through the proximity of puruṣha (VB) some natural alteration occurs in the buddhi enabling it to cognize.
2. A certain other alteration (*pariṇāma*) occurs (VB, NB) in the buddhi upon the proximity of an object, whereby the buddhi subtly takes on the very form of the object thus perceived. That alteration is called the vṛtti.

But what exactly is the relationship between the mind-field and the self, and what causes their union? Vyāsa says:

> The mind-field is like a magnet. It renders benefits and service by its mere presence in the proximity [of the spiritual self].

It is not possible, however, (VM) for something material to benefit the pure spiritual self. If the mind, a material evolute, were to affect the self in any way, that would subject the self to a certain corruptibility. The word *upa-kāra* in its conventional signification (*ruḍhi*) means "benefit," but here it can only signify "service," with a derivative meaning (*yaugika*): *upa* 'near', *kāra* 'to do'—"to simply act in a certain way by mere presence." The buddhi (HA) serves as the self's instrument for yoga and liberation by its mere proximity, without ever touching the latter, as a magnet (VB, NB) pulls out a pin stuck in the body without an active effort of its own. The mind-field (VM) is not in any way joined to puruṣha.

The service that buddhi performs for puruṣha is to be its "perceptible" (*dṛśhya*), that is, its object of perception, so that *khyāti* may occur and consequently puruṣha's capacity to be the master over matter may be made manifest. To serve as a *dṛśhya* means (VM) to be the self's object of experience when the mind-field is converted into the forms of the objects it experiences from the external world. For example, a sight or sound presented to the mind-field is refined into the mind's vṛtti. In the *khyāti* process such a vṛtti commingles with the light of self and serves the latter by its proximity without ever touching or affecting it.

The term "proximity" (*sānnidhya*) needs to be understood. It does not mean (VM, HA) proximity in space and time because according to Sāṅkhya philosophy the spiritual self is beyond space and time altogether, and matter, too, is beyond space and time in its unmanifest prakṛti (*pradhāna*) state. The proximity consists of compatibility (*yogyatā*) of qualities inherent in the two. That is, puruṣha has the power to make matter its servant, and matter has the capacity to serve. The locus of this proximity, the merger of the compatibilities, is in the "singularity of a cognition" (*pratyaya*), which is explained by Vyāsa as:

> Being an object of (puruṣha's) view, it [matter as its evolute the mind-field or buddhi] becomes the property and possession (*svam*) of puruṣha, who is its master and proprietor (*svāmin*). Therefore, the cause of puruṣha's cognition of the vṛttis of the mind-field is his beginningless connection (therewith).

This "beginningless connection" needs to be understood. The Sanskrit word used is not *saṁyoga* 'union'. A union is normally defined as "a coming together of those that were separate." This definition cannot apply to the union of eternal factors such as the spiritual self and unmanifest matter. Hence Vyāsa uses the word *sambandha* 'relationship or connection (rather than union with)'. The self has known eternally that matter is his domain, his possession and property. In that context he knows, "Buddhi is mine." The fact (HA) that the self is the seer, and the matter is seen, is eternal; it is the innate nature of the relationship. The eternal entities have eternal natures and the connections between such are, therefore, eternal. This answers (VM) the question: If the bondage is caused by ignorance (which is defined in *YS* II.3,5), what causes the beginning of such ignorance? That ignorance is merely the relationship between the seer and the seen, beginningless, known to puruṣha, and eternal; it has no other extrinsic cause.

Another question is: If the relationship is eternal, what happens during the dissolution of the universe (*pralaya*), the alternate of creation in the endless cycles of creation and dissolution? VB answers: When a person sleeps, he still remains the proprietor of his treasure. Furthermore, when a relationship is not any factor or process apart from the inherent attributes of the *relata* or the correlates, such problems do not arise. The relationship between self and matter is not a process that begins or occurs under certain conditions, such as creation, and ceases under certain other conditions, such as dissolution. The inherent quality remains as a seed. The recurrence of *khyāti* is not caused by any external factor but is retained as a seed, a potential, as part of the inherence of the attributes of each entity. The effectiveness of such inherence continues only through the impressions (saṁskāras) in the buddhi, the inclinations that their strength produces, becoming propensities (*vāsanās*) and leading to the pacific, fierce or stupefied vṛttis. *Sāṅkhya-pravachana-sūtra* I.104 and VI.55 say (VB) that such effectiveness of the inherent attribute ceases at the pure consciousness when isolation (*kaivalya*) occurs and *khyāti* ceases.

But, asks an objector, how is it possible (VB) that an eternal or beginningless relationship can exist as inherent in something (i.e., mahat or buddhi) which is a non-eternal evolute of matter? The problem is solved by reminding ourselves of the Sāṅkhya tenet of *sat-kārya-vāda,* that an effect always exists within its cause, and the cause does not cease simply because the cause has been transmuted into an effect. Consequently mahat or buddhi never cease to partake of an inherent relationship which is an eternal attribute of their cause, prakṛti.

As stated in *YS* I.22 and confirmed elsewhere (VB), the relationship discussed above exists only between the individual puruṣha and his personal mind-field and not between the said individual and all mind-fields, nor between the universal puruṣha and a specific mind-field. Vṛttis and the spiritual self's awareness of them (*YS* IV.18) are two separate factors, like a candle illuminating the interior of a jar into which it has been placed, but from which it maintains a separate identity. At no stage do they become one, like a jewel and its light. In this context the reader should deeply contemplate the two analogies of a candle in a jar and of a jewel and its luminosity. Vyāsa's quotation from Pañchaśhikha,

> There is only one perception; reflective cognition (*khyāti*) alone is the perception,

was explained and discussed on pp. 129-31 and need not be repeated here. To conclude, then:

> As the moon does not break up even though its reflection in turbulent water appears fragmented,
> so puruṣha (BR) remains unaltered in the *khyāti* process of buddhi.[9]

9. For a summary of the discussion on this sūtra please read the paraphrase of Vyāsa's commentary and the first hypothesis regarding subjective composite personality defined on p. 124. The rereading of this material will establish that puruṣha always remains a neutral witness. It is thus always in samādhi (refer to p. 108 and subsequent discussion). In *vyutthāna,* puruṣha appears to be involved in vṛttis but is not really so because the process of *khyāti* occurs in the buddhi and not in the spiritual self. Any statements or arguments proposing that vṛttis reflect into, or that *khyāti* occurs in, puruṣha are experientially fallacious as well as untenable in the light of the basic Sāṅkhya-yoga tenet that puruṣha is incorruptible. BG, NB, NBB reflect VB's opinions on these matters for the most part and are therefore not quoted extensively.

Sūtra I.5 वृत्तयः पञ्चतय्यः क्लिष्टाक्लिष्टाः।

vṛttayaḥ pañchatayyaḥ klişhṭākliṣhṭāḥ

vṛttayaḥ: the vṛttis (are)
pañchatayyaḥ: fivefold (and of two kinds)
kliṣhṭa-: afflicted, painful and impure, imbued with *kleśhas,* and
a-kliṣhṭāḥ: not afflicted, not painful, pure, not imbued with *kleśhas*

The vṛttis are fivefold (and of two kinds): afflicted, painful and impure, imbued with *kleśhas* (*kliṣhṭa*); and not afflicted, not painful, pure, not imbued with *kleśhas* (*a-kliṣhṭa*).

Vyāsa's Commentary

Now, those (vṛttis) must be controlled. Though many, the mind-field's

> [*Sūtra:*] vṛttis are fivefold (and of two kinds): afflicted . . . and not afflicted.

The afflicted, painful and impure vṛttis are caused by the *kleśhas* and are causes of the *kleśhas*. These become the field for the abundant growth of the domain of karmas (*karmāśhaya*).

The unafflicted vṛttis are those whose subject is discernment (*viveka-khyāti*), and which impede the power of guṇas. These remain unafflicted even when fallen in the currents of the afflicted ones. They remain unafflicted also in the intervals of the afflicted ones.

The afflicted vṛttis also (appear) in the intervals of the unafflicted ones.

The vṛttis produce their own kind of saṁskāras, and in turn, the saṁskāras produce identical vṛttis. Thus the wheel of vṛttis and saṁskāras revolves incessantly.

When the mind-field becomes such that it has completed the work within its authority, it stands on its own.

Or it even goes into dissolution.

Paraphrase of Vyāsa's Commentary

The vṛttis with which puruṣha appears to be assimilated (*YS* I.4) need to be brought under control according to the definition of yoga (*YS* I.2). The vṛttis are innumerable but can be classified into a fivefold division of categories (*YS* I.6). Furthermore, all these five categories of vṛttis are of two types: (*a*) afflicted, painful, impure (*kliṣhṭa*), and (*b*) unafflicted, not painful, pure (*a-kliṣhṭa*). The afflicted vṛttis are caused by *kleśhas* and produce further *kleśhas* (*YS* II.3) and cause the growth of the domain of karma (*karmāśhaya*), which leads to continued bondage (*YS* II.12).

The unafflicted, sattvic, vṛttis are those that lead to discernment (*viveka-khyāti*) by impeding the power of the guṇas. Even when the unafflicted vṛttis are experienced within the streams of the afflicted ones, they yet remain unafflicted. Also, when they appear in the intervals between the periods of afflicted ones, they remain unaffected by the latter.

Similarly, the afflicted vṛttis make their appearance in the intervals between the periods of unafflicted ones.

The vṛttis produce on the mind-field their own kinds of impressions (saṁskāras), which in turn create similar vṛttis, and the vicious circle continues without ceasing.

The mind, however, is purified through the practice of yoga. Furthermore, the sattvic vṛttis are encouraged so that the mind progresses towards *samprajñāta* samādhi, which leads to *viveka-khyāti,* the discrimination, discernment, of the separateness of the composite personality and the spiritual self.

At this point the mind has served its purpose; it has completed the work that is within its authority. Now the vṛttis are of no further service. Mind alone remains, entirely on its own, without reference to external objects.

The relationship between the spiritual self and all the material evolutes, including the mind-field, is now severed and all the evolutes dissolve into the equilibrium of prakṛti. Puruṣha's isolation, *kaivalya,* is now complete.

Discussion

We begin with Vyāsa's sentences:

> Now, those (vṛttis) must be controlled. Though many, the mind-field's
>
> [*Sūtra:*] vṛttis are fivefold (and of two kinds): afflicted . . . and unafflicted

The *Yoga-sūtras* instruct one to control the vṛttis of the mind-field. Now, one can be taught only what is possible (VM), and the control of vṛttis is not possible without first knowing them. But they are too numerous to be counted even in a thousand lifetimes. They are innumerable not only within a single person's mind-field but all together in the mind-fields of many persons (VM, VB, SS, RY, NB). How then can these innumerable vṛttis be known in order to be controlled (VM,VB)? This sūtra solves the problem by classifying the innumerable vṛttis into five categories (VM, VB). All the other vṛttis are products of these five (VB). Through control of the five, all their derivatives, the totality of innumerable vṛttis, are controlled. Vṛttis such as *rāga* (attraction) and *dveṣha* (aversion) are automatically prevented from arising (BG) when their causes, the five major vṛttis, are brought under control.

The list of five is not exhaustive (VM and RY on *YS* I.6). No statement is made to exclude such vṛttis as, for example, the loss of a sense of direction, or the false impression of a single line or a circle of fire that is induced when a torch is moved rapidly (*alāta-chakra*). Even though it may be difficult to place such mental activity within any of the five categories of vṛttis, any exclusion is of a *paryudāsa* type (negation by omission) rather than *prasajya-pratiṣhedha* (negation by direct statement) against a possibility. A *paryudāsa* negation is not very strong and implies that an entity omitted may be included to fulfil the original intent (*ākāṅkṣhā*). The *ākāṅkṣhā* here is to include rather than exclude, as indicated by the fact that the words used are *pañchatayyaḥ* 'fivefold' and *pañchadhā* (see Vyāsa on *YS* I.6) 'divided in five ways', and not simply *pañcha* 'five'.

The sūtra makes these five vṛttis known. "Vṛttis of the mind-field" refers to the genus mind-field, so that all the specific mind-fields are included. The vṛtti is a single entity, a whole, with five parts (VM, RY), namely, *pramāṇa,* etc. enumerated in the next sūtra. Hence the term "fivefold" (*pañchatayī*).

At this point VB gives a new twist to the word *vṛtti*. The original meaning of this word is as we have translated it, but its secondary meaning is "means of livelihood." Vṛttis are the mind-field's means of livelihood (*vṛttis*); it is by these that the mind continues to survive. Without them it has no existence.

To provide practical application (VM) to the theory and to ascertain which of the vṛttis are desirable and which are to be avoided (RY), the five are further subdivided into two: *klishṭa* and *a-klishṭa*. The mind functions (HA) both as

pra-vartaka: involver, engager, initiator, promoter, inducer, producer, instigator, urging and prompting one towards X, and
ni-vartaka: disinvolver, terminator, inhibitor, abstainer, abolisher, urging and prompting one away from X.

Thus the fivefold vṛttis are positivistic or negativistic, leading to bondage or to liberation. For example, a proof (*pramāṇa*) leading the mind (HA) to favour, to an attraction or any *kleśha* is considered *klishṭa*. A proof leading one to rise beyond attraction or aversion is *a-klishṭa*.

One may argue that a proof is neutral and the conclusions impersonal, but yoga psychology would reply that this is not the case. Because of the force of unconsciously stored past impressions (saṁskāras), and because of the resultant personal propensities (*vāsanās*), the mind is inclined towards a certain use of the proof, and draws its own favoured conclusions. For example: (*a*) a wolf's mind receives proof, through its eye, that a woman is present in the forest. It concludes: "Flesh to eat"; (*b*) a passionate youth's mind receives proof, through his eye, that a woman is present. He concludes: "A beauty to ravish"; (*c*) a yogi's mind receives proof, through his eye, that a woman is present. He concludes: "What otherwise would have been a corpse is here imbued with the luminosity and the consequent beauty of the spiritual self. The spiritual self is to be realized." The first two examples are *pramāṇa* processes in the afflicted and impure category, *kliṣhṭa*. The last example is in the unafflicted category, *a-kliṣhṭa*.

Whether *kliṣhṭa* or *a-kliṣhṭa*, the vṛttis of both kinds (VB, BG) have to be brought under control. By fostering the *a-kliṣhṭas*, one controls the *kliṣhṭas* (VM,VB), and then one vanquishes the *a-kliṣhṭa* vṛttis in turn through transcendental dispassion (*para-vairāgya*) (*YS* I.16). As we read elsewhere,

> Vanquish the others by sattva, then that sattva by (higher) sattva.
> *Bhāgavata-purāṇa* XI.13.1.

Since all vṛttis consist of the three guṇas and are therefore *kliṣhṭa* (VB), it might seem inappropriate to divide them into *kliṣhṭa* and *a-kliṣhṭa*. The subclassification, though, indicates only the particular degree of the relationship between the vṛttis and the *kleśhas*. Vyāsa explains this relationship:

> The afflicted, painful and impure vṛttis are caused by the *kleśhas* and are causes of the *kleśhas*.

The single, compound word *kleśha-hetukāḥ* may be translated as "caused by the *kleśhas*" and "causes of the *kleśhas*." Some commentators have stood by the first reading, and others have accepted the second. It is probably more correct, however, to side with those who have tried to include and reconcile both. The *kleśhas*, such as *asmitā* (VM) and *avidyā* (HA), are the causes that bring about the advent of vṛttis. Or (VM) it may be said that as prakṛti serves puruṣha, only its rajasic and tamasic vṛttis are the cause of *kleśha*. This view of VM is, however, a limited one, as it contradicts the statements made just above with regard to the need for vanquishing the sattvic vṛttis also. In any case, vṛttis (VM) caused by the *kleśhas* lead to further *kleśhas*.

According to VB the word *hetu* (cause) actually means a purpose, an effect. *Kleśhas*, too, are the effects of the vṛttis. The main *kleśha* (VB) is pain (*duḥkha*), which is the effect produced by the vṛttis that take the form of objects experienced; hence, it is *kliṣhṭa*.

The *kleśhas* cause affliction and pain by causing inversion (HA) of awareness (*viparyastra-pratyaya*), turning the inward consciousness outward so that awareness does not dwell in the seer's own (MA) nature. These *kliṣhṭa* vṛttis are a particular mutation of the mind-field (AD) invaded (BR, AD) by the *kleśhas,* rooted in (HA) and consisting of the *kleśhas.*

Again, Vyāsa:

> These (vṛttis) become the field for the abundant growth of the domain of karmas (*karmāśhaya*).

Here the word *karmāśhaya* needs to be understood. It is that domain of the mind-field on which are left the impressions of all (*a*) experiences from the objective world without, and (*b*) vṛttis from the mental world within. These impressions, saṁskāras, have internal currents of their own. When certain saṁskāras, by constant addition of like impressions, become strong enough, the propensities they create impel a person in a certain direction. The choices thus made produce pain or pleasure in the process of reincarnation (*YS* II.13). The substratum of this process within the mind-field is called the *karmāśhaya,* or the domain of karmas.

Because vṛttis arise only for the purpose of acquisition of *kleśhas,* they become the field for abundant growth of the *karmāśhaya* (VM). The person in this pursuit makes his determination with vṛttis such as valid proof (*pramāṇa*), etc. (*YS* I.6). Then, whether attracted or repelled, he adds to the *karmāśhaya.* Thus it is that vṛttis can serve as the ground for the generation of an abundance of virtue or vice (VM). These (VB) vṛttis become the supporting ground for a multitude of propensities (*vāsanās*) for virtue or vice. A person smitten by a craving caused by vṛttis that take the form of objects of experience undertakes to overcome the craving by pursuits such as injuriousness or compassion, thereby gathering vice or virtue. Thus begins the stream of sorrow. This, then, is the nature of *kliṣhṭa* vṛttis, which are (RY) the cause of afflictions like attraction and aversion (*rāga* and *dveṣha*) (*YS* II.7,8), with bondage as their fruit. That is, every being is

- bound to pleasure and so on
- by having performed actions (karma)
- because of attraction, aversion, etc.
- towards the matters that he has come to know
- with vṛttis such as valid proof.

We need to remember that virtue arising from sattva is only relatively desirable. Virtue exists only in comparison to vice. A yogi's action, however, is beyond all concepts of black and white (*YS* IV.7), and the sattva of the lower samādhi is transcended in higher samādhi when the relationship with all guṇas is terminated. Here the *a-kliṣhṭa* vṛttis replace the former afflicted ones. These unafflicted vṛttis are as purely sattvic as it is possible for a material evolute to be. Hence they, unlike the afflicted ones, produce no further *kleśhas*. Vyāsa's commentary reads:

> The unafflicted vṛttis are those whose subject is discernment (*viveka-khyāti*), and which impede the power of guṇas.

A-kliṣhṭa vṛttis (VB) do not result in *kleśhas*. The *kleśhas* arise from activity of the guṇas, for it is the latter's prerogative or empowerment (*adhikāra*) to initiate action, which (VM, VB) continues up to discernment (*khyāti*).[10] *Khyāti* (VM), which means "clarity of wisdom" (*prajñā-prasāda*), occurs when the sattvic aspect of buddhi has been washed of rajas and tamas and flows tranquilly. By whatever means discernment (*khyāti*) between the spiritual self and the sattva of buddhi is realized, those means are included (VB) in the clause "whose subject is discernment." The unafflicted vṛttis help bring about the discernment and reduce the power of the guṇas until the latter have finally fulfilled their purpose. They do so by opposing or blocking the activation of ignorance (*avidyā*), desire (*kāma*) and the attendant actions (karmas). The result of *a-kliṣhṭa* vṛttis is liberation (mokṣha), says RY; but this is technically incorrect. *A-kliṣhṭa* vṛttis lead only to discernment, which in turn leads to *asamprajñāta* samādhi and final liberation.

---

10. *Khyāti* is used here in the sense of *viveka-khyāti* and not as in Vyāsa's commentary quoting Pañchaśhikha (see pp. 129ff.).

What are these unafflicted vṛttis? They are the same as *pramāṇa,* etc. enumerated in the next sūtra. When these are directed towards worldly objects, they are *klishṭa,* and when they are directed inwards, they are *a-klishṭa.*

It is clear that tamasic vṛttis are afflicted (*klishṭa*) and sattvic vṛttis are unafflicted (*a-klishṭa*). The question arises regarding the category to which rajasic vṛttis might belong. BG says that they are unafflicted at best or mixed into and included in either sattvic or tamasic in a specific mental situation. VB also regards them as mixed, both *klishṭa* and *a-klishṭa.* However, this disagreement is solved by remembering that in Sāṅkhya philosophy the function of rajas is always to impel both sattva and tamas. Without the impelling force of rajas the other two guṇas are ineffective and not efficacious. In this sense the rajasic element may be considered to be mixed with either sattva or tamas, whichever is dominant, and therefore sattva or tamas is served or supported by rajas. The progress of the mind-field towards pure sattva is not possible without the operational capacity of rajas.

A counterargument posed is as follows: Since the liberated ones seldom incarnate (*Nyāya-sūtra* of Gotama III.1.25), it is understood that all beings, with the exception of liberated incarnations, bear afflicted vṛttis. It would be rare if unafflicted vṛttis should arise in the constant stream of such afflicted vṛttis. And even if unafflicted vṛttis were to arise among the afflicted ones, they would be powerless, having fallen among powerful opponents. Therefore, it is illogical that afflicted vṛttis could be controlled through unafflicted ones, and the latter, again, through transcendental dispassion (*para-vairāgya*) (VM). Against this pessimism, however, Vyāsa shows optimism:

> These (unafflicted vṛttis) remain unafflicted even when fallen in the currents of the afflicted ones. They remain unafflicted also in the intervals of the afflicted ones.
>
> The afflicted vṛttis also (appear) in the intervals of the unafflicted ones.

Practice and dispassion (*abhyāsa* and *vairāgya*) (*YS* I.12-16) are the unafflicted vṛttis par excellence, even though not enumerated among the five. Or it may be said that these two arise (VM, HA, RY) from *a-klishṭa* vṛttis, for example (VM), from

- *āgama:* textual authority, one of the valid proofs (*pramāṇas*), or
- *anumāna:* inference, another *pramāṇa* leading to a spiritual conclusion, or
- the instruction of a teacher and contemplation thereon.

When practice and dispassion cause a break (HA) in the flow of afflictions, the vṛttis leading to a higher good (*paramārtha*) arise. Even though these latter vṛttis arise in the stream of afflictions and afflicted vṛttis, they remain untouched by them (VM, VB, HA) and are not corrupted. The same applies to unafflicted vṛttis that appear in intervals between afflicted vṛttis.

Similarly, when unafflicted vṛttis begin to flow, their stream is often interrupted by afflicted ones. However, these corrupt vṛttis have no power to alter the purer ones; rather, as the purer vṛttis grow in strength through repeated practice, their saṁskāras gradually mature, and the impure vṛttis are brought under control. Then as dispassion grows and becomes *para-vairāgya,* even the pure vṛttis are discarded (VM, VB, HA, RY, MA). A few examples of vṛttis becoming unafflicted (*a-klishta*) may be given as follows (NTC):

pramāṇa: proof—is unafflicted when it leads to perception of the self.

viparyaya: perverse cognition—helps one to gain merit when one superimposes the idea of divinity upon an icon.

vikalpa: imaginary cognition—is beneficial when the great sentences (*mahā-vākyas*) of Vedānta, such as "Thou art That," leave some purificatory imprint on the mind, even when they have not been fully understood.

nidrā: sleep (cf. Sūtra I.38)—is of value when it causes one to experience sattvic pleasure.

smṛti: memory—helps when, upon seeing worldly objects such as the blue sky, one is reminded of the descriptions of appearances of one's favourite incarnation of the Deity.

Does it necessarily mean, then, that once an aspirant has begun his or her practice success is assured, and that the vṛttis associated with *kleśhas* have no more power over the aspirant? This may be answered in two ways:

1. Vyāsa has rejected the disciples with distracted (*vikṣhipta*) minds as unworthy of consideration as serious yogis (*YS* I.1). He is not talking about them.
2. The wording of most commentators suggests that unafflicted vṛttis have to be strengthened through practice and dispassion until they cease to be intermittent and create a flow (*pravāha*). Then the *kliṣhṭa* vṛttis arising intermittently have no more power and will soon be conquered.

This is the essence of what Vyāsa says:

> The vṛttis produce their own kind of saṁskāras, and in turn, the saṁskāras produce identical vṛttis. Thus the wheel of vṛttis and saṁskāras revolves incessantly.

Saṁskāras are the intangible and inactive state of vṛttis, and the vṛttis are the tangible and active outcome of saṁskāras (HA). The only way this wheel of saṁskāras and vṛttis can be stopped (*stambhana*) and the mind-field dissolved (*pralaya*) is through the practice of *nirodha*. Until then the struggle for supremacy continues between the afflicted and the unafflicted vṛttis.

This process may be further elaborated upon: Even when a person's mind-field is filled with impure vṛttis, the purer vṛttis arise in many ways. For example: saṁskāras of pure vṛttis from past lives remain dormant. While the karmas are maturing in the current life, and some impure karmas have already matured and fructified, the purer saṁskāras from the past arise and produce purer vṛttis. This may occur (*a*) when some external stimulant of a pure nature is presented to the mind (e.g., a sattvic or beautiful view, an "accidental" glance at an uplifting text, an inspiring sermon heard upon the invitation or insistence of friends, and so forth) or (*b*) when the pain and sorrow produced through worldly pursuits jolts one into dispassion and renunciation, or even a mild re-examination of one's values. These processes may occur (*a*) spontaneously, even in the middle of an impure stream, or (*b*) during the interruptions that occur in the impure flow. The impure vṛttis still arise during the interruptions in the flow of pure ones (*YS* IV.27), but eventually—after the practice of austerities, restraints, *yamas* and *niyamas* and meditation ceases to be a painful discipline and becomes a habit and a natural inclination—negative emotions and painful thoughts seldom arise. Finally, the power of impure vṛttis is broken and the pure vṛttis form a stream; the intermittent appearance of impure vṛttis no longer threatens the spiritual inclination and is soon conquered.

Again, Vyāsa:

> When the mind-field becomes such that it has completed the work within its authority, it stands on its own.
>
> Or it even goes into dissolution.

"When the mind-field becomes such" means that it is controlled and progressing towards *nirodha*-samādhi. It has completed the work of (*a*) *bhoga*—presenting experiences to the spiritual self—and (*b*) *apavarga*—serving as vehicle of the thoughts of liberation. Now the mind-field withdraws from its domain of authority and the field of service in three stages:

1. Only the saṁskāras remain without activating vṛttis (*YS* I.18). There are (VB) no more conflicts and pains in the mind. Then it reaches the samādhi of the raincloud of virtue and of the knowledge of the nature of all things (*dharma-megha*) (*YS* IV.29) (HA), in which (VM) the mind dwells in itself, by itself. But this stage (VM) is not the goal; it is merely incidental (*āpātataḥ*) on the way to the final step.
2. We have translated Vyāsa's phrase *ātma-kalpena* to mean "stands on its own"; that is, the mind dwells in itself, by itself. Here we can go further.
   a) The mind, being sattvic, is reflective. It reflects the light of the pure self, and all the objects of experience reflect in it, becoming vṛttis. It takes the form of whatever reflects in it and identifies with it.

b) In samādhi there are no objects of experience, but only the light of the spiritual self reflecting in the mind, with the result that it now identifies only with the spiritual self. At this stage Vyāsa's phrase, *ātma-kalpena,* is understood to mean: identifying with the self (ātman), imagining itself to be the self, as close to self in purity as it is capable of becoming (*YS* III.55).

3. As the practice deepens further (VB) (*abhyāsa-pāṭavena*), the saṁskāras are burnt (NB) from the individual mind-field, which now goes through the process of *prati-prasava,* dissolution into final prakṛti (*YS* IV.34), following the Sāṅkhya scheme of *prati-sañchara,* the cosmic principle of the orderly dissolution of evolutes (*TSS* 7). This is the total and permanent (*ātyantika*) termination of the relationship between self and non-self.

This dissolution of the mind-field may be mistaken for liberation (*mokṣha* or *mukti*) (as in RY), and may be referred to as *videha-kaivalya* (as in VB), the state of becoming bodiless even when dwelling in the body. The point needs to be made that *YS* I.19 considers the *videha* state to be far lower than final isolation (*kaivalya*), although the dissolution of the individual mind-field into the original and final prakṛti is an inevitable stage in the process of liberation. The individual yogi who has accomplished this is called *jīvan-mukta,* liberated yet not disincarnate, still maintaining the body; this state is known as *jīvan-mukti,* liberation while yet incarnate.

The final dissolution (*pralaya*) of the mind-field cannot occur in a *jīvan-mukta,* who yet needs the mind as an instrument of keeping the physical body operative, although the mind does come very close to the *pralaya* state in the samādhi of a *jīvan-mukta.* The *videha-mukti* by itself, however, is not the definition of *asamprajñāta* or seedless (*nir-bīja*) samādhi (*YS* I.18,51) or of *kaivalya* (*YS* IV.34), which are not states of mind but simply the self dwelling in the self, without reference to a material evolute such as the mind. The final liberation while the self is yet incarnate means not ever (VB) leaving the state of samādhi, the self dwelling in the self, even when carrying on the mental, corporeal, and social duties, which the yogi continues to perform, out of compassion, to help liberate others.

In conclusion: In *dharma-megha,* mind dwells in itself, and then identifies with the spiritual self. In *asamprajñāta* and *kaivalya,* the self dwells in the self.

Sūtra I.6 प्रमाणविपर्ययविकल्पनिद्रास्मृतयः।

pramāṇa-viparyaya-vikalpa-nidrā-smṛtayaḥ

pramāṇa-: valid proofs
viparyaya-: perversive cognition
vikalpa-: imaginary cognition, linguistic misconception
nidrā-: sleep, and
smṛtayaḥ: (*smṛti*) memory

The fivefold vṛttis of the mind are: valid proofs, perversive cognition, imaginary cognition, sleep and memory.

Vyāsa's Commentary

Those afflicted and unafflicted vṛttis divided into five are

[*Sūtra:*] valid proofs, perversive cognition, imaginary cognition, sleep and memory.

Sūtra I.7 प्रत्यक्षानुमानागमाः प्रमाणानि।

pratyakṣhānumānāgamāḥ pramāṇāni

pratyakṣha-: direct perception
anumāna-: inference
āgamāḥ: and (textual, scriptural, inspired, revealed) authority
pramāṇāni: proofs

Direct perception, inference and revealed authority are the three categories of the vṛtti called valid proof (*pramāṇa*).

Vyāsa's Commentary

The mind-field is drawn towards, attracted to and coloured by an external (*upa-rāga*) substance through the channels of the senses. With that as its object, a modification (vṛtti) is produced in the mind-field; this vṛtti is the valid proof (*pramāṇa*) called direct perception (*pratyakṣha*). It determines, primarily, the specific in a matter that consists of the general and the specific.

The result is the puruṣha-originated, undistinguished apprehension of the vṛtti in the mind-field. Puruṣha is the cause of buddhi's accurate apprehension. This we shall establish later.

Inference (*anumāna*) is the vṛtti determining primarily the general, having as its object that connection of the inferable which conforms to the homogeneous and excludes the non-homogeneous. For example, "The moon and the star have movement because they are seen to arrive at another locus," or "The Vindhya mountain does not move, for it is not seen to arrive at another locus."

A matter seen or inferred by an accomplished person is taught in the form of words in order to transfer one's knowledge into another. The vṛtti from that word, with its matter and meaning as the object, is the listener's acquisition (*āgama*).

That *āgama* overwhelms one whose teacher has not seen or inferred the matter correctly and whose presentation of the matter cannot be trusted. But the *āgama* is without such disturbance in the case of the original teacher.

Paraphrase of Vyāsa's Commentary

When the senses present certain information to the mind-field, there occurs in the mind a certain modification (vṛtti) whose object is the sense data. However, there arises a doubt as to the actual properties of an object, which also shares certain of its properties with other objects. The determinative process (*ava-dhāraṇa*) helps the mind to eliminate general shared properties so that it focuses on the specific. For example, "Is that a person or a post?" In this question the general shared properties of the person and the post are eliminated, and by focusing on the specific properties one determines the visible object to be either a person or a post. This vṛtti, the chief determinant of the specifics, is a valid proof (*pramāṇa*) called direct perception (*pratyakṣha*).

Such an apprehension in the mind-field is possible because the origin of awareness is in puruṣha, who transmits to the mind its capacity to perceive. In such an apprehension or perception of a vṛtti, the mind-field itself does not distinguish between its experience of the object from the external world and the awareness imparted by puruṣha. In other words, the objects, the experience, the vṛtti, the mind-field and the awareness of the spiritual self are not distinguishable one from another. Puruṣha, however, is the cause of buddhi's accurate apprehension.

Discussion

Throughout the history of Indian philosophy there have been intense debates concerning how many categories of valid proof there might be. Different schools have each accepted a varying number according to the internal needs of the particular philosophical system. Numerous scholarly treatises have detailed the preferences of these systems and the arguments that developed among them. The yoga system accepts only three categories of valid proof (*pramāṇa*) since these suffice for its purposes:

pratyakṣha: direct perception
anumāna: inference
āgama: scriptural or revealed authority

The functions of the valid proofs (*pramāṇas*) accepted by other systems can be subsumed under these three in one way or another (VB, NTC) and need not be individually dealt with here (VM, NTC).

Neither the *Yoga-sūtras* nor Vyāsa has defined *pramāṇa* itself separately because the derivation of the word is clear and applicable to all three *pramāṇas.* First, the word *pramā* means "apprehension of a state, condition, fact, object or entity (*tattva*) heretofore not obtained" (VM, VB). Because the mind is an evolute of matter, all of its operations such as the logical processes, vṛttis like *pramāṇas* and acceptance or rejection of a postulate or a conclusion are in themselves devoid of consciousness. Like matter itself they are all unconscious (*jaḍa*) except through the presence of the consciousness of the spiritual self (*chit*) (RS); hence *pramā* may be defined not merely as the apprehension of a state, condition, etc. as just stated above, but also as the reflection of puruṣha falling upon the vṛtti, whereby exploration of a matter formerly not known—that is, an apprehension—occurs (RY, SS). A *pramāṇa* is the instrument, means or method for reaching that apprehension (*pramā*). That proof (*pramāṇa*) is a knowledge that is consistent and cannot be challenged (*a-vi-saṁ-vādin*) (BR, NB).

Direct perception (*pratyakṣha*) is the root of all other proofs, which in turn depend on it; and therefore *pratyakṣha* comes first (VM).

Vyāsa states:

> The mind-field is drawn towards, attracted to and coloured by an external (*upa-rāga*) substance through the channels of the senses. With that as its object, a modification (vṛtti) is produced in the mind-field; this vṛtti is the valid proof (*pramāṇa*) called direct perception (*pratyakṣha*).

An external substance (*vastu*) is a requisite in the above statement (VM), so that the type of superimposition that occurs in the perversive (*viparyaya*) vṛtti (*YS* I.8) may be excluded.

Contact between the mind and objects occurs through the senses. Without (*a*) the objects, (*b*) the senses as channels of contact, and (*c*) the process of contact, the mind cannot be transmuted into the form of a given vṛtti (VB). The formed apprehension then becomes the means of verification and the final determinant. The senses are an important constituent of this process, as we find, for example, that if a jaundiced eye sees a white conch shell as yellow, there ensues in the mind the vṛtti of a yellow conch shell, which is contradicted only by the logical processes of induction and deduction (*anvaya* and *vyatireka*) (VB, NB).

The single word *upa-rāga* is translated here as "drawn towards, attracted to and coloured by." This threefold process is included in the meaning of the prefix *upa* 'near, closely' and the verb root *rañj* 'to colour, to be drawn towards, to be attracted to'. The primary meaning of the verb root *rañj* is "to colour." The way a clear crystal is coloured yellow in the proximity of a yellow object is suggested by *upa* + *rañj* = noun, *upa-rāga*. Similarly, when a person is drawn towards another person or a mind is drawn towards the experience of an object, the same *upa-rāga* takes place, with the colours of the nearby person or object reflecting in the mind. In the case of *pratyakṣha,* the "colours" of the object of experience pass through the channels of the senses. The phrase *tad-viṣhayaḥ* 'with that as its object' refers in Vyāsa's commentary to the entire process of colouring the mind in this way, with the mind taking the form of the vṛtti that is being produced. If it were only a mental perception without an external object and without contact through the senses, the realist philosophers of the Sāṅkhya-yoga school would not classify it as a valid direct perception of the *pratyakṣha* type.

Vyāsa states:

> It (*pratyakṣha*) determines, primarily, the specific in a matter that consists of the general and the specific.

An object of experience or an entity has two aspects:

sāmānya: universal, generic, general
viśheṣha: particular, specific, individual

The word "cow" expresses the cow nature shared by all cows, without which a specific cow would not be a cow. It also refers to a specific cow.

The (HA) general, generic, universal (*sāmānya*), is often signified by words and is maintained as a mental image referring to the totality and collectivity of all the possible individuals of that genus. The specific, particular, individual (*viśheṣha*), may be experienced without any verbal signification. An age-old problem in all philosophical systems, Eastern or Western, is whether the mind's experience of an object is of its universal or particular aspect. For instance, does the mind experience the universal cow, which might exist in the unmanifest even if all individual cows ceased to exist, or does it experience the specific cow seen grazing in a particular pasture?

The philosophers (VM, RS) who subscribe to Kumārila Bhaṭṭa's interpretation of the Mīmāṁsā school believe that only the universals are experienced. On the other hand, Buddhist philosophers accept no universals, experiencing, as they maintain, only the particular. Nyāya, the school of logic, believes that an object is endowed with both universal and particular attributes. Each cow has both universal "cowness" and its individual "cowness" present in its configuration.

Vyāsa's view is that the object is not endowed (VM, RS, HA) with some universal or particular attributes, but that there exists (VM, RY)

> *tādātmyam:* the object in question is both universal and particular.

In other words, the object denoted by the word "cow," and/or observed with the senses, producing a vṛtti in the mind, incorporates all the universal "cowness" and the individual "cowness," not apart from the fact that it is a cow. However, for the purpose of defining *pratyakṣha,* Vyāsa states:

> It determines . . . the specific in a matter (*artha*) that consists of the general and the specific.

This simply reinforces Sāṅkhya-yoga realism, which holds that when the senses contact an object, no observation of the universal is possible. Even though the universal is present (VM) in the particular, it is secondary for the purpose of the observation.

We have translated the phrase *viśheṣha-avadhāraṇa-pradhāna* as "it determines, primarily, the specific." The word "primarily" indicates that the universal is considered secondary in this instance. Without its inclusion in *pratyakṣha,* the universal would fail to serve as a basis for and an aid to inference (*anumāna*), which is the chief determinant of the concealed universal aspect from the observation of the particulars.

This realism presents a problem because all the major schools of Indian philosophy consider *yogi-pratyakṣha* to be the supremely valid proof. The ordinary person's direct perception (*pratyakṣha*) is covered by the statements made so far, and that direct perception definitely requires the presence of external objects and the mind's contact with them through the channels of the senses. But what is the definition and the process of *yogi-pratyakṣha*? Does Patañjali intend to include it? Is it Vyāsa's intent to define it here? Even a cursory reading of Vyāsa's words leads one to understand that *yogi-pratyakṣha* is not meant to be included here and that it will be described in the *Yoga-sūtras* elsewhere (for example, *YS* III.1,17-19,25-29,33-36,43,49,52,54). Nonetheless, commentators VM, VB, NB, RY and SS have attempted to classify *yogi-pratyakṣha* here as a type of direct perception.

The definition of *pratyakṣha* as given by Vyāsa on this sūtra is only a pointer (*upa-lakṣhaṇa*), (VM, NB) stating a part to include a larger whole. It is a pointer to the implicit, complete idea of realization (*sākṣhāt-kāra*) and the (VM) *viveka-khyāti.*

Phrases or words like *upa-rāga* 'colouring' are used for the purpose of stating the cause and process of the vṛttis produced (VB) in the mind from external sources. These phrases and words should not be taken as part of the definition of *yogi-pratyakṣha;* otherwise the direct experience of self (ātman) and of God (īśhvara) could not occur, not being a product of, and not having been induced through, the contact between objects and senses.

In the deeper meditation of *samprajñāta* samādhi, when the mind is no longer dependent on externals and is clear, there appears a reflection of the pure consciousness (*chiti-śhakti*) (RY, SS). This is direct perception, *yogi-pratyakṣha.*

Even though this sūtra and Vyāsa's commentary thereupon do not speak of *yogi-pratyakṣha,* the view expressed by various commentators is in conformity with and supported by the *Yoga-sūtras* philosophy in general.

Returning to the common person's direct perception (*pratyakṣha*), Vyāsa says:

> The result is the puruṣha-originated, undistinguished apprehension of the vṛtti in the mind-field. Puruṣha is the cause of buddhi's accurate apprehension. This we shall establish later (*YS* II.20, IV.22).

This extract from Vyāsa's commentary was clarified earlier, but is here presented again. The emphasis in Vyāsa's text is on the result (*phalam*). The above sentences are meant to convey the result of the process of observation and direct perception, which is that a vṛtti occurs in the mind-field. But in and of itself it would be a "dead" process, because the mind is an unconscious material evolute. What gives this process of perception and the resultant vṛtti a semblance of life, awareness and consciousness—an apprehension—is the fact that the vṛtti and its substratum, the mind-field, are being illuminated by the spiritual self (puruṣha).

The process of proof, any valid experience, is called *pramā.* It occurs as follows: When the senses are in the proximity of objects, they cause the mind to become occluded by the tamas of those objects. At once sattva arises to counter that tamas and an illumination occurs. Such a mingling of tamas and sattva is the valid experience (*pramā*). Sattva cannot rise all by itself except when impelled by the power of consciousness (*chiti-śhakti*). In other words it is the grace of this spiritual force alone that causes valid experience. The light of consciousness from within reflecting in buddhi and illuminating the tamas of the objects being reflected therein from outside constitutes the experience. Buddhi by itself is incapable of creating such a process (AD). This is what is meant by

> the puruṣha-originated . . . apprehension of the vṛtti in the mind-field.

The complete phrase, however, is:

> the puruṣha-originated, *undistinguished* apprehension of the vṛtti in the mind-field.

What is meant by "undistinguished" (*a-viśhiṣhṭa*)? It means simply that (HA) the mind then sees itself as not distinguished from the puruṣha, through whose illumination the mind-field experiences apprehension of the vṛtti. The vṛtti and the puruṣha's illumination thereof thus becoming undistinguished, the mind then says, "I am the conscious seer." Thus the mental processes of the person are mistaken as being processes of the self, the illumination, the mind and the vṛtti becoming one. This is the end result, called *pramā*, and the means thereto is *pramāṇa*, the process of the proof. This is the explanation offered by the commentators (VM, HA, SS) who are true to the original intent of Vyāsa. VB takes up the word *pauruṣheya*, which can be translated as "puruṣha-originated" (as has been done here) or as "puruṣha's own." In the case of the latter, Vyāsa's sentence would be translated as:

> The result is puruṣha's undistinguished apprehension of the vṛtti *of* the mind-field.

But VB says that is not possible. If a vṛtti occurs in the mind-field, how can it affect puruṣha? If an axe is being used to cut an oak tree, how can that activity fell a maple tree instead? It is not the self who becomes undistinguished from the mind and its vṛttis; it is rather the mind that assumes the characteristics of the self's illumination.

> Puruṣha is the cause of buddhi's accurate apprehension. This we shall establish later (*YS* II.20, IV.22).

Just as a flame is but the tip, the end result, of the process called the lamp—with its vessel, oil and wick—so a vṛtti is but the tip of the buddhi (NB). It is for this reason that a concentrated (*ekāgra*) mind is compared to a lamp where there is no breeze (*BhG* VI.19). When, for example, a vṛtti concerning a jar occurs, the mind knows only "this is a jar." But that "I know a jar" is a wholly different vṛtti, in which the mind's assuming the role of the self is clearer. It is a servant pretending to be the master, rather than only serving him.

As explained earlier, VB holds the view that a reflection of buddhi with its vṛttis falling on the puruṣha causes puruṣha to know the vṛttis. We have already refuted that view as not being in conformity with the formal Sāṅkhya-yoga view. Therefore his explanations (supported by NB, BG) of the phrases

> *pauruṣheyaḥ chitta-vṛtti-bodhaḥ:* puruṣha's knowledge of the vṛttis of the mind
>
> and
>
> *buddeḥ pratisaṁvedī puruṣhaḥ:* puruṣha apprehends in association with buddhi

are also inaccurate.

VB also seems to resent the realism of Sāṅkhya as the major philosophical approach of the *Yoga-sūtras* and throughout attempts an interpretation whereby the *Yoga-sūtras* may be read in the light of the idealism of Vedānta, stopping a few steps short of the extreme idealism of the Vijñāna-vāda school of Buddhism. VB's view is that the spiritual self has a myriad rays that it radiates . Some of these rays illuminating the mind produce vṛttis. Like a lamp's flame illuminating many objects, the vṛttis' lights emanate outwards through the senses and take the form of the objects perceived. The vṛttis that are experienced in dream and meditation do not arise from memories of prior experiences induced externally. They are vṛttis emanating from the light of the self remaining in the mind-field. They have not radiated further out through the sense channels to become one with the world of objects.

This is in conformity with the Vedānta view that all experiences are emanations of Brahman. It should not, however, be confused with the view of the Vijñāna-vāda Buddhists, as the following quotation clearly shows: "We believe," says VB, "that the objects perceived are also independent emanations with which the vṛtti-emanations join in the phenomenal world." The *Vijñāna-vādin* does not accept the independent real existence of objects of perception in the phenomenal world.

This stand seems to negate the necessity for the entire process of the reflection of objects falling upon the mind-field through the senses. VB might well have written an independent philosophical treatise of his own rather than presenting his own thoughts as an exposition of Vyāsa's commentary. Therefore throughout the remainder of this work his comments in regard to this question will be ignored.

Now, to inference (*anumāna*). Vyāsa says:

> Inference (*anumāna*) is the vṛtti determining primarily the general . . .

As explained in the case of direct perception (*pratyakṣha*), the senses perceive a specific object. This is not the case with inference (*anumāna*). Seeing a specific flood of waters in a stream, one infers that there is snow melting in the mountains. The snow, whose existence and melting is inferred, is not any specific snow that has been seen; it is the universal idea "snow" that is present in the mind. It is not the particular snowfall we saw last year while hiking in the mountains. This does not preclude the fact that a specific snow is melting. If we were perceiving it with our eyes, it would be that specific snow, but the specific is subordinate to the general in the process of inference and occurs only after the inference is completed. We have translated the phrase *sāmānya-ava-dhāraṇa-pradhānā* as "determining primarily." A reading of the explanation of a similar phrase regarding *pratyakṣha,* above, will clarify this translation.

Now, again, according to Vyāsa, inference (*anumāna*) has

> as its object that connection of the inferable which conforms to the homogeneous and excludes the non-homogeneous.

This can be illustrated by the standard example of a five-membered syllogism of Nyāya, the Indian system of logic:

1. proposition (*pratijñā*): The mountain has fire.
2. cause (*hetu*): Because it has smoke.
3. exemplification (*dṛṣhṭānta*): Whatever has smoke has fire,
   - like a kitchen hearth,
   - unlike a body of water.
4. recapitulation of cause (*upanaya*): The mountain has smoke.
5. conclusion (*nigamana*): The mountain has fire.

Or another example:

> A pot is non-eternal.
> Because it is a product.
> Like other objects, such as a cloth, which being products, are non-eternal.
> A pot is a product.
> Being a product, a pot is non-eternal.

In both of these examples the attributes—"having smoke" and "being a product"—indicate an invariant association (a commonality, a homogeneity) inherent between the cause and the exemplification. Any one of the elements of the syllogism by itself has no potency—called *śhakti* in formal logic—to produce any conclusion. It is the invariant association (such as the association implicit in the statement that "where there is smoke there is fire"), the homogeneity, that helps to produce a conclusion.

Now, to the third valid proof (*āgama*). Vyāsa says:

> A matter seen or inferred by an accomplished person (*āpta*) is taught in the form of words to transfer one's knowledge into another. The vṛtti from that word, with its matter and meaning as the object, is the listener's acquisition (*āgama*).

Some of the original words in these sentences are important to understand: An *āpta* is an accomplished one, he who has attained. The word *āpta* is from the verb root *ap* 'to attain, accomplish, find'. The attainment (*āpti*) in this sense is more technically defined as connecting together (*a*) the realization of reality (*tattva-darśhana*), (*b*) compassion (*kāruṇya*), that is, the motivation to eradicate the suffering of others, and (*c*) strength of the senses and body and expertise in the use thereof (*karaṇa-pāṭava*). This defines the qualifications of a realized teacher. He has to be (VB) free of weaknesses and faults such as confusion, negligence, desire for personal gain, failure in control over the senses and inability to use the senses properly. One with such an attainment is an *āpta,* a noble teacher. It is also said that one is an *āpta* (HA) to a student by whose words that particular student is able to reach a conclusion, determination or conviction to which the student's own rational thought (*vichāra*) had not yet led him. Vyāsa's words,

> A matter seen or inferred by an *āpta,*

mean that inference alone, that is, rational or logical processes of thought, does not make one an authority (*āpta*). First comes the fact of *dṛṣhṭa,* having seen, realized in the state of samādhi. It is because of such an *in*sight (a realization within) that a school of philosophy is called *darśhana:* a vision, insight, a realization (from the verb root *dṛṣh* 'to see'). The matter thus seen, says Vyāsa,

> is taught in the form of words

or by the means (HA) of silent gesture, etc., as many yogis do. *Śhabdena* means "through words," "in the form of words," and "with the accompaniment of words." All of these meanings are applicable here. The last one is especially significant because verbal guidance may often accompany an initiation in which a guru's knowledge is transferred to another—often without words. This transfusion of knowledge is not emphasized here, but merely suggested to those who have gone through the experience and can therefore read between the lines.

The matter is taught in the form of words, says Vyāsa,

> to transfer one's knowledge into another.

Not "to another" but "*into* (*paratra*) another." This means (VM, VB, NB, HA, RY) that the knowledge similar to that in the teacher's own thought waves of the mind-field (chitta-vṛtti) should appear in the chitta-vṛtti of the listener (*śhrotṛ*), that is, a student. In the tradition, the first stage of the study is listening to the teaching. This teaching should be imparted with the intention (VM) that what is beneficial to the student should accrue, and what is not beneficial should be prevented. It is all of these qualifications and processes that constitute valid proof (*āgama*), which literally means "that which comes" *into* the student. The vṛtti of the words, with their (*a*) intended and (*b*) inherent meanings arising in the student's mind, is *āgama*. That is the noble authority, a revealed knowledge, conveyed into the student directly by the teacher into whom it was revealed, or through a lineage, or in the form of sacred texts.

Further, Vyāsa says:

> That *āgama* overwhelms one whose teacher has not seen or inferred the matter correctly and whose presentation of the matter cannot be trusted.

On the other hand, there may be teachers who are trusted and accepted even though they have neither realized nor inferred the matter themselves, but are faithfully presenting the knowledge originally imparted by the founder of the lineage. Vyāsa says:

> But the *āgama* is without such disturbance in the case of the original teacher.

These lines can be read both as (*a*) in the case of an original teacher, a human founder of the lineage, and (*b*) in the case of the original teacher (God), whose revealed knowledge (Veda) is conveyed through teachers who themselves may not have realized or inferred the contents thereof. This is *āgama,* revealed authority, the third valid proof.

Sūtra I.8 विपर्ययो मिथ्याज्ञानमतद्रूपप्रतिष्ठम्।

viparyayo mithyā-jñānam a-tad-rūpa-pratiṣhṭham

viparyayaḥ: perversive cognition
mithyā-jñānam: false knowledge
a-tad-rūpa-: not in the nature, form, of that (object)
pratiṣhṭham: established

False knowledge without a basis in the nature or form of the respective object is the vṛtti called perversive cognition (*viparyaya*).[11]

Vyāsa's Commentary

Why is this not a valid proof? Because it is refuted, contradicted and annulled by a valid proof. A valid proof has a real substance for its object. It is commonly seen that a non-proof is contradicted by a proof. For example, if someone with double vision sees two moons, this perception is refuted by the sight of the single moon.

This ignorance (*avidyā*) consists of five sections:

avidyā: nescience
asmitā: I-am-ness
rāga: attachment
dveṣha: aversion
abhiniveśha: fear of death

the five afflictions (*kleśhas*) (*YS* II.3). These very five bear their real names as follows:

darkness,
stupor,
great stupor,
nocturnal, and
blind nocturnal!

11. We have borrowed the phrase "perversive cognition" as the translation of *viparyaya* from the translation of Bangali Baba.

We shall speak of these further in the context of the impurities (*mala*) of the mind-field.

Discussion

Perversive cognition (*viparyaya*) is false knowledge (*mithyā-jñāna*) not established, having no basis (*pratiṣhṭhā*) in the nature or form of that object of which this purports to be the knowledge.

Perversive cognition (*viparyaya*) is defined as false knowledge (*mithyā-jñāna*) (VM, VB, BG, NB), which is then explained as "not established," etc. It gives the impression of being a cognition or a knowledge, but is (VM) either

tad-rūpa-a-pratiṣhṭham: not established in, having no basis in, the form of that which is,
or
a-tad-rūpa-pratiṣhṭham: established in a form or nature *not* of that object.

In other words, (VB) perversive cognition has its basis in some other object, which does not correspond to the given object's true aspect. It does not reveal the ultimate (*pāramārthika*) nature of that object (BR), as when a seashell appears to be a silver coin (BR). But this type of cognition is simply a flow within the mind (HA) whereby a vṛtti of buddhi is attributed to (VB, BG, NB) the object in question. It means that when such a superimposition is further examined and thereby contradicted, the object is found to be unable to perform the functions that it would have been capable of had the false impression been accurate (SS). Only if, though it may be contradicted, it is nonetheless efficacious in practice, can it (RY) be considered accurate.

Lest the definition and the discussion be regarded as irrelevant to the needs of a spiritual aspirant, BR employs the term *param-ārtha,* the ultimate nature (of an object). This suggests that we are interested not merely in ordinary objects of our sense experience but in the totality of the universe. All our cognition of the universe turns out to be false, impractical and inefficacious when, following

Sāṅkhya, we finally discover its ultimate nature to be the equilibrium of prakṛti, and, following Vedānta, we find Brahman, the transcendental (which is also a translation of *paramārtha*), to be the true reality onto which this universe has been superimposed. The definition of *viparyaya* also includes doubt (*saṁśhaya*), except that the fact of "not being established" applies only to the mental process (e.g., "Is that a man or a post?") (BR). Here the possibility of something opposite to its nature is present until the determination is made.

The question arises as to why the definition of *viparyaya* as given in this sūtra does not include also linguistic misconception (*vikalpa*), which is defined in the next sūtra. Since *vikalpa,* too, is a false cognition, one might expect it to be included here. The answer is given (VM, NB, RY, SS) that in the case of *viparyaya* it must be possible for an ordinary, non-philosophical person to be able to contradict the false impression by simple practical experience. In *vikalpa* we are dealing with matters open only to the philosophically conversant, as will be seen in the next sūtra. In *viparyaya* there has to be an object whose form or nature can be experienced (NB). In the case of *vikalpa,* if one says, for example, "rabbit's horn," there is no particular object that is being misconstrued as that horn, nor does the experience confirm the existence of some object in the place of that non-existent horn. The horn is merely a word referring to nothing. Hence *vikalpa* cannot be included in *viparyaya.*

Furthermore, in the case of *viparyaya* there has to be an agreement among all the viewers who have good vision (for example, "there was no silver, only a glinting seashell"). In the case of philosophical positions of the type presented by Vyāsa on *YS* I.9 and considered by him as *vikalpa,* there is never an agreement among different philosophers (RY, SS).

In other words, all intellectually held philosophical positions and purely mental experiences which have been proved false are considered *vikalpa.* When, for instance, a text says, "All things, such as the earth, are all in the mind and never outside; the experience of them as real is as in dreams, delusions and intoxication," the experience described is a *vikalpa* (BG, NB). Thus dreams also fall in the category of *vikalpa* (VB, BG, NB) because they are purely mental and no specific object replaces a dream object.

Now to Vyāsa:

> Why is this (*viparyaya*) not a valid proof? Because it is . . . contradicted . . . by a valid proof.

This question and answer means that the imaginary experience produced by *viparyaya* is not valid, because it is later contradicted by a valid proof. Here the logicians may argue with regard to the relative strength of an anterior and posterior statement and experience. Between a prior or a posterior experience, which is the more reliable? The rules as established by the Mīmāṁsā school are that

> where the posterior originates from the anterior, or the posterior's (*a*) existence as an object or (*b*) validity as an idea in some way depends on the anterior, it is the anterior that is considered more powerful.

Mīmāṁsā also states that

> an anterior is normally contradicted by the posterior, the posterior arising after contradicting the anterior. But it is inconceivable for an anterior to arise or be established by contradicting a not-yet-experienced posterior.

In other words,

> where the posterior does not arise directly from an anterior and its existence as an object or the validity as an idea is not dependent thereupon, then the posterior is stronger than the anterior and has the power to contradict it and to establish itself. When two intelligent suggestions or impressions arise independently of each other, the posterior overpowers and condemns the anterior.

Applied to *viparyaya* this means that when for example a perceiver has the impression that he saw a silver coin (the anterior impression), it is not out of that impression that the latter impression ("It is a seashell and not a silver coin") originates. The posterior impression, that it is a seashell, rises from a fresh examination. The silver coin impression is not the originating cause of the seashell impression. Thus, according to the rules of Mīmāṁsā, the posterior is the valid proof proving the anterior to be a false impression. The posterior is the *pramāṇa,* the anterior is *viparyaya.* Hence, one must concur with Vyāsa:

> Why is this (*viparyaya*) not a valid proof? Because it is refuted, contradicted and annulled by a valid proof. A valid proof has a real substance for its object. It is commonly seen that a non-proof is contradicted by a proof. For example, if someone with double vision sees two moons, this perception is refuted by the sight of the single moon.

The Sāṅkhya-yoga philosophers are realists. As was seen in the discussion on *pratyakṣha* in Sūtra I.7, the reality of a substance or object must be confirmed by all the senses involved. For example, silver must be seen with the eyes to be so, must tinkle like silver to the ear and must feel like silver to the tactile sense. The perception must be consistent; that is, all the senses must experience the object the same way at all times, and the observations of all the perceivers must be consistent. All the senses of all the observers must confirm the reality the same way at all times. Such a proof contradicts any perception of lesser consistence and proves the latter to be a *viparyaya.*

It is the natural inclination of intelligence to be partial to, to be inclined towards, reality (VB); hence this *viparyaya* is rejected, is treated as contemptible, and needs to be eradicated in all cases. Until the experience (VB) of an object or entity so occurs that it would not be contradicted later, the nature of that entity cannot be considered as finally ascertained.

It is well here to explain differences among selected Sanskrit words dealing with the concept of error. Knowledge (*khyāti*) is the opposite of error. An error may be

a-khyāti: non-apprehension
or
anyathā-khyāti: misapprehension

The Sāṅkhya system proper uses the term *a-viveka,* "an absence of the correct knowledge" of the nature of puruṣha, which the teachers of formal logic then place under the category of non-perception (*a-khyāti*). It appears that the yoga system is a little different in this regard. It considers error to be a misapprehension (VB), the definition of ignorance or nescience (*avidyā*) being "mistaking the self to be non-self," as in *YS* II.3.[12]

Now Vyāsa:

> This ignorance (*avidyā*) consists of five sections.

In other words, ignorance (*avidyā*), which from here on will be referred to as nescience, defined in *YS* II.3 and II.5, falls within the category of *viparyaya.* This nescience is *pañcha-parvā,* "having five sections." The word *parvan* 'section' refers to segments of a bamboo or sections of mountain chains. It is used where an object consists of many segments but constitutes a single object. It is not that many segments are brought from different places to put together a bamboo, but the bamboo itself consists of the segments. So, nescience is not made up of its five sections, but they are all part of the same one ignorance or nescience. These are the very five afflictions (*kleśhas*) enumerated in *YS* II.3 as

avidyā: nescience or ignorance
asmitā: I-am-ness
rāga: attachment
dveṣha: aversion
abhiniveśha: fear of death

Nescience is a factor (VM) common to all the afflictions, hence the rest are considered its segments. It is (VB) the seed of the calamity called *saṁsāra,* the revolving cycles of the great wheel, including transmigration. The vṛtti *viparyaya,* misapprehension, therefore must be brought under control (*nirodha*).

12. Many different theories regarding erroneous perception have been discussed in different schools of Indian philosophy and refuted by the various commentators but need not be recounted here. Students interested in such detail may refer to the various texts on Indian philosophy.

Now to Vyāsa's enumeration of the five segments of nescience. The other more poetic terms, darkness, etc., follow the scheme of *Sāṅkhya-kārikā* 48, which states:

tamas: darkness (eight kinds),
moha: stupor (eight kinds),
mahā-moha: great stupor (ten types),
tāmisra: nocturnal (eighteenfold), and
andha-tāmisra: blind nocturnal (eighteenfold).

These divisions are explained (VM, VB) as follows:

1. *Avidyā:* nescience (*YS* II.5): *tamas* (darkness) is eightfold: The error of mistaking as ātman (the self) the eight that are:

    i. *a-vyakta:* unmanifest prakṛti and its evolutes
    ii. *mahat:* buddhi
    iii. *ahaṁkāra:* ego
    iv-viii. *tan-mātrās:* the five subtle elements

    It is darkness because (VB) it veils *jñāna* (knowledge). It includes the error of identifying (VB) body, etc. as self because body, etc. are the products of the eight listed above. *Viparyayas* (perversive cognitions), such as between silver and a seashell, are not included in this category. *Sāṅkhya-kārikā* 44 says that bondage is caused by *viparyaya.* Hence *avidyā,* the major cause of bondage, is included here and not the minor confusions.
2. *Asmitā:* I-am-ness (*YS* II.6): *moha* (delusion) is eightfold: The error of considering the eight *siddhis* (*YS* III.45), powers or accomplishments, as though they were something benevolent and belonging to the self (*ātmīya*) (VB), whereas they are actually the opposite (RY):

aṇimā: the power to become minute
laghimā: the power to become light
prāpti: the power to reach or touch the most distant things
prākāmya: the power by which all that one may wish can be fulfilled

mahimā: the power to become large
īśhitva: physical, vocal and mental lordship, not impeded by any
vaśhitva: control over all elements and beings; ability to create, rearrange or dissolve them
kāmāvasāyitā: whatever one says or intends with the mind comes true (whereas in others' case it conflicts and is not fulfilled)

I-am-ness and possession (*svatva*) are synonymous and therefore the above divisions apply, the *siddhis* being a form of possessive power.

3. *Rāga:* attraction (*YS* II.7): *mahā-moha* (great stupor) is tenfold: "I shall attain the eightfold *siddhis* through yoga. I shall attain a lordship, becoming an adept *siddha.* Thereby I shall enjoy the objects of the ten senses, such as sounds, both that are commonly tangible (*dṛṣhṭa*) and that are ordinarily intangible but which are spoken of by the authoritative sources (*ānuśhravika*)." Any such other inclination is included in the tenfold great stupor (*mahā-moha*) or attraction (*rāga*).
4. *Dveṣha:* aversion (*YS* II.8): *tāmisra* (nocturnal) is eighteenfold: When one is bent upon the above pursuits and some (VB) impediment prevents the attainment of *asmitā* (the eight *siddhis*) and *rāga* (the ten enjoyments of the senses), then the anger arising with regard to that failure and towards its cause is nocturnal (*tāmisra*) or aversion (*dveṣha*).
5. *Abhiniveśha:* fear of death (*YS* II.9): *andha-tāmisra* (blind nocturnal) is eighteenfold: *asmitā* (the eight *siddhis*) and *rāga* (the ten objects of the senses) having been attained, there yet comes the realization that all this will perish at the (VB) end of a cycle of creation (*kalpa*). Such fear is that of the blind night (*andha-tāmisra*) or the fear of death (*abhiniveśha*). The night, here, is that of the period of dissolution in a single cycle of creation.

In the above order of five, each succeeding *kleśha* is considered more undesirable and of a lower grade than its predecessor, indicating progressively lower and yet lower levels of spiritual realization. It is also interesting to note that the above definitions seem to be of concern only to the advanced yogi. The definitions as provided under *YS* II.5-9 are wider and are applicable even to the majority of people, who are in *kṣhipta* and *mūḍha* states of mind. The following scheme shows *viparyaya* from the common person's viewpoint compared to the viewpoint of one whose consciousness has become more refined and subtle, whose horizons of space and time, though far wider, have not yet reached final isolation (*kaivalya*):

Kleśha	Common View	Imperfect Yogi's View
avidyā	I am the body, male or female, with consequent pleasures and attractions.	I am prakṛti and its evolutes.
asmitā	I have an identity; I desire success, power and wealth.	I desire *siddhis*.
rāga	I desire the objects of my immediate pleasure.	I will use my *siddhis* to obtain the intangible universals of refined pleasures.
dveṣha	I am averse to specific objects, persons or situations that have caused me pain.	I am angry at causes, persons or situations that have prevented my fulfilment of *siddhis* and consequent enjoyments.
abhiniveśha	I fear my death, that is, the death of this body that I am.	I fear that all my powers and consequent pleasures and enjoyments of the universal evolutes will cease at the end of a *kalpa*.

Even when a whole universe is provided as the body of a highly evolved yogi, the above *viparyayas* or *kleśhas* remain at the indicated scale until pure liberation is reached. In the mythological literature of India called the Purāṇas, the five alternative names of *viparyayas* (*tamas, moha, mahā-moha, tāmisra* and *andha-tāmisra*) are five of the numerous hells into which the least evolved beings are said to fall and suffer the results of their actions.

Sūtra I.9 शब्दज्ञानानुपाती वस्तुशून्यो विकल्पः।

śhabda-jñānānupātī vastu-śhūnyo vikalpaḥ

śhabda-: word *jñāna-:* knowledge *anupātī:* following, dependent upon	dependent only upon a verbal conception
vastu-: real object *śhūnyaḥ:* devoid of	devoid of a real object
vikalpaḥ: imaginary cognition	

Dependent upon a verbal knowledge only but devoid of a real object is the vṛtti called imaginary cognition (*vikalpa*).

Vyāsa's Commentary

That imaginary cognition arises neither in association with valid proof nor in association with perversive cognition. A usage appears, confined to an exaltation in the knowledge of words, even though devoid of substance. For example: "Consciousness is the form and nature of puruṣha." When consciousness itself is puruṣha, what is being designated by what? Normally there has to be an operative relationship in a designation, e.g., "Chaitra's cow."

Similarly, the attributes of a substance being denied as belonging to puruṣha, it (puruṣha) is inactive. Or, "Someone named Bāṇa stops (or will stop, or has stopped)"; here, upon the cessation of movement, only the meaning of the verb is conveyed. Or, "Puruṣha's characteristic is to be devoid of birth"; here merely the absence of the characteristic of being born is understood and not a particular attribute associated with puruṣha. Therefore (it is obvious that) this characteristic is imagined (*vikalpita*) and by that imagination a usage in practice prevails.

Paraphrase of Vyāsa's Commentary

Vikalpa neither arises from nor is in any way dependent on or associated with *pramāṇa* or *viparyaya.* It is not grounded in either of them. Because there exists a certain sense of exaltation about the knowledge of words, people bring words into usage even when there is no actual substance signified by the words, no actual object designated by such a definition. For example, the statement

> Consciousness (*chaitanya*) is the form and nature of puruṣha (the spiritual self)

is meaningless or fallacious. When the actual position of our philosophy is that consciousness itself is the spiritual self, what consciousness, other than the very puruṣha, could be designated as the nature of that puruṣha? Otherwise it is as though one were talking of a cow belonging to a person named Chaitra, who as the owner is other than his possession. Similarly, the sentence

> The attributes of a substance being denied as belonging to puruṣha, it (puruṣha) is inactive

is making no positive statement about any substance; only the attributes of matter as pertaining to puruṣha are denied.

Similarly, the sentences "A person named Bāṇa stops," "A person named Bāṇa will stop," and "A person named Bāṇa has stopped" are philosophically irrelevant because the true reality of a person is the spiritual self (puruṣha) who neither moves in the confines of space nor stops, nor is the concept of time applicable to him. Yet the verb "stop" implies arrested motion, and when coupled with varying tense configurations, also carries the notion of arrested motion in time and space. By definition, this is philosophical nonsense since Bāṇa's true nature is pure consciousness, puruṣha, and as such is without name or form and is quite unaffected by human limitations of time, space and motion. In another example, the content of the sentence

> Puruṣha's characteristic is to be devoid of birth

is also insubstantial because to be devoid of something cannot be a positive or a substantial characteristic. The sentence makes no statement about any attributes of puruṣha. The usage of words in this way is expressive of imagination (*vikalpa*).

Discussion

We have translated the compound phrase *śhabda-jñāna-anupātī* as "dependent upon a verbal knowledge only." Explaining this in somewhat greater detail, *vikalpa* is that modification (vṛtti) of the mind-field which follows

> words, knowledge of words, and the knowledge produced by words, and is productive of the same,

where no actual object or substance (*vastu-śhūnyaḥ*) exists. The question arises that if it is verbal knowledge (VM), why can it not be included in *āgama pramāṇa,* which in other systems of philosophy is known as *śhabda pramāṇa,* or verbal proof? The answer is that according to Vyāsa on the preceding sūtra, there has to be an actual substance (*arthaḥ*) that is corroborated by an *āpta,* to be called *āgama pramāṇa. Vikalpa* relates to no substance.

Then why not include it under perversive cognition (*viparyaya*)? Because in *viparyaya* there is a substance which is at first wrongly cognized but then when the error is refuted, is seen in its own true nature. In *vikalpa,* however, there is no object at all.

A certain vṛtti, imagination, arises, and a word expresses it. The word also produces that very vṛtti when used again by the same speaker or by another. This particular vṛtti is then bound to the exalted power of verbal knowledge. So Vyāsa says:

> That imaginary cognition arises neither in association with a valid proof nor in association with perversive cognition. A usage appears, confined to an exaltation in the knowledge of words. . . .

The mind is exalted by the fact that it knows words and uses them. The word *māhātmya,* translated here as "exaltation," may also mean "glory" and "power." Words have a power of their own to convey the imagined meaning (VB) and therefore a certain usage develops.

The word *vyavahāra,* translated as "usage," also means "practical application" or "efficacy." In *viparyaya* (VB) the object erroneously perceived has no practical application. A seashell perceived as silver cannot be used by a silversmith to make silver earrings. Also in *viparyaya* words do not express (VB) the actual object. An observer says "silver" when first seeing a seashell, but the word "silver" in this case does not convey the truth of the object. It might safely be said that *viparyaya* is a cognition that does not follow a verbal conception (*śhabda-jñāna-an-anupātī*). In *vikalpa* there is no refuting of an error, and the imagination expressed by appropriate words still serves practical purposes, as we shall see below. Even the most learned continue to make use of *vikalpa* in practice. There is no succession of error and refutation, and one word does not replace another; no "seashell" replaces "silver." In other words, *vikalpa* has a greater practical reality than has *viparyaya.* For example (HA), consider the word "time," which is not a substance, but generates an imaginary idea, a vṛtti, which produces the vṛtti—a concept of "time"—a word used consistently by the most learned.

There are many different types of *vikalpa* which have not been separately categorized by the commentators. Sometimes this imagination produces (VM) non-distinction among distinct objects, and sometimes it produces distinction where there is no distinction, and so forth. Sometimes the distinction of the qualification and the qualified, where the two are actually one, is unreal. "Distinction" and "non-distinction," not being substances, fall under the category of *vikalpa.* The examples given by Vyāsa are as follows:

> "Consciousness is the form and nature of puruṣha." When consciousness itself is puruṣha, what is being designated by what? Normally there has to be an operative relationship in a designation. . . .

The word "designation" (*vyapadeśha*) has been translated as "predication" (RP) and as "the relationship of qualification with the qualified" (BB). Both translations are equally accurate. But what is being qualified, designated by what, when consciousness is the same as the spiritual self? When we say a person named Chaitra has cows, the cows are something different from the owner, and there is an operational, functional relationship between them. This simply does not apply when we know consciousness and puruṣha to bear a single identity. This is an example of *vikalpa* producing a distinction where none exists and (VM, VB) when the conception of a relationship of qualification with something qualified is artificial and imaginary. The use of the genitive case is not *vikalpa* in the case of, say, "Devadatta's blanket" (BR), but it is so in the case of "puruṣha's consciousness." Again, Vyāsa says:

> Similarly, the attributes of a substance being denied as belonging to puruṣha, it (puruṣha) is inactive.

Another rendering of the original would be as follows (VB):

> *pratiṣhiddha-vastu-dharmā:* the attributes of a substance are denied in the case of puruṣha;
> *niṣhkriyaḥ puruṣhaḥ:* puruṣha is inactive.

This latter rendering presents one with two examples of *vikalpa*. The attributes that are normally ascribed to a substance are denied in the case of puruṣha because this says nothing about puruṣha. The Sanskrit adjectival compound *pratiṣhiddha-vastu-dharmā* which is supposed to be qualifying puruṣha is actually no qualification at all. Similarly, the adjective "inactive" (*niṣhkriya*), denying any possible activity in the case of puruṣha, expresses no qualification. These are pseudo-adjectives, works of imagination (*vikalpas*) dependent on words alone. Another rendering is based on a different reading of the text:

> *pratiṣhiddhā vastu-dharmāḥ:* the attributes of substances are denied;
> *nishkriyaḥ puruṣhaḥ:* puruṣha is inactive.

The first part here criticises the Buddhist view that "all attributes (*dharmas*) are painful, impermanent and devoid of a self." If there are no attributes, how can any statement be made about them and, especially, how can they be denied? It is all verbal activity (*vikalpa*). The followers of the Buddhist and Nyāya schools accept negation (*a-bhāva*) as a proof or a category in their systems, but Sāṅkhya-yoga denies it as a *vikalpa*.

Next Vyāsa says:

> "Someone named Bāṇa stops (or will stop, or has stopped)"; here, upon the cessation of movement, only the meaning of the verb is conveyed.

Stopping (VM, VB) is a cessation of movement, an absence thereof. A verb normally expresses an activity of some kind, but stopping denotes an absence, a negation of the activity called movement. This cessation of movement is further ascribed to Bāṇa, who is supposed to be the doer, an agent (*kartṛ*), performing this activity called the cessation of activity as he "stops." To confound by compounding it further, an insubstantial concept like time—present, future or perfect (or past)—is attached to it. So we say Bāṇa stops, will stop, has stopped. First there is an absence of movement; then the verb "stop" is given a positive state (*bhāva*); and then that absent *bhāva,* which is actually a negative (*a-bhāva*), is attached to the idea of succession, an anterior or posterior incidence expressed by a tense; this produces a triple *vikalpa*! But to go yet deeper, the person Bāṇa is merely a false identification of the nameless, formless puruṣha who, not being subject to the space-evolute of matter, does not move from place to place, so no question of the cessation of movement arises. The fourth *vikalpa*! Not being subject to space, it is not subject to time, time itself being a *vikalpa*. Therefore, the present, future and past tenses do not apply. "Bāṇa stopped" is an example of a fivefold *vikalpa*!

"Puruṣha's characteristic is to be devoid of birth" is the translation of Vyāsa's *an-utpatti-dharmā puruṣhaḥ*. The first of these two words is a compound adjectival phrase with the literal meaning of "one-with-the-characteristic-of-not-being-born." Here also the same argument applies as with the example given above, "puruṣha is inactive." The negative adjective is false. It has no substance and is a mere verbal expression of the vṛtti called *vikalpa*. It is an absence, imagined as though a positive state, then attached to puruṣha as though his attribute—yet it expresses no attribute of puruṣha. Hence Vyāsa says:

> Here merely the absence of the characteristic of being born is understood and not a particular attribute associated with puruṣha. Therefore (it is obvious that) this characteristic is imagined (*vikal-pita*), and by that imagination a usage in practice prevails.

The criticism of the examples of *vikalpa* given above is directed at fallacious philosophical concepts which cannot be substantiated. Some examples of the grossest form of *vikalpa,* the non-philosophical imagination, are (BG) brought together in the following verse:

> There goes the son of a barren woman;
> He has worn a crown of sky-flowers
> After bathing in the waters of a mirage.
> He carries a bow made of a hare's horns.

Sūtra I.10 अभावप्रत्ययालम्बना वृत्तिर्निद्रा।

abhāva-pratyayālambanā vṛttir nidrā

abhāva-: absence, negation
pratyaya-: cognition principle, cognition, causal principle
ālambanā: resorting to, supported by, leaning on, dependent on, having as a base
vṛttiḥ: modification, mental state, operation, fluctuation, activity
nidrā: sleep

Sleep is the modification or operation of the mind-field resorting to the cognition principle of absence or negation and to the cause thereof.

Vyāsa's Commentary

Sleep is to be considered a particular type of cognition because one reflects about it. "I slept comfortably; my mind is clear; it brightens up my discernment." "I slept uncomfortably; my mind is sluggish; it is wandering, unsteady; I am unable to concentrate." "I slept heavily and in a stupor; my mind is tired, indolent; it feels stagnant and lost."

This kind of reflection would not occur if there were no experience of cognition (during sleep), nor would there be memories based on that sleep and relating to the subjects of these reflections. Therefore sleep is a particular type of cognition. And for the purpose of samādhi, this (vṛtti called) sleep, too, should be brought under control (*nirodha*) just like other cognitions.

Discussion

In all sūtra texts there occurs a method known as implicit succession (*anu-vṛtti*), whereby the presence of a word that occurs in a given sūtra is implied also to function as part of a number of subsequent sūtras until no longer needed. An example of *anu-vṛtti* is the word *vṛtti* that occurred in *YS* I.5 and is understood in *YS* I.6-9. For example, the full translation of *YS* I.9 is:

> Dependent upon a verbal knowledge only but devoid of a real object is the vṛtti called imaginary cognition (*vikalpa*).

Even though the word *vṛtti* does not occur in the sūtra, it is brought down from *YS* I.5. Since the topic of the five vṛttis continues until *YS* I.11, the word *vṛtti* would be implicit up to that sūtra by the rule of *anu-vṛtti.*

Then why is the word *vṛtti* repeated in the current sūtra? The answer is that this additional confirmation of sleep as a vṛtti is essential because one normally does not consider sleep to be a modification, fluctuation, wave, operation or activity of the mind-field. About the other four vṛttis there is no question, but even experts (VM, NB) are doubtful about sleep being an operation of the mind-field. The repetition of the word *vṛtti* in the sūtra is for the purpose of challenging and refuting the possible view (RY) that sleep is an absence of awareness.

The compound phrase *abhāva-pratyaya-ālambanā* is to be explained as follows: *Abhāva* is absence of the vṛttis that occur in wakefulness and dream states (VM, VB, HA); that is, it is the absence of all the other vṛttis (BG, NB) enumerated in these sūtras. Absence means non-production or non-appearance (BG). The word *pratyaya* means cognition (*pratīti*) as well as the cause or origin; it is that from which any cognition as an effect proceeds. The cognition that causes the absence of other vṛttis (VM, VB, BR, NB, HA, RY, RS) is the guṇa of prakṛti called tamas. Tamas veils sattva, the essential nature of buddhi (VB) and of the mind-field (VM). When tamas becomes dominant (BR) and overpowers the sattva and rajas of buddhi (VB, VM), veiling the chitta (NB), it covers all the senses (VB, VM). However, this does not mean that the senses are absent, as the Vedāntins would have us believe (RS).

Then, because there are no other objects to reflect in the mind to give the mind their form (VM, VB), the substance tamas (*tamo-dravyam*), which is as real as any darkness (VB), overwhelms the mind which, obscured with this defilement (*malina*) (VB), consequently becomes impure. The mind then takes the form of this very tamas as its object (VM,VB, BG, NB, RY, SS) and identifies with it (the experience and the vṛtti arising therefrom) as it would with external objects. Here the mind observes "I am sleeping" and enjoys the tamasic pleasure that ensues. The sleeping person is then called inwardly conscious (*antaḥ-sañjña*) (VM, VB, NB). The statement about the sleep state being inwardly conscious occurs in verses 4 and 7 of the *Māṇḍūkya Upaniṣhad,* where it is called *antaḥ-prajña.* The subject of this Upaniṣhad is the four states of consciousness (wakefulness, dream, sleep and superconsciousness) as inherent in the experience of the word *OM* or *AUM.* This relates not to personal consciousness alone but also to the consciousness of the cosmic Person, His wakefulness, dream, sleep and superconsciousness, how these reflect in the states of individual consciousness, and how the individual states may become the means for understanding, experiencing and realizing the states of the cosmic Person. The 12 verses of the *Māṇḍūkya Upaniṣhad,* 215 verses of expository text by Gauḍapāda—who was the guru of the guru of Śhankarāchārya—as well as Śhankara's own commentary on the same are a very detailed and profound body of philosophy, which cannot be treated here even succinctly. In addition, many other texts like the *Yoga-vāsiṣhṭha* provide us with further detailed material. It is earnestly recommended that the reader gain access to these sources of the great teachings concerning the nature of cosmic as well as individual sleep in which the sleeping person is termed inwardly conscious.

Before continuing, it is well to understand some facts about sleep. It is obvious that sleep cannot be considered a state of unconsciousness, for these reasons:

- Only the surface layer of mind, that is, the conscious mind, is overcome by tamas.
- Only that part of the mind sleeps which normally undergoes alterations of wakefulness, dream and sleep. The rest of the mind continues its normal operations (which are enumerated in *YS* III.15).
- The entire mind never sleeps during one's lifetime.

If the entire mind were to sleep, who would continue operating the lungs so one may breathe while asleep? Who would maintain the heartbeat and keep the process of digestion going and keep the blood circulating? Who would arrange for the mind to float in and out of dreams? A person sleeps, wakes up feeling cold, covers up with a blanket, falls asleep again, and remembers nothing of it in the morning. Who tells the sleeping mind that the skin is feeling cold? A person sleeps, rolls to the edge of the bed, but, unlike an infant, does not fall off. Who tells the sleeper to roll away from the edge and back to a safer part of the bed? If the entire mind slept, having lost consciousness, who would answer, however slowly, to the person's name being called and wake up? If the entire mind slept, who could awaken whom? One would never wake up; one could not even remain alive.

It is obvious, then, that the part of the mind that experiences vṛttis is the very one that experiences tamas, the pall of mist or fog which deactivates the senses temporarily and induces sleep. All the commentators agree that during sleep (*a*) the mind identifies with tamas, which replaces the objects of other vṛttis, and (*b*) the mind observes "I am sleeping" and experiences this absence and this observation as a tamasic pleasure. This is what is meant by the phrase *abhāva-pratyaya-ālambanā* 'resorting to or being dependent on the cognition of absence and to the cause thereof'. Vyāsa's commentary reads:

> Sleep is to be considered a particular type of cognition because one reflects about it.

In other words, (HA) sleep is that vṛtti of the mind in which awareness is very indistinct (*a-sphuṭa*). The object of this vṛtti, like the objects of our other experiences and their consequent vṛttis, is tamas with its dullness and stupefaction which causes the occlusion or subjugation of normal cognitions that occur in wakefulness and dream. As darkness has the characteristic of indistinctness, causing the features of all objects in it to become indistinct, as though unified, so also has sleep the quality of dullness and stupefaction (*jaḍatā*) that becomes the common feature of the body, the senses and the mind-field (HA). If sleep were an absence of experience

(HA), one could not have recollections (BB) of it, because a recollection implies memory or an imprint of an event or of an experience (HA, BR).

A logician might say that one recalls an absence. For example, one might state, "There was no elephant in the hall." Whether or not this can be termed the memory of an absence of an elephant or simply a conclusion drawn on the basis of the memory one had of the actual experience of the positive conditions of the hall has been a subject of intense and complex debates among logicians of many schools. What is relevant to the point here is the fact that one does not have the recollection of a vague absence of vṛttis but reflects about the quality of various types of sleep. This proves that sleep is indeed a positive vṛtti. It should be noted that neither Vyāsa nor the subsequent commentators have raised the possibility that the quality of sleep is not a matter of recollection, but is inferred from how one feels upon awakening. This question leads to the various categories of sleep spoken of by the commentators. NTC, in fact, discusses in considerable detail various philosophical views on the nature of sleep, a full description of which would require a separate treatise.

Even though sleep means that the mind is overcome by tamas, it does not mean that the other two guṇas (sattva and rajas) are altogether absent. They are subservient to tamas in the experience of sleep. Vyāsa gives examples of the sattvic, rajasic and tamasic sleep (VM, VB, RY). Vyāsa's commentary reads:

> . . . one reflects about it. "I slept comfortably; my mind is clear; it brightens up my discernment." "I slept uncomfortably; my mind is sluggish; it is wandering, unsteady; I am unable to concentrate." "I slept heavily and in a stupor; my mind is tired, indolent; it feels stagnant and lost (literally, as though stolen)."

These three types of recollection or reflection indicate sattvic, rajasic and tamasic sleep respectively. In the first example, the tamas of sleep is aided by sattva; that is, even though sleep is primarily a tamasic experience, sattva is serving as a minister (VM, VB) to tamas the king. The person waking from such a sleep feels that the mind is clear (*prasanna*). The word *prasanna* suggests the quality of clear, still water and a pleasantness of mind that results from such clarity. (VB) In such a clear mind, with a pleasant mood, the intelligence functions with perfect discernment and is expanded and made sharp to grasp subtle matter and detail.

(VM, VB) Rising from rajasic sleep one observes that the mind is feeling a laziness (*styāna*). (This will be defined further in *YS* I.30 among the nine obstacles in yoga.) The sleep in which tamas has altogether overpowered sattva and rajas (VM) leaves one feeling that the energy of the mind has been stolen (VB), as though plundered by others. The mind loses its initiative and becomes disinclined to undertake action. As a result, one is unable to concentrate and becomes ineffective.

We have already commented on Vyāsa's statement that

> this kind of reflection would not occur if there were no experience of cognition (during sleep), nor would there be memories based on that sleep and relating to the subjects of these reflections. Therefore sleep is a particular type of cognition.

This is understood. Now Vyāsa says:

> And for the purpose of samadhi, this (vṛtti called) sleep, too, should be brought under control (*nirodha*) just like other cognitions (*pratyayas*).

The question might arise that since sleep (*nidrā*) is a vṛtti in which the mind is concentrated (*ekāgra*) (see Sūtra I.1), why is it required that one practise *nirodha* of other vṛttis, such as *pramāṇa,* which occur in the wakeful state? Is the *ekāgra* of sleep all that one needs? In sleep the mind is concentrated on tamas and free from painful attractions to objects which a yogi should avoid (VB). Why, then, should he practise the *nirodha* of sleep? Because even though sleep appears like a concentration (VM), it is yet tamasic. Samādhi results from the conquest of the three guṇas, the least desirable of which is tamas. Sleep is, therefore, an adversary of samādhi. The purpose of samādhi is to raise one above the attributes of the three guṇas:

sukha: pleasure (from sattva)
duḥkha: pain (from rajas)
moha: somnolence and stupor (from tamas)

It has been seen that the three types of recollections about one's sleep indicate the presence of these three attributes, and it is therefore obvious that sleep is an adversary (VB) of samādhi and must be brought under control. Furthermore, samādhi is not defined merely (HA) as a state of mind (*a*) devoid of external awareness, (*b*) under the power of stupor, (*c*) merely carrying on the functions of the body, (*d*) without any remembrance of past experiences. Rather, samādhi is total absorption in the object of meditation and consequently is accompanied with restraint over activities of the body and senses. Hence *nirodha* of sleep is as requisite as that of the other vṛttis insofar as the pursuit of samādhi is concerned.

Sūtra I.11 अनुभूतविषयासम्प्रमोषः स्मृतिः।

anubhūta-viṣhayāsampramoṣhaḥ smṛtiḥ

anu-bhūta-: experienced
viṣhaya-: objects of experience
a-sampramoṣhaḥ: non-theft, not being stolen, not being lost
smṛtiḥ: memory

Objects experienced not being lost is the vṛtti called memory (*smṛti*).

Vyāsa's Commentary

Does the mind-field remember the cognition (*pratyaya*) or the object of experience? A cognition is associated with and coloured by the object of an apprehension and resembles and manifests (*nir-bhāsa*) the features of both the object apprehended and the process and instrument of apprehension. Such cognition then produces an imprint (saṁskāra) that is similar to them both.

That saṁskāra then manifests its identity with its own manifes-tative cause; it generates a memory. This memory is identical in form to the same (saṁskāra, its manifested identity, and the mani-festative cause). It consists of both the object apprehended and the process and instrument of apprehension.

There, when the process and instrument of apprehension is the primary feature, it is intelligence (buddhi). When the form of the object of experience is primary, it becomes memory (*smṛti*). This memory is of two kinds: (*a*) where something imaginary is remem-bered, and (*b*) where something not imaginary is remembered. Of these, the former manifests in dream and the latter during wakeful-ness. All these memories arise from the experience of valid proof, perversive cognition, imaginary cognition, sleep and memory.

Also, all these vṛttis consist of pleasure, pain and stupefaction. The pleasure, pain and stupefaction, however, are to be explained under the afflictions (*kleśhas*). Attraction (*rāga*) is attendant upon pleasure. Aversion (*dveṣha*) is attendant upon pain. And ignorance (*avidyā*) is stupefaction.

All these vṛttis are to be brought under control (*nirodha*). Upon accomplishment of their *nirodha,* there ensues the samādhi of wisdom (*samprajñāta*) or even the acognitive (*asamprajñāta*) samādhi.

Discussion

The first part of the discussion will clarify the compound phrase *anubhūta-viṣhaya-asampramoṣhaḥ.*

a-sampramoṣhaḥ: from the verb root *muṣh* 'to steal'; not being stolen, non-theft, not being lost—of
viṣhaya: a subject, or an object, which
anu-bhūta: has been experienced.

The phrase can be explained in many different ways.

A non-theft pertains to (VM, BR, AD) a subject, or an object experienced through valid proof, etc. Non-theft means (BR) the arising of such a subject in the buddhi by way of saṁskāras. The word *viṣhaya* means a subject or an object of experience, that is to say, *the subject of a memory as the object of a past experience.* This entire phrase should be substituted for "subject" or "object of experience" in reading this discussion where the *viṣhaya* of a memory is being discussed.

Only the experience based on *pramā,* etc. (see Sūtra I.7) is the father (RY) of memory. Only the subject of that experience is akin to, or, as it were, "a kin to" the memory and can be included in the process of memory. The term being translated here as "akin to" or "a kin to" is *ātmīya* (VM, RY), which means "belonging to; related to, like a relative or a kinsman; something to be included in the process as belonging to a particular realm." A subject (VM) belongs to the realm of the awareness (*jñāna*) born of a particular saṁskāra when it is projected forth from the experience that caused the saṁskāra in the first place. Incorporating any more of a subject than that is like a theft (VM, NB). Where such a theft does not occur and no more than the object of the experience is grasped as the subject (NB), such a vṛtti is called memory. Memory must be limited to that subject which has been absorbed by the chitta and not stealing, as it were, another's possession (HA). It could be less than that subject, due to failure of recall, but never more (VM, NB). This "another's possession" includes even the original object that was experienced (RY). It is not the subject of memory for the purposes of the sūtra. The sūtra does not mean to include a recognition, which requires an external object being experienced afresh with the senses even though they are also serving as an aid to the past impression. Memory, as a technical term here, is entirely an internal mental process produced from the saṁskāras (VB). The intent of Vyāsa appears to be that the subject of memory is the vṛtti that was experienced together with the substance (*artha*) of that vṛtti, but not the external object (VB, BG, NB).

Vyāsa's commentary reads:

> Does the mind-field remember the cognition (*pratyaya*) or the object of experience?

In a memory, does the mind remember the fact of a cognition (the consciousness of a perception) (VM, NB), like "I know the vessel" (HA), or does it remember the form of the object? Is it the experience that is remembered (VM) or the object of the experience? Vyāsa's answer is:

> A cognition is associated with and coloured by the object of an apprehension and resembles and manifests the features of both the object apprehended and the process and instrument of apprehension. Such cognition then produces an imprint (saṁskāra) that is similar to them both.

The Sanskrit phrases here should be examined with care:

> *pratyayaḥ:* a cognition
> *grāhya-uparaktaḥ:* (is) associated with and coloured by the object of an apprehension.

Upa-rañj means "to be coloured by something because of its proximity." A cognition is coloured and its nature determined by the proximity of the object that is being experienced, apprehended. Therefore a cognition carries the features or natures (*rūpa*) of the object as well as the process or the fact of that apprehension. It contains both the *grāhya,* the object of experience, and the *grahaṇa,* the instrument, the process and the fact of experience. "It resembles the features and natures of both of these and manifests them"—this entire idea is expressed by the word *nir-bhāsa* 'shining forth as'.

The cognition then leaves a saṁskāra in which both features are included: (1) the fact that the person cognizes the object, has gained experience thereof; and (2) the object as it actually is. *Smṛti* does not arise by itself. An experience first becomes a saṁskāra, an imprint, in the *āśhaya* (which is to be explained). From the saṁskāra it rises again as a mental operation (vṛtti). This process of the rising of vṛttis through the saṁskāra of a past experience is memory (*smṛti*) (AD). The object itself therefore ceases to be present, but the saṁskāra produces the memory. So Vyāsa states:

> That saṁskāra then manifests its identity with its own manifestative cause; it generates a memory. This memory is identical in form to the same (saṁskāra, its manifested identity, and the manifestative cause). It consists of both the object apprehended and the process and instrument of apprehension.

We have translated the phrase *sva-vyañjaka-añjanaḥ* as "manifests its identity with its own manifestative cause." Concerning the way the saṁskāra was formed, the cause of its manifestation was the original cognition. So when it re-produces the experience in the form of memory, the memory also is identical to (*a*) the saṁskāra, as it manifests, shows itself to be identical with, the original experience, and (*b*) the experience itself that was the manifestative cause of the saṁskāra (although the memory has now been triggered by (VB) some other manifestative cause, such as an appropriate time).

The memory, then, just like the original cognition, and the saṁskāra it had formed, consists of both the object apprehended, and the process and fact of apprehension. This is the chain of causation here:

(*a*) the experience, from which is produced
(*b*) the saṁskāra, which generates
(*c*) the memory,

each with the twofold process: (1) cognition that "I know the object," and (2) cognition of the nature of the object itself.

This is a synopsis of what the commentators have said about Vyāsa's paragraph. Obviously, unless the mind knows that it knows, it cannot re-produce as memory the experience of the original object. In this process the faculty of discrimination (buddhi) plays its part. Vyāsa says:

> There, when the process and instrument of apprehension is the primary feature, it is intelligence (buddhi).

A more literal translation of the text would be:

> When the feature of the process of apprehension is primary, it is intelligence.

But the first rendering is preferred as being better English. The word "intelligence" (buddhi) is not used here in the sense of the entire buddhi faculty but rather one of its functions, the process of apprehension. Once again, let us clarify "I know the vessel." This is an apprehension, an act of intelligence. This particular type of apprehension is called *anu-vyavasāya,* the awareness that buddhi has that it cognizes or apprehends or experiences. It is an important part of the process of memory, in which the other part of the cognition is the object (in this case, the vessel). However, when one sees the vessel a second time and says, "This is that vessel," this is not technically included under memory for the purpose of this sūtra. It is called "re-cognition" (*pratyabhijñā*). In the apprehension "I know the vessel," one vṛtti—"the vessel"—is the subject (*viṣhaya*) of the other vṛtti—"I know." Knowing here is the primary feature. Then, says Vyāsa:

> When the form of the object of experience is the primary feature, it becomes memory.

Even though the *anu-vyavasāya* is an important part of the process of memory, the memory proper is a single vṛtti—"the vessel." Here the awareness, "I know," is secondary.

Vyāsa says:

> This memory is of two kinds: (*a*) where something imaginary is remembered, and (*b*) where something not imaginary is remembered. Of these, the former manifests in dream and the latter during wakefulness.

In fact what appears in the dream is not memory proper because the entire scene of space, time and relationships is warped. A person familiar in one setting may be seen associated with a completely different setting, which is imaginary, of which there has been no former experience and, therefore, from which no memory could evolve. For this reason many commentators (VM, NB, RY) place the dream under memory only because (VM) it appears to be *like* a memory; however, strictly speaking, dreams fall under the category of *viparyaya* (*YS* I.8), having no substance (VM).

It may be safely said that some constituents of a dream are certainly pure memory, while the rest are imagination. VB is of the opinion that Vyāsa meant to include here only those parts that are true memory. This view is supported by Vyāsa because of the locative case "in dream," which obviously does not mean that the dream is entirely imagination. Nor does Vyāsa himself equate the dream with imagination (*viparyaya*), although it must be agreed that those parts of the dream which are not pure memory do fall under the definition of *viparyaya* (*YS* I.8):

> False knowledge without a basis in the nature or form of the respective object is the vṛtti called perversive cognition (*viparyaya*).

In the list of five vṛttis (*YS* I.5-11), memory has been placed last (VM, VB) because in Vyāsa's words:

> All these memories arise from the experience of valid proof, perversive cognition, imaginary cognition, sleep and memory.

"The experience" means the buddhi's first (VM) cognition of or involvement with the object (VM); thereafter it becomes (VB) the awareness of the apprehension that buddhi has (*anu-vyavasāya*), as explained above. It is also clear from Vyāsa's passage that a memory may be remembered, as the first-time experience of that memory. Thus there may occur the memory of a memory.

Of the five vṛttis (BR), *pramāṇa, viparyaya* and *vikalpa* occur in the wakeful state. The experience of these three combined, masquerading as direct perception (*pratyakṣha*), becomes the dream. Sleep is a unique state in that it is marked by the absence of other vṛttis even though it is in itself a vṛtti. Memory is the effect of any or all of these vṛttis.

Buddhi is the raw material from which these vṛttis are shaped, as images are shaped from gold (VB). These vṛttis are the mutations (*pariṇāmas*) of buddhi. Because buddhi is made of prakṛti, which consists of the three guṇas, Vyāsa says:

> Also, all these vṛttis consist of pleasure, pain and stupefaction. The pleasure, pain and stupefaction, however, are to be explained under the afflictions (*kleśhas*).

However, for the sake of brevity here, he quotes *YS* II.7-8:

> Attraction is attendant upon pleasure. Aversion is attendant upon pain.

As to stupefaction, he says:

> And ignorance (*avidyā*) is stupefaction.

This will be defined further in *YS* II.5.

Although the desirability of avoiding stupefaction and pain is obvious, a question arises as to why the pleasure of the vṛttis should also be avoided. The traditional reply is that nowhere does pleasure exist in the vṛttis as pure and unalloyed, free from pain and stupefaction. It is, in fact, pleasures and attractions (*rāgas*) that are the direct causes of aversions.

As to *moha* (stupefaction, somnolence, delusion), it is of three kinds (HA):

1. *vichāra-moha:* confusion of thought processes
2. *cheṣhṭā-moha:* confusion in the physical posture, gait, movement, effort, as though one's limbs are not being moved under one's own observation or by one's own clarity of will
3. *vedanā-moha:* confusion of feelings and emotions where one does not know even what is painful or pleasant to him

It is such confusion that produces all pain and grief. For this reason, says Vyāsa:

> All these vṛttis are to be brought under control (*nirodha*). Upon accomplishment of their *nirodha,* there ensues the samādhi of wisdom (*samprajñāta*) or even the acognitive (*asamprajñāta*) samādhi.

Sūtra I.12 अभ्यासवैराग्याभ्यां तन्निरोधः।

abhyāsa-vairāgyābhyāṁ tan-nirodhaḥ

abhyāsa-: (with) practice and
vairāgyābhyāṁ: with dispassion
tat-: of those
nirodhaḥ: control (occurs)

The control of those vṛttis occurs through practice and dispassion.

Vyāsa's Commentary

Now, what is the method for establishing control over these (vṛttis)?

> [*Sūtra:*] The control of those vṛttis occurs through practice and dispassion.

The river of the mind-field indeed flows both ways. It flows towards beatitude (BB) and it flows towards evil (BB). The part sloping down the domain of discernment (*viveka*) towards the reservoir of isolation (*kaivalya*) flows towards beatitude. The one sloping down the domain of indiscrimination (*a-viveka*) towards the reservoir of worldly transmigrations flows towards evil.

There, the stream of worldly attractions is blocked, reduced, through dispassion (*vairāgya*). The stream of discriminative wisdom (*viveka*) is opened up through the practice (*abhyāsa*) of realizing (*darśhana*) discernment (*viveka*).

Thus the *nirodha* of the vṛttis of the mind-field is dependent upon both (*abhyāsa* and *vairāgya*).

Discussion

The mind-field is like a river (HA). As some rivers (VB)[13] flow towards the ocean and some simply become lost into the ground, so the mind flows both ways. Vyāsa expresses it as follows:

13. VB says, "As the river sometimes flows towards the ocean and sometimes towards the ground, or else it might just dry up." His explanation of the metaphor is not clear.

> The river of the mind-field indeed flows both ways. It flows towards beatitude and it flows towards evil. The part sloping down the domain of discernment (*viveka*) towards the reservoir of isolation (*kaivalya*) flows towards beatitude. The part sloping down the domain of indiscrimination (*a-viveka*) towards the reservoir of worldly transmigrations flows towards evil.

The phrases

> *kaivalya-prāg-bhāra:* towards the reservoir of isolation
> and
> *saṁsāra-prāg-bhāra:* towards the reservoir of worldly transmigrations

present some difficulty in translation. *Prāg-bhāra* is a dam or dyke (*prabandha*). Its *yaugika,* derivative meaning (see p. 18), could also be "bearing a weight or load tipping in favour of (as on a scale); carrying a momentum towards; predisposed towards." So the complete translation would be: "It is predisposed towards, carrying a moment towards, bearing its weight towards isolation (*kaivalya*) so its flow creates a reservoir at the dam of *kaivalya,* and similarly . . . at the dam of *saṁsāra.*" The word *viṣhaya* is a double-entendre. It means "a domain; a subject and/or an object of experience." The river of mind flows in the domain of discernment (*viveka*) when the subject it is occupied with and the object of its experience is that *viveka.* The same applies in the case of non-discernment, indiscrimination (*a-viveka*). The mind-river is inclined (BB) down the slope of its domain (*viṣhaya*), subject or object—whether it be discrimination or indiscrimination.

Saṁsāra is the antonym of *kaivalya, nirvāṇa,* or *mokṣha.* The word expresses involvement with the world that leads one to gather karma so that one remains entangled in the continuous moving wheel of the world through the cycles of creation and dissolution and many transmigrations through birth and death.

When the mind-river is inclined towards *kaivalya,* it leads to *kalyāṇa,* all that is beautiful, benevolent, propitious and desirable, to the noble way, the way of beatitude (BB), in short, to liberation (*mokṣha*) (VB). Otherwise it leads one towards the evil way and the evil result (*pāpa*).

Pertaining to practice and dispassion (*abhyāsa* and *vairāgya*) Vyāsa says:

> The stream of worldly attractions is blocked, reduced, through dispassion (*vairāgya*). The stream of discriminative wisdom (*viveka*) is opened up through the practice (*abhyāsa*) of realizing (*darśhana*) discernment (*viveka*).

Thus far the definition of yoga has been given, and Sūtras 5-11 were an exposition on the word *vṛtti* that occurred in the definition, the *lakṣhaṇa-sūtra* I.2. Now the means thereto, the method thereof (VB), are to be explained.

The practitioner is being advised to choose not just one (VM, VB, RS) of the two methods, either practice (*abhyāsa*) *or* dispassion (*vairāgya*), but the two together. Each of the two fulfils an essential part of the purpose (VM, VB, RS, BG). This is very clear from Vyāsa's words:

> Thus the *nirodha* of the vṛttis of the mind-field is dependent upon both (*abhyāsa* and *vairāgya*).

Ordinarily (RY) the average person's mind-stream flows in the domain and down the slope of worldly interest towards the ocean of *saṁsāra*. One breaks the momentum of that flow through dispassion and turns the stream upwards through practice (*abhyāsa*) of the discrimination between puruṣha and the sattva of the mind.

The stream of the mind-field flowing towards the worldly involvements is turned off (SS), reduced (VB, HA), blocked (RS, BG, NB), its flow stemmed (RY), stopped (HA), through dispassion (*vairāgya*). Dispassion arises as one sees (BR, NB) the evil of worldly ways and interests, and consequently the mind's inclination is turned off from them (BR).

Practice is cultivating and nurturing *viveka*, a view of life, of reality and of oneself and one's attitudes and works in the light of the philosophy and experience of discernment or discriminating wisdom (VB, BG, NB, HA). This view is referred to as *darśhana,* the common Indian word for philosophy. Frequently repeated observance of the means and methods of attaining *viveka* (HA), as well as practice of meditation all the way up to samādhi (SS), is to be included in this practice of the view of discernment (*abhyāsa* of the *darśhana* of *viveka*).

Through *abhyāsa* the stream of those vṛttis is unblocked, opened up and made increasingly stronger, leading to *viveka,* so that the stream may enter the ocean of *nirodha* (VB). In other words, it is through practice that the stream of *viveka* is opened up, releasing its flow (HA, NTC). Thus the turbulence of the mind is calmed so that it may flow pacifically (SS). The experience shows the mind that the way of peacefulness leads to comfort (BR). The result is a firmness and strength in one's practice as well as in one's dispassion.

NTC has described this process as follows: A flooded river causes havoc and at the same time provides a service. On one hand it devastates villages and towns; on the other hand it irrigates the fields. The devastation is prevented by building dams and so forth, and the irrigation is controlled and directed by digging canals and the like. Similar is the case of the river of the mind-field (*chitta-nadī*). Its flow upon the ground of objects towards the ocean of transmigratory cycles into the world (*saṁsāra*) is broken through dispassion (*vairāgya*). And its flow on the ground of spirituality towards the ocean of the joy of liberation increases through practice (*abhyāsa*) by bringing into control the obstacles like sleep.

The mind-field has two natures (RY): agitation as well as submersion (*laya*). If one has disinterest in the world (*vairāgya*) but no practice of discernment or of meditation, the mind's agitations will be pacified but the mind will enter into sleep. The yoga of samādhi will not be fulfilled. It is a well-known fact in the oral and experiential tradition that many people who have not prepared themselves by practice fall asleep during mental exercises while in the corpse posture (*śhavāsana*). Some also fall asleep during meditation or when in the presence of a master's mental and pranic energy. Only with gradual practice are they able to absorb and assimilate the energy of prāṇa, kuṇḍalinī and consciousness into themselves so that their meditations may be elevated to greater heights.

Therefore it is to be concluded that *both abhyāsa* and *vairāgya* are prerequisite for attaining *nirodha.* Hence (VB) we read:

> No doubt, O mighty-armed Arjuna, the mind is fickle and difficult to restrain, but, O Son of Kunti, it is brought under control through practice (*abhyāsa*) and through dispassion (*vairāgya*).
>
> *Bhagavad-gītā* VI.35

Even though *nirodha* was defined in *YS* I.2, the word occurs again in this sūtra as the stated goal. Practice and dispassion bring about the *nirodha* of the vṛttis (BR), whose normal nature, based in the guṇas, is *prakāśha,* illumination; *pra-vṛtti,* involvement, initiative, adventurousness; and *niyama,* stability, restraint, control. When (BR, NB) their predisposition to flow outwards has been stemmed and they are turned inwards, the vṛttis submerge into their originating cause, the mind-field. Then they dwell within their origin, chitta, as *śhakti,* power, energy, potentia. This having occurred, the river of the mind also merges into *nirodha,* which is the same (NB) as *kaivalya* (isolation).

Sūtra I.13 तत्र स्थितौ यत्नोऽभ्यासः।

tatra sthitau yatno'bhyāsaḥ

tatra: there, between those (two, practice and dispassion)
sthitau: in the matter of, towards, settling, stabilising, coming to rest (of the mind-field); as regards stilling, steadiness
yatnaḥ: endeavour, effort
abhyāsaḥ: practice

Between those two, practice and dispassion, the endeavour towards stillness and stability (*sthiti*) of the mind-field is called practice.

Vyāsa's Commentary

Stillness or stability (*sthiti*) means the mind-field flowing pacifically when it is without vṛttis.

The endeavour tending towards this purpose is virility or exertion.

Practice is the observance of the means thereto, with the will to achieve its fulfilment.

Discussion

The definition of practice is given (VB) by way of stating its nature and purpose. That is, the endeavour with regard to, for the purpose of, stilling the mind is called practice.

It may be asked (SS): One has to make the effort of a mental activity when practising the repetition of mantra for *japa* and so forth, but what could be the endeavour involved in stillness? Although Vyāsa says that

> stillness or stability (*sthiti*) means the mind-field flowing pacifically when it is without vṛttis,

it does not mean a total absence of vṛttis (VM, VB). As we shall see under *YS* I.42, (VB) one does not begin even *samprajñāta* samādhi until after this stillness (*sthiti*) is experienced. This *sthiti*—

"stillness, stability, settling down, coming to rest, steadiness"—means either that the mind-field is free of any vṛtti other than that which is the object of concentration (VB), or that it is free of the rajasic and tamasic vṛttis (VM, NB, RY), and sattvic vṛttis alone (NB, RS) remain. Stillness is the one-pointedness of the mind-field when it is without the rajasic and tamasic vṛttis (RY).

Other commentators are more ambitious. According to them (BR, AD), that mutation (*pariṇāma*) of the mind, when it is without vṛttis and dwelling in its own nature, is to be called *sthiti.* However, VB is correct in stating that this definition would raise *sthiti* beyond the experience of *samprajñāta* samādhi; the path would then come after the goal, the endeavour would supersede its own purpose. The intent of the sūtra seems to be to state implicitly that the endeavour in meditation means bringing the mind to stillness or stability, which means freedom from the rajasic and tamasic turbulences, the mind's one-pointed concentration on a single sattvic vṛtti remaining uninterrupted so that the mind flows in a calm, pacific, smooth stream. The mind then flows calmly because it is not interrupted by other vṛttis (VB) and not disturbed by emotional waves of exhilaration, grief and so forth. The word *śhānta* 'pacific, calm' used by Vyāsa is explained (VB):

> One who upon hearing, touching, seeing, tasting or smelling whatever pleasant or unpleasant is neither pleased nor displeased is called pacific, calm (*śhānta*).
>
> *Mahopaniṣhad* IV.32

The endeavour is directed towards *sthiti,* and is explained by Vyāsa by offering two synonyms:

vīrya: virility, vigour, strength, energy, potency, the qualities of a hero
utsāha: enthusiasm, perseverance, fortitude, firmness, exertion, vigourous pursuit

Obviously an endeavour should be undertaken with these heroic qualities turned inwards and their intense concentration directed at the effort to bring the mind to stillness. One says to oneself again and again: "Even though the mind naturally flows outwards, I shall definitely bring it under control" (SS).

On this sūtra NTC says stability (*sthiti*) means one-pointedness (*ekāgratā*) upon the transcendental self (*para*-ātman) whose nature is essence (*sat*) and consciousness (*chit*). The effort (*prayatna*) means:

> *utsāha:* zeal and enthusiasm that "I shall certainly restrain the mind which constantly flows outwards."
> *sāhasa:* courage, that is, embarking upon the endeavour without considering "It can be done," "It can't be done," etc.
> *dhairya:* steadfastness and patience that "If not in this life then in some future one this will definitely succeed." It should be such that one is willing to try to empty the ocean by catching its drops on the end of a blade of grass!
> *adhyātma-vidyā:* pursuit of spiritual science. It means that the mind-field (chitta) is extinguished like fire when it is provided no more fuel. It occurs when one sees the purposelessness and falsity of objects and a true purpose in ātman.
> *mahat-sevā:* service of the great, which consists of prostrating before them, asking them questions and serving their person.

In addition, *yamas,* etc. will be explained in subsequent sūtras.

Returning to Vyāsa:

> Practice is the observance of the means thereto. . . .

The means towards this stillness are (VM) the eight limbs (*aṅgas*) of yoga (*YS* II.29ff.) and others such as (VB, BG) faith, etc. (*YS* I.20). This state of stillness is further strengthened by following the methods taught in *YS* I.35-39. This observance of the method, says Vyāsa, is undertaken

> with the will to achieve its fulfilment.

This phrase is a translation of the single word *sam-pipādayiṣhayā,* the instrumental case of the desiderative nominal form *sam-pidādayiṣhā,* which implies a desire, an intent, a will. Without a definite resolve and the exertion of will, one will not fulfil one's purpose, and the effort will not bear fruit. To reverse Vyāsa's sequence:

- A will and intent to fulfil the purpose is required
  so one may undertake
- the observance of the means and methods of yoga
- with heroic perseverance, vigour, power and virility,
  so that
- the mind may become one-pointed on a sattvic vṛtti,
  alone, and
- flow in a calm, pacific, unturbulent, smooth stream.

Another possible translation of the sūtra is: "The effort to remain there is practice." It is a common experience that whatever depth of meditation one reaches remains a temporary experience at first. No sooner does one reach it during a meditation session than he or she slips down, and during the activity of daily life meditative depth remains elusive. Only by continuous application of will and constancy of practice does it become possible for one to learn to "remain there" at first during the meditation, and later to maintain that depth in daily life. This is further discussed in the next sūtra.

Sūtra I.14 स तु दीर्घकालनैरन्तर्यसत्कारासेवितो दृढभूमिः।

sa tu dīrgha-kāla-nairantarya-satkārāsevito dṛḍha-bhūmiḥ

saḥ: that (practice)
tu: however
dīrgha-kāla-: (for) a long time
nairantarya-: without interval, without interruption
satkāra-: respect, positive attitude, reverence, adoration, devotion
ā-sevitaḥ: pursued, thoroughly served, maintained in assiduous and complete observance
dṛḍha-bhūmiḥ: (becomes) firm of ground

That practice, however, becomes firm of ground only when pursued and maintained in assiduous and complete observance for a long time, without interruption and with a positive and devout attitude.

Vyāsa's Commentary

Assiduously undertaken for a long time (*ā-sevitaḥ*), assiduously undertaken without interruption, cultivated with ascetic observance (*tapas*), celibacy (*brahmacharya*), knowledge (*vidyā*) and devotion (*śhraddhā*) and thus with a positive and devout attitude, it becomes firm of ground. That is to say, it is then not suddenly overpowered by a worldly, non-meditative (*vyutthāna*) saṁskāra.

Discussion

The firmness of practice is being advised (BG). The question arises that since the *vyutthāna*-saṁskāras, saṁskāras of worldly involvements, have accumulated much strength in people from beginningless time (VM, VB, NB, SS), as have the impressions of rajasic and tamasic vṛttis (RY), how is it possible that a commonly infirm and weak practice, undertaken relatively recently (SS), will overpower the force of these saṁskāras (VM, VB, NB, RY) which await to waylay one (VM) and by which the practice is often blocked (VM, VB) and constricted (RY)? The answer is as follows.

The practice needs the three qualifications (VM) stated. It must be observed (*a*) for a long time, (*b*) without interruption, (*c*) with due respect, adoration, devotion and positive feeling. In other words, the practice must be consistent, frequent, repeated—for a long time, every day, without interruption and with a positive feeling. Yoga should be practised every day and every moment (HA). If one practises for some time and then allows an interruption, it permits an accumulation of opposite vṛttis again, which then overpower the meagre yoga-saṁskāras which had been gathered (VB, SS). To practise for a few days or months and to expect accomplishment is like a parent's saying "There are only four Vedas. My son went to study them five days ago and hasn't returned yet!" (SS). In this regard (SS) one may quote:

> Reaching accomplishment after many life spans, one then arrives at the transcendental state.
>
> *Bhagavad-gītā* VI.45

Therefore one should be prepared to practise for years and lifetimes.

As for a positive attitude: without it there will arise at the time of meditation or during meditation the problems of (SS) sleep, distraction, and the smearing of mind with the worldly dirt of attractions. A positive attitude of adoration and reverence for the path must be constantly affirmed. (This will be further discussed under Sūtra I.30, which speaks of the impediments in the way of attaining firm ground.) A positive attitude exhibits itself in very substantial ways:

tapas: ascetic practice, austerity, reducing one's material and physical pleasures and luxuries and the body's dependence on objects (to be discussed under *YS* II.1,32).

brahmacharya: celibacy, maintaining control over sexual passion (to be discussed under *YS* II.30).

vidyā: knowledge, proficiency (*a*) in the tradition, (*b*) in the texts, and, more importantly, (*c*) in the systematic method of practice.

śhraddhā: faith and devotion that "Samādhi is the only worthy goal, the path I am on is the correct one, the lineage of my gurus is authentic, I shall certainly reach samādhi, and I revere, honour, adore, have faith in my goal, my path, my gurus, and myself." This faith shows itself in the way of (*a*) service given to the gurus, (*b*) humility towards all, (*c*) constant examining and curbing of one's ego, and (*d*) attitudes and acts expressive of devotion.

If one does not practise for a long time, or if one breaks off one's practice many times over an extended period, it shows the absence of sufficient faith and devotion; as a result, distractions (*vikṣhepas*), despoiling emotions (*kaṣhāyas*), inclinations to pleasure, etc. are not countered (NTC). When the practice becomes firm of ground, one cannot be moved from it even by the strongest adversity or pain (SS), nor can one be distracted from it by the subtlest pleasure or the most powerful attraction, nor, as Vyāsa says, can it be

> suddenly overpowered by a *vyutthāna*-saṁskāra.

When a certain level of practice is thus firm of ground, one recognizes the greatest depth of experience it is capable of imparting. Then

> one can go to that depth in an instant at any time
> under any condition or situation, and gradually
> that becomes the natural plateau of awareness
> in which one remains at all times.

From here one attempts to gain yet higher ground by the same rules of this sūtra which have brought one this far.

Sūtra I.15 दृष्टानुश्रविकविषयवितृष्णस्य वशीकारसंज्ञा वैराग्यम्।

dṛṣhṭānuśhravika-viṣhaya-vitṛṣhṇasya vaśhīkāra-sañjñā vairāgyam

dṛṣhṭa-: seen, perceived with physical senses
ānuśhravika-: heard of in a tradition or scripture
viṣhaya-: subjects, matters, objects of enjoyment or experience
vitṛṣhṇasya: of one who has lost craving for
vaśhīkāra-: mastery, bringing under total control
sañjñā: term, definition, name
vairāgyam: dispassion

The mastery established by someone who has lost all craving for the matters of experience or enjoyment, whether perceived with physical senses or heard of in the tradition and scriptures (as of the subtle worlds), is called dispassion.

Vyāsa's Commentary

When one has lost the craving for matters perceptible, such as women [i.e., the opposite sex], food, drink, power and affluence (*aiśhvarya*), as well as when one has lost the craving in matters that are heard of in traditions and scriptures, such as the attainment of heaven or of the states of *videha* and *prakṛti-laya* (*YS* I.19), then the mind,

> seeing the fault or the blemish that accrues in involvement,

its state,

> devoid of a concept of rejectables or acceptables even in the presence of celestial and non-celestial objects and comprising a disinterest in enjoyments, which occurs through the power of *pra-saṅkhyāna* (the realization of the difference between matter and the spiritual self),

is termed *vaśhīkāra,* mastery and control, that is, dispassion (*vairāgya*).

Discussion

The verb root *rañj* 'to colour', from which is derived the word *vairāgya,* was discussed earlier (p. 152) and should be reviewed before proceeding with this reading.

Vairāgya means "the state of being devoid of, free from, *rāga,* the attraction that accrues, as it were, from the objects of attraction reflecting in and colouring the mind." Even though this is the expanded, derivative meaning of the word, it is not a complete definition of *vairāgya* for the purpose of yoga.

(VB) Simply the absence of this colouring process will not suffice, nor will even the freedom from attractions that is gained from seeing their faults; such a simple *vairāgya* is not conducive to the goal that is *nirodha.* Mere disinterest in certain objects of experience and enjoyment is of no value for this purpose, as for example a disinterest in objects in the case of an illness. We also see that often an attraction towards objects remains even after intelligence becomes aware of their attendant faults. Therefore, the definition of *vairāgya* here is not merely turning away from a craving, becoming indifferent (*vi-tṛṣhṇa*), but rather total mastery and control (*vaśhīkāra*). NTC says that control (*vaśhīkāra*) is an essential part of dispassion. If this were not so one might mistakenly think he had attained *vairāgya* when he had only not found the objects of his desire or lacked the capacity to enjoy them.

The first step is to overcome the craving for the objects of this world which are perceived with the senses, such as the enjoyment of the opposite sex, food and drink; also to be overcome are affluence, success, luxury, power—all of which are expressed by the word *aiśhvarya.* Although this word was discussed earlier (p. 101), here it is not used in the same sense of achieving spiritual lordship, but rather of achieving worldly success. It may also be said that even though spiritually attained lordship is naturally attendant upon a person of sattvic buddhi, the ambitious attraction towards it, which is not sattvic, is to be avoided.

The word "women" from Vyāsa's commentary is being paraphrased here as "the opposite sex," out of consideration for contemporary concerns. These texts were composed and taught in monasteries by yoga masters for whose male disciples the attraction of women must have been a common problem. Although there have been many great women yogis (*yoginis*) known to the tradition, it is thought that men are not as strong an attraction to aspiring women as women are to aspiring men. This is the only explanation that can be offered at this point; and wherever such allusions appear, they will be translated as "the opposite sex."

The perceptible objects of attraction may be conscious, such as persons of the opposite sex, or unconscious, such as food, drink, garments, etc. (VM, RS), or attractive sounds and so forth (BR). Then there are also imperceptible attractions, of which we hear only in spiritual traditions. These are experiences such as paradise or heaven, the subtle worlds of the shining ones, or *devas,* the energy realms, the so-called astral planes, the sounds of angelic music and so forth. Often human beings are taught to turn their minds from worldly objects so they may reap these heavenly experiences and such as rewards. In the yoga tradition a promise of these other-worldly enjoyments of subtle matter with the aid of a subtler mind may occasionally be used to draw a disciple's attention away from grosser worldly objects of material forms perceptible with the senses. However, as soon as this purpose has been accomplished, the spiritual teacher works towards turning the disciple's mind away from these subtle pleasures also. (The classic example of this approach is the epic by the poet Aśhvaghhoṣha of the first century A.D. narrating the stratagems of this nature used by the Buddha to liberate his cousin, Nanda.)

The chief attractions of the subtle nature enumerated by the commentators are (NB) the eight *siddhis* (discussed on *YS* III.45), heaven, and the states of *videha* and *prakṛti-laya.* The last two deserve some attention here, although they will be discussed in greater detail under Sūtra I.19.

The word *videha* means "bodiless." The yogis who, after abandoning the physical body, continue to maintain the body constituted of mahat, ahaṁkāra and mind are called *videhas* (VM, RS). Others say that the *videhas* maintain the *liṅga* body (VB), which by the definition of the word *liṅga* given in Sūtra II.19 would be considered constituted of the mahat evolute alone, the first evolute of prakṛti.

Concerning the *prakṛti-layas,* the word means "those who are absorbed in prakṛti," which is unmanifest matter, an equilibrium of sattva, rajas and tamas. This is the state of matter before creation, that is, before the equilibrium of the three guṇas is disturbed to produce even the subtlest evolute. Only a minute portion of prakṛti is at any time passing through the mutation of forms that constitute the universe and its phenomena. The *prakṛti-layas* are those yogis, those spiritual selves

- who have risen beyond all attractions of the mutative phenomena
- who have dissolved—unlike the *videhas*—even the *manas,* ahaṁkāra and mahat (or buddhi) into the equilibrium of unmanifest prakṛti
- but who have not yet reached *kaivalya.* They use the unmanifest, non-phenomenal matter beyond the universe as their playground.

(VB) The *videhas* enjoy still the sullied form of prakṛti, whereas the *prakṛti-layas* have mastery over pure prakṛti. As ordinary beings in bondage identify with the body, and *videhas* identify with the mind, ahaṁkāra and mahat (buddhi), so the *prakṛti-layas* identify solely with pure prakṛti. They may create whatever universes they wish out of the domain of their mastery and thus be the *īśhvaras* (lords or gods) of a given universe. But this is not yet *kaivalya.* Through this misidentification they may again enter (VM) cycles of *saṁsāra,* even though the cycle is at the scale of a universe and their incarnations span the cycles of creations and dissolutions.

A truly liberated being is beyond any interest even of this ambitious scale. True dispassion is beyond an interest in even the subtlest form, beyond even a desire to drink the ambrosia of the gods (NB). This is the explanation of the condition of *vairāgya* as given by Vyāsa:

> When one has lost the craving for matters perceptible, such as the opposite sex, food, drink, power and affluence, as well as

when one has lost the craving in matters that are heard of in traditions and scriptures, such as the attainment of heaven or of the states of *videha* and *prakṛti-laya* . . .

Furthermore, there are two levels of *vairāgya:*

apara: not transcending
para: transcending, beyond

The current sūtra deals with *apara-vairāgya,* which is an attempt at dispassion towards the attractions described above. *Para-vairāgya* will be dealt with in the next sūtra. *Apara-vairāgya* is divided into four steps (*bhūmikās*):

1. *yatamāna:* the initial effort
2. *vyatireka:* ascertainment
3. *ekendriya:* "pertaining to the single sense (i.e., mind) only"
4. *vaśhīkāra:* control and mastery

Yatamāna, the initial effort, is explained as follows:

- Resolving to discover from the gurus and the scriptures as to what is of essence and meaning and what is not so in this world (SS).
- Uprooting the mind from attractions (*rāga*) (HA).
- Understanding the nature of the freedom from craving (*vi-tṛṣhṇa*) and through knowledge the practice of the means of developing dispassion, such as seeing that worldly objects involve endless troubles (such as gaining, guarding, loss and consequent grief) and blemishes (such as violence to others in the entire process) (VB, BG, NB).
- Seeing that the despoilers (*kaṣhāyas*) such as attraction (*rāga*) dwell in the mind, that they cause the senses to be drawn towards worldly objects. "May the senses no longer be drawn towards these objects"—this resolution, and an endeavour to bring about the maturity of emotions (*kaṣhāyas*) (VM, RY).
- Reducing desires (*yatamāna*) even though one is unable to give up the objects of desire (NTC).

Vyatireka, the second step, is explained as follows:

- Developing the ability to ascertain which of the despoilers, blemishes, present in the mind, the emotions, have been brought to maturation through the practice of discernment (*viveka*) (SS), which are now in the process of maturing, and which have to begin maturing at some time in the future (VM, RY, SS).
- Ascertaining which of the senses have been conquered and which are yet to be conquered (VB, BG, NB).
- Ascertaining in which domains of attraction the dispassion has been accomplished, and in which domains it is yet to be perfected (HA).
- Abandoning those objects of desire towards which one has the least attraction until finally only the one, the most attractive, remains (NTC).

Ekendriya, the third step, is limited only to one sense, the mind. It is further characterized as follows:

- One knows that involvement in perceptible and non-perceptible objects is synonymous with suffering (SS).
- One's mental energies behind the attractions, aversions, etc. have matured so that they are incapable of activating the senses towards the external forms and so forth (VM, VB, BG, NB, RY, NTC).
- These attractions have become very weak (HA) and dwell only in the mind as mere interest (*autsukya*) (VM, RY, SS).
- One knows that there remain only the mental conditions, such as desire for honour and aversion to dishonour, so that one works towards and finally accomplishes dispassion towards these (VB, BG, NB).

Vaśhīkāra, control and mastery, is defined by Vyāsa:

> The mind,
>
> > seeing the fault or the blemish that accrues in involvement,
>
> its state,
>
> > devoid of a concept of rejectables or acceptables even in the presence of celestial and non-celestial objects and comprising a disinterest in enjoyments, which occurs through the power of *pra-saṅkhyāna* (the realization of the difference between matter and the spiritual self),
>
> is termed *vaśhīkāra,* mastery and control, that is, dispassion (*vairāgya*).

(Some of the defects and blemishes (*doṣhas*) one sees in the worldly involvement have been explained above, but a more complete statement about them is made in Sūtra II.15.) When this view has been perfected, one rises above the first three steps of dispassion, in the last of which there remained yet a mental interest in the objects of the world even though the inclination of the senses to indulge has been withheld or restrained. Up to that point one should stay away from the presence and sight of temptations because in their presence the mental interest might, and often does, awaken and activate the sense, making the practitioner open to the danger of abandoning (NB) the path altogether. This, however, is not the situation in the case of *vaśhīkāra.* Here, even in the presence of objects there is neither attraction nor aversion. It is important that there be neither acceptance nor rejection, but rather indifference. In *vaśhīkāra* there are no more injunctions to and from, no commandments or prohibitions, no idea of "rejectables and acceptables," but total neutrality (NTC). When such neutrality is accomplished, even the closest presence of the objects of enjoyment does not distract the mind (BG, NB, RY). One says that "I am not under the control of these objects, but rather they are the objects of my control (*vaśha*)" (BR, NB, RY)—not merely because one has seen the faults of worldly pursuits, but because the power of internal discrimination, the knowledge of the difference between prakṛti and the spiritual self, is gathering strength. Because this last step, *vaśhīkāra,* is the culmination of the previous three, they are not separately stated in the *Yoga-sūtras* or by Vyāsa (VM). Furthermore, this lower dispassion (*apara-vairāgya*) falls within the practice of *samprajñāta* samādhi but is external to *asamprajñāta,* which is beyond, and in which the higher dispassion (*para-vairāgya*) develops. Of that, in the next sūtra.

Sūtra I.16 तत् परं पुरुषख्यातेर्गुणवैतृष्ण्यम्।

tat paraṁ purușha-khyāter guṇa-vaitṛṣhṇyam

tat: that (dispassion) (is)
paraṁ: supreme, transcendent, of higher kind
purușha-: (as regards) the conscious being, the spiritual self, spiritual noumenon
khyāteḥ: through discernment
guṇa-: (for) the attributes of matter (that is, prakṛti), namely, sattva, rajas, tamas
vaitṛṣhṇyam: state of being free of all craving

That dispassion is of the higher kind, transcendent, supreme, when it is the freedom from all craving for the attributes, guṇas, arising through the realization of the spiritual self, purușha.

Vyāsa's Commentary

One who sees the faults and blemishes of objects perceptible and of those heard of in the traditions and scriptures, is dispassionate (*virakta*).

One whose buddhi is filled, expanded and satiated with increased and strengthened discriminating wisdom because of the purification that occurs through repeated practice of realizing and seeing (*darśhana*) the spiritual self is dispassionate (*virakta*) towards the guṇas, whether with manifest or unmanifest attributes.

These are the two kinds of dispassion (*vairāgya*). Of these two, the latter is no other but clarity (*prasāda*) of knowledge. When it arises, discernment (*khyāti*) rises equally and then (the yogi) contemplates and observes thus:

- Whatever was to be attained has been attained.
- The afflictions which were to be eliminated have been eliminated.
- The fast-jointed (RP), transitional (*saṅkramaḥ*) chain of birth (BB) and becoming has been broken, without the breaking of which one is born and dies, one dies and is born, again and again.

The ultimate limit of knowledge itself is dispassion. Immediately after this very dispassion follows isolation (*kaivalya*).

Discussion

The last sūtra explained the lower dispassion (*apara-vairāgya*). Up to here (VM) the growth of sattva has washed off the inertia of tamas, but the dust of rajas yet clings to the mind-field. It is reiterated by Vyāsa here:

> One who sees the faults and blemishes of objects perceptible and of those heard of in the traditions and scriptures, is dispassionate (*virakta*).

When (RY) the practice of the eight limbs (*aṅgas*) of yoga has led to partial purification of the mind, when one has seen the flaws in involvement with worldly objects, and has finally reached the *vairāgya* of the level called mastery (*vaśhīkāra*), then this lower *vairāgya* serves as the means (VM, RS) to the higher dispassion. In other words (VB), the lower dispassion is only with regard to *viṣhayas,* the objects of the world. The higher dispassion (*para-vairāgya*) is with regard to guṇas (VB, BG, NB) and with regard to knowledge (*jñāna*) (VB, NB) and the means thereof (BG). Even knowledge has some similarity with the *viṣhayas.* Even though knowledge shows that worldly objects are perishable, its purpose is to remove ignorance (VB, BG, NB); it may even lead to temptations like the *siddhi* of omniscience (HA). The knowledge that causes awareness of the faults of the *viṣhayas* does not by itself lead to that *vairāgya* (VB, BG, NB) in which one might say "Enough!" ("*Alam!*") to even *viveka-khyāti,* the knowledge of the separateness of the self and the non-self. This sūtra points out that when the correct knowledge (*samyak-jñāna*) has eradicated ignorance, then there develops indifference (*upekṣhā*) towards even the fact of that knowledge, towards the means which led to that knowledge (VB, BG, NB) and towards the causes of all effects because now the yogi has reached the satiety (*tṛpti*) of dwelling within the self (VB, BG).

That is to say (BG), when one has mastered the lower *vairāgya,* he now further firms up his knowledge of the separateness of the guṇas and the spiritual self (*viveka*). This is *dharma-megha,* the samādhi of the raincloud of virtue and of the knowledge of the nature of all things. As a result, one abandons all craving for the guṇas, which had hitherto served as the instruments (*upa-karaṇas*) of self. That self is no longer interested even in the fact of being separate *from* anything such as those guṇas. This is the culmination, perfection, of that state in which knowledge is at its clearest (*jñāna-prasāda*). This is self-knowledge (*ātma-jñāna*). This is the higher dispassion.[14] Vyāsa says:

> One whose buddhi is filled, expanded and satiated with increased and strengthened discriminating wisdom because of the purification that occurs through repeated practice of realizing and seeing (*darśhana*) the spiritual self is dispassionate (*virakta*) towards the guṇas, whether with manifest or unmanifest attributes.

In the above reading the phrase *puruṣha-darśhana-abhyāsa* 'the repeated practice of realizing and seeing the spiritual self' means that (VB) one has received knowledge through *āgama,* scriptural authority, *anumāna,* one's own inference, and *āchārya,* a realized teacher who has himself experienced self-realization. Thereby occurs (VB) the purification of intelligence (buddhi) as rajas and tamas are eliminated and one-pointed concentration on sattva in a single, unbroken stream (*eka-tānatā*) is accomplished. The buddhi thus purified is

ā-pyāyita: filled and expanded with
pra-viveka: increased and strengthened (prefix *pra*) discriminating knowledge

that (VB) puruṣha is pure and infinite, that the guṇas are just the opposite, and that (BG) the power called consciousness (*chiti-śhakti*) is immutable, etc. (*YS* I.2). There accrues a satiety (*tṛpti*) in such a buddhi, for it has now completed its purpose of serving the puruṣha.

14. VB tries to reconcile Sāṅkhya-yoga with Vedānta by saying that this means the realization of either individual self or the Supreme Self.

> [Being] dispassionate (*virakta*) towards the guṇas, whether with manifest or unmanifest attributes,

means that (HA) one is indifferent towards (*a*) their manifest attributes: those that constitute knowledge of, and consequent activity in, the gross, visible world as well as the subtle, invisible worlds; and (*b*) the unmanifest attributes as experienced by the *videha* and *prakṛti-laya* yogis.

It is this lower-level *vairāgya* that is said to be the means of reaching the *prakṛti-laya* state in texts such as *Sāṅkhya-kārikā*. The yogis of these categories, then, do not go beyond *apara-vairāgya* to *para-vairāgya;* they have not reached (VM) dispassion towards the unmanifest attributes. Vyāsa says:

> Of these two [levels of *vairāgya*], the latter is no other but clarity (*prasāda*) of knowledge.

To summarize (VM): Even though the mind-field's primary constituent is sattva, it becomes smeared with rajas and tamas. We have stated above that tamas is overcome by lower dispassion. Higher dispassion also eliminates the effects of rajas. (The word *rajas* in Sanskrit also means "dust.") Thus washed by the pure streams of practice and dispassion and free of the dust of rajas, the mind is now clear. This clarity is expressed by the word *prasāda,* which (*a*) suggests the image of clear, flowing water in which no dust swirls about, and (*b*) indicates a state of happiness, joyfulness and intense pleasantness felt in the mind. The suffix *mātra,* translated here as "no other but," expresses the fact that this clarity of mind is such that the mind in meditation now requires no external objects, not even as objects of concentration.

This is the explanation of Vyāsa's passage offered by VM, but it is incorrect. No matter how much the clarity of sattva may be emphasized, the passage cannot refer to a state of mind. The passage fits the definition of higher dispassion in which all three guṇas, including sattva, have been transcended and all dependence on the evolutes of prakṛti, including the mind-field, has ceased. The knowledge *of* guṇas is certainly not indicated here. The correct reading is that the passage refers only to the pure state of self-knowledge, which is (VB) synonymous with that freedom from all craving (*vaitṛṣhṇya*), the other definition of higher dispassion. This purity of self-knowledge constitutes freedom from attraction to the manifest or unmanifest forms of the guṇas. When such purity of knowledge arises, says Vyāsa,

> discernment (*khyāti*) rises equally and then (the yogi) contemplates and observes thus:
>
> - Whatever was to be attained has been attained.
> - The afflictions which were to be eliminated have been eliminated.
> - The fast-jointed (RP), transitional (*saṅkramaḥ*) chain of birth (BB) and becoming has been broken, without the breaking of which one is born and dies, one dies and is born, again and again.
>
> The ultimate limit of knowledge itself is dispassion.

The three fulfilments or accomplishments appear to be a summary of the seven grounds of attainment described in *YS* II.27. "Whatever was to be attained [that is, self-knowledge] has been attained." "The afflictions" (*kleśhas*), together with all the propensities (*vāsanās*) produced by them, have been eliminated. As to the "fast-jointed, transitional chain of birth and becoming," it refers to the continuous cycle of birth and death (*saṁsāra*), which is part of the cycles of creations and dissolutions, resulting from the accumulation of good and evil actions. Its segments or joints (*parvas*) are the very states of transition through which one passes, wandering from body to body to become one person or another through numberless series of transmigrations. (More of this process is explained in the discussion on Sūtras II.12 and II.13.) This cycle continues until the final dispassion is reached. According to Vyāsa, again:

> The ultimate limit of knowledge itself is dispassion. Immediately after this very dispassion follows isolation (*kaivalya*).

The samādhi which is synonymous with *kaivalya* is *a-samprajñāta. Asamprajñāta* follows *dharma-megha* (*YS* IV.29-31), the samādhi of the raincloud of virtue and of the knowledge of the nature of all things. The higher dispassion is the condition of *dharma-megha* (VM), and without it *asamprajñāta* cannot be reached either by knowledge or by the practice of *yamas, niyamas* and the other limbs of yoga (VB). RY summarizes the entire process as follows:

- A person receives authoritative knowledge from the guru.
- He develops discernment (*khyāti*).
- By the practice of *khyāti,* the initial stage of *dharma-megha* develops.
- This destroys the blemishes (*mala*) (compare the Latin word *macula*) of rajas and tamas from the mind-field, causing the mind to be purely sattvic and filled with *prasāda.*
- The higher state of *dharma-megha* is then realized, which is the same as the dispassion towards guṇas.
- The concomitant of this dispassion is the awareness that the reservoir of karma is cleared, all *kleśhas* have been eliminated and total self-knowledge has been gained.
- Then the highest dispassion of *asamprajñāta* samādhi ensues.

Sūtra I.17 **वितर्कविचारानन्दास्मितारूपानुगमात् सम्प्रज्ञातः।**

vitarka-vichārānandāsmitā-rūpānugamāt samprajñātaḥ

vitarka-: gross thought
vichāra-: subtle thought
ānanda-: ecstasy, rapture
asmitā-: I-am-ness
rūpa-[15]: nature, form, appearance (of)
anugamāt: through accompaniment (of)
samprajñātaḥ: samprajñāta, lower samādhi, cognitive samādhi, samādhi of wisdom

***Samprajñāta,* the samādhi of wisdom, occurs through the accompaniment of the appearances (RP, BB) of gross thought (*vitarka*), subtle thought (*vichāra*), ecstasy (*ānanda*) and I-amness (*asmitā*).**

Vyāsa's Commentary

Now, when one's vṛttis of the mind-field have been brought under control (*niruddha*) through the two means (*abhyāsa* and *vairāgya*), in what ways is *samprajñāta* samādhi said (to ensue)?

> [*Sūtra:*] *Samprajñāta,* the samādhi of wisdom, occurs through the accompaniment of the appearances of gross thought (*vitarka*), subtle thought (*vichāra*), ecstasy (*ānanda*) and I-am-ness (*asmitā*).

The mind-field's gross expansion (*ābhoga*) towards the supportive factor is called the gross thought (*vitarka*). The same when it is subtle is the subtle thought (*vichāra*). Rapture is ecstasy (*ānanda*). The perception of a unified self is I-am-ness (*asmitā*).

There the *vitarka*-conjoint samādhi actually accompanies all four.

15. Some texts do not include the word *rūpa* (nature, form, appearances) as part of the sūtra.

The second one, with the gross thought (*vitarka*) having been terminated, is accompanied by the subtle thought (*vichāra*). The third one, with the subtle thought having been terminated, is accompanied by ecstasy (*ānanda*). The fourth one, with that ecstasy having been terminated, is merely I-am-ness (*asmitā*). All these samādhis are dependent on, conjoint with, or accompanied by supportive factors.

Discussion

I. The Stages of Samādhi

So far yoga in general has been defined in Sūtras 2-16. In Vyāsa's commentary on Sūtra 1 it was stated that

> Yoga is samādhi.

Now (VB) the specifics of that samādhi are being described. When one has brought the rajasic and tamasic vṛttis under control (*nirodha*) by means of practice and dispassion (RY, SS), what are the different ways or kinds of samādhi that follow? This is how Vyāsa introduces the sūtra:

> Now, when one's vṛttis of the mind-field have been brought under control (*niruddha*) through the two means (*abhyāsa* and *vairāgya*), in what ways is *samprajñāta* samādhi said (to ensue)?
>
> > [*Sūtra:*] *Samprajñāta,* the samādhi of wisdom, occurs through the accompaniment of the appearances of gross thought (*vitarka*), subtle thought (*vichāra*), ecstasy (*ānanda*), and I-amness (*asmitā*).

The definitions of *samprajñāta* in general are based on the derivations of the word from:

sam: well, proper, deep, harmonized, balanced, holistic
pra: forth, expansive, perfect, complete
jñā: knowing

As realization (*sākṣhāt-kāra*) increases through its four stages (BG, NB), *samprajñāta,* the samādhi in which wisdom (*prajñā*) comes to its most harmonized, perfect expansion, is gained (VB). It is a special type of cultivated concentration (*bhāvanā*) (BR, NB, AD, SS). *Bhāvanā* means impressing the object of concentration (*bhāvya*) again and again onto the mind-field (BR) by preventing any other object from entering the mind (NB). It is by *bhāvanā* that the form and nature of the object of meditation is completely realized (*prajñā*) so fully as to leave no residue of doubt or the possibility of *viparyaya* (*YS* I.8) (BR, NB). This realization of the true nature of the objects of meditation is called *pra-jñā,* the process of awakening of wisdom, and *prajñā,* the wisdom itself.

Samprajñāta samādhi differs from *asamprajñāta,* the acognitive samādhi, in that the former requires *ālambanas.* The word *ālambana* is translated here as "supportive factor." In *samprajñāta* the mind needs an object, whether of a gross or subtle nature, until *dharma-megha* samādhi is reached. These objects on which the concentrated thought of the mind is dependent are termed here the supportive factors (*ālambanas*).

Any of the categories of reality from the Sāṅkhya system of philosophy may be employed as an *ālambana.* For these categories see *TSS* 2, 3 and *YS* II.19. Briefly, these can be (VB, NB, BR) any of the following:

- Unconscious categories:
  - prakṛti, primordial matter — 1.
  - 23 evolutes of matter — 2-24.
- Conscious categories:
  - puruṣha; individual self — 25.
  - an aspect or incarnation of godhead } 26.
  - God }

Theistic Sāṅkhya philosophers as well as most commentators on the *Yoga-sūtras* include the twenty-sixth category, God. An *ālambana,* supportive factor, can be any combination of the above categories, individual or cosmic. For example, in meditation on a gross thought (*vitarka*), one may concentrate

- on the five gross elements, or
- on any material forms (such as a flame, the sun, the moon, a star, etc.) or

- on the physical form of an aspect, or
- on the incarnation of the godhead (such as Viṣhṇu, or Śhiva, or Jesus, etc., as venerated in Christian countries, or forms of Buddha as taught in Buddhist lands) or
- on *Virāṭ,* the Cosmic Immanent form of the godhead (an example of which may be seen in *BhG* chaps. IX, X, XI).

However, when we look closely at the question on concentration, it is found that among the conscious categories:

- only the physical, incarnate form, or *Virāṭ,* the cosmic form of the godhead
- but not the formless consciousness of the pure spiritual self, nor the formless transcendental Supreme Self

can be an *ālambana* of the mind-field. The mind, an evolute of unconscious matter, has no capability to grasp the pure consciousness principle. Even a semblance of such grasping does not begin until *asmitā* is realized, and only upon reaching discriminating wisdom (*viveka*) (VB) does mind come within reach of the spiritual principle, which is realized not as an *ālambana* of the mind but as the free self. This is so in the case of the individual self; the transcendental Supreme Self is far beyond.

The experiences to be realized in the four stages exist in everyone as a potency (*śhakti*). The potency of each is realized and then abandoned, left behind, till the final samādhi is reached (BR). The mind cannot enter the subtlest stages at once—at least it is not the common experience (*prāyaśhaḥ*) (NB). Hence it is said: The mind, conquered at the grosser level, should then be led slowly to the subtler factors. It is not likely that an average practitioner could leap to the highest samādhi and gather the processes of the intermediate states as part of such an instantaneous development. If such an instantaneous process should occur, there would be no need for such an order (NB) as described in this sūtra. Only by starting from gross objects does the mind gradually move to harmony with the subtlest and settle there (BG).

It is not that the realization of a relatively grosser object of concentration by itself leads to the higher ground of a subtler object. A material object cannot lead to spiritual realization because even in its thought form only a vṛtti is produced. Realization of the true nature and form of an object of concentration only leads to the *siddhis* which are described in *YS* III and which are declared (in the discussions on sūtras such as *YS* I.8, I.15, and III.37) to be undesirable goals for a true yogi's pursuit.

What then is the purpose of such realization at these various levels in *samprajñāta* samādhi? They are to fulfil the purpose described in *YS* I.15,16: to develop dispassion towards each level of the material evolutes. At each level one feels that the next subtler level is purer. But upon examination by realization it is found that the purity is only relative, at best derived from sattva, which is an attribute of matter. Each level is successively found to be attended by some faults and blemishes (NB) that have been described earlier. Thus a *vairāgya* towards each successive state develops. Simply perfecting the level of realization is not conducive to progress towards isolation and liberation. It is only when full dispassion develops towards that very experience and realization that the next step can be taken towards a yet subtler object of concentration.

A basic principle of the Sāṅkhya philosophy is that the categories of evolutes are divided in the order of causational succession (VM, NB, RY):

- Each cause produces an effect.
- An effect is grosser, coarser—that is, more tangible, closer to the world of senses and to the gross elements—than its cause.
- Concentration on each effect leads to the realization of the form and nature of that effect.
- When the mind's vṛttis concerning that effect are controlled, the mind's doors open to the cause of that effect.

A tangible object is seen, experienced, thought of, contemplated, but its cause is hidden, intangible. When we see a jar, we normally do not think of the clay the jar is made of. But when the realization of the nature of the jar reaches a certain fulness, the clay becomes more real and the jar becomes more a subsidiary of clay. As the mind focuses on the normally experienced, conventional nature of an object, it slowly transcends its tangible nature and grasps the intangible, the cause which was previously not seen, experienced, thought of, or contemplated (NB). This is the meaning of progress in Sāṅkhya-yoga: When the mind becomes as unified with the object of concentration as a red-hot ball of iron is with fire, the former ground is abandoned and the next exercise to gain the yet higher ground begins (VB, NB).

Another Sāṅkhya principle is:

> An effect is less real, durable, stable;
> a cause is more real, durable, stable (NB).

A jar breaks easily; its durability and stability is minimal compared to that of its cause, the clay. It is for this reason that the subtler objects of concentration lead to greater stability of the mind.

- The vṛtti of the effect is
  - brought to *nirodha,* fully controlled, and
  - dissolved into (*laya*) the vṛtti of its cause.
- Because a cause is always subtler, that is,
  - less tangible,
  - closer to the mind, buddhi and ahaṁkāra, and thus to the spiritual self,
- the next step in meditation is also always subtler.

Thus a process of *nirodha* and *laya* of the

- gross into subtle, and
- effects into causes,

continues until one reaches prakṛti. According to Sāṅkhya philosophy

- each effect carries within it the properties of all the successive causes in a chain of causation which has led to that particular effect as its end-product. But
- each cause carries within it only the potential of all the effects likely to be produced within the chain of the succession of effects starting from the given cause.

For example,

- clay includes a jar only as a potential, but
- a jar includes both the nature of the jar as an effect
- and its cause, the clay itself.

Since the various levels of the samādhi of wisdom (*samprajñāta*) lead from the vṛttis of grosser effects to those of subtler causes, the lower-level meditations include the subtler levels, but at each level the former coarse experience is abandoned. The four levels of *samprajñāta* are respectively:

sa-vitarka or *vitarka-anugata:* with *vitarka* or accompanied by *vitarka*
sa-vichāra or *vichāra-anugata:* with *vichāra* or accompanied by *vichāra*
sānanda or *ānanda-anugata:* with *ānanda* or accompanied by *ānanda*
sāsmita or *asmitā-anugata:* with *asmitā* or accompanied by *asmitā*

By the argument presented above concerning the chains of causation and their relevance to the different levels of samādhi, it is clear that (VM, RS)

- *sa-vitarka* samādhi actually accompanies all the other subsequent factors also, namely, *vichāra, ānanda,* and *asmitā.*
- *sa-vichāra* samādhi has abandoned *vitarka* but also accompanies *ānanda* and *asmitā.*
- *sānanda* samādhi abandons *vitarka* and *vichāra* but includes *asmitā.*
- *sāsmita* samādhi has no other accompaniments.

As to objects of concentration, since the mind must be brought to gradual refinement, it must move along the scale of the various evolutes of matter until it reaches an identification with the subtlest, finest possible state. The twenty-four states of matter with which the mind may identify are divided fourfold (*YS* II.19):

1. The sixteen *viśeṣhas,* distinct, specific forms of matter:
   - the five gross elements: earth, water, fire, air, space

- the five active senses: hands; feet; organs of speech, elimination and generation
- the five cognitive senses: smell, taste, sight, touch, sound
- the lower mind (*manas*)

2. The six *a-viśheṣhas*, the general causes of the *viśheṣhas*, namely
   - the five subtle elements (*tan-mātrās*), the 'merest measures of those' that produce the five gross elements; and
   - ego (ahaṁkāra), the identifying principle by which the composite sentience (*asmitā*) begins to identify itself as such-and-such being.
3. *Liṅga-mātra*, the 'barest sign' of the presence of matter, the subtlest evolute, mahat, the universal and individual buddhi. It is the receptacle of the spiritual self, the point where a material evolute first appears to unite with the spiritual self, producing *asmitā*, I-am-ness, the composite sentience further defined in *YS* II.6.
4. *A-liṅga* 'without a mark' prakṛti—principal matter—in the state of equilibrium, not manifest as the phenomena of the universe.

Of these, the *viśheṣhas*, *a-viśheṣhas*, and *liṅga-mātra* are the *ālambanas* in *samprajñāta* samādhi. As the components of a sentient personality, they are further divided into a scheme of apprehension as follows:

- *Viśheṣhas*, the objects apprehended by *asmitā*, are *grāhya*, objects of apprehension. Ahaṁkāra, ego, is the instrument by which *asmitā* apprehends the *grāhyas*. Ahaṁkāra is *grahaṇa*, the instrument of apprehension.
- *A-viśheṣhas*, the five subtle elements, are also *grāhya*.
- *Liṅga-mātra*—buddhi or mahat—receives and reflects consciousness from puruṣha, thus creating *asmitā*, the composite sentience. This, and not puruṣha, is the agent of apprehension. This is *grahītṛ*, the one who apprehends.

This scheme of apprehension is important in the classification of samādhis, as will be shown in *YS* I.41 and throughout this sūtra:

- *Grāhyas* (objects of apprehension) are the field of concentration in *vitarka*-accompanied samādhi and in *vichāra*-accompanied samādhi.

- *Grahaṇa* (the instrument of apprehension) is the field of concentration in the *ānanda*-accompanied samādhi.
- *Grahītṛ* (that which apprehends) is the field of concentration in the *asmitā*-accompanied samādhi.

The earlier yoga tradition, that of Patañjali and Vyāsa, states these to be the objects of concentration. Any other objects are only either parts or composites of these. Vyāsa states:

> The mind-field's gross expansion (*ābhoga*) towards the supportive factor is called the gross thought (*vitarka*).

The word *ābhoga* 'expansion' means the awakening of a wisdom (*prajñā*) in which a realization of the true nature of an object of concentration has occurred (VM). It is a fulness or perfection of the mind-field with regard to that object (VB). At the first level it is considered gross (*sthūla*) because the object of concentration is in its gross form (VM), thereby giving to the mind the like vṛtti, the mind identifying with that form.

A note of care and caution should be given here regarding *samprajñāta* concentrations, especially those on the sixteen *viśheṣhas,* and particularly the five gross elements. One may mistake these to be concentrations on the *external* earth and earthly forms, etc., with all the gross elements. It should be remembered that (*a*) a perception of gross elements in the ordinary world falls within the category of *pratyakṣha-pramāṇa,* direct perception, a vṛtti to be controlled, and (*b*) holding the perception in the mind is memory, another vṛtti to be controlled. For the practice of samādhi the concentration on these factors is *internal,* as they exist, operate and are apprehended within the sentient personality. It is therein that their nature is observed and mastered.

It needs to be noted that this concentration consists of the convergence of the particular evolute, as one of the subjectively inherent components of the inner sense, *antaḥ-karaṇa* (see p. 230) or chitta, with its counterpart in the objective world. For example, since mind is the controller of all the senses, their powers and those of the objects of the senses are all included in the mind. The mind concentrates on the objects and assimilates the vṛtti arising from the same; thus the lower-level agent of concentration, the lower mind (*manas*), and the object of concentration converge and merge, establishing a unity, a fulness and perfection of the wisdom of that level. This applies not only to *sa-vitarka* but to all the levels of samādhi.

II. Sa-vitarka Samādhi

As an archer under training first learns to shoot at a wider and more visible target, so the yogi first develops his attention on a grosser form and then moves towards a subtler one (VM, RY). *Virāṭ* as well as the manifest or incarnate forms of a deity and also the sixteen *viśheṣhas* are the gross objects of concentration. Taking such an *ālambana,* one concentrates on its (NB, BR, BG)

- whole aspect and
- parts,
- past, present and future manifestation(s),
- nearness to one (as within the person or in the proximity of the senses), or
- distance,
- desirable or undesirable qualities, or the faults inherent in the fact that it is constituted of the guṇas,
- even those manifestations that one has
  - not seen personally,
  - not heard of in the teachings,
  - not contemplated with the mind.

The concentration includes

- examining all relevant order and sequences, and
- cultivating the full grasp of
  - words or names,
  - their meanings (that is, the object denoted by the word), and
  - the knowledge consisting of the relationship between the word and the meaning.

A process of thought examining these details of an object is called *vitarka* in the normal language. In yoga it has the technical sense of concentration on the sixteen *viśheṣhas,* with attention to these aspects, with the goal of finally realizing the whole nature of the object. One need not at first concern oneself with regard to those aspects of the object of concentration which may not be within one's reach; for example:

- being too subtly hidden within the personality,
- too distant,
- not seen,
- not heard of, or
- not ever contemplated!

As concentration is mastered and refined, the next step comes into view and the hidden nature of the *ālambana* is gradually revealed (NB) in the natural process of yoga. The concentration should remain constant, continuously maintained (*ava-dhāraṇa*) (VB). By cultivating it thus, the *bhāvanā* then causes the object, the sense of its perception, and the mind to become one. This entire process explained hitherto is called *vitarka.* In the final realization of the nature of the object the knowledge of all the aspects listed above occurs at once, not in sequence, not in parts, not apart from the perceiving mind. When such a total, whole realization is maintained without a break, that state is termed "the samādhi accompanied by *vitarka.*" It is *grāhya-samāpatti* (*YS* I.41); its field of command is *grāhya,* the objects grasped, within the gross body. It is further divided into *sa-vitarka* samādhi and *nir-vitarka* samādhi, which will be explained in Sūtras I.42 and I.43.

III. Sa-vichāra Samādhi

Seeing that *sa-vitarka* samādhi is still involved only with guṇas and their products, the yogi rejects it and thereby opens the doors to the next, *sa-vichāra* samādhi. Vyāsa says:

> . . . the gross thought (*vitarka*). The same when it is subtle is the subtle thought (*vichāra*).

The *vitarka* refined becomes *vichāra.* The word should not be taken in its dictionary meaning of "thought." It is used here in a sense specific to this science (VB).

The word *vi-chāra* is derived from *vi + char,* expressing a progressive movement. Here it means the movement of the mind away from gross objects to subtler objects of concentration (VB). Having seen the faults of the involvement in gross objects, however perfectly realized in *sa-vitarka,* one looks at the causes of those gross objects, which inhere in them. The yogi thus moves from the sixteen *viśheṣhas* (products of the *a-viśheṣhas*) to the six *a-viśheṣhas* themselves. He concentrates on these subtler essences of the elements and on the senses (NB, BG)

- with each of their parts, and
- the totality of their wholeness (NB, BG), including their
- space,
- time, and
- attributes,

} and their relationships,

together with all the details explained on p. 227. The mind takes the form of the vṛtti of concentration and becomes identified with it. *Vichāra* then becomes the expansion (*ābhoga*) of chitta towards the subtle *ālambanas,* awakening wisdom (*prajñā*), in which the realization of the true nature of an object of concentration occurs. It is the same fulness and perfection of the mind-field with regard to subtle objects of concentration as has already been described with regard to the gross objects on pp. 226-27.

It is well here to examine a point made by a commentator in relation to *sa-vichāra* samādhi. HA(E) suggests that *vichāra* is a refined analytical process. The philosophical analysis of the relationship of prakṛti evolutes with ātman and Brahman finally leads to the realization that "I am none of these prakṛti evolutes with which I have identified the self." But such an analytical process is part of the practice of intense *vichāra* contemplations on the path of *jñāna*-yoga as taught in the Vedānta lineage. For the purpose of yoga practice according to Patañjali and Vyāsa, it will fall within (*a*) the *anumāna-pramāṇa,* inference as valid proof, a vṛtti to be brought under control, or (*b*) *svādhyāya,* the study of scriptural sentences leading to liberation, the fourth of the *niyamas* (which are the second *aṅga* of yoga) (*YS* II.32). Both of these, the *pramāṇa* vṛtti and *svādhyāya,* are left far behind when one begins to enter samādhi. Therefore *vichāra* here does not denote an analytical thought process. It is a technical term (*tāntrikī paribhāṣhā*) for a particular concentration on certain evolutes in order to master their nature and then to negate their influence on the ego (ahaṁkāra).

Among the subtle evolutes, the objects of this realization are

- the five *tan-mātrās,* subtle elements in the subtle body, the causes of the five gross elements and the subtle essences of the five cognitive senses (smell or odour, flavour or taste, sight or illumination of forms, touch, sound), and
- ahaṁkāra, ego.

As the immediate cause of the *tan-mātrās,* ahaṁkāra begins to be brought under control in this samādhi, but primarily it is the object of concentration in the next samādhi.

Some commentators (BR, SS) prefer to replace ahaṁkāra with the total *antaḥ-karaṇa,* the inner sense, which is collectively called *chitta* in yoga and is threefold in Sāṅkhya:

1. *manas,* mind, which is one of the sixteen *viśheṣhas,* the objects of concentration and realization in *sa-vitarka* samādhi
2. ahaṁkāra, ego, included by all commentators as one of the six *a-viśheṣhas,* objects of concentration and realization in the later stages of *sa-vichāra* samādhi, and in *sānanda* samādhi
3. mahat, buddhi, intelligence, *liṅga-mātra,* the first evolute of prakṛti, the object of concentration and realization in *sāsmita* samādhi

It is obvious, however, in the light of the above definitions of the various levels of *samprajñāta* which specify the different components of the *antaḥ-karaṇa* involved, that it would be erroneous to assume that the entire *antaḥ-karaṇa* is an *ālambana* of *sa-vichāra* samādhi.

Even though the primary objects of concentration in *sa-vichāra* are five of the *a-viśheṣhas,* with ahaṁkāra only beginning to be touched, it must be remembered, as explained on p. 223, that effects include causes; therefore, the subtler causes of the *a-viśheṣhas* are included: mahat (*liṅga-mātra*) and prakṛti (*a-liṅga*). The *sa-vichāra* samādhi is also *grāhya-samāpatti* (*YS* I.41); its field of command is *grāhya,* the objects grasped, not in the gross body, which is the field of *sa-vitarka,* but in the subtle body. *Sa-vichāra* is further divided into *sa-vichāra* samādhi and *nir-vichāra* samādhi, which will be explained in Sūtras I.42 and I.43.

IV. Sānanda Samādhi

About the third samādhi, Vyāsa says:

Rapture is ecstasy.

The word for ecstasy, *ānanda,* does not denote here bliss, the *ānanda* of Brahman, who is the Supreme Self. It is initially the property called *sukha,* pleasure inherent in the sattva-guṇa. In *ānanda*-accompanied samādhi the yogi captures the pleasure of sattva.

Sattva, as one of the three guṇas, is part of the entire scheme of prakṛti and its evolutes. Even though that scheme includes the delusion of tamas and the pain of rajas as well as the pleasure of sattva, beings involve themselves with the world only in pursuit of the pleasure of sattva. It is that attachment to the pleasure derived from sattva which causes bondage and which initiates the continuance of *saṁsāra.* In *sa-vitarka* and *sa-vichāra* samādhis the realized wisdom shows one the futility of pursuing the various objects of concentration, starting from the *vitarka* of the earth element and going up to the *vichāra* of the subtle elements and possibly the initial stages of ahaṁkāra, the ego. As the evolutes gradually dissolve into their subtler and yet subtler causes, in *sānanda* samādhi they dissolve into ahaṁkāra. Since tamasic ahaṁkāra produces the elements, and sattvic ahaṁkāra produces the mind and cognitive senses, both with the aid of rajas, it can be seen that a gradual refinement of awareness would lead a yogi to the more subtle sattva of ahaṁkāra. Even though like all other evolutes it consists of all three guṇas, rajas and tamas here are subordinated to sattva (SS), especially now that the yogi has ascended beyond the *vitarka* and *vichāra* grounds. The essence of pleasure that was tasted through the lower evolutes has its fount here. The yogi then concentrates on the pleasure of sattva of ahaṁkāra and enjoys a state of rapture (VB). Most mystics have mistaken this to be the bliss of God, which is yet far beyond.

This pleasure, *ānanda,* must also be seen (BG, NB)

- in its parts, and
- as a whole,

until the oneness of the enjoyer and the enjoyed is perceived and the expansion (*ābhoga*) of awareness to a fulness occurs, that is, its nature is fully realized.

In the *ānanda-anugata* samādhi the only vṛtti (VB) that prevails is,

> "I am in pleasure, happy, enraptured."

VB quotes:

> He knows that ultimate pleasure which is grasped by intelligence (buddhi), and which is beyond the senses. It is that settled wherein he is no longer shaken from reality. . . . Know that to be the freedom from the contact with pain; it is called yoga.
>
> *Bhagavad-gītā* VI.21,23

Even though mahat or buddhi proper is not reached until the next (*asmitā*-accompanied) samādhi, the sattvic nature of mahat here filters through into ahaṁkāra, adding to the rapture.

Those who reach only this far (to *sānanda* samādhi) are lost in mystic ecstasy and consider that to be the supreme attainment. Many powers (*siddhis*) may attend upon them. They have mastered the ego of the body—everything from the body made up of the *viśheṣhas* to the ahaṁkāra—and are called *videha,* the bodiless ones (for which see the discussion in Sūtras I.15 and I.19).

The field of this *sānanda* samādhi is *grahaṇa,* the instruments of apprehension (to be discussed in Sūtra I.41), and includes in the object of concentration its inherent causes, *asmitā* and the *a-liṅga* prakṛti. Unlike *sa-vitarka, nir-vitarka, sa-vichāra* and *nir-vichāra,* this samādhi is not subdivided (for example, into *sānanda* and *nir-ānanda*).

A summary discussion of selected commentators on the subject of *sānanda* and *sāsmita* samādhis follows. Even though *ānanda*-accompanied samādhi is still the topic, the question under discussion below will not be understood without defining *asmitā*-accompanied samādhi. It must be clearly pointed out here that there is little agreement among the commentators with regard to the objects of concentration in both *ānanda*-accompanied samādhi and the next, *asmitā*-accompanied, samādhi. Table 1 presents a summary of their views. These views will be examined one by one in the order shown in the table, according to the object of concentration in *ānanda*-accompanied samādhi.

Rapture inherent in the senses. VM (and RY) have given completely erroneous explanations of the cause and nature of the rapture in this samādhi. VM says:

> Because the nature of sattva is illumination—mahat is predominantly sattvic and all the senses are derivatives of mahat—the chitta's expansion (*ābhoga*) in concentration on the sattvic pleasures inherent in the senses is the rapture of this samādhi.

TABLE 1 Objects of Concentration, According to Various Commentators

	Object of Concentration	
Commentators	Ānanda-*accompanied Samādhi*	Asmitā-*accompanied Samādhi*
VM, RY, BM	Rapture inherent in the senses	Puruṣha qualified by ahaṁkāra
VB, BG, NTC	Rapture	Puruṣha both as *jīva* and īśhvara
SS	Mahat with dominant sattva penetrated with a residue of rajas and tamas	Mahat with pure sattva
NTB	Senses	Puruṣha qualified by ahaṁkāra
HA(E)	Rapture experienced in total relaxation of senses and *antaḥ-karaṇa*	Buddhi whose vṛtti is intent upon puruṣha
BR	Ahaṁkāra	Buddhi

While this statement is correct in pointing out the source of the pleasure in the senses, it is absolutely incorrect in suggesting that the object of concentration here might be that pleasure inherent in the senses. VB, in refuting VM's view, points out that such a suggestion confuses this *ānanda*-accompanied samādhi with *sa-vitarka* and *sa-vichāra,* in which the full realization of the nature of senses has already occurred and they have been abandoned as unworthy of pursuit. If the pleasure inherent in the senses were the object of concentration in this samādhi, they would produce the kind of vṛttis in which attraction and aversion are implied. This would—like the *sa-vitarka* and *nir-vitarka* samādhis, and the *sa-vichāra* and *nir-vichāra* samādhis—necessitate two levels in the *ānanda*-accompanied samādhi:

- one with the vṛtti, and then
- a higher one without the vṛtti of the rapture.

Neither Patañjali nor Vyāsa has suggested two divisions of this samādhi, and therefore VM's interpretation is erroneous.

VM, RY and BM, stating the rapture inherent in the senses to be the object of the *ānanda*-accompanied samādhi, consider puruṣha, qualified by ahaṁkāra, to be the object of the *asmitā*-accompanied samādhi.This raises a question about mahat, the first and finest evolute in the order of manifestation and the last to be mastered. If ahaṁkāra, the product of mahat, is the object in the *āsmita*-accompanied samādhi, in what other samādhi would mahat (buddhi) be mastered? Again, in what samādhi would *asmitā* be realized? There are no further samādhis after the *asmitā*-accompanied with any supportive factors (*ālambanas*) or objects of concentration. Nor does this conform to the scheme of apprehension, which for the sake of clarity is repeated here:

- Sixteen *viśheṣhas,* gross objects of apprehension (*grāhya*) in *sa-vitarka*
- Five *a-viśheṣhas,* subtle objects of apprehension (*grāhya*) in *sa-vichāra*
- Ahaṁkāra (the sixth *a-viśheṣha*), the instrument of apprehension (*grahaṇa*) in later stages of *sa-vichāra* and in *sānanda*

- *Liṅga-mātra,* mahat or buddhi, *asmitā,* the agent of apprehension (*grahītṛ*) in *sāsmita*

Rapture alone. This view of VB, BG and NTC does not sufficiently explain the source and nature of the rapture. VB states that the realization of the increase of sattva, as the mind rises to higher grounds in the *vichāra*-accompanied samādhi, is the rapture. According to BG the rapture also consists of the pleasure which is identical to the realization of the general and particular aspects of the objects of the *vichāra*-accompanied samādhi. The same view is supported by NTC. They all include ahaṁkāra and mahat among the objects of *sa-vichāra* samādhi. In this case, again, the *grāhya* and *grahaṇa* become confused. Since *ānanda*-accompanied samādhi has *grahaṇa* as its field, rapture (*hlada*) alone cannot be its object of concentration; an instrument of apprehension like ahaṁkāra must find a place herein.

Mahat. The view held by SS that

> mahat with dominant sattva penetrated with a residue of rajas and tamas is the object in *sānanda,* and mahat with pure sattva is the object in *sāsmita,*

is closer to the truth. However, this view places ahaṁkāra in *sa-vichāra,* which again confuses *grāhya* and *grahaṇa.* Since buddhi or mahat forming *asmitā* is the true agent of apprehension (*grahītṛ*) and *grahītṛ* is the field of *sāsmita* samādhi, it cannot be the object of concentration in *sānanda,* which holds *grahaṇa*—ahaṁkāra—as its field.

Senses alone. The objections presented to oppose the view that rapture inherent in the senses is the object of concentration in *sānanda* apply equally to the view of NTB that senses alone are the object. Furthermore, NTB's view that puruṣha qualified by ahaṁkāra is the object of concentration in *sāsmita* samādhi is untenable because it presents ahaṁkāra as *grahītṛ,* whereas it is actually buddhi among the evolutes that unites with the reflection of puruṣha to produce *asmitā,* the true *grahītṛ.* Moreover, NTB's view is incorrect because (*a*) puruṣha, being immutable, cannot be qualified, and (*b*) it could not in any case be qualified by ahaṁkāra at all because purușha has no direct contact with ahaṁkāra in the universally accepted Sāṅkhya scheme below:

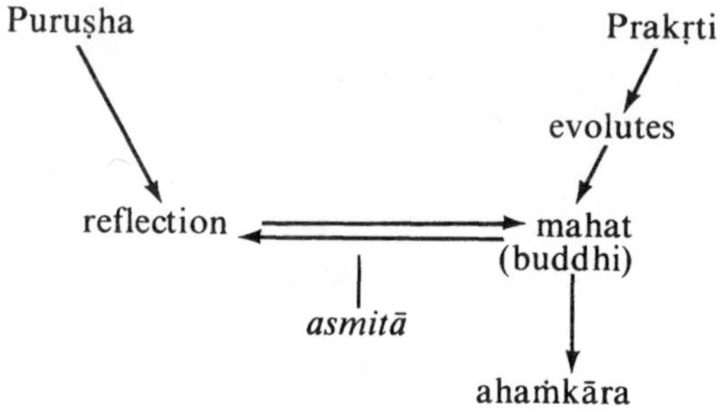

Asmitā, the composite sentience, is produced by the union of purușha's reflection with mahat (buddhi). Ahaṁkāra is a product of mahat and can have no direct contact with purușha. That being the case, how can purușha be qualified by ahaṁkāra?

Rapture of relaxation. HA(E) has presented the view that the rapture arises from the feeling of relaxation in the five active senses, the five cognitive senses and the three constituents of the inner senses: *manas,* ahaṁkāra and buddhi. There is no doubt experientially that such is the case, but this view confuses the careful classification scheme of apprehension related to these samādhis and therefore remains incomplete with regard to the *ānanda*-accompanied samādhi. His statement, however, that the object of concentration in the *asmitā*-accompanied samādhi is buddhi intent upon purușha is absolutely correct.

Ahaṁkāra. Similarly BR's view that ahaṁkāra is the object in *sānanda* and buddhi in *sāsmita* is what we have accepted. However, BR errs in a different direction from the other commentators in defining *ānanda.* He seems to consider the pleasure of this samādhi to be the attribute of consciousness (*chiti-śhakti*) which is without guṇas. BR says:

> When (concentration on the) sattva of the *antaḥ-karaṇa* somewhat penetrated by a residue of rajas and tamas is cultivated (*bhāvyate*), then, there being no guṇas in the *chiti-śhakti,* the

> excellence of its essence (sattva), whose nature is pleasure and illumination, being cultivated, is called the *ānanda*-accompanied samādhi.

The entire statement seems self-contradictory. If the concentration is still on the sattva of the *antaḥ-karaṇa,* then the pure consciousness (*chiti-śhakti*) has not yet been realized. Furthermore, sattva, whose nature is pleasure and illumination, is a part of prakṛti and not an attribute of *chiti-śhakti.* The reader can stretch the statement somewhat and read it to mean that one is now closer to *chiti-śhakti,* whose own bliss (*sukha,* pleasure in the case of the sattva guṇa) and illumination have begun to penetrate the sattva of the inner sense, causing the excellence of the latter's pleasure and illumination to expand, thus overcoming the residue of rajas and tamas. In any case BR's comment suggests that in the *ānanda*-accompanied samādhi sattva is still somewhat alloyed with a trace of rajas and tamas.

V. Ahaṁkāra and Asmitā

Some commentators (e.g., BR) consider *asmitā* to be the counterpart of the ahaṁkāra evolute in Sāṅkhya philosophy, but they are mistaken. Ahaṁkāra has been left behind in the *ānanda*-accompanied samādhi. The "samādhi of rapture" has been completed, in which the concentration on the ahaṁkāra evolute has been accomplished. If *asmitā* and ahaṁkāra were at all identical, there would be no possibility of the *asmitā*-accompanied samādhi.

Like many other commentators of the *Yoga-sūtras,* BR insists upon maintaining the identity of ahaṁkāra and *asmitā* but divides them by function, saying:

> The identity of ahaṁkāra and *asmitā* should not be doubted. Where the inner sense (*antaḥ-karaṇa*) referring to itself as "I" (*aham*) apprehends the objects of experience, it is called ahaṁkāra. When the mind-field is turned inwards in the process of the dissolution of the evolutes and in it a mere reflection of "presence," "existence," appears, that is called *asmitā.*

While it is accurate that ahaṁkāra is outward-going towards the mind, the senses and the objects of the senses and that *asmitā* is an inward process that occurs in the inner face of buddhi, there still cannot be an identity of ahaṁkāra and *asmitā*. *Asmitā* occurs in mahat, which is subtler than its product, ahaṁkāra.

VM also equates *asmitā* with ahaṁkāra, even though in Sāṅkhya the senses are an evolute of ahaṁkāra, not of mahat. VM says:

> Senses are products of *asmitā*. Therefore *asmitā* is their subtler form. That buddhi unified with the self (ātman) is referred to as the "perception of a unified self."

Here he confuses buddhi with ahaṁkāra. The criticism directed at BR also applies to VM in this regard.

Vyāsa uses the term *asmitā* clearly as the equivalent of ahaṁkāra on *YS* II.19. Yet it is shown above in the present sūtra that ahaṁkāra is the object of concentration in the *ānanda*-accompanied samādhi, and mahat is the object of concentration in the *asmitā*-accompanied samādhi. This seeming contradiction will be resolved in the discussion on Sūtra II.19. The definition of *asmitā* given here is accurate for the purposes of the present sūtra.

VI. Sāsmita Samādhi

Having fully realized ahaṁkāra in *sānanda* samādhi, the yogi sees the flaws of the guṇas present therein (NB). He therefore develops distaste and dispassion (*vairāgya*) towards the powers over matter (*siddhis*) and moves to the yet higher ground of the *asmitā*-accompanied samādhi. Just as the products among the evolutes are gradually dissolved into subtler and yet subtler causes, ahaṁkāra dissolves into mahat, the universal and individual buddhi, the evolute called intelligence. Since

- all the coarser evolutes have been dissolved, and
- mahat is the first evolute of prakṛti,

it has no other object of concentration but itself. It is *liṅga-mātra,* a bare presence, 'the first sign' that prakṛti gives of its presence. The principle of convergence and unification of the object and the agent of concentration (pp. 226-27) reaches its finest dimension here. Vyāsa says:

The perception of a unified self is I-am-ness (*asmitā*).

Since the inner face of buddhi is the most sattvic, purest part of the evolutes of prakṛti, it is closest to the consciousness principle. The rays of the consciousness principle reflect in buddhi as into a clear crystal. They are amalgamated like a piece of white marble thrown into milk, or milk poured into a clear, marble cup (RS). It is here and nowhere else that puruṣha and prakṛti meet. Just as the sun seen in a mirror is not really the sun and is not affected by the flaws in and the colours of the mirror in which its reflection is seen, so also puruṣha is not affected by its reflection in the buddhi. It is here in the union of the reflected ray and buddhi that ignorance and bondage begins and ends, a process with which puruṣha has no association. This is the primary constituent of the "person"; all else are its projections, adjuncts and instruments. Here the person first says "I am." (This I-am-ness is *asmitā*.) "I am this conditioned, delimited being, a composite of spirit and matter" (VB, VM, RY). In realizing the nature of *asmitā,* one understands it as being the final break between spirit and matter, whereby the two constituents of the composite sentience,

- matter in its finest essence of the sattva of buddhi, and
- the reflection of puruṣha therein,

dissolve their marriage. The phrase "composite sentience" will be used interchangeably with "I-am-ness" to translate the word *asmitā*. (*Asmitā* will be explained in detail under Sūtra II.6.)

Thus the *asmitā*-accompanied samādhi means (SS) the realization of mahat in which sattva is predominant. BR elucidates this by contrasting it with the preceding samādhi as follows: In the *ānanda*-accompanied samādhi, as BR pointed out (p. 236f.), sattva is still somewhat penetrated by residual rajas and tamas. In *asmitā* the rajas and tamas have been completely subdued and only the purity of sattva dominates. With this purity the sattvic inward face of mahat is turned away from its outward-facing evolute, ahaṁkāra or ego. When facing outwards it produces the ego, which in turn produces mind, senses and their objects. When it is turned inwards, the purity of its sattva receives the reflection of puruṣha, because of whose life-force and consciousness channelled through the buddhi all the processes of the personality are initiated and sustained. In the *asmitā*-accompanied samādhi (BR) even this sattva becomes subsidiary (*nyag-bhāva*) and the presence of *chiti-śhakti* is exalted. There is only an awareness of existence (*sattā-mātra*) alone without any conditions, productions, evolutions or devolutions.

We have translated Vyāsa's *eka-ātmikā saṁvit* as "the perception of a united self." The sattvic illumination of the mirror of buddhi and the reflected light of puruṣha are unified in *asmitā.* VB says that the word *eka* 'one' here signifies "only one," that is to say: "Only one, the self (ātman), is its object." He interprets this to mean that in this samādhi there is only one *ālambana,* the mind-field's perception of only the puruṣha, by which one realizes that "I am." As the object of concentration merges with the agent thereof, the agent, mahat or buddhi in this case, sees itself unified with the spiritual self. In this view it is correct that buddhi is seen unified with the spiritual self, but it is incorrect that the pure, unreflected ātman is its object of concentration. Commentators such as VB and NB have erred in stating that in *sāsmita* samādhi one knows "I am thus—thus alone," that there is nothing further to know, and that this is the ultimate ground of realization. Actually the realization of ātman does not begin until *asamprajñāta,* the acognitive samādhi.

In the *asmitā*-accompanied samādhi,

- first the object of concentration is *asmitā* itself.
- When *asmitā* has been examined
  - in all its parts, and
  - as the complete whole,
- its nature is fully realized.

That realization means *viveka-khyāti,* re-cognition of the separateness of buddhi and puruṣha, and of the separateness of puruṣha from the evolutes of prakṛti—mind, body, etc. Puruṣha, the conscious principle, is twofold:

1. the individual *jīva*
2. the universal īśhvara, godhead

Both of these reflect in the buddhi (VB, NB, BG). Of these, first the realization of the *jīva*-self as apart from the false identifications of buddhi occurs. Whereas the conditioned, manifest deity in a pseudo-material visual image is an object of concentration only in the first two samādhis, here the quest for the formless God ensues and an awareness of the presence of the Supreme Self occurs. However, statements by the commentators that the *final* God-realization takes place here are erroneous and at this point they must simply have been carried away to make such stipulations.

This is *grahītṛ-samāpatti;* the field of this samādhi is the agent of all apprehensions (to be explained in Sūtra I.41). Because of the unified awareness, this samādhi also is not divided into *sāsmita* and *nir-asmitā.* Here mahat is finally dissolved into the unmanifest, *a-liṅga* prakṛti. Those who attain this state and consider it to be the final destination are called *prakṛti-laya* yogis. They have dissolved the evolutes into prakṛti but not realized the self or the Self. (For further details see the discussion on Sūtras I.15 and I.19.)

For those who continue further, the ultimate in the *asmitā*-accompanied samādhi is the beginning of *dharma-megha,* the samādhi of the raincloud of virtue and of the knowledge of the nature of all things (*YS* IV.29). The lower dispassion (*apara-vairāgya*) (*YS* I.15) is accomplished and the transcendent *para-vairāgya* (*YS* I.15) commences.

To recapture the four samādhis in the words of Vyāsa:

> There the *vitarka*-conjoint samādhi actually accompanies all four. The second one, with the gross thought (*vitarka*) having been terminated, is accompanied by the subtle thought (*vichāra*). The third one, with the subtle thought having been terminated, is accompanied by ecstasy (*ānanda*). The fourth one, with that ecstasy having been terminated, is merely I-am-ness (*asmitā*). All these samādhis are dependent on, conjoint with, or accompanied by supportive factors.

These samādhis with supportive factors (*sālambana*) are also called seeded (*sa-bīja*) samādhis, which will be explained in *YS* I.46. The terms *sālambana* and *sa-bīja* separate (VM) the samādhi of wisdom (*samprajñāta*) from the acognitive samādhi (*asamprajñāta*), which is seedless (*nir-bīja*), and which will be explained in Sūtra I.51. Of the five states of the mind explained in Sūtra I.1, the samādhi of wisdom constitutes the fourth—*ekāgra,* one-pointed—because it requires objects of one-pointed concentration.

VII. Concentrations on a Deity

The question arises as to whether this methodical and analytical approach is essential in order to prepare the aspirant for *asamprajñāta* samādhi. Is an allowance made for concentration on, devotion to and an uplifting grace from God? What is the guidance given in this matter?

In discussing the matter of godhead, the commentators have mostly expressed their own religious credos and have tried to find a place for it within the scheme of the *Yoga-sūtras* and Vyāsa's commentary. (See *YS* I.23,24 and II.1,32,45.) According to them, the realization of the various aspects or incarnations of the godhead may fall into two categories (NB):

- In one the yogi develops his concentration to such a degree that his expanded consciousness may ascend and project itself to the subtle worlds which are the domains of particular aspects of the godhead.
- In the other the godhead is so pleased by the devotee's *japa* (mental concentration on a mantra) and meditation that he projects an appearance of himself to grant the grace of his descent and presence to the devotee.[16]

As an experiential fact, however, the two cannot be separated. The ascent of the devotee's consciousness is the same as the descent of the divine grace.

As has been stated above, if a devotee's *bhāvanā* is on a par-

16. See the authors' book *God* (Honesdale, Pa.: Himalayan International Institute of Yoga Science and Philosophy, 1979).

ticular deity, it is indeed required that the mind take this same *ālambana* through all the four stages of *samprajñāta* (VB, BG, NB) in the order in which they occur. A failure to maintain this consistency would, for example, mean (NB) repeatedly abandoning one form of deity for worship of another, leading to constant unsteadiness and fickleness of the mind, which is obviously contrary to the pursuit of samādhi.

The order in which the four stages are practised and mastered is important (BG, NB). It is clearly stated, however (BG), that if a yogi makes a spontaneous ascent to a higher ground by the grace of God, he then need not climb methodically and laboriously over the lower steps (BG). Grace, then, is a shortcut which bypasses the method. It must be remembered, however, that when one climbs to a higher plateau through the force of such grace, the lower *siddhis* attendant upon the practice of the earlier steps do not accrue. It is only if for some reason one needs those *siddhis*—even though they are irrelevant to one's spiritual attainment, station and progress—that he may go back down and practise the lower methods (NB)! Although the possibility of such instantaneous realization of a higher state is acknowledged, for the purposes here it is assumed that a method is generally requisite for mental purification and mastery in order that one may become a deserving vessel for grace.

As was mentioned earlier, in the tradition of Patañjali and Vyāsa all objects of concentration are either parts or composites of *grāhya, grahaṇa,* or *grahītṛ*. For example, a candle flame for concentration is part of the fire element. An icon may be considered a composite product of all the five gross elements. The theism of yoga as acknowledged in *YS* I.23-28, II.1,32,45 also encouraged the later commentators to state more clearly that the mental image of *Virāṭ,* the universe-form of God, or the figure of a deity or incarnation is often used as the object of concentration. Even though at first glance these mental images may appear not to be included in the scheme of Patañjali and Vyāsa, the theology of the Purāṇa texts explains that Īśhvara, God, may take forms that appear material to the devotees, even though the energy used for such appearances is actually non-material. From the point of view of a devotee seeking *samprajñāta* samādhi, the form of such a divine manifestation is a visible one, subject to experience with the senses; therefore, concentration on such an image is concentration on the *viśheṣhas*. One begins concentration with mental devotions offered to the deity in manifest forms. Hindus may devote the concentration to figures like Viṣhṇu and Śhiva, Buddhists to the various forms of Buddha, Christians to Christ, and so forth. In Sūtras I.23-29 the subject of devotion to God is explained more elaborately. Here commentators primarily include among the objects of concentration a physical appearance of the divine being or some other cosmic form manifest in the material universe. Neither Patañjali nor Vyāsa has dealt with this form of concentration at this point, so it appears that the concentration here is not on the Supreme Being as the Transcendental Spirit as such but only on those manifestations of Him which are possible among the evolutes which comprise the objects of concentration in the *sa-vitarka* and *sa-vichāra* stages.

It is well to clarify how concentrations on a deity differ in the first and second samādhis. In the discussions on the objects of concentration in *sa-vitarka* the manifestations of Īśhvara are included. In *sa-vichāra,* when a deity is still the object of concentration, the visual image of a pseudo-material form is abandoned and a subtler presence, perhaps with an appearance consisting of the universal *tan-mātrās,* is invoked, to which mental worship is offered.

On the other hand, a *sādhaka* not attracted to such mental images of a deity may begin his concentration on other parts or composites of the *viśheṣhas.* As already mentioned, a single object of concentration used as an *ālambana* begins at the level of a gross form and continues through the various stages of *samprajñāta.*

VIII. The Systems of the Śharīras and the Koṣhas

Before bringing this sūtra to a conclusion, it needs to be shown how the samādhis relate to the systems of the three bodies (*śharīras*) and five sheaths (*koṣhas*) within the composite sentience (*asmitā*). It must be borne in mind, however, that the classifications of the various evolutes and faculties as apportioned among the different bodies and sheaths are not unanimously agreed to and may differ greatly in various texts.

As the light of puruṣha filters down through *asmitā,* the ego process (ahaṁkāra) causes one to mistake puruṣha or ātman, the spiritual self, to be a delimited and mutable being.

- In *ānandamaya koṣha* the self, by nature devoid of the dichotomy of pain and pleasure, is mistaken to be happy or unhappy, suffering pain or enjoying pleasure.
- In *vijñānamaya koṣha* an assumption of delimited knowledge and ignorance accrues.
- In *manomaya koṣha* the processes of mentation are attributed to the self.
- In *prāṇamaya koṣha* the self is thought to be the agent of actions.
- In *annamaya koṣha* a mortal personality, passing through various physical states, is erroneously identified as the self.

As the process of samādhi advances, the assumptions of false identifications with each sheath are dropped and gradual freedom from mortality, action, mentation, ignorance, pain and bondage is achieved. One is sequentially freed from each level of assumed bondage. This is the wisdom (*prajñā*) of the samādhi of wisdom (*samprajñāta*). In the acognitive (*asamprajñāta*) samādhi the final enlightenment occurs.

TABLE 2 Samādhis in the Three Bodies

Samādhi	*Supportive Factor* (Ālambana)	*Body*
asmitā-accompanied	*asmitā* (mahat; higher buddhi)	causal (*kāraṇa śharīra* or *liṅga śharīra*)
ānanda-accompanied	lower buddhi ego (ahaṁkāra)	
vichāra-accompanied	subtle elements	subtle (*sūkṣhma śharīra*)
vitarka-accompanied	mind subtle senses *prāṇas* external senses five gross elements	gross (*sthūla śharīra*)

TABLE 3 Samādhis in the Five *Koṣhas* (Sheaths)

Koṣha *(Sheath)*	*Supportive Factor (*Ālambana*)*	*Samādhi*
anandamaya (bliss)	*asmitā* (mahat; higher buddhi)	*asmitā*-accompanied
vijñānamaya (knowledge)	lower buddhi ego	*ānanda*-accompanied
manomaya (mind)	subtle elements mind	*vichāra*-accompanied
prāṇamaya (*prāṇa*)	subtle senses *prāṇas*	*vitarka*-accompanied
annamaya (food)	gross elements gross senses	

TABLE 4 Composite Interrelationships

Causative Schema

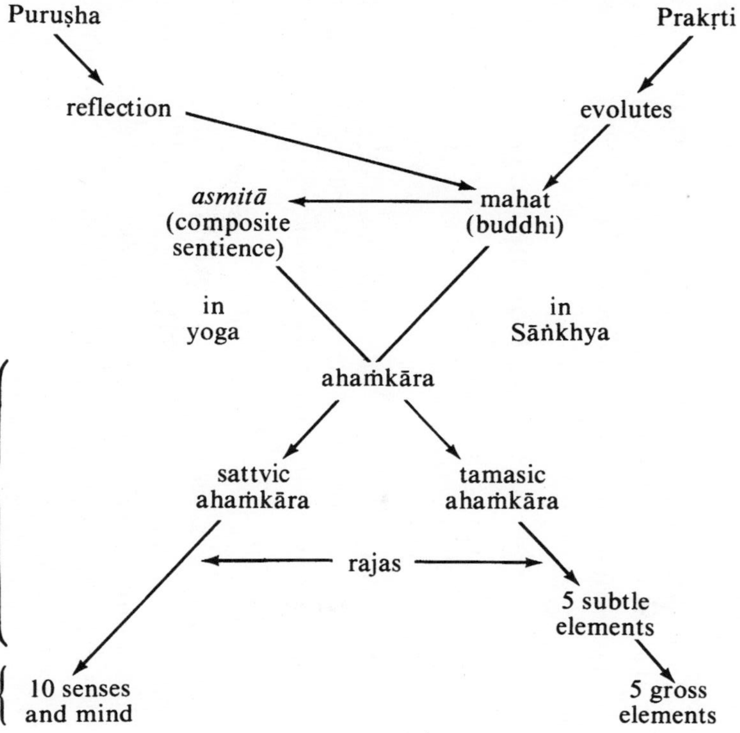

YS Classification	*Causative Schema*	*Field of Concentration*	*Samādhi*
liṅga-mātra	*asmitā* (composite sentience) ← mahat (buddhi)	*grahītṛ* →	*asmitā*-accompanied
6 *a-viśheṣhas*	ahaṁkāra	*grahaṇa* →	*ānanda*-accompanied
	sattvic ahaṁkāra; tamasic ahaṁkāra; rajas		
	5 subtle elements	*grāhya* →	*vichāra*-accompanied
16 *viśheṣhas*	10 senses and mind; 5 gross elements	*grāhya* →	*vitarka*-accompanied

Sūtra I.18 विरामप्रत्ययाभ्यासपूर्वः संस्कारशेषोऽन्यः।

virāma-pratyayābhyāsa-pūrvaḥ saṁskāra-śheṣho'nyaḥ

virāma-: cessation
pratyaya-: cognition principle, cognition, causal principle
abhyāsa-: practice
pūrvaḥ: preceded by, having as a prerequisite
saṁskāra-śheṣhaḥ: leaving its saṁskāra as residue
anyaḥ: the other

(*Asamprajñāta*) is the other (samādhi), having as its prerequisite the practice of the cognition and causal principle of cessation and leaving its saṁskāra as residue.

Vyāsa's Commentary

Now, what are the means to the acognitive samādhi (*asamprajñāta*) and what is its nature?

> [*Sūtra:*] (*Asamprajnāta*) is the other (samādhi), having as its prerequisite the practice of the cognition and causal principle of cessation and leaving its saṁskāra as residue.

When all the vṛttis of the mind-field have submerged and only the saṁskāras remain as a residue, such control (*nirodha*) is the acognitive (*asamprajñāta*) samādhi. [Or: When all the vṛttis have ceased, the control (*nirodha*) wherein only the saṁskāras remain as a residue is the samādhi of the mind-field called the acognitive (*asamprajñāta*).]

The means thereof is the transcendent dispassion (*para-vairāgya*); the practice with supportive factors (*ālambanas*) is not efficacious as a means of achieving it. Therefore the awareness of cessation, devoid of object, is used as the supportive factor, and it is without a substance, without interest[17] or purpose.

Preceded by such a practice, the mind-field which is without a

17. BB translates *artha-śhūnva* as "devoid of interests."

supportive factor becomes as though it has reached a state of non-being (*abhāva*). This is the seedless (*nir-bīja*), acognitive (*asam-prajñāta*) samādhi.

Discussion

This sūtra continues with the definitions of samādhis. Going back to the last two of the samādhis of wisdom:

- In the *ānanda*-accompanied samādhi the mind's identification was, "I am happy."
- In the *asmitā*-accompanied samādhi, the mind's identification with its vṛtti of puruṣha's reflection falling into mahat or buddhi was simply, "I am."

These thoughts are also supports (*ālambanas*) for the mind. So long as these vṛttis remain, dispassion (*vairāgya*) has not yet transcended the lower limitations of prakṛti, and the highest samādhi is not reached. This sūtra presupposes two questions:

1. What are the means to attain the acognitive samādhi?
2. What is the nature of this samādhi?

The first compound phrase in the sūtra, *virāma-pratyaya-abhyāsa-pūrvaḥ,* answers the first question, and the remainder of the sūtra (a phrase and a word), *saṁskāra-śheṣhaḥ anyaḥ,* answers the second question (VM). Or we may surmise that (VB)

- the first phrase explains the means (*upāya*),
- the second phrase defines (*lakṣhaṇa*), and
- the last word names the state aimed for (*lakṣhya*).

First let us take part of the phrase *virāma-pratyaya-abhyāsa-pūrvaḥ*. This is explained in different ways:

- (VM) *Virāma* is the absence of all vṛttis. The awareness which is its cause is *virāma-pratyaya.*
- (VB) That even the vṛtti may cease, such an awareness is *virāma-pratyaya.* The transcendent dispassion says even to the wisdom

of *samprajñāta,* "Enough!" ("Let even the disturbance of such knowledge come to pacification.") Such an awareness is *virāma-pratyaya.*

- (HA) *Virāma* itself is the causal awareness of the absence of all cognition. This transcendent dispassion itself is *virāma-pratyaya.*
- (BR, AD) That by means of which one reaches cessation, that is, one abandons all concern with *vitarka* and such supports, is in itself (as the causal cognition) *virāma-pratyaya.*
- (BG) That even the vṛtti signified as the knowledge of reality may cease—this is *virāma-pratyaya.*
- (SS) Even the effort to turn the vṛttis off (*uparama*) is *virāma-pratyaya.*

The practice of *virāma-pratyaya* means constantly, repeatedly, entering into that awareness (VM, VB). The process of *virāma-pratyaya-abhyāsa* is establishing it again and again into the mind-field (BR, AD, BG, SS). It is brought to perfection when even the vṛtti "I am" from *asmitā* is abandoned (HA). In other words, whatever vṛtti arises in the mind is rejected as

neti, neti: not this, not this.

The phrase "preceded by such a practice" means that this cessation is the prerequisite of the acognitive samādhi. This samādhi is characterised by the presence of residual saṁskāras only (*saṁskāra-śheṣha*).

We have translated a single sentence of Vyāsa in two ways:

- When all the vṛttis of the mind-field have submerged and only the saṁskāras remain as a residue, such control (*nirodha*) is the acognitive (*asamprajñāta*) samādhi.

Or

- When all the vṛttis have ceased, the control (*nirodha*) wherein only the saṁskāras remain as a residue is the samādhi of the mind-field called the acognitive (*asamprajñāta*).

Both clauses, "vṛttis of the mind-field have submerged" and "vṛttis have ceased," are renderings for the image produced by the original word, *pratyastamaye.* That is, they have set like the sun into the very source from which they had arisen.

While the main intent of both possible translations of the complete sentence appears to be the same, the most important difference in the second translation is in the phrase "samādhi of the mind-field." Actually, *samprajñāta* is a samādhi of the mind-field and *asamprajñāta* is not. *Asamprajñāta* is only the self dwelling in the self. This was made clear in Sūtra I.3 and will be further clarified in the fourth chapter of *YS.* This sūtra, however, only seems to contrast *asamprajñāta* with the *samprajñāta* of the preceding sūtra by indicating not the nature of self in *asamprajñāta* but what happens to the mind-field *after samprajñāta:* simply that it receives *nirodha*-saṁskāras.

In the second translation, therefore, "samādhi of the mind-field" does not mean *samādhi* in the sense in which we generally use the term; rather, the word *samādhi* in this instance signifies the derivative meaning from *sam-ā-dhā,* that is, "harmonizing all conflict, bringing together of all contrastive factors" so that the juxtaposition between the mind and its supports (*ālambanas*) also ceases. Vyāsa says:

> The means thereof is the transcendent dispassion (*para-vairāgya*); the practice with supportive factors (*ālambanas*) is not efficacious as a means of achieving it.

It was explained earlier in Sūtra I.5 that the saṁskāras themselves produce vṛttis, which in turn feed the saṁskāras. It was also explained that saṁskāras are the dormant form of vṛttis and that vṛttis are the operative form of saṁskāras. When the vṛttis are brought totally under control and are pacified, they are no longer fed into the saṁskāras. The saṁskāras cease to produce the operations of vṛttis but simply lie as inoperative residue. The progressive stages of the mind-field are as follows (BR):

- *vyutthāna:* absence of concentration, as in *kṣhipta* and *mūḍha* (see Sūtra I.1., p. 78)
- *samādhi-prārambha:* the beginnings of samādhi, as in *vikṣhipta*

(ibid.) when sāttva gains ascendancy
- *ekāgratā:* one-pointedness
- *nirodha:* total control

The saṁskāras of *vyutthāna,* worldly activity and stupefaction, are brought under control as the saṁskāras of the next stage (the beginnings of samādhi, however distracted) are nurtured. The saṁskāras of this second stage are replaced by those of one-pointedness. Even the one-pointed vṛtti must be pacified when final *nirodha* gains strength. When total *nirodha* has occurred in the acognitive samādhi, the transcendent dispassion produces no saṁskāras other than its own imprints on the mind. The mind has now left the neighborhood of the world and has begun to dwell close to the spiritual self. All the former saṁskāras have been replaced by those of *nirodha.* There being no next stage after this, no other saṁskāras can replace the *nirodha*-saṁskāras, which then remain as the residue.

We read from Vyāsa:

> The practice with supportive factors (*ālambanas*) is not efficacious as a means of achieving it. Therefore the awareness of cessation, devoid of object, is used as the supportive factor, and it is without a substance, without interest or purpose.

This awareness is practised under two conditions:

During samādhi.
During ordinary involvement in the world.

One constantly bears in mind that worldly phenomena and relationships are not conducive to samādhi. While performing all the necessary duties of the world, the yogi continues to turn the awareness of the self on the self until the mind's ordinary saṁskāras become so weakened that samādhi is integrated with the wakeful state. Up to this time it is interrupted constantly by the world but now, even remaining open to the world, the yogi finds repose in an uninterrupted samādhi. Such an awareness must be diligently cultivated by whittling away the saṁskāras of objects, even of the objects of concentration.

It must be borne in mind that between *samprajñāta* and *asamprajñāta* comes *dharma-megha,* the samādhi of the raincloud of virtue and of the knowledge of the nature of all things. It is both

- the higher stage of the *asmitā*-accompanied, and
- the initial stage of the acognitive (*asamprajñāta*).

This will be more clearly defined in *YS* IV.29. (VM) It cannot be reached with supportive factors (*ālambanas*) of the preceding samādhis. The lower *vairāgya* cannot lead to it. A cause and its effect must be homogeneous. The lower dispassion needs some objects of concentration to lead to the lower samādhi. *Dharma-megha* samādhi is described (VM) as arising from that state of buddhi in which rajas and tamas have been completely washed off and the objects of buddhi are transcended. It is the endless state wherein the yogi perceives worldly objects as totally unworthy of attention and, abandoning them, he dwells only in his own essential nature. Thus, denying all supports, *dharma-megha* serves as the supportless (*nirālambana*) acognitive samādhi.

(VB) Mere one-pointedness can never produce such a state. There is no object, short of puruṣha's own abiding in his own nature, that can lead to the acognitive samādhi. Even buddhi's vṛtti with regard to the nature of puruṣha, as experienced in *asmitā,* must cease. To all such knowledge it must say, "Enough!" At this point it seems Vyāsa's intent to say that the objectlessness becomes the object of concentration. Whatever vṛtti arises in the mind is negated by *neti, neti:* that is, "This is not the self, this is not the self." The mind is thus left behind and puruṣha's pure awareness is turned inwards.

Vyāsa says:

> Preceded by such a practice, the mind-field which is without a supportive factor becomes as though it has reached a state of non-being (*abhāva*).

The mind has not ceased to exist. But

- because its vṛttis have become inoperative, its presence is not noticeable;
- the awareness of spiritual self is so centered in the self that the mind is no longer being used.

The yogi's mind and body appear to have died. The lower awareness has ceased. The mind is now truly objectless. One might think that the mind was in a state of sleep; however, the word *abhāva* 'non-being' used here reminds the reader of the definition of sleep in Sūtra I.10:

> Sleep is the modification or operation of the mind-field resorting to the cognition principle of absence or negation and to the cause thereof.

In Sūtra I.10 it was made clear that sleep is tamasic, whereas samādhi is beyond the guṇas. However, the yogi may often resort to the *abhāva* of vṛttis in the mind for his rest rather than subject himself to the tamas of ordinary sleep. This *abhāva*-like state of the mind, known to the Buddhist tradition as "no-mind," is the true *nirodha*. Its saṁskāras completely transform the nature of the yogi's mind.

The purpose of the *nirodha*-saṁskāra remaining even as a residue in the mind is so that the yogi may be able to get up from samādhi (NB, BG) when he chooses and attend to simple bodily needs in order to maintain his physical presence and thereby help the world. He maintains total control over his mind so that he may continue to use it as an instrument in the world. In this aspect also *nirodha* means control, as all of the yogi's personality systems are operated by his yoga (*yoga-yantrita*) (NB).

Vyāsa says:

> This is the seedless, acognitive, samādhi.

The term "seedless" (*nir-bija*) will be explained further in Sūtra I.51, but here it may be understood to mean that, there being no further objects in the mind, the saṁskāras can no longer produce vṛttis, *kleśhas,* karmas, and consequent cycles. (BG, NB) This presence of the *nirodha*-saṁskāras remains in the mind so long as the yogi is embodied because the spiritual self needs a mind to operate the body. When the spiritual self is disembodied and dwells in total liberation (*mokṣha*), all dependence on material evolutes, including the mind-field, is dissolved, and there are not even *nirodha*-saṁskāras. This is the meaning of Vyāsa's statement *artha-śhūnyaḥ,* which has been translated as "without a substance, without interest or purpose." The spiritual self is freed of contact with all delimiting "substantiality." Self has no more "interest" in prakṛti, which has already served its "purpose" (*puruṣhārtha*) and withdrawn. The seeds of ignorance have been burnt in the fire of realization. [18]

18. We strongly recommend to the student that he add to his reading on this sūtra from the commentary in English by Swami Hariharānanda Āraṇya, *Yoga Philosophy of Patañjali* (Calcutta: University of Calcutta, 1977).

Sūtra I.19 भवप्रत्ययो विदेहप्रकृतिलयानाम्।

bhava-pratyayo videha-prakṛti-layānām

bhava-pratyayaḥ: (the samādhi) of causal cognition of being, at (re)birth
videha-: (of) *videha,* bodiless, yogis, and
prakṛti-layānām: of the *prakṛti-laya* yogis, those who have merged (the awareness) into prakṛti

The samādhi of the bodiless (*videha*) yogis and of those who have merged into prakṛti (*prakṛti-layas*) is called *bhava-pratyaya,* the samādhi of the causal cognition of being. [Or: Samādhi naturally experienced at rebirth comes to the *videha* and *prakṛti-laya* yogis. Or: *Bhava-pratyaya,* the samādhi of the causal cognition of being, accrues to the bodiless (*videhas*) and to the prakṛti-dissolved (*prakṛti-layas*).]

Vyāsa's Commentary

Now this samādhi is indeed of two kinds:

- *upāya-pratyaya:* the causal cognition of which develops from method
- *bhava-pratyaya:* the causal cognition of which develops into the continuity of worldly being and at (re)birth

Of these, *upāya-pratyaya* accrues to the yogis, and

[*Sūtra:*] *bhava-pratyaya* accrues to the bodiless (*videhas*) and to the prakṛti-dissolved (*prakṛti-layas*).

Bhava-pratyaya samādhi is (the experience) of the bodiless shining gods (*videha devas*). Their mind-field using only its saṁskāras, they experience what only appears to be the state of absolute isolation (*kaivalya*). They carry over the same kind of maturation and fruition (*vipāka*) of the saṁskāras.

Similarly when the mind-field is still active in its domain and is merged into prakṛti, the *prakṛti-layas* experience what only appears like the state of absolute isolation (*kaivalya*), and then only until the mind, active in its domain, returns again (into re-incarnation).

Discussion

The state of the *videhas* and the *prakṛti-layas* was discussed in Sūtras I.15 and I.17. In this sūtra we encounter a very special problem. The sūtra follows the one on the acognitive (*asamprajñāta*) samādhi, which has been described as

- *nirodha*-samādhi: the samādhi of total control and final cessation of vṛttis, and
- *nir-bīja:* seedless, so that the saṁskāras can no longer produce *kleṣhas,* karmas, and their fruition.

Yet Sūtra I.19 appears to indicate that the seedless final samādhi of the last sūtra is further subdivided into

- *upāya-pratyaya* of the true yogis, and
- *bhava-pratyaya* of the *videhas* and *prakṛti-layas.*

However, *bhava-pratyaya* samādhi described by Vyāsa does not match the descriptions of the seedless, acognitive, *nirodha*-samādhi. A second look at the definitions and explanations already presented on the *videhas* and *prakṛti-layas* clearly shows that

- the *videhas* stop at *ānanda*-accompanied samādhi, and
- the *prakṛti-layas* stop at *asmitā*-accompanied samādhi.

It is not possible that the samādhi of *videhas* and *prakṛti-layas* could be a division of *asamprajñāta,* yet with the exception of BR and AD all the commentators have considered *upāya-pratyaya* and *bhava-pratyaya* to be so. It is inconceivable that a yogi who has already reached *asamprajñāta* now needs to develop the methods (*upāyas*) to be described in Sūtra I.20. It is further inconceivable that one in *asamprajñāta* still has the mind active in its domain, causing re-incarnation! It is obvious that these commentators have failed to establish proper connection among the sūtras:

Sūtra 17 describes *samprajñāta* samādhi.
Sūtra 18 points out that there is another (*anyaḥ*) samādhi (*asamprajñāta*).
Sūtras 19-50 continue on the topic of *samprajñāta* with intermittent secondary references to *asamprajñāta* where relevant.
Sūtra 51 finally returns to the topic of *asamprajñāta*.

In other words, Sūtras 17 and 18 list the two kinds of samādhi. Then the following sūtra explains the first one on the list, *samprajñāta*. Only when that one has been explained is the second one dealt with, in Sūtra 20. The commentators have erroneously applied Sūtra 19 to qualifying the second topic on the list. Only BR and AD imply that Sūtra 19 follows 17. BR says:

> *Videhas* and *prakṛti-layas* have been explained in the sūtra dealing with *vitarka* and so forth. Their samādhi is *bhava-pratyaya*, a samādhi the causal cognition of which is of the worldly being (*bhāva*) of *saṁsāra*. They are yet confined to worldly power (*adhimātra*) in the cycle of *saṁsāra*. They are qualified to attain only a samādhi of a like kind. Because they are unable to see the supreme reality, this samādhi of theirs is merely a semblance of yoga. Therefore, one who seeks liberation should with great exertion strive for the knowledge of the supreme reality and cultivate it in meditation.

This indeed is the true intent of Patañjali and Vyāsa. All the commentators excepting BR and AD have produced confused arguments trying to fit *upāya-pratyaya* and *bhava-pratyaya* samādhis into *asamprajñāta*. They all in one way or another confirm especially *bhava-pratyaya* not to be yoga proper. It is not necessary to present their divergent views, and only a summary of what is acceptable in the light of what has been established above will be given.

Right from the beginning of one's practice one needs to avoid erroneous philosophical views such as those that fall into the category of *vikalpa* (Sūtra I.9) and confusion of philosophies (*bhrānti-darśhana*) (Sūtra I.30); otherwise one is prone to fall into philosophical complacencies (*tuṣhṭis*) (see *TSS* 15), which are elaborated by NTC as follows:

- Everything happens from nature or matter (prakṛti), and if only I realize all the modes of its evolution, I will be liberated.
- The householders cannot attain liberation; renunciation by becoming a monk will give me liberation.
- Everything happens in its own time; thus time will give me liberation.
- Everything is predestined; I'll be liberated when it is my destiny to be so.

When one holds such erroneous views from the very beginning, the ground is laid for stopping one's spiritual practice at the state of *videhas* and *prakṛti-layas.*

The Videhas

The word *videha* means "bodiless," that is to say:

- While yet embodied, the *videhas* have eliminated identification with all evolutes—from the five gross elements that constitute the physical body, up to ahaṁkāra.
- When they depart from the body, they remain bodiless, achieving the status of *videha devas:* 'the bodiless shining ones'.

As was seen in Sūtras I.15 and I.17, the status of *videha* accrues only upon reaching the *ānanda*-accompanied samādhi. Here the *siddhis* of the subtle worlds made up of the six *a-viśheṣhas* are mastered. When one conquers a higher peak, it is understood that one has climbed the lower peaks also. The *videhas* are not merely masters of ahaṁkāra and the rapture of the third *samprajñāta:* they have under their command the lower pleasures also. Without needing a physical body the *videhas* may yet control all (*a*) gross and subtle elements, (*b*) senses and their powers, (*c*) subtle celestial essences of fragrances, etc., and, of course, (*d*) ahaṁkāra. In the subtle worlds they become masters of the rapturous and ecstatic pleasures of celestial fragrances, flavours, sights, forms, lights and visions, tactile sensations and incomparable music.

We can explain *bhava-pratyaya* in five ways:

1. The cause of the *videhas'* cognition of these rapturous conditions is their continued involvement with *bhāva,* the existence

limited to evolutes of prakṛti which maintain *saṁsāra*.

2. Their actual experience is also not spiritual but of *bhāva*, delimited material existence.
3. The result of this cognition is their continued involvement in the *saṁsāra* cycle. They are reborn after a time.
4. Upon birth they naturally remember the samādhi they had already attained.
5. But they are still bound to ignorance (*avidyā*) as both the cause and the content of worldly continuity (*bhava*).

All of these five explanations are implicit in the compound phrase *bhava-pratyaya*.

Vyāsa says:

> Now this samadhi is indeed of two kinds:
>
> - *upāya-pratyaya:* the causal cognition of which develops from method
> - *bhava-pratyaya:* the causal cognition of which develops into the continuity of worldly being and at (re)birth

Thus, samādhi may be attained in two ways:

1. By the practice of a method.
2. By birth as a result of saṁskāras continuing from previous lives.

Further, Vyāsa says:

> Of these, *ūpaya-pratyaya* accrues to the yogis, and
>
> [*Sūtra:*] *bhava-pratyaya* accrues to the bodiless (*videhas*) and to the prakṛti-dissolved (*prakṛti-layas*).
>
> *Bhava-pratyaya* samādhi is (the experience) of the bodiless shining gods (*videha devas*). Their mind-field using only its saṁskāras, they experience what only appears to be the state of absolute isolation (*kaivalya*). They carry over the same kind of maturation and fruition (*vipāka*) of the saṁskāras.

Samādhi gained by the observance of method is the subject of the next sūtra. Here the concern is with the *videhas* and *prakṛti-layas*, whose samādhi is *bhava-pratyaya*. The mind of the *videhas* is not occupied with external objects but uses past saṁskāras. This is implicit in the phrase *sva-saṁskāra-mātra-upayoga*.

Some readings of the text change *upayoga* to *upabhoga*, which expresses that such yogis enjoy only their saṁskāras. In such a mind involved with past saṁskāras, the fresh saṁskāras formed are those of the samādhi of one-pointed concentration. Their concentration on these objects continues to bind them and produces like saṁskāras. Here the fact of the pacification of other vṛttis constitutes the experience of samādhi. The fact that unmatured saṁskāras are still active keeps such yogis from the purest samādhi. Because of the rapture of their experience and the vast time scales of their subtle, celestial plane of existence, they think they have reached absolute isolation (*kaivalya*), which is the true goal of yoga. Because saṁskāras of the elements, senses and subtle, rapturous enjoyments keep becoming stronger, they need to go through the death process and attain the state of *devas*, celestial shining ones or angelic beings without physical bodies composed of gross elements. While in that celestial station they continue to maintain mastery over the world of subtle senses and enjoy the rapturous experiences of subtle, celestial fragrances; flavours; forms, visions and lights; tactile sensations; sounds and music; and the works of ego and cosmic power.

However benevolent, they are delimited and not one with the infinite. Vyāsa uses the verb *ati-vāhayanti* 'they carry over'. It suggests that these yogis maintain their *ātivāhika śharīras*, their subtle bodies, as vehicles of migration in which the saṁskāras continue to be maintained. It is the force of these saṁskāras that determines the mode and the place of their rebirth (country, parentage, condition, and so forth). No matter under which condition they are born, they do not have to make an effort to learn the ways of samādhi. What they had already attained comes naturally to them, but since theirs was not a seedless (*nir-bīja*) samādhi, they must bear the fruition of the remaining saṁskāras (per *YS* II.13) while progressing further on the path of samādhi.

The Prakṛti-Layas

Vyāsa says:

> Similarly when the mind-field is still active in its domain and is merged into prakṛti, the *prakṛti-layas* experience what only appears like the state of absolute isolation (*kaivalya*), and then only until the mind, active in its domain, returns again (into re-incarnation).

The mind of the *prakṛti-layas* is still active in its domain, continuing with its *adhikāra* (which was discussed under Sūtra I.5). The *prakṛti-layas* have accomplished *asmitā*-accompanied samādhi. The chitta in its mahat or buddhi aspect has reached the finest evolute and has touched prakṛti. There appears to be nothing further to attain at this point. The *sādhaka* does not realize, without a guru, that this actually is not the end. The constituents of the material personality have been dissolved into their causes, but at this point the direction of meditation changes. There are no objects. The spiritual self must now turn towards itself. However, if this direction does not become clear and the proper guidance is not available or accepted, the yogi takes this point to be the end. His mind-field touches unconscious prakṛti. It finds an absence of consciousness there, reaching the samādhi of the unconscious (*jaḍa*-samādhi). Just as the awareness had progressively identified itself with the various evolutes, it now identifies with prakṛti. All the other vṛttis have been eliminated, but *avidyā* is not yet conquered. These yogis dwell in the causal body (*liṅga śharīra*), which consists of mahat alone.

While the *videhas* control various evolutes in the cosmos, *prakṛti-layas* are beyond that cosmic consciousness. They are involved only with unevolved prakṛti, from which (like the sage Viśhvāmitra) they may create their own universes over which they are as Brahmā, the creator, with *devas* under their control. However, this state of godhood is yet not supreme consciousness. Their ignorance is still a type of *viparyaya* (Sūtra I.8), and they still need to purify themselves beyond the desire to control prakṛti and to create universes. The cosmic ego must also be dissolved. To do this they must again incarnate as human beings and practise *asamprajñāta* samādhi. Upon rebirth they also, like the *videhas,* remember the practice of samādhi and can proceed to *asamprajñāta.*

Both the *videhas* and *prakṛti-layas*—sometimes together referred to as "the shining ones bound to action (*karma-devas*)"—are called *taushṭikas* in the Sāṅkhya system. They have experienced *tushṭi,* a feeling of satisfaction while yet short of the goal. (For details see *TSS* 15 and *Sāṅkhya-kārikā* 47, 50.) Neither the *prakṛti-laya* nor the *videha* is considered to be a yogi proper by Vyāsa. Only those who go into *asamprajñāta* are to be considered true yogis.

How long do these *videhas* and *prakṛti-layas* remain in their particular station? We paraphrase the answer (VM, VB) from *Vāyu-purāṇa:*

- Those who have become masters of concentration on the senses dwell at their station as *videhas* for the duration of ten Manu-intervals, the masters of elements for a hundred, and the masters of ego for a full thousand.
- Those who have mastered buddhi dwell there free of fever for ten thousand Manu-intervals, and those who contemplate the unmanifest prakṛti stay for a hundred thousand. After reaching purusha, who is beyond the guṇas, there is no further measure of time.

The commentators suggest that the order of sūtras here follows the maxim of the needle and the cauldron. If one has to clean both, it is expedient to take first the smaller and easier object, the needle, and then go on to cleaning the cauldron. The sūtra on *bhava-pratyaya* came first, by that maxim, and now we come to the sūtra on *upāya-pratyaya* samādhi.

Sūtra I.20 **श्रद्धावीर्यस्मृतिसमाधिप्रज्ञापूर्वक इतरेषाम्।**

śhraddhā-vīrya-smṛti-samādhi-prajñā-pūrvaka itareṣhām

śhraddhā-: faith
vīrya-: strength
smṛti-: mindfulness, memory, remembrance, intentness or presence of mind
samādhi-: meditation
prajñā-: awakening of wisdom, *samprajñāta*
pūrvakaḥ: preceded by, having them as a precondition or prerequisite
itareṣhām: of others

The samādhi of (some) others has as its preconditions faith, strength, intentness, meditation and the awakening of wisdom in *samprajñāta.*

Vyāsa's Commentary

Samādhi, the causal cognition of which is cultivated through method (*upāya-pratyaya*), accrues to the yogis.

- Faith (*śhraddhā*) means full clarity and pleasantness of the mind-field. Benevolent like a mother, she protects the yogi.
- When that yogi holds to faith and seeks discriminating wisdom (*viveka*), strength (*vīrya*) gathers in him.
- As strength gathers in him, intentness attends upon him.
- At the presence of intentness the mind, free of disturbance, becomes harmonized and established in samādhi.
- When the yogi's mind-field has become harmonized and established in samādhi, the discrimination from awakening wisdom (*prajñā-viveka*) appears, and one then knows the exact reality (*yathārthaṁ vastu*).

By the practice (*abhyāsa*) of that and through dispassion (*vairāgya*) concerning it, the *asamprajñāta* samādhi occurs.

Discussion

In introducing Sūtra 19 Vyāsa said that samādhi is attained in two ways: by birth, as continuity from previous lives; and by practice of a method. The *videhas* and *prakṛti-layas* are rejected as unworthy of being included among the yogis until, upon rebirth, they practise the method to its ultimate conclusion, the *asamprajñāta* samādhi. To reassert that only those who allow the method to lead them up to *asamprajñāta* are true yogis, Vyāsa says:

> Samādhi, the causal cognition of which is cultivated through method (*upāya-pratyaya*), accrues to the yogis.

As we read on, we find that the method (*upāya*) does not mean merely the techniques of concentration but also attitudes of mind and the philosophy of life expressed in words like "faith (*śhraddhā*)," "strength (*vīrya*)," "intentness (*smṛti*)," and so forth. This is the path (SS) for one desiring liberation (*mumukṣhu*). It is the path of the fivefold means shown in this sūtra.

The question arises (VM, HA, RY): Since those who follow the path up to becoming *videhas* and *prakṛti-layas* also do so by having faith, then why is it included only among the methods for those who pursue the *upāya-pratyaya*? The answer is in the way *śhraddhā* is to be defined. It was partly explained in Sūtra I.14, but here it will be explained further. It is said that (RS)

> having *śhraddhā* as his wealth, one would see the self by the self.

This imples that *śhraddhā* is faith in the fact that one has chosen the way of self-realization (RS). This is a particular mutation (*pariṇāma*) of the mind (RS). Vyāsa says:

> Faith (*śhraddhā*) means full clarity and pleasantness of the mind-field.

This clarity and pleasantness is called *prasāda,* discussed earlier in Sūtra I.16. It arises when (VM) the mind begins to feel an interest in and attraction towards knowledge of true reality through

> *āgama:* tradition and scriptural authority that one accepts,
> *anumāna:* rational processes one applies, and
> *upadeśha:* the teaching of one's guru.

It is the happy and pleasant feeling that comes with the intention to achieve discernment (*viveka*) (HA). It is a sattvic quality (RY). It is an enthusiasm (BD) and a pleasant-mindedness and feeling of love (*prīti*) with which one feels the desire, "May I attain yoga" (VB). Such *prasāda* comes from *āstika*-buddhi, an attitude of affirmation (NB) and recognition that "This yoga I undertake is indeed the way to the highest purpose of being" (SS). Such an attitude or view often arises by hearing of its eminence, as, for example:

> The yogi is greater than the ascetic, greater than those on the path of knowledge, even greater than the ones involved in action. Therefore become a yogi, O Arjuna.
>
> *Bhagavad-gītā* VI.46

Śhraddhā is a feminine word, expressive of a gentle quality, associated with humility and reverence, and not overassertiveness or fanaticism. Vyāsa says:

> Benevolent like a mother, she protects the yogi.

She is a capable and strong (*samartha*) mother (VB, NB), who protects the yogi from the possible calamity of falling onto the wrong path (VM) and from becoming attracted to allurements of pleasure (NB). She crushes the power of a thousand impediments (NB, VB) so that no breach in the process of yoga may occur (VB).

Such is not the *śhraddhā* of those who have wavered and gone off the path to become *videhas* and *prakṛti-layas.* Even though they may have started off with a certain strength of faith and all the rest, they have weakened and turned away from unwavering pursuit of self-realization. This *śhraddhā,* the will to attain the final objective (VM), produces endeavour, maturing in a certain virility and vigour (*vīrya*). Says Vyasa:

> When that yogi holds to faith and seeks discriminating wisdom (*viveka*), strength (*vīrya*) gathers in him.

One becomes enthusiastic (SS), puts forth effort (RY), does not quit, and maintains firmness (NB) in his practice of yoga as he seeks knowledge of the reality of either the individual self (*jīva*) or God (īśhvara) (VM). He consequently develops the capability to guide his students (RS). He endures.

It will be seen later that *vīrya* means "the capacity to initiate," and does not develop without the practice of celibacy. The word is related to the Latin *vir* 'a man', to the Sanskrit words *vīra* 'a brave hero' and *vīrya* 'the seminal strength of a celibate', and also to the English word "virility." *Vīrya* will be discussed further in Sūtra II.38, which says:

> Through the practice of celibacy one gains *vīrya.*

There the commentators define *vīrya* (*inter alia*) as "the capacity to initiate." This *vīrya* produces *smṛti.* We have translated the word *smṛti* as "intentness" in Vyāsa's sentence:

> As strength (*vīrya*) gathers in him, intentness (*smṛti*) attends upon him.

The word is derived from *smṛ* 'to remember' and its conventional meaning is "memory." In the context of yoga it is seldom common memory, but rather memory in the way Arjuna, the hero of the *Bhagavad-gītā,* uses the term when he says:

> I have gained memory.
>
> *Bhagavad-gītā* XVIII.73

Upaniṣhad-Brahma-yogin explains this statement to mean:

> I have gained the recollection of my true nature that I am Brahman.

The *YS* commentators say *smṛti* means contemplation (RS) or meditation (*dhyāna*) (VM, VB, NB, RY) to which one has been led by *vīrya,* the endeavour with regard to the eight *aṅgas* of yoga (*YS* II.29ff.). It is the awakening of one-pointedness (BD). According to HA, it means that one is always mindful, aware.

The fivefold method of this sūtra is identical to the Buddhist tradition of cultivating five strengths (*indriyas*), among which *smṛti*—*sati* in Pali—is the most important. Practising mindfulness (*sati-paṭṭhāna*) of

body: *kāya,*
emotions: *vedanā,*
mind: *chitta,* and
conditions: *dhamma,*

as well as cultivating repeated awareness (*anu-smṛti—anussati* in Pali), which includes the paramount

ānāpāna-sati: mindfulness of exhalation and inhalation,

is perhaps the most central part of Buddhist meditation practice. Thus it appears that the true meaning of the word *smṛti* as it occurs in this sūtra is preserved in the Buddhist practice of *sati-paṭṭhāna,* a mindfulness that is maintained not only on one's meditation seat but throughout daily endeavours. This practice of constant mindfulness is taught universally by the yogis of the Himalayas, irrespective of their affiliations. There is no doubt, therefore, that *smṛti* in this sūtra is not ordinary memory, remembrance or recollection, but rather the practice of remaining intent upon self-observation, such as being mindful of breathing. In the next sentence, Vyāsa's phrase *smṛti-upasthāna* is identical to the Buddhist Pali phrase *sati-paṭṭhāna.*

Vyāsa says:

> At the presence of intentness the mind, free of disturbance, becomes harmonized and established in samādhi.

We have translated *smṛti-upasthāna* as "the presence of intentness." No commentator has anything more to say about it. *An-ākula* 'free of disturbance' means that the mind rises from the *vikṣhipta* state (see p. 83) to the higher ground of one-pointedness (NBB). "Becomes harmonized and established in samādhi" is expressed in the original by one word: *sam-ā-dhīyate.* It means that the mind becomes free of polarities and conflicts. At this point there is a convergence of the method of *śhraddhā, vīrya, smṛti,* and so forth, with that of the eight *aṅgas* of yoga (*YS* II.29ff.) that begin with restraints (*yamas*) (VM, HA, RS, VB, RY), without which no samādhi is possible (VM). The fivefold method is clearly supportive of the eight limbs even at the *smṛti* stage, which might mean mindfulness of the practice of *yamas,* etc., (SS) which finally leads to samādhi. When one orders a servant to go shopping, arrangement for a necessary vehicle is automatically implied (RS)—this is a common analogy in Sanskrit texts. Since no samādhi is possible without the *yamas,* etc., the sūtra implies their practice in mentioning samādhi.

With the convergence of *upāyas* and *aṅgas,* realization of the objects of concentration occurs as discussed in Sūtra I.17. Since the word *samprajñāta* includes wisdom (*prajñā*), it is obvious that this sūtra separates the actual practice of samādhi or concentration from the resulting wisdom (*prajñā*). According to Vyāsa:

> When the yogi's mind-field has become harmonized and established in samādhi, the discrimination from awakening wisdom (*prajñā-viveka*) appears, and one then knows the exact reality (*yathārthaṁ vastu*).

According to BR, the yogi then realizes the nature of the object of his *bhāvanā* (see Sūtra I.17, p. 220). This realization must first be effected. Then, as concentration grows, the separateness of the evolutes from the spiritual self (*jīva*) or īśhvara is seen (VM, VB, RY). Knowing the exact reality, then, means that

- initially the nature of the objects of concentration is realized,
- then *viveka-khyāti* occurs, and
- that leads to *dharma-megha* samādhi.

Vyāsa says:

> By the practice of that and through dispassion (*vairāgya*) concerning it, the *asamprajñāta* samādhi occurs.

From *śhraddhā* to *prajñā* are the means (*upāyas*) for attaining *samprajñāta* samādhi and its resulting wisdom. When one develops dispassion even towards this knowledge, as in *YS* I.16, *asamprajñāta* samādhi ensues. *Samprajñāta*, then, serves as the *upāya* for *asamprajñāta*.

Sūtra I.21 तीव्रसंवेगानामासन्नः।

tīvra-saṁvegānām āsannaḥ

tīvra-: acute, intense, fast, speedy
saṁvegānāṁ: of those with vehemence, speed, velocity, force, momentum, progress
āsannaḥ: near, very close, impending, imminent

For those whose rate of progress is fast and whose momentum is great, samādhi is very near and even imminent.

Vyāsa's Commentary

There are indeed nine kinds of yogis by virtue of the fact that their observance of the methods (*upāyas*) is mild, medium or intense. So that there are:

mṛdu-upāya: those of mild *upāya*
madhya-upāya: those of medium *upāya*
tīvra-upāya: those of intense *upāya*

Among these, again, those of mild *upāya* are divided threefold:

mṛdu-saṁvega: those of mild progress
madhya-saṁvega: those of medium progress
tīvra-saṁvega: those of speedy progress

Those of the medium *upāya* and intense *upāya* (are divided threefold) similarly. Among these, for those whose *upāya* is intense,

[*Sūtra:*] whose rate of progress is fast and whose momentum is great,

the attainment of samādhi as well as the fruit of samādhi

is very near and even imminent.

Discussion

If *śhraddhā,* etc. are the normal methods (*upāyas*), then samādhi and its fruits should accrue equally to everyone who undertakes to travel on the path of yoga (VM); but it is seen that some succeed, some fail, some take a very long time, some yet longer, while some others attain very quickly. It is stated (RS):

> Of all the yogis whose inner self is intent on me, the one who devotes himself to me with *śhraddhā* is the one most favoured by me.
>
> *Bhagavad-gītā* VI.47

> No one who takes to the blessed way suffers misfortune.
>
> *Bhagavad-gītā* VI.40

Thus we are assured that anyone actually undertaking the observance of *śhraddhā,* etc. is bound to reach the final goal. Yet we are told that success does not attend upon everyone equally. Some have to pass through many lifetimes.

> One who has not completed yoga in this life, a *yoga-bhraṣhṭa,* is born in the home of the pure ones endowed by grace.
>
> *Bhagavad-gītā* VI.41

> At the end of many births the knowing one reaches me.
>
> *Bhagavad-gītā* VII.19

This sūtra explains the way of progress. Vyāsa's introdution to the sūtra can be summarized. These are the nine grades of yogis: those of

mild *upāya* and mild momentum,
mild *upāya* and medium momentum,
mild *upāya* and great momentum,
medium *upāya* and mild momentum,
medium *upāya* and medium momentum,
medium *upāya* and great momentum,
intense *upāya* and mild momentum,
intense *upāya* and medium momentum,
intense *upāya* and great momentum.

Many practitioners are impatient and anxious concerning the rate of their progress. One's rate of progress is dependent upon the intensity of one's *upāya* and the degree of one's momentum (*saṁvega*). The *upāyas* were explained in the last sūtra. Their strength in a person depends on the past saṁskāras (VM). The commentators have not explained what constitutes that strength in the varying degrees of mildness or intensity. If one has practised the *upāyas* in past lives, he is capable of undertaking advanced practices in depth with a certain intensity. For example, if one has practised the *smṛti upāya* of breath awareness in past lives, when he begins the practice in this life,

he will naturally sit steady and for a prolonged period,
his awareness of the breath will be uninterrupted and
the breath will flow smooth and fine,
leading to a higher awareness.

That being the case, he can be taught a higher method of breath awareness, which a person of mild *upāya* is not qualified to receive. A person of mild *upāya* cannot undertake his practice for any extended length of time:

- his body is an obstacle,
- his mind is interrupted by extraneous thoughts and emotions,
- the excuses of worldly duties cause him *vyutthāna*—he must get up,
- he does not reach the depths of awareness.

This brings us to *saṁvega*. VM and RY consider this word to mean the strength and the degree of *vairāgya*. No other commentators have explained it this way. No doubt a person's rate of progress and momentum do depend on his degree of *vairāgya*. However, the derivative meaning of the word *saṁvega* includes vehemence, speed, velocity, force, momentum, rate of progress. By implication it means a strong saṁskāra from the past (BR) and a strong (HA) *ichchhā*—desire and will—to make fast progress. BG considers this to include the fact that the practice remains uninterrupted. The importance of this has been explained in Sūtra I.14.

All the commentators are agreed that both the intensity of the *upāya* and the momentum of progress depend on the accumulated saṁskāras from past lives (VM, VB, RS, NB, RY), and when the strength of *upāya* and *saṁvega* reaches its peak, samādhi is imminent. Vyāsa says that this includes

> the attainment of samādhi as well as the fruit of samādhi,

that is, (VM) *samprajñāta* and its fruit, *asamprajñāta*. The fruit of *asamprajñāta* (VM, VB) is *kaivalya,* as it is said:

> One who has attained samādhi gains *mokṣha* in that very life.
> *Viṣhṇu-purāṇa* VI.7.35

Sūtra I.22 मृदुमध्याधिमात्रत्वात् ततोऽपि विशेषः।

mṛdu-madhyādhimātratvāt tato'pi viśheṣhaḥ

mṛdu-: mild, slow
madhya-: medium
adhimātra-: extreme, ultimate
(*mṛdu-madhya-adhimātratvāt*): because there exists a division of slow, medium and ultimate
tataḥ: from that
api: even, also
viśheṣhaḥ: distinction

Even from among those of great momentum there is a distinction of the slow, medium and ultimate.

Vyāsa's Commentary

Even from among those (of great momentum described in Sūtra I.21) there is a distinction of those with

- mild intensity,
- medium intensity and
- ultimate intensity.

With this distinction

- the attainment of samādhi and
- the fruit of samādhi

are

- imminent for those of mild intensity,
- more imminent for those of medium intensity, and
- most imminent for those of ultimate intensity and extreme *upāya.*

Discussion

In the last sūtra nine grades of yogis were described. Of these, the last ones, those of intense *upāya* and great momentum, are further subdivided here. At the ultimate stage the effort is most intense (BR); the ground becomes completely firm; the mind becomes completely incapable of causing *vyutthāna* and simply dissolves (SS). The yogi then remains in the glory of the inward conscious self without any interruption ever, and with no further impediments.

The word *api* has two meanings: "even" and "also." Translated as "even," it refers to those whose *upāyas* and rates of progress have been mentioned in Sūtras I.20 and I.21. "Also" implies that there is yet some other category of yogis to be considered: namely, those who follow the methods to be mentioned in Sūtras I.23 and I.33-39. This especially includes yogis who are at the ultimate stage of receiving the grace of God as in Sūtra I.23 (VB, NB). In other words, the subdivisions established in this Sūtra I.22 apply to yogis who practise methods propounded in all these sūtras: I.20,21,23 and 33-39.

Sūtra I.23 ईश्वरप्रणिधानाद् वा।

īśhvara-praṇidhānād vā

īśhvara-: God's
praṇidhānāt: by practising the presence
vā: or

Or, samādhi can be attained quickly[19] through practising the presence of God.

Vyāsa's Commentary

Does samādhi become imminent by this fivefold method (*upāya*) alone? Now, is there some other way (*upāya*) for its attainment or not?

The practice of the presence of God (*praṇidhāna*) is a specific form of devotion (*bhakti-viśheṣha*). Through this practice God is won over and turns towards the yogi, and when the yogi merely directs his thought (*abhi-dhyāna*) towards Him, He favours him with grace.

Also, merely by the yogi's turning his thought towards Him, his attainment of samādhi as well as the fruit of samādhi becomes closer, imminent (*āsannatara*).

Discussion

Is (HA) the samādhi for the attainment of wisdom (*samprajñāta*) concerning the

- objects of apprehension (*grāhya*),
- instruments of apprehension (*grahaṇa*) and
- the agent of apprehension (*grahītṛ*)

imminent only by these methods of *śhraddhā,* etc., and only through the extreme practice of these with great momentum? No; another

19. The word *āsannaḥ* is brought down to this sūtra from Sūtra I.21 by way of *anu-vṛtti* (see Sūtra I.10, p. 178).

way is by practising the presence of God (*īśhvara-praṇidhāna*).

Īśhvara-praṇidhāna in this sūtra is not to be confused with the definition of the term to be given in *YS* II.1. Here it means *dhāraṇā, dhyāna* and *samādhi* with regard to the practice as taught in Sūtra I.28 (BG, NB), the result of which is stated in Sūtra I.29. If one does not read the present sūtra in light of Sūtras I.28 and 29 but looks at it by itself, he would correctly see that its intent is to state that the grace of God when invoked by a true devotee leads to samādhi. But he would also mistakenly think that faith, etc. are of no consequence. The real intent is that samādhi through the grace of God is within reach of yogis of the ninth category, those of intense *upāya* and great momentum (Sūtra I.21), who are further subdivided in Sūtra I.22. To reach that grade of intensity, one does need to practise the five *upāyas.* However, the sūtra does not present a choice between the five *upāyas* and the practice of the presence of God. Lest the word "or" (*vā*) in this sūtra give the impression of a choice, it has been preempted by the word "also" (*api*) in the preceding sūtra (see p. 276). The practice of the presence of God needs to start right from the beginning as part of faith (*śhraddhā*) and continue to develop. When all of these together reach a certain peak of intensity, all other practices may be dropped, and at the last stage God's grace alone suffices to help the yogi reach the final samādhi.

The *Yoga-sūtras'* definition of God follows in the next sūtra. Some commentators (BG, NB) prefer to state that Īśhvara is the Supreme Self (*parama-ātman*), bearing appellations such as "Brahman." According to BG, Īśhvara is the non-qualified pure consciousness. According to NB, Īśhvara is the special puruṣha who is pure consciousness, identical to the *qualified* Brahman. These discussions have no bearing on the theory of the *Yoga-sūtras,* which do not concern themselves with the transcendental nature of Brahman. The *Yoga-sutras'* main concern is the *kaivalya* of the one who is in ignorance and in suffering. Because the nature of the transcendent most likely will become known to the individual puruṣha only after *kaivalya* has been attained, one should not concern oneself too much with this type of controversy concerning the nature of God.

According to VB and NB, *samprajñāta* samādhi leading to the knowledge of the individual self (*jīva*-ātman) then leads to *asamprajñāta* through perfection of the *upāyas* like *śhraddhā,* whereas a yogi reaches *asamprajñāta* of the Supreme Self even without those *upāyas.* It is thus (VM, NB) that all the textual traditions insist that liberation (*mokṣha*) is attained through knowledge of Brahman.

For those who do not believe in God and cannot practise His presence or surrender to His will, it has been seen that the path of *upāyas* is available, in which the definition of *śhraddhā* incorporates no such requisite belief or surrender (see Sūtra I.20). For those endowed with a high degree of intensity it is possible that the practice of *praṇidhāna* may serve as a shortcut so that the other *upāyas* present themselves on the journey without effort and serve as secondary supports for the practice of the presence of God. This also explains the difference between concentration on aspects of God in *sa-vitarka,* etc. and *īśhvara-praṇidhāna* itself.

Vyāsa says:

> The practice of the presence of God (*praṇidhāna*) is a specific form of devotion (*bhakti-viśheṣha*).

Praṇidhāna means "placing something near, in the proximity of; putting something down." *Īśhvara-praṇidhāna* is to place oneself down in all humility and egolessness in the proximity of God, to dwell near and close to God, to surrender and place oneself at the disposal of God even though one will not know the nature of God till after *asamprajñāta* samādhi is reached. This devotion should be (VM, RY) (1) mental, (2) vocal, and (3) physical.

This is the secret (NB) and easy path (NB, AD). It is (BR) to reject all other desires of worldly pleasures and to offer all one's actions to Him who is the Supreme Guru (BR, RS). It is not merely the surrender of an action after the fact but *bhāvanā* (as explained in Sūtra I.17) before and during the acts also (HA).

While one practises this *bhāvanā* through daily acts, it also involves another *bhāvanā,* that of cultivating the object of concentration in meditation. Even though one does not know the nature of God until after *asamprajñāta* samādhi has been perfected, one fills oneself with love, invokes His presence and concentrates on Him in the heart lotus, offering one's entire self to Him without any other concern or worry. A yogi does not limit this practice to his separate meditation alone but applies it to his entire life. Such *bhakti* indeed leads to samādhi. Vyāsa says:

> Through this practice God is won over and turns towards the yogi, and when the yogi merely directs his thought (*abhi-dhyāna*) towards Him, He favours him with grace.
>
> Also, merely by the yogi's turning his thought towards Him, his attainment of samādhi as well as the fruit of samādhi becomes closer, imminent (*āsannatara*).

All the commentators prefer this passage to be translated thus:

> Through this practice God is won over and turns towards the yogi and, by His mere will and thought directed towards him, graces him. By God's mere will and thought directed towards him, the yogi's attainment of samādhi and the fruit of samādhi becomes closer, imminent.

The commentators are correct here in explaining that *abhi-dhyāna* (will and thought directed towards Him) is a reciprocal process. The yogi directs his thought towards God, who then directs His grace towards the yogi, whereby the yogi receives God's grace and attains samādhi. The grace of realization may come by this alone, without any other effort (VM). It is stated in the Upaniṣhads (RS):

> Whomsoever He chooses, by him is He to be found.
> Unto him this Self of his own reveals His person.
>
> *Muṇḍaka Upaniṣhad* III.2.3

Whosoever wins God over and thus becomes qualified is chosen by God, who deems, "May he know Me." By such a qualified one (*adhikārin*) is God to be found. The devotee, a yogi, wins God's favour through that devotion (RS) which causes him to lovingly think of God constantly (NB). God directs His will towards him—"May his wish be fulfilled," "May his desire be fulfilled" (VM, RY, SS)—thus He graces the person who was burning on the embers of worldly cycles (*saṁsāra*) (SS). Even if the devotee is unable to follow the rules and observances because of physical illness, problems, impediments or any incapacity, God remains favourable to him and wills that he may attain samādhi and *mokṣha* (VM, NB).

God often graces devotees by assuming an incarnate form, *nirmāṇa-kāya*, a Buddhist term used by SS for the historical, physical body of the Incarnate One. HA says God has promised in many texts (as also stated by Vyāsa in *YS* I.25): "Throughout the cycles of creations, dissolutions and great dissolutions through my teaching of knowledge and virtue I shall deliver the puruṣhas who are transmigrating in *saṁsāra*." And a quotation from Pañcha-śhikha (also given by Vyāsa in *YS* I.25) confirms: "The first wise being, the illustrious supreme sage, directing a produced mind, taught the tradition (*tantra*) out of compassion to Āsuri, a seeker after knowledge." Thus God favours devotees by assuming a *nirmāṇa*-chitta (see *YS* IV.4), which is not a physically incarnate form but an incarnation of God into an individual mind. This He does through the Golden Womb (Hiraṇya-garbha), the first guru (Sūtras I.1 and I.26). Thus God's grace can descend in many different ways. He may incarnate in a physical body or send His grace through the Golden Womb or incarnate into an individual guru's mind or into the mind of the devotee himself. This is also the meaning of surrender to the guru. If one is unable to find the mental way of surrender to God, he begins with surrender to the guru, who in turn leads him to the Supreme Guru of whom Sūtra I.26 speaks.

Attainment of samādhi and the fruit of samādhi in Vyāsa's commentary on this sūtra are the same as in the preceding sūtra. The yogi gains *samprajñāta* when he practises the presence of the incarnate form of the guru and God. The fruit thereof is *asamprajñāta* samādhi in the presence of the Supreme Being, whose grace is the final liberation (*mokṣha*).

The following sūtras will explain *īśhvara-praṇidhāna* further.

Sūtra I.24 **क्लेशकर्मविपाकाशयैरपरामृष्टः पुरुषविशेष ईश्वरः।**

kleśha-karma-vipākāśhayair a-parā-mṛṣhṭaḥ puruṣha-viśheṣha īśhvaraḥ

kleśha-: afflictions
karma-: actions
vipāka-: maturing, ripening, fruition of actions
āśhayaiḥ: with propensities, accumulations, domains
a-parā-mṛṣhṭaḥ: unsmeared
puruṣha-viśheṣhaḥ: a special puruṣha
īśhvaraḥ: God

A special puruṣha not smeared by afflictions, actions, their fruitions and the domains of their accumulated propensities is God.

Vyāsa's Commentary

Now, in addition to prakṛti and puruṣha, who is this one named God (īśhvara)?

> [*Sūtra:*] A special puruṣha not smeared by afflictions, actions, their fruitions and the domains of their accumulated propensities is God.

The afflictions (*kleśhas*) are ignorance (*avidyā*) and so forth. The actions (karmas) are well or ill (*kuśhala* or *a-kuśhala*). Their fruit is the maturation (*vipāka*). The propensities of like nature are the accumulations in their domain (*āśhaya*). Though operative in the mind, they are attributed to puruṣha as though he were the experiencer of their fruits, as defeat or victory actually occurring to the fighting warriors is attributed to the king. The one who is not smeared by such experience of the results of actions (*bhoga*) is God (īśhvara), the special puruṣha.

There are many absolute entities[20] who have attained isolation

20. BB's translation of *kevala;* the word literally means "one alone; one who has attained *kaivalya,* or isolation of self from matter."

(*kaivalya*). They attained *kaivalya* after rending the three bondages. For God, however, there never was any connection with those bondages nor will there ever be.

Though a liberated one's preceding condition of bondage is known, such is not the case with God. Similarly, though the way the succeeding condition of bondage of one who has entered *prakṛti-laya* is known, such is not the case with God. He is indeed always free (*mukta*), always the Lord (īśhvara).

Does this perennial supremacy of the Lord (īśhvara), which is derived from the fact that in Him obtains the excellence of essence and intelligence (sattva), have a purpose and a proof (*nimitta*) or not? Its proof and purpose is the Law, the revealed teaching and the scriptures (*śhāstra*).

What is the purpose and the proof of the scriptures (*śhāstra*)? Its purpose and proof is the excellence of its essence and intelligence. These—the Law, its teaching and the scriptures (*śhāstra*) on the one hand and the supremacy on the other—subsisting in the essence and intelligence of the Lord (īśhvara), have a beginningless, mutual relationship. That is why it is thus: always the Lord, always free (*mukta*).

This Lordship of His is without equality to another and without being exceeded in excellence by another. It is not exceeded by some other lordship. Whatever could be the unexceeded excellence, that would be That Lordship. Therefore, wherever the Lordship (*aiśhvarya*) reaches its extremity, that is God (īśhvara).

Nor is there a Lordship equal to His. Wherefore? If there were two equals who had simultaneous intentions with regard to a certain matter, one would say, "Let it happen in the new way," and the other would say, "Let it be in the old way," and the wish of only one of them would be fulfilled while thwarting the other's power of fulfilling a wish (*prākāmya*); this would occasion the contingency of one of the two "equal" īśhvaras being the less. And between two equals it is impossible to attain a simultaneous fulfilment of the wish of both because they have contradictory purposes.

Therefore, whose Lordship is free of any other equal or someone excelling, only He is the Lord (īśhvara) and He is the special Conscious Being (*puruṣha-viśheṣha*).

Discussion

This is a *lakṣhaṇa*-sūtra, a sūtra of definition, defining īśhvara. From the last sūtra, where surrender to God is enjoined, a question arises. The Sāṅkhya-yoga system believes in two entities, the conscious puruṣha and the unconscious prakṛti. If īśhvara is unconscious, He is prakṛti; if He is conscious, He is no other than puruṣha. If He is unconscious prakṛti, how can He be won over? If He is conscious puruṣha, or consciousness-force (*chiti-śhakti*), being neutral and unaffected, how can He be won over by any observance (VM)? Obviously then, this īśhvara is neither prakṛti nor the entity normally referred to as puruṣha. Hence Vyāsa asks:

> Now, in addition to prakṛti and puruṣha, who is this one named God (īśhvara)?

The sūtra provides the answer:

> A special puruṣha not smeared by afflictions, actions, their fruitions and the domains of their accumulated propensities is God.

This definition is sufficient so far as the needs of the *Yoga-sūtras* are concerned.

Commentators like VB have used enormous amounts of space trying to fit this definition of īśhvara within the framework of the Vedāntic discussions of Brahman. We shall not try here to summarize or reproduce VB's discussion because it has no direct bearing on the aims of the Sāṅkhya-yoga system. The Sāṅkhya system gives a questioning human being an insight into the facts of his ignorance, bondage and pain by defining its causes and explaining the relationship between prakṛti and puruṣha. In the oral tradition (as taught by Swami Rama) the *Yoga-sūtras* is a *prayoga-śhāstra,* a text to teach a practical method by which puruṣha's connection with prakṛti may be sundered so that puruṣha may dwell in his own nature and (as in the current sūtra) so that a qualified aspirant may receive the grace of God that leads to liberation. The *Yoga-sūtras* end with *kaivalya;* however, the nature of God as experienced in *kaivalya* is definitely not a *Yoga-sūtras'* topic. It is sufficient for the individual puruṣha in bondage to know that there is a God who, unlike himself, is free of afflictions and whose grace can help to liberate him. Where Īśhvara fits within the scheme of Brahman and Its emanations is certainly not the topic of the *Yoga-sūtras.* Other texts, such as some of the Upaniṣhads—especially *Kaṭha, Muṇḍaka, Māṇḍūkya* and *Śhvetāśhvatara*—as well as the *Bhagavad-gītā* and the Purāṇas, have with varying degrees of success developed ways of fitting the Sāṅkhya-yoga and Vedānta systems together.[21]

Returning to the sūtra proper, Vyāsa says:

> The afflictions (*kleśhas*) are ignorance (*avidyā*) and so forth.

The word *kleśha* (BR) is derived from the verb root *kliṣh,* meaning "to cause pain." The *kleśhas* afflict and cause pain and are the five (*avidyā* and so forth) which were partly discussed as the five perversive cognitions (HA) (*viparyayas*) in Sūtra I.8 and which will be further enumerated in Sūtra II.3. They afflict a puruṣha by attacking him with all kinds of worldly sorrows (VM). Their attack means only their attaching themselves to him (RS). Again, Vyāsa:

> The actions (karmas) are well or ill (*kuśhala* or *a-kuśhala*).

The actions are virtue and vice (*dharma* and *a-dharma*) (VM, VB, BG, NB, HA), those (BR) (*a*) enjoined and prescribed, (*b*) prohibited and (*c*) mixed. Because they cause the well or the ill, they are referred to as *kuśhala* and *a-kuśhala,* respectively. The word *kuśhala* normally means "wellness." Even in the spoken language one normally asks, "Are you *kuśhala*?"—that is, "Are you well?" To be *kuśhala* is to be free of all ill condition—physical, mental or situational—to be a person whom no calamity or accident befalls.

21. The most commonly accepted arrangement of the combined Vedānta and Sāṅkhya categories has been charted and may be studied in the author's work *God* (Honesdale, Pa.: Himalayan International Institute of Yoga Science and Philosophy, 1981).

Such a condition is not arrived at by chance or predestination but as the result of one's acts (karma) which cause the wellness or illness. Therefore the word developed a secondary meaning: to be skillful, an expert, proficient in any area. Thus, someone expert at surgery is *śhalya-kriyā-kuśhala.* Wellness in life requires an expertise, a proficiency, in the exact science called life. Hence *Bhagavad-gītā* II.50 states:

> *yogaḥ karmasu kauśhalam.*
> Yoga is skillfulness (*kauśhala*) in actions (*karmas*).

Some commentators (e.g., HA) say that saṁskāras are included in karmas here, but that would be redundant since *āśhaya,* the domain of karmas, is about to be mentioned. More about karmas will be discussed in Sūtras II.12-14, II.22, IV.2 and IV.6-9. Vyāsa says that

> Their fruit is the maturation (*vipāka*).

The derivative meaning of the word *vipāka* is "ripening (like a fruit)." The karmic seed ripens, comes to fruition and maturation. The *vipākas,* accordingly, are (VB, VM, BR, BG, NB, RY, AD, SS) (*a*) the species in which one is reborn (*jāti*), (*b*) the life span after the birth (*āyus*), and (*c*) the pleasant or painful experiences (*bhoga*) during that life span. This will be discussed further in conjunction with Sūtra II.12. Vyāsa says:

> The propensities of like nature are the accumulations in their domain.

Or more literally:

> The *vāsanās* of like qualities are the *āśhayas.*

The *vāsanās* are the saṁskāras, imprints of actions left in the mind, and the propensities towards the like *vipāka* that develop in the mind. The word *āśhaya* means "that which lies dormant" or "that wherein something lies dormant; a storehouse." The *vāsanās* lie dormant in the mind (VB, VM, RY) until the maturity of karma (BR, AD); hence they are the *āśhayas.*

The presence of a saṁskāra in the mind begins to produce certain mental tendencies, fantasies, thoughts, wishes, images and so forth even before the maturity of a karma. Thus they provide a certain momentum and propensity towards the external choices one makes. These choices, apparently conscious but in fact the results of the propensity from the dormant and unconscious *āśhaya,* expose one to the immediate external causes of maturation, which are then credited with or blamed for one's fortune or misfortune, wellness or illness. As a matter of fact, in the propensities inhere the qualities of past action and of the fruits that are to ripen in due time. They may consist of tendencies towards knowledge (BG) or the opposite. These are, like the *vipāka,* the *vāsanās* of (HA) the species in which one will be born, the life span after that birth, and the pleasures and pains during that life span.

These very *vāsanās* also produce the basic instincts. A human being to be reborn as an elephant *unconsciously* begins to develop certain mechanisms, momentum and propensities within the internal world of his dormant saṁskāras. When he is finally born as an elephant, he already knows how to act towards, for instance, trees, without which knowledge he would not be able to survive (RY).

The word *āśhaya* is also translated as "the domain wherein something lies dormant." The aspect of chitta in the subtle body, where the saṁskāras and *vāsanās* dwell, is their domain (*āśhaya*). Hence the words

> *karmāśhaya:* (*karma* + *āśhaya*),
> *vipākāśhaya:* (*vipāka* + *āśhaya*),

or as in this sūtra, after parsing the euphony, *karma-vipāka-āśhaya.*

A question can be raised here: (VM) Since all these *kleśhas,* karmas and so forth are the attributes (*dharmas*) only of buddhi and do not in any case smear the puruṣha, why is it that only the special puruṣha named Īśhvara is mentioned as not being smeared by them? Vyāsa replies:

> Though operative in the mind, they are attributed to puruṣha as though he were the experiencer of their fruits, as defeat or victory actually occurring to the fighting warriors is attributed to the king.

It is not that puruṣha is truly the experiencer (*bhoktṛ*), but rather that it is the source and cause of the mind's awareness (*chetayitṛ*) (VM). The experience (*bhoga*) simply means feeding chitta with the sattva of the objects of experience and causing it to take on like vṛttis (VB). It is only for practical purposes (HA) that *kleśhas,* etc. are attributed to puruṣha. When it is said "The king is victorious" or "The man is wealthy," these are not statements concerning the actual person (VB). On *YS* II.19 Vyāsa says:

> Devadatta is becoming impoverished because his cattle are dying out. Devadatta's impoverishment is due to the death of his cows but there is no actual loss in his own person.

Similarly, when we say that puruṣha is, for instance, happy, or unhappy, or stupefied, these are not statements regarding puruṣha's own being at all. Thinking that there is any relationship of inherence (*samavāya-sambandha*) between puruṣha and the experience of happiness, etc. is indeed ignorance (*avidyā*) (VB). Any attributing of such qualifications is mere speculation for practical purposes. Yet the individual *jīvas* are considered as owners (*svāmin*) of their individual buddhis and chittas and thereby also the owners of the happy, unhappy or stupefied conditions and *kleśhas,* etc. that smear the minds.

Then there is a special puruṣha, concerning whom even such hypotheses for practical purposes are not possible. Vyāsa says:

> The one who is not smeared by such experience of the results of actions (*bhoga*) is God (īśhvara), the special puruṣha.

He is unique in that the qualifications and conditions of the buddhi and chitta cannot be attributed to Him (VM, VB, BR, RY) in past, present or future (BR, BG, NB, RY, HA). Even though the *kleśhas,* etc. cannot touch Him, He may associate Himself with a *nirmāṇa-*

chitta, a mind-field specially created to serve as a vehicle of incarnation (HA). The word *īśhvara* is derived from the verb root *īśh* 'to govern', which includes the capacity to impart grace (see discussion on p. 101, Sūtra I.2). He is able to save all the worlds simply by His will (NB, BR); hence, "īśhvara."

That His freedom from *kleśhas,* etc. is not in any way subject to time is emphasized in the next statement of Vyāsa:

> There are many absolute entities (*kevalin*) who have attained isolation (*kaivalya*). They attained *kaivalya* after rending the three bondages. For God, however, there never was any connection with those bondages nor will there ever be.

The word *kevalin* used by Vyāsa has been translated as "absolute entities" for want of a better phrase. Those who attain *kaivalya,* according to the *Yoga-sūtras'* definition, are called *kaivalin* and not *kevalin. Kevalin* is a Jaina term. It appears that Vyāsa is challenging the view of the Jainas, who do not believe in a creator God but do believe that those who reach the highest perfection through yoga and are called *kevalin* become īśhvaras after death. In Vyāsa's view, Patañjali's definition of īśhvara does not apply to them.

VB recognizes that some Vyāsa manuscripts have the reading *kaivalin,* which means those who have attained *kaivalya.* He considers Hiraṇya-garbha as an example of those who have attained *kaivalya,* are leaders among the liberated ones and might possibly qualify for the title "īśhvarā." VB seems to regard Hiraṇya-garbha as an historical personage who attained *kaivalya.* This mistaken assumption will be refuted in the discussion on Sūtra I.26.

In any case, neither the Jaina *kevalins* nor the *kaivalins* can be considered equal to īśhvara, on the ground that at one time, unlike īśhvara, they had to free themselves from the three kinds of bondage. These three kinds of bondage (*bandha*) in the Sāṅkhya system are as follows:

- *Prakṛta* (or *prakṛtika*) *bandha,* by which one identifies the self with prakṛti or with any of its evolutes. The *prakṛti-layas* are at the highest rung of the ladder of this bondage.

- *Vaikṛta* (or *vaikārika*) *bandha,* by which one becomes attracted to celestial pleasures, as do the *videhas,* or by which a renunciate may be drawn to the ordinary, worldly attractions.
- *Dākṣhiṇa* (or *dākṣhiṇika*) *bandha,* by which worldly people remain involved with desires and hope for liberation through ritual practices. Also included in this category of bondage is the dependence of renunciates on the offerings of basic necessities received from householders.

For God there was never any connection with such bondages nor will there ever be. Vyāsa continues:

> Though a liberated one's preceding condition of bondage is known, such is not the case with God. Similarly, though the way the succeeding condition of bondage of one who has entered *prakṛti-laya* is known, such is not the case with God. He is indeed always free (*mukta*), always the Lord (īśhvara).

At this point the fact of Lordship (*aiśhvarya*) is defined in various ways. The Lord (īśhvara) is endowed with a will that can never be impeded and is always efficacious (VB). His Lordship refers to His ability to save the entire world and all the worlds by mere will (NB). This Lordship means to possess the supreme power of (VM, RY, VB, NB) knowledge (*jñāna*) and action (*kriyā*), which remains even when the world is dissolved in *pralaya* (VB) and renders possible the Lord's capability as a saviour of the worlds (NB). Again we read Vyāsa:

> Does this perennial supremacy of the Lord (īśhvara), which is derived from the fact that in Him obtains the excellence of essence and intelligence (sattva), have a purpose and a proof (*nimitta*) or not? Its proof and purpose is the Law, the revealed teaching and the scriptures (*śhāstra*).
>
> What is the purpose and the proof of the scriptures (*śhāstra*)? Its purpose and proof is the excellence of its essence and intelligence. These—the Law, its teaching and the scriptures (*śhāstra*) on the one hand and the supremacy on the other—subsisting in the essence and intelligence of the Lord (īśhvara), have a beginningless, mutual relationship. That is why it is thus: always the Lord, always free (*mukta*).

The single word *sattva* has been translated as

- essence (that is, being) and
- intelligence (that is, knowing)

both as intertwined, one not subsisting without the other. The word *sattva* in this sense is not to be confused with that sattva which is a guṇa of prakṛti, but rather refers to the very essence and intelligence, being and knowing, which is an innate attribute of the Lord.

The single word *śhāstra* is translated here as (1) the eternal Law, which is synonymous with God's knowledge and the application of which is manifest in the power of action (*kriyā-śhakti*), creativity, by which the world comes into existence and is maintained within the Law, (2) the revealed teaching, which is conveyed from the Lord to the individual *jīva* so the latter may be raised and saved, and (3) the scripture itself in that verbal form which is conveyed by *jīva* to *jīva,* from teacher to disciple. The scripture in this tradition is the Veda, as well as any knowledge passed on as revealed authority (*āgama pramāṇa*) (*YS* I.7).

Vyāsa means to say here that the purpose of the Lord's essence and knowledge is manifest in the fact that from His compassionate grace He gives this knowledge to the *jīvas* to help raise and liberate them. The proof of this fact lies in the statements given in the Vedas and by other revealed authorities. The purpose of the Vedas, the other scriptures and revealed words is to lead the *jīva* to the knowledge of God. God reveals the texts; the texts reveal God. Because God reveals the scriptures, they are authoritative—and God is the supreme authority because of scriptural testimony. One is the proof of the other and vice versa. Even though this appears to be a circular argument, the eternal relationship of God and His revelation is a fundamental tenet of all traditional spiritual paths. When one follows the steps prescribed by the *Yoga-sūtras,* the truth of the revealed statements is verified by individual experience.

It is fitting at this point to reread the last quotation from Vyāsa because all the commentators have interpreted the first paragraph in a way different from Vyāsa's intention. This difference is based on the term *sattva,* which in this case is properly translated as "God's own essence and intelligence." All the other commentators use the term to express the usual guṇa of prakṛti. However, if *sattva* were to be read as a guṇa, Vyāsa's paragraph would be translated as follows:

> Does this perennial supremacy of the Lord, which is arising from His taking up and holding to the excelling sattva, have a purpose and proof or not?

This translation will not be challenged because it does not conflict with our own interpretation. The Lord's essence and intelligence reaches out and touches the sattva of prakṛti, which He knows as His *sva* (own property), and over which now He acts as *svāmin* (owner).

The argument now develops further. It is understood that the Lord is the saviour of all and that He cannot function as saviour without the powers of knowledge and action (NB). But (VM, RY) how can these powers become operative in the consciousness-force (*chiti-śhakti*), which is stated to be immutable? It is answered (VM, NB) thus: Out of compassion for the *jīvas* the Lord, as it were, reaches down and touches the pure sattva of prakṛti, the power of sattva excelling beyond the reach of rajas and tamas. The Lord touches this sattva as it prevails in the chitta. The Lord thus asserts His proprietorship over this aspect of prakṛti. But unlike us, He does not thereby become subject to *avidyā* and bondage. He sees—the texts do not say that He desires—He sees that

> I shall raise these beings from the oceans of the sorrows of rebirth and threefold pains.
>
> I shall do so by revealing the true knowledge to them.
>
> It is not possible to reveal the true knowledge without extending forth my preeminent power of knowledge and action.
>
> I can extend it forth only by touching that pure sattva of the chitta which is free of rajas and tamas.

Thus He touches the sattva without identifying with it, unlike the ordinary *jīvas.* One becomes ignorant (*a-vidvān*) only when he identifies with that ignorance (*avidyā*) that is constituted of mistaking the self for the non-self. One is not ignorant when he *uses avidyā* qua *avidyā,* knowing it to be so. An actor representing a hero on the stage does not become confused as to his own true identity. The Lord, unlike the *jīva,* does not identify with *avidyā* on the stage of a sattva-dominated chitta. Thus His power of knowledge and action continues to send His grace into the chitta to liberate beings.

Another difficulty (VM, NB) arises here. Only by touching the chitta can the Lord see that a being needs to be liberated. On the other hand, it has just been stated that the Lord touches the chitta in order to liberate it. The answer to this logical dilemma lies in the fact that the relation of the Lord and prakṛti is *śhāśhvatika* (perennial), as Vyāsa says. At the time of each dissolution of the universe the Lord knows: "Even in the next cycle of creation shall I similarly liberate beings" (see Sūtra I.25 commentary). This compassion and grace is synonymous with the Lord's powers (*śhakti*) of knowledge and action. In such perennial relationship, the question does not arise as to whether the compassion to liberate comes before touching a chitta, or after.

Here it needs to be remembered that the cosmic chitta is the instrument of that grace which flows from the Lord to the individual chitta of a *jīva.* In fact, the *Yoga-sūtras'* philosophy, in contrast to that of Sāṅkhya, recognizes only the cosmic chitta, which, becoming operative in an individual personality, appears individuated. Īśhvara assumes the cosmic chitta to be His mind wherewith to run the universe and to grace individual beings out of compassion. Because īśhvara is always the Lord and always free, unlike individual *jīvas,* there is no question of His falling into ignorance and identifying Himself with the cosmic chitta. When (NB) He takes hold of the sattva of prakṛti, the universe is created, and in touch with that sattva-chitta the Lord expresses His knowledge and action. When the Lord takes hold of the tamas of prakṛti, the universe is dissolved and the Lord rests in his yoga sleep (*yoga-nidrā*). This perennial and perpetual cycle continues because īśhvara is forever and always the Lord and ever free.

Vyāsa's next three paragraphs are self-explanatory and need no comment.

> This Lordship of His is without equality to another and without being exceeded in excellence by another. It is not exceeded by some other Lordship. Whatever could be the unexceeded excellence, that would be That Lordship. Therefore, wherever the Lordship (*aiśhvarya*) reaches its extremity, that is God (īśhvara).
>
> Nor is there a Lordship equal to His. Wherefore? If there were two equals who had simultaneous intentions with regard to a certain matter, one would say, "Let it happen in the new way," and the other would say, "Let it be in the old way," and the wish of only one of them would be fulfilled while thwarting the other's power of fulfilling a wish (*prākāmya*); this would occasion the contingency of one of the two "equal" īśhvaras being the less. And between two equals it is impossible to attain a simultaneous fulfilment of the wish of both because they have contradictory purposes.
>
> Therefore, whose Lordship is free of any other equal or someone excelling, only He is the Lord (īśhvara) and He is the special Conscious Being (*puruṣha-viśheṣha*).

The paragraphs establish that there is only one God. If there were many Gods acting in concert, adds VM, none of them would be īśhvara, as in a committee no single person has the supreme power. On the other hand, in a battle of wills between two hypothetical Gods, the one whose will is proved to be paramount will emerge as that one īśhvara. Beyond the extreme preeminence of Lordship there can be no other God. By practising the presence of that one God and surrendering all mental, vocal and physical acts to His will, one receives the ever-flowing grace, enters samādhi and is liberated.

Sūtra I.25 तत्र निरतिशयं सर्वज्ञबीजम्।

tatra nir-atiśhayaṁ sarvajña-bījam

tatra: there, in that (God)
nir-atiśhayaṁ: ultimate, not exceeded (by any other), unexcelled
sarvajña-: of omniscient
bījam: seed

In Him the seed of the omniscient is unexcelled and ultimate.

Vyāsa's Commentary

Furthermore,

[*Sūtra:*] In Him the seed of the omniscient is unexcelled and ultimate.

All this lesser or greater apprehension and the process of apprehension arising from the past, future or the immediate, relating to each severally or collectively as well as supersensually, is the seed of the omniscient. Expanding gradually, the one in whom it reaches its ultimate and is unexcelled, is the omniscient one. The seed of the omniscient has a limited measure and does excel; hence (it is to be concluded that) it also reaches its ultimate dimension.

The one in whom knowledge reaches its ultimate dimension is the omniscient one. He is the special puruṣha; this is it.

The power of inference is exhausted in producing a conclusion regarding only the general. It has not the power to help determine the particular. Therefore one should seek out the particulars concerning Him, such as His names, from the authoritative textual tradition (*āgama*).

Even though He has no reason to benefit (*anu-graha*) Himself, His purpose is to confer grace (*anu-graha*) to the beings, (deeming) that "Throughout the cycles of creations, dissolutions and great dissolutions through my teaching of knowledge and virtue I shall deliver the puruṣhas who are transmigrating in *saṁsāra.*"

As is said, "The first wise being, the illustrious supreme sage, directing a produced mind, taught the tradition (*tantra*) out of compassion to Āsuri, a seeker after knowledge."

A Review of Vyasa's Commentary

Vyāsa lists the various limitations of the knowledge of delimited beings. Their knowledge may be

(*a*) of the past, the future, or the immediate present,
(*b*) in relation to a single object, entity or experience, or to a collective, aggregrate or composite of many,
(*c*) gained through the senses, or supersensual (*atīndriya*).

The word *atīndriya* means that the knowledge may be gained by means other than the senses, as in the case of yogis. Yet this type of knowledge has its limitations and does not make the accomplished yogi into an omniscient being. The word *atīndriya* also refers to the knowledge of objects which cannot be perceived with the senses because they are too small (RS) (for example, atoms), too distant, or concealed in some other way.

The knowledge of beings may be extremely little or may increase in degrees. *Grahaṇa* is translated to mean both the process of apprehension as well as the instruments of apprehension. The degree of knowledge of each living entity depends on the limit of the instruments of apprehension that it possesses. With each degree of knowledge manifest in delimited beings it is assumed that a higher degree of knowledge exists. Knowledge itself may be little or its scope may be of little things and thus delimited. Similarly it may become expanded and become greater knowledge, or the knowledge may be of things larger in scope.

All of this knowledge in the delimited entities is yet the seed of omniscience, in that it contains knowledge from the omniscient one. We observe the fact that knowledge increases and expands, the higher knowledge excelling the lower. The one in whom this excelling reaches its ultimate limit, beyond which there is no higher excellence, is the omniscient, special puruṣha. We reach this conclusion about His omniscience through inference; seeing the gradual expansion of knowledge among beings, we infer the existence of a Being in whom it reaches its ultimate excellence.

An inference leads to a conclusion about the general only. For specific knowledge concerning the names and so forth of Īśhvara, our source of information is in the scriptures and traditions. This knowledge found in the scriptures and traditions is not arrived at through inference but is conferred upon realized beings by Īśhvara, who has no reason to benefit Himself but benefits beings only as a way of compassionate grace. It is not a desire or a want on His part; rather, He sees within His omniscient nature that "Throughout the cycles of creations, dissolutions and the larger cycles of the same I shall cause deliverance of puruṣhas who are transmigrating in the world. I shall do so by inspiring into them the teachings of knowledge and virtue." It is thus that the sage Pañchaśhikha states that the first wise one, Hiraṇya-garbha, created a great mind into whom He incarnated, becoming the sage Kapila, the founder of the Sāṅkhya-yoga system. Kapila then taught his disciple, named Āsuri, and the tradition continues even to the present day.

Now, in the light of this review, the various points need to be discussed.

Discussion

It is first necessary to settle on a correct reading of the sūtra. Vyāsa and most other commentators (VM, VB, BR, BG, Sh, RY, AD, NTB, BM) have preferred the reading

sarvajña-bījam: seed of the omniscient.

NB, AD and SS clearly favour

sārvajñya-bījam: seed of omniscience.

Because Vyāsa is the ancientmost commentator, and himself a *ṛṣhi,* his reading will be adhered to. Some commentators, however, failing to follow Vyāsa's explanation, do not fully understand the meaning of the phrase "seed of the omniscient," which is clarified in the review above. Although VB acknowledges the alternative rendering "seed of omniscience," he feels that the two readings have the same intent. NB and SS accept only "seed of omniscience."

It is clear that the phrase "seed of the omniscient" indicates the presence of the omniscient one as a seed within all, because of which a *little* knowledge is manifest in delimited beings. That knowledge is the seed of the omniscient one (*sarva-jña*), the īśhvara Himself, who is then called (in the next sūtra) the guru of all. The rendering "seed of omniscience" indicates the presence of only one power, that of omniscience, in living beings, and consequently there is no doubt that Vyāsa's original reading, *sarvajña-bījam* 'seed of the omniscient', is accurate.

The (NTB) knowledge of entities like ourselves has as its sine qua non (*a-vinā-bhāva*) the presence of the knowledge of the omniscient one, for anything delimited is always dependent upon a homogeneous unlimited, the excelled dependent upon the unexcelled of its own kind. For example, the larger space is the sine qua non of the lesser space in a jar (NTB, RY, SS). The increase or decrease of tamas, which normally veils the buddhi, determines one's capacity for more or less knowledge (VM). As the moon is naturally overpowered by the sun, so rajas and tamas are easily overcome by sattva (RS). This enhanced sattva increases the capacity for knowledge among the various beings. Thus there exist varying capacities for knowledge, the limitations of which have been delineated by Vyāsa as follows: Some know only the past or the present or the future or some very minute items like atoms or vast things like space; some know these a little, some know them more and some others know them yet more; some know a single object, others know objects collectively, compounded or aggregated; some know few, others know many; some know the objects that are within the grasp of the senses, others know suprasensual objects also.

The fact remains in any case that small things indicate the existence of objects of larger dimensions. The small size of a berry (VM) indicates the possibility of the existence of a larger fruit. But if we keep enlarging our vision, the idea of greatness and expansion eventually reaches the point where there is no possibility of any greater excellence. There has to be some final entity beyond which excellence and expansion cannot be thought of (NB). There the finitude ceases. Such is the case with ātman, the self (VM), or with īśhvara. The knowledge in each delimited entity has within it a seed of the omniscient; it grows till each being reaches īśhvara.

The word *bīja* (seed) is also explained as *liṅga* (the sign, an indicator) (VB, NB, BM) to help in an inference. The degrees (RS) of finitude help one to infer an infinitude. An inch, a foot, a yard, a mile, a light-year finally go on to support the idea of an unexcelled distance—infinite space. The degrees of material objects starting from the minutest atom to the vastest radical matter, prakṛti itself, are thus inferable, the vast from the minute. The finitude is excelled by larger finitudes, but infinitude is unexcelled by any beyond. Similarly, the capacity of knowledge begins with small degrees, such as that of an insect, and goes on to that of a human being, all excelled by the relatively higher knowledge, till we reach, by inference alone, that one whose knowledge is infinite. Here RS blunders by saying:

> Īśhvara is the one who possesses the mind-field, chitta, with the capacity of infinite knowledge.

Mind being a material evolute, God cannot be dependent on such an evolute for His knowledge. He may rule over the universe through a universal mind (*samaṣhṭi*-chitta), but within Himself His omniscience cannot be dependent on the capacity of such a mind.

According to BR, AD and SS, *bīja* means the root. The root of all knowledge, even that seen in small degrees among beings of varying capacities, exists in that īśhvara. Obviously this pertains to such statements as:

> The universe is the *aśhvattha* tree with its roots above, branches below.
>
> *Bhagavad-gītā* XV.1

The above concludes the discussion on the following paragraphs from Vyāsa's commentary on Sūtra I.25:

> All this lesser or greater apprehension and the process of apprehension arising from the past, future or the immediate, relating to each severally or collectively as well as supersensually, is the seed of the omniscient. Expanding gradually, the one in whom it reaches its ultimate and is unexcelled, is the omniscient one. The seed of the omniscient has a limited measure and does excel; hence (it is to be concluded that) it also reaches its ultimate dimension.
>
> The one in whom knowledge reaches its ultimate dimension is the omniscient one. He is the special purușha; this is it.

Further, we read from Vyāsa:

> The power of inference is exhausted in producing a conclusion regarding only the general. It has not the power to help determine the particular. Therefore one should seek out the particulars concerning Him, such as His names, from the authoritative textual tradition (*āgama*).

Seeing that in degrees of knowledge, the lesser is always excelled by the greater, we infer in general that there must be some omniscient being in whom knowledge reaches its highest excellence. The particulars of the nature of such a being are to be learned only from the authority of *āgama,* statements of realized ones whether in person, in a tradition or in the scriptures. For a discussion on the self-authenticated veracity of *āgama,* see Sūtra I.7.

Vyāsa says that

> One should seek out the particulars concerning Him, such as His names.

Names such as śhiva (the Benevolent One), īśhvara (the Lord) (VM), brahman (the Expansive One), *antar-yāmin* (Pervading Within All Things and Beings), *parama-ātman* (the Supreme Self) (VB) and others preferred by different commentators which are referred to in various texts. The phrase "such as His names" implies that not only the names but other facts also can be known. These facts might be, for instance, statements regarding His *șhaḍ-aṅgatā,* "being constituted of six complements," or His *avyayatā,* "immutabilities." For example, it is said that

Those who know His order, ordinance or system (*vidhi*) state that

sarvajñatā: omniscience
tṛpti: satiety
anādhi-bodha: beginningless wisdom (enlightenment)
svatantratā: sovereignty
nityam a-lupta-śhakti: power, potentia (*śhakti*) that never suffers a loss or reduction
ananta-śhakti: infinite power, potentia (*śhakti*)

these six constitute the complements, *aṅgas,* of the Great Lord.
Vāyu-purāṇa XII.33

Furthermore,

jnāna: knowledge
vairāgya: dispassion
aiśhvarya: lordship
tapas: ascetic power
satya: truth
kṣhamā: forgiveness
dhṛti: fortitude
sraṣhṭṛtva: creativity
ātma-sambodha: full self-awareness
adhiṣhṭhātṛtva: command over the dominion

these ten immutables are definite in the Lord.
Vāyu-purāṇa X.65-66

Such are the powers of the Lord (VM, NB, NTC, RY) as expressed in the scriptures. Similarly (VB) the attributes such as perfect bliss, perfect compassion, transcendence, and being the cause and support of the universe are to be included and understood on scriptural authority.

This raises the question as to the true identity of the Lord. There are (VB, NB, NTC) numerous names and forms to which the divinity is attributed. These include the trinity of Brahmā, Viṣhṇu, Śhiva, their incarnations (*avatāras*) such as Rāma and Kṛṣhṇa, the various celestial beings, and so forth. Which of these beings is the true Lord? The question is answered by quoting *Viṣhṇu-purāṇa* I.22.58 and stating that all these are simply the powers, *śhaktis,* of the One Lord (VM, NB, NTC). No distinction can ever be made between the power and the powerful one, between the potentia (*śhakti*) and the omnipotent (*śhaktimān*). It is thus that all these beings, manifestations of one Lord, are said to possess the attributes of the One. By themselves they are not the Lord. For example, among the trinity of Brahmā (the Creator), Viṣhṇu (the Preserver), and Rudra (Śhiva) (the Dissolver), Brahmā takes the universe as his body much as the little *jīvas,* individual souls, identify with their limited bodies. He is not the Lord (HA). As explained in Sūtra I.19, such beings are simply advanced souls. Often these souls identify with the Lord (NTC), and attaining such a height, serve as vehicles for the Lord's descending power and become *avatāras.*[22] Such ones are worshipped and honoured only as the various powers of the one God, sharing in His identity, inseparable from Him as His powers. Thus only the one God is praised when they are praised. Ultimately they, too, have to liberate themselves from their universe-bodies, returning into the Supreme One, whose *śhaktis* they are and who never enters into the play (*līlā*) of the universe. It is He whose name is *OM.*

The question arises: Since God is ever free (VB), ever satiated (VM, NB) and maintains supreme *vairāgya* (VM), how can He have any craving to achieve anything? Being compassionate, He can produce only happiness, and it would be unthinkable that He could create a world full of pain for the beings therein (VM, NB). Even though He has the total power of activity (*kriyā*), there seems to be no reason or purpose for any endeavour on His part with respect to producing the universe or revealing knowledge. Vyāsa answers:

> Even though He has no reason to benefit (*anu-graha*) Himself, His purpose is to confer grace (*anu-graha*) to the beings, (deeming) that "Throughout the cycles of creations, dissolutions and great dissolutions through my teaching of knowledge and virtue I shall deliver the puruṣhas who are transmigrating in *saṁsāra.*"

The Lord has no reason to act in order to accomplish anything to favour or satisfy Himself. His endeavour arising from His knowledge

22. For further discussion see pp. 121-28, including chart 1, of the author's book *God* (Honesdale, Pa.: Himalayan International Institute of Yoga Science and Philosophy, 1979).

and will, however, continues eternally through the cycles (*pravāha-anādi*) (NB). The fact of His compassion cannot be challenged simply on the grounds that beings suffer in His creation. He provides knowledge all the way from scriptural revelation to discriminating wisdom. Beings enjoy pleasure when acting in accordance with that knowledge and suffer pain when failing to do so. Discriminating wisdom in beings matures only through the combination (*samucchaya*) of *jñāna* (knowledge) and *dharma* (virtue), and not by either one separately. These beings transmigrate in *saṁsāra,* die and are reborn within *kalpas* (cycles of creation), *pralayas* (partial dissolutions of universes), and *mahā-pralayas* (total dissolutions after one thousand cycles). It is not that the Lord takes a vow or makes a declaration to bring deliverance in the future, but rather that His will, knowledge and compassion being eternal, He simply knows that He is to help their deliverance continuously by imparting the scriptural revealed knowledge and discriminating wisdom (*viveka-khyāti*) (VM, NB, HA). Obviously, the revealed knowledge is open to all, but *viveka-khyāti* is arrived at only through the practice of *dhyāna* and samādhi, which cannot be achieved without the Lord's grace.

In the current *kalpa* the revealed knowledge was imparted by Kapila, an incarnation of God. Vyāsa quotes an ancient saying of Pañchaśhikha:

> "The first wise being, the illustrious supreme sage, directing a produced mind, taught the tradition (*tantra*) out of compassion to Āsuri, a seeker after knowledge."

According to the tradition, knowledge is revealed in the minds of great sages in the beginning of each cycle of creation. However, the revelation may be granted again and again to wise beings in samādhi throughout the cycle.[23] Kapila is the first *ṛṣhi* to whom the knowledge of Sāṅkhya-yoga was given; he is therefore the first wise being, the illustrious supreme sage of this lineage. He is regarded as one of the twenty-four incarnations of Viṣhṇu, and the

23. For further information see pp. 17-19, 65-102, and 147-76 of the author's book *Mantra and Meditation* (Honesdale, Pa.: Himalayan International Institute of Yoga Science and Philosophy, 1981).

story of his birth and teaching is given in the *Bhāgavata-purāṇa*.

The phrase "produced mind" (*nirmāṇa*-chitta)[24] will be explained in Sutra IV.4. An incarnation, sage or guru may send forth a spark of his *asmitā* into the mind of a disciple in an initiatory process whereby the reality and the experience of the object of teaching is transferred into the disciple's mind, the disciple then being known as the teacher's "mental offspring" (*mānasa-putra*),[25] the pure part of his mind having been produced from a spark of the guru's mind. It is thus that the lineage of produced minds, the mental offsprings, continues to impart knowledge down through the generations. Kapila thus taught Āsuri, whose disciple was Pañchaśhikha, from whom the sage Vyāsa quotes:

> "The first wise being, the illustrious supreme sage, directing a produced mind, taught the tradition (*tantra*) out of compassion to Āsuri, a seeker after knowledge."

24. Ibid., pp. 147-76, for a detailed description of the initiatory process.

25. Ibid.

Sūtra I.26 पूर्वेषामपि गुरुः कालेनानवच्छेदात्।

pūrveṣhām api guruḥ kālena an-avachchhedāt[26]

pūrveṣhām: of the first, ancient, former (teachers)
api: even, also
guruḥ: guru
kālena: by time
an-avachchhedāt: there being no delimitation, break, division

He is the guru even of the very first, the ancient and the former teachers, because in Him there is no delimitation by time.

Vyāsa's Commentary

The same one

> [*Sūtra:*] is the guru even of the very first, the ancient and the former teachers, because in Him there is no delimitation by time.

The past and ancient teachers, even the very first ones, are delimited by time. The one in whom time does not approach and revolve as a condition (RP) with the effect of delimitation is the guru of even the past, the ancient and the very first ones. Just as this is proved in the beginning of the current creation on the grounds of His supremacy, which initiates and propels the process of creation and revelation, so also the same should be understood with regard to the creations that have already transpired, and so forth.

Discussion

The word *pūrva* can mean "anything past, former, anterior, preceding," "ancient," and "the very first one." God is the guru of all the ones who have preceded us: those of the immediate past; the

26. Some texts read the sūtra as
sa eṣha pūrveṣhām api guruḥ kālena an-avachchhedāt
but we concur with VM that the words *sa eṣhaḥ* are Vyāsa's introduction to the sūtra.

ancient ones; as well as the very first gurus of the creation,[27] even of those like Hiraṇya-garbha (BG, NTB, HA), Brahmā, Vişhṇu, Śhiva (VB, NBB, AD, SS, BM) and others. He is the guru of Brahmā, etc. and of the preceding creations as well (NB). The word *api* 'also' is meant to include both prakṛti and the individual souls (*jīvas*) because He is their true self (ātman). The ruling power (*adhiṣhṭhātṛ*) of any entity is often called its self (ātman); for example, the sun is the ātman of the eye, and the soul (*jīva*) is the ātman of the body (NB). Being the ātman of souls, God pervades them, is their indweller (*antar-yāmin*) (VB, NB, NBB) and their father (VB, NBB). In the Vedāntic interpretation this fatherhood simply means that souls are to God as sons and daughters are to a father or sparks are to a fire. Being the dweller within (*antar-yāmin*) them, He gives them the eye of knowledge (VB, BG, NB, NBB). Souls are delimited by the divisions of time, from which He is free. The universe and the universal mind from which individual minds are further created are all His creation and partake of His knowledge. They become conditioned by time, but He remains untouched. They have a beginning through Him, but He is beginningless (BR et al.).

This applies not merely to this creation but to all the past creations. We have translated the single, compound word *prakarṣha-gati* as:

> His supremacy, which initiates and propels the process of creation and revelation.

Prakarṣha means supremacy (from *pra* + *kṛṣh* 'to draw forth'). He draws the universe forth from prakṛti and is therefore supreme over it. The prefix *pra* expresses "initiating" and "propelling"; the propulsion from Īśhvara continues through the entire process of producing the modifications of prakṛti, from mahat to the very earth element. This is creation. Within the same creation occurs

27. For further detail see the rendering of the verses from chapter 1 of the *Laws of Manu* in the author's book *Mantra and Meditation* (Honesdale, Pa.: Himalayan International Institute of Yoga Science and Philosophy, 1981), pp. 135-38.

the multiplying of soul sparks to whom knowledge is revealed and through whom it is transmitted in the guru lineage. The sense of this movement in creation and revelation is expressed by the word *gati,* from the verb root *gam* 'to know; to move; to reach', normally translated into English as "to go."

VB, NB, NBB have raised a question here. The Sāṅkhya philosophy upholds the sovereignty of both puruṣha and prakṛti as two independent, coequal entities. How is it possible then that puruṣha draws nature forth into the process of creation and propels its modifications? This is answered by referring to *YS* IV.3. An efficient cause does not produce an effect out of the material cause but rather provides the condition to which the inherent nature of the material cause responds and thereby produces its own modification. For example, a farmer does not create the essence of his plants. He merely opens the water channel; the water flows naturally and irrigates the plants. Or, the fact that a potter, the efficient cause, turns the potter's wheel does not detract from the inherent capacity of the wheel to help shape the pot. Similarly, God's presence as the efficient cause of the universe does not detract from prakṛti's inherent capacity for the modifications that occur in the process of creation, in which revelations also occur (VB, NB, NBB).

In this context, the beginnings of the yoga lineage in the current creation have already been stated in Vyāsa's commentary on the last sūtra. The tradition and texts (*āgama*) also tell us that the same process has occurred in the preceding creations (*pūrva*) and that God is the guru of the gurus (such as Brahmā, Viṣhṇu, Śhiva, and others) of those creations as well (NB). As Vyāsa says,

> The same should be understood with regard to the creations that have already transpired, and so forth.

Obviously "and so forth" has the force of including any future creations, because what is past or future to us is not so to God; time as a condition of delimitation has no connection with God, does not approach or revolve as a condition which might delimit His will, knowledge, and action by any division of time. In future creations the substance of this very sūtra will be revealed within the self of the sages again and again, so that the term *pūrva,* "the preceding gurus," may refer also to those who are yet to come even in any current or future creations.

Sūtra I.27 तस्य वाचकः प्रणवः।

tasya vāchakaḥ praṇavaḥ

tasya: his
vāchakaḥ: signifier, signifying word or name (is)
praṇavaḥ: the word *OM*

The word *OM* is His significator (name).

Vyāsa's Commentary

God (īśhvara) is the signified meaning of *OM*. Now, is this relationship of the signified with the signifier established by convention or is it like the lamp and the light?

This relationship of the signified with the signifier is permanent. God's convention, however, carries forward only the permanent meaning, just as an already established relationship of a father and a son is elucidated by conventionally indicating, This is his father, This is his son.

So in different creations too the convention, being dependent upon the inherent power (*śhakti*) of the signified and the signifier, is indicated the same way as before. Those who know the tradition categorically assert that the relationship of the word and the meaning is eternal because the perception of knowledge in consciousness as well as the continuity of usage is eternal.

Discussion

Because Sūtra I.23 asserted the possibility that samādhi may be attained through the practice of the presence of God (*īśhvara-praṇidhāna*), Sūtras I.24-26 were devoted to explaining īśhvara. Sūtra I.27 is preparatory to Sūtra I.28, which explains *praṇidhāna.*

The name of God is *OM*. It is a tradition of the mantra science that certain mantras are given specific names. The mantra *OM* is called *praṇava.* Many different etymological derivations are suggested by various commentators. For instance:

1. From prefix *pra* and verb *nu:* "whereby He is eminently eulogized" (BR, SS, Sh), or "that which eulogizes Him" (BR, Sh).
2. From prefixes *pra* and *ni* and verb *dhā,* as in *praṇidhāna:* "whereby He is placed close, brought close, by those who practise His presence (*pra-ni-dhātṛs*)" (Sh). Or "whereby one places God in the mind," for it is by a word or a name that one bears those in mind who are absent or intangible (Sh).
3. From *pra* + *ni* + *dhā* and *av:* "He who protects from *saṁsāra* the devotees (*pra-ni-dhātṛs*) who practise His presence," or "He who leads (*pra* + *nir* + *vā*) the devotees to nirvāṇa" (Sh).

The only way one who has not yet realized God can practise His presence is through His name, which is *OM.* The perennial question of Indian philosophy is raised again here: What is the relationship of the word and its meaning?[28] Although this is answered in greater detail under *Yoga-sūtras* III.17, here only the relevant part is briefly discussed. In this regard (HA) there are two kinds of objects: (1) Those which can be experienced without a name. For example, even if one does not know the word "blue," the colour is experienced with the eye. (2) Those which cannot be experienced without a word and its inherent meaning. For example, one cannot know a certain John as the son of Jack and Jack as John's father without the words "father" and "son" and the meaning that these words connote. Since God, unlike the colour blue, is not tangible to the senses, He cannot be experienced by the unrealized. He can only be signified by His name, *OM.* Only thus can *praṇidhāna,* His presence, be practised.

Now, there are some philosophers of language who believe that the relationship of words and meanings is established by the convention of usage alone. So Vyāsa raises the question:

> God (īśhvara) is the signified meaning of *OM.* Now, is this relationship of the signified with the signifier established by convention or is it like the lamp and the light?

28. A detailed examination of the origins, levels and significances of words is found in chapters 3, 5, 7, and 8, and pp. 75-77 and 121-31 of the author's book *Mantra and Meditation* (Honesdale, Pa.: Himalayan International Institute of Yoga Science and Philosophy, 1981).

If this relationship between the word and the meaning were eternal, inherent or natural and not a conventional one, a word should need no other pointer than "This word signifies this object"; it should simply convey itself. Thus where a word was not applicable, it would simply not signify the unrelated object. A thousand lamps cannot illuminate a jar that is simply not there (VM, NB). It is obvious, however, that if one so wishes, one can use the word "elephant" for a camel and start a fresh convention (VM). Similarly, is not God's name, *OM,* simply a matter of usage and convention, the way a father gives his son the appellation, say, "Devadatta" (VB)?

In other words, one may ask (RY) whether the relationship between word and meaning is produced by convention or only expressed by it. It is not produced, because then Īśhvara would have to produce it by fitting together the words and the meanings in the beginning of each cycle of creation, independent of the convention of the preceding cycle, thus contradicting the convention. Nor can it merely be expressed, because if it already exists, its expression (for example, by a father indicating about his son that "This is the son") is superfluous insofar as its effect on the relationship is concerned.

To resolve these doubts and contradictions, Vyāsa says:

> This relationship of the signified with the signifier is permanent. God's convention, however, carries forward only the permanent meaning, just as the already established relationship of a father and a son is elucidated by conventionally indicating, This is his father, This is his son.

The relationship of the word and the meaning is like the lamp and its light, sine qua non, indivisible (NBB).

The superimposition (*adhyāsa*) of one on the other (NB, NBB) will be explained further in Sūtra III.17. Even though in the *Mahābhāṣhya* Patañjali the grammarian has said that ordinarily *sarve sarvārtha-vāchakāḥ,* "all words may denote all meanings," yet it is God's convention and revelation that is determinative and elucidative (VM). He carries forward an eternally established power from one creation to the next, each time connecting the words to their meanings and revealing the same in the Vedas in passages such as:

OM KHAM BRAHMA
OM SPACE BRAHMAN

Yajur-veda XL.17

The relation between the two is one of identity. The two are identical, inseparable. This is their inherent power (*śhakti*) (VB, NB, NBB), which is not a third, separate factor. This, however, does not rule out the human freedom to establish fresh conventions so long as they do not transgress the eternal, divine ones; a father may still name his son "Devadatta," which is not his eternal name. But God has to reveal the eternal words and meanings in the beginning of each creation because during the dissolution period the saṁskāras gathered around the *jīvas* also are dissolved and there is no continuation of memory (RY).

It is a principle of Sāṅkhya philosophy that a word or sound is one of the five *tan-mātrās,* subtle elements, modifications of prakṛti. At the dissolution of the universe they all dissolve, together with their meanings, which are the objects related to them and connoted by them. Their *śhakti,* thus having been dissolved, is by no means permanently destroyed. As some plants become dormant in the hot season but regenerate at the touch of the rain in the season of the monsoons, so the objects—the meanings signified—and the words as their signifiers reappear together with their inherent *śhakti* upon the moment of the new creation. God's will alone (BM) then indicates, Let this be the word; let this be the meaning. Vyāsa says:

> So in different creations too the convention, being dependent upon the inherent power (*śhakti*) of the signified and the signifier, is indicated the same way as before. Those who know the tradition categorically assert that the relationship of the word and the meaning is eternal because the perception of knowledge in consciousness as well as the continuity of usage is eternal.

Āgamin, those who are versed in the *āgama,* the textual authority as the tradition of the yoga lineage, uphold the view that

> *nityaḥ śhabdārtha-sambandhaḥ.*
> The relationship of the word and the meaning is eternal.

This echoes Vararuchi's first *vārttika* in Patañjali's *Mahābhāṣhya* (I.1) on Pāṇini's grammar:

> *siddhe śhabdārtha-sambandhe,*

which has the identical translation.

In Vyāsa's passage we have translated the word *sam-prati-patti* as:

> the perception of knowledge in consciousness as well as the continuity of usage.

Of these two meanings, the first is the derivative (*yaugika*) meaning and the second is the conventional (*rūḍhi*) meaning. The commentators (VM, VB, NB, NBB, RY, HA) have all translated the word *sam-prati-patti* only as the equivalent of *vyavahāra-paramparā,* "continuity of usage," but we have chosen to give prominence to the derivative meaning. In Sūtra I.25 it was stated that God's names, etc. should be learned from *āgama,* the textual authority and the tradition of the lineage. Such authority begins and the lineage is derived from the fact of revelation, the perception of knowledge in consciousness. Especially with regard to the name of God, the usage has no other basis and its continuity in the usage is dependent thereupon.

We have said above that the sound is a modification of prakṛti and is subject to creation and dissolution. However, knowledge of God is eternal. The spoken word is its grossest vehicle. The knowledge, which is not a possession of God as an object separate from Him but rather is one with His self-nature, uses the sound and the word as His vehicle. The knowledge part of the word is *kūṭastha-nitya:* eternal as an Absolute; immutable and never modified. It is the half mora of *OM,* the silence, beyond the three—*a, u, m*—which the yogis experience in samādhi. Only the physical sound is the modifiable eternal (*pravāha-nitya*) which is manifested and unmanifested, appears and disappears, with creations and dissolutions.

At a transcendent level to say that "God" is the meaning of the word *OM* falls within the category of linguistic misconception or imaginary cognition (*vikalpa*) defined in Sūtra I.9 (NB). *OM* as the eternal and immutable knowledge is not a name of God, separate from Him. It is the same as God, just as its syllabic components *a,u,m* are the very Brahmā, Vishṇu and Śhiva who revolve in and with the cycles of *saṁsāra*. These sounds are their sonar bodies, as the silent knowledge beyond them is God's own knowledge-self. This truly is the essence of this sūtra but it can be understood only by studying the *Māṇḍūkya Upanishad* with Gauḍapāda's *kārikā* verses and Śhankarāchārya's commentary thereupon.

VB and BGG quote Yajñavalkya:

> He is the Divine Being, deva, with intangible form,
> to be grasped only by intent concentration,
> unified with the mind.
> His name is *OM*.
> Called by this name, pleased,
> He confers grace.
>
> *Bṛhad-yogi-yajñavalkya-smṛti* II.61

"Unified with the mind" in the above passage means that His power is drawn into the mind when the meditator calls upon Him in particular, advanced meditative processes (NTC). This being the origin and the end of all mantras renders to the devotee the fruit of the practice of all other mantras.

Sūtra I.28 तज्जपस्तदर्थभावनम्।

taj-japas tad-artha-bhāvanam

tat-japaḥ: repetition, recitation of that (and)
tat-: of that
artha-: meaning
bhāvanam: absorbing, cultivating
} cultivating, absorbing, the meaning of that

The japa[29] of that name, and cultivating and absorbing its meaning (is called *īśhvara-praṇidhāna,* the practice of the presence of God).[30]

Vyāsa's Commentary

When the yogi has understood the nature of the signifier and the signified, his

> [*Sūtra:*] *japa* of that name and cultivating and absorbing its meaning (is called *īśhvara-praṇidhāna,* the practice of the presence of God).

(This means) the *japa* of *OM,* and cultivating, impressing upon one's mind and absorbing it into God who is the *significatum* (*abhidheya*) of the word *OM.* As the yogi performs the *japa* of *OM* and becomes intent upon cultivating and impressing upon the mind the meaning of the word *OM,* his mind-field succeeds in becoming one-pointed. As is said:

> With the aid of silent recitation (*svādhyāya*) let one establish the posture, sitting in yoga. Through yoga too they sit for silent recitation. By perfecting silent recitation and yoga together the Supreme Self shines forth.

29. The word *japa* is left untranslated for want of an appropriate Western equivalent. Chant, mantra recitation, contemplation, are all parts of the complete process of *japa.* For the various progressively refined states of *japa,* see chapter 13 in the author's book *Mantra and Meditation* (Honesdale, Pa.: Himalayan International Institute of Yoga Science and Philosophy, 1981).

30. The parenthetical addition in the translation is an *anu-vṛtti,* a word brought forward (in this instance, from Sūtra I.23).

Discussion

As explained in the previous sūtra, since it is not possible for an ordinary person to practise the presence of God (*īśhvara-praṇidhāna*) without having reached the samādhi of God-realization, some other medium within reach of the mind has to be resorted to. The sound that is God's name, and is identical with Him, is within reach of the mind so far as its first three components, *a, u, m,* are the objects of concentration. The tradition of the Upaniṣhads and the lineage of the yogis speaks of the silent half mora that follows the three articulate components and is experienced only beyond the mind. The last sūtra defined this medium, *OM,* as the name of God, and the current sūtra explains practising the presence (*praṇidhāna*) of God. Says Vyāsa:

> When the yogi has understood the nature of the signifier and the signified,

only then does the actual *praṇidhāna* which is *japa* begin.

Patañjali equates *praṇidhāna* with the practice of *bhāvana,* which is translated as "cultivating or absorbing the real meaning (in meditation)" (VM, BR, AD, BM). It begins at a level within the limits of a practitioner's capacity. One may recite the word methodically or let it become a silent mental contemplation (BM). But *japa* must not be purely the recitation of the word, but rather *bhāvana* of the meaning of the word, that is, of the God who is signified by that word and is one with it. The *japa must* be accompanied with meditation (*dhyāna*) on Brahman (VB), or the Supreme Self, with faith and devotion (NB). In fact the *bhāvana,* contemplation of Brahman, should continue all the way through *dhāraṇā, dhyāna* and *samādhi* (BG). In other words the *japa* of the word, through its association, reminds one of that which it signifies, and the mind begins to dwell upon Him whose omniscience and other attributes are known to the practitioner (HA). *Japa* cannot be done without this association of the word and its meaning. (The significance of *bhāvana* has also been explained and discussed in Sūtra I.17, q.v.).

VB and NBB explain that *bhāvana* or *praṇidhāna* is experienced at two levels. First, the practitioner knows that parts and a whole are inseparable, effect and cause are unified, the power and the powerful (*śhakti* and *śhaktimān*) are one, and thus he contemplates and then experiences himself permeated by and unified with Brahman—like heat and fire in a hot iron ball, the heat and the hot object being unified. Later, the practitioner discriminates between prakṛti and puruṣha and then knows "I am Brahman." This explanation of *bhāvana* is Vedāntic and is not mentioned by Patañjali or Vyāsa.

As the yogi undertakes this practice, says Vyāsa:

> his mind-field succeeds in becoming one-pointed.

In the gross, recitative level of the articulate *japa*—even if the tongue is silent and the mind alone recites the word—the mind is in the *vikṣhipta* state, distracted by other thoughts. As the meaning, the very presence of God, becomes the primary experience, the first stages of samādhi ensue. In *sa-vitarka* the relationship of the word and the meaning is maintained. As one approaches *nir-vitarka* (samādhi without *vitarkas*), the separation of the word, the meaning and their relationship ceases, and the experience is unified. This entry into samādhi is what is meant by referring to the mind-field's becoming one-pointed, moving away from *vikṣhipta* to *ekāgra*.

Even if the meditation is on the lesser components of the meaning of *OM* (on Brahmā, Viṣhṇu, Śhiva and so forth, who are signified parts of *OM—a, u, m*) the same process of development occurs, for that concentration also is on the divine consciousness that pervades these deific presences (NB). We have translated *sampadyate* as "succeeds." The meaning is actually much richer: "one prospers, reaches the desired enrichment, finds fulfilment in all directions (NB); one comes to rest in the Supreme Self, becomes filled with the Supreme Self."

In the last sūtra we spoke of the power (*śhakti*) of the word and the meaning of the word, respectively known as *vāchaka* (that which enunciates, signifies) and *vāchya* (that which is enunciated, signified). As the *japa* becomes more and more refined, the power of the *vāchaka* is reduced till only the *vāchya* remains; the word ceases and meaning alone shines so as to totally occupy the mind until even the mind becomes, as it were, absent, taking the form of the object of concentration as stated in *YS* I.43 and III.3.

Following this thought comes the verse quoted by Vyāsa, attributed to his father, Parāśhara, in *Vișhṇu-purāṇa* III.6.2:

> With the aid of silent recitation (*svādhyāya*) let one establish the posture, sitting in yoga. Through yoga too they sit for silent recitation. By perfecting silent recitation and yoga together the Supreme Self shines forth.

The word *svādhyāya* is defined by Vyāsa in *YS* II.1 as

> *japa* of the purificatories like *OM*, and the study of scriptures that lead to liberation,

and again in *YS* II.32 in almost identical words. Its effects are described in *YS* II.2 and II.44. The background meaning of the term is in *adhyāya* 'study' (in the formal sense of the study of the Vedas), which traditionally has required reciting the Vedas, adhering to strict principles of enunciation and accentuation, and memorizing each word and annotation accurately. In fact both for the purpose of study and the rituals, the Vedas must be recited aloud. In this sense mere *adhyāya* is not *japa*. However, when the recitation is to oneself only, then it becomes *sva-adhyāya*, self-study, and then as a mental act it is called *japa*.

The term *yoga* in the verse under discussion means samādhi as it was explained by Vyāsa in *YS* I.1.

It can be experientially proved that as one begins *japa*, the mind is stilled and thereby the posture becomes steady. The verb form *āsīta* has been translated as

> Let one establish the posture, sitting in yoga.

As the *bhāvana* of the meaning of the mantra becomes firm, the presence of God is experienced and samādhi ensues. Repeated experience of deep meditation thus firms the practice of *japa* in turn. It is felt by some commentators that *svādhyāya* and yoga, that is, *japa* and samādhi, cannot be simultaneous (VB); the thought here is that one begins a meditation session with *japa*, which leads into samādhi, and at the end one emerges from samādhi into *japa* (VB, BM). This indeed is the case for a beginner in samādhi. But the verse states clearly that fulfilment, enrichment, perfection (*sampatti*) of both *japa* and samādhi leads to illumination of the Supreme Self. At that level *praṇidhāna* or *bhāvana* reaches the silent mora, the half that is beyond the articulate three. There *japa* is not even a mental endeavour and becomes one with samādhi.

Before we move on to the next sūtra, let us recapture the process that has occurred so far.

- One has engaged in *japa* and *bhāvana* (Sūtra I.28) of *OM*, for a long time, without interruption and with deep faith and commitment (Sūtra I.14).
- The articulate form of the word has ceased.
- The power of that which enunciates (*vāchaka*) has been extinguished by that which is enunciated (*vāchya*).
- All *vikṣhepas* having been eliminated, the mind-field has become *ekāgra*.
- All external objects of concentration have been abandoned.
- No further saṁskāras are gathered.
- Only the past saṁskāras maintain the momentum of physical continuity.
- The self now dwells in the self.

The next sūtra explains the natural concomitants of the yogi's development to such a degree.

Sūtra I.29 ततः प्रत्यक्चेतनाधिगमोऽप्यन्तरायाभावश्च।

tataḥ pratyak-chetanādhigamo'py antarāyābhāvaśh cha

tataḥ: then, through that (practice of the presence of God)
pratyak-: inward
chetanā-: consciousness
adhigamaḥ: attainment, realization
} attainment of inward consciousness, or realization of the inwardly conscious (self)
api: too
antarāya-: (of) obstacles, impediments, obstructions
abhāvaḥ: absence, removal
cha: also

Then through the practice of the presence of God accrues the attainment of inward consciousness and the realization of the inwardly conscious self; also the impediments are removed, made absent.

Vyāsa's Commentary

As to the impediments such as illness: well, through the practice of the presence of God (*īśhvara-praṇidhāna*) they cease to be. And the realization of one's true nature occurs. Just as God (īśhvara) is pure, joyful, absolute (*kevala*), without encumbrances, so also this (little) puruṣha, who is the cause of buddhi's accurate apprehension, is of the same nature—this is what he realizes.

Discussion

Patañjali and Vyāsa are aware of many questions, doubts, problems, obstacles and impediments that appear all along the path. No doubt their own disciples asked many questions. This can be surmised from Vyāsa's wording here:

> As to the impediments such as illness: well, through the practice of the presence of God, they cease to be.

This is by way of assurance so that disciples would continue the practice of *japa* following the prescriptions of Sūtra I.14.

There is, however, a slight discrepancy between the sūtra and Vyāsa's commentary. The order in the sūtra is, first, the realization of the inward consciousness and, second, the absence of impediments. Vyāsa, however, starts with removal of impediments, which is, of course, more logical because only when the impediments are removed can there ensue self-realization. The order in the sūtra, however, has its own reason. The first phrase of the sūtra,

> *pratyak-chetanā-adhigamaḥ,*
> the attainment of inward consciousness and the realization of the inwardly conscious self,

states the natural end result of what has been discussed from Sūtras I.23 to I.28.

The grace of God, invited through the practice of *japa* and so forth, naturally reverses the outward flow of awareness and draws it inwards until it finally reaches the ultimate goal of self-realization. All along the way the obstacles and impediments are removed through the same continuous practice and by the same grace that responds and uplifts and clears the paths and channels. This is what the experience of initiates confirms. Since the inward flow of consciousness and the removal of obstacles are concomitants of each other, either one could be stated first.

Since a commentator's work consists of clarifying subtleties for those who are naturally more concerned about the present impediments and obstacles, Vyāsa assures them that these obstacles will be overcome by continued practice of *japa* and so forth until final realization is reached. For those of greater experience he says that grace turns the consciousness inwards, and thereby the impediments are naturally removed. In this order, the next sūtra naming the impediments naturally follows.

There are differences of opinion on the meaning of the compound phrase *pratyak-chetanā,* which has been translated here as attainment of inward consciousness, or realization of the inwardly conscious, the self. The word *pratyak* is derived from the prefix *prati* 'towards' and the verb root *añch* 'to be directed; pointed or turned towards a certain direction'. VM (and NB, RY, NTC) sees *prati* to be a shortened form of *pratīpam* 'opposite'. So *pratyañch* or *pratyak* to him means not "turned towards the spiritual self," but the opposite, "outwards," and thus *pratyak-chetanā* is that little, ignorant self who is turned outwards because of *avidyā* away from the Supreme One.

But others (BR, AD) see it differently. *Pratīpam* 'opposite' to them means the opposite of the common outward consciousness; it means the power of the seer (*dṛk-śhakti*) as explained in Sūtras II.6,20. This is more in accordance with the tradition. In the *Kaṭha Upaniṣhad* IV.1,2 the outward consciousness is referred to as *parāñch* or *parāk,* from *para* + *añch* ('turned away, directed away' from the inward self towards distant objects). The word *parañch* or *parāk* is used in that sense elsewhere too (e.g., *Āitareya Upaniṣhad* III.3, *Chhāndogya Upaniṣhad* I.6.8 and *Bṛhadāraṇyaka Upaniṣhad* IV.4.1). Thus *parāñch* or *parāk* and *pratyañch* or *pratyak* are antonyms. *Pratyak* is, thus, definitely inward consciousness. Even if *prati* is short for *pratīpam* 'opposite', it indicates to an initiate that state whereby and wherein all previously held values are literally turned inside out. What was previously held to be reality now loses its significance and the reality that is experienced inwards alone holds sway over one's awareness.

VB and NBB explain *prati* in *pratyak* to mean "each." Thus God (īśhvara) is *pratyak-chetanā,* the consciousness that is turned towards each object. This explanation does not appear to fit the context or the intent of the sūtra. The realization intended is not of that consciousness which is turned towards all objects, but rather the one withdrawn, turned towards the self. Granting that omniscience ensues after self-realization, the current sūtra is not referring to that *siddhi.* The intent of the sūtra is simply to state that through *īśhvara-praṇidhāna* the consciousness is drawn inwards by divine grace, naturally leading to realization of the inwardly conscious self. This is the same (RS) as the seer dwelling in his own nature, explained in Sūtra I.3. So Vyāsa says:

> And the realization of one's true nature occurs.

What exactly is meant by this realization? What does the yogi see as the nature of the self? Vyāsa explains:

> Just as God is pure, joyful, absolute (*kevala*), without encumbrances, so also this (little) puruṣha, who is the cause of buddhi's accurate apprehension, is of the same nature—this is what he realizes.

(The phrase qualifying puruṣha as "the cause of buddhi's accurate apprehension" was discussed in Sūtra I.7 and need not be repeated here.) That puruṣha who was thus qualified hitherto is now seen beyond buddhi and other evolutes. It has re-cognized that it is *kevala,* alone and without prakṛti and free of the encumbrances (*upasargas*) of the karmic cycles such as birth in a species, life spans and pains and pleasures in those species and life spans (*YS* II.13). The divine nature in the self is perceived. VB interprets the statement in accordance with the Vedāntic doctrine of the unity of the little self and the Supreme Self. Here Vyāsa comes closest to stating the identity of the lower and the higher puruṣha but does not quite do so. The particles *yathā* 'just as' and *tathā* 'so also' indicate similarity but not identity.

The sūtra, it appears, means to say that *īśhvara-praṇidhāna* leads to self-realization; in self-realization one sees the similarity of the natures of the little self and īśhvara. The sūtra says nothing of the next step, which may be the Brahman-realization of Vedānta but is not stated here to be so.

The question arises: How is it that the practice of the presence of God can bring forth the realization of the nature of the individual self? How can attention directed towards one entity or object ever bring forth the closeness of another? The answer (VB, VM, NB, NBB, RY) is that attention directed towards something of a totally contradictory or nonhomogeneous nature cannot bring forth the understanding or the presence of its opposite. But, for example, the study of one science helps us to understand another related science also. That is why Vyāsa has drawn attention to the similarity of natures of the little and the greater puruṣhas. The attention directed towards the greater puruṣha naturally brings about the realization of the nature of the little puruṣha.

Sūtra I.30 **व्याधिस्त्यानसंशयप्रमादालस्याविरति-भ्रान्तिदर्शनालब्धभूमिकत्वानवस्थितत्वानि चित्तविक्षेपास्तेऽन्तरायाः।**

vyādhi-styāna-saṁśhaya-pramādālasyāvirati-bhrāntidarśhanālabdhabhūmikatvānavasthitatvāni chitta-vikṣhepās te'ntarāyāḥ

vyādhi-: illness
styāna-: mental laziness, procrastination, mind's idleness
saṁśhaya-: doubt
pramāda-: negligence
ālasya-: laziness, languor, sloth
a-virati-: failing to turn away from the world and the senses, non-abstention
bhrānti-darśhana-: wrong views, confusion of philosophies
a-labdha-bhūmikatva-: failing to gain a ground (and)
an-avasthitatvāni: instability, inability to maintain the ground or level
chitta-vikṣhepāḥ: (are) distractions of the mind-field
te: they (are)
antarāyāḥ: obstacles, impediments

Illness, mental idleness, doubt, negligence, sloth, non-abstention, confusion of philosophies, failure to gain a ground and instability are the distractions of the mind-field; they are the impediments.

Vyāsa's Commentary

Now, what are the impediments? The same as the distractions of the mind-field. Again, what are those and how many?

> [*Sūtra:*] Illness, mental idleness, doubt, negligence, sloth, non-abstention, confusion of philosophies, failure to gain a ground and instability are the distractions of the mind-field; they are the impediments.

The nine impediments are the distractions of the mind-field. They exist together with the vṛttis of the mind-field. In their absence the vṛttis of the mind-field explained before do not exist. Of these:

- Illness is the imbalance of the body constituents, fluid essences and senses.
- *Styāna* is the mind's idleness and procrastination.
- Doubt is the observation touching both ends: "It might be thus, it might not be thus."
- Negligence is not cultivating (*bhāvana*) the means that lead to samādhi.
- Sloth is the lack of initiative, propensity and perseverance because of heaviness of the body and the mind-field.
- Non-abstention is the mind-field's failure to turn away from the world and the senses, lustfulness consisting of involvement in sensuality arising from proximity of and contact with sense objects.
- Confusion of philosophies is the condition called *viparyaya.*
- Failure to gain ground means not reaching the ground of samādhi.
- Instability is the mind-field's failure to be sustained in the ground that has been attained.

Only upon achieving samādhi would that, the mind-field, stabilise.

These distractions (*vikṣhepas*) of the mind-field are called the nine impurities of yoga, adversaries of yoga, obstacles or impediments to yoga.

Discussion

These impediments are called *vikṣhepas* because they throw the mind off (*vi* + *kṣhip*) from the path of yoga (VM, VB). They cause it to fall from yoga (RY, SS), thus causing the aspirant to become a *yoga-brahṣhṭa* (one who has fallen from the path of yoga), which is discussed in chapter 6 of the *Bhagavad-gītā.* They appear with the growth of the power of rajas and tamas (BR, NB, BM) and prevent accomplishment of one-pointedness (BR), the *ekāgra* state, which is the fourth of the five grounds (*bhūmis*) of the mind-field explained in Sūtra I.1. Unless the *vikṣhepas* are mastered, the mind-field cannot progress from *vikṣhipta* to the *ekāgra* state because *vikṣhepa* consists of the presence of a variety of vṛttis (NBB).

Some of the nine impediments, *antarāyas,* are by themselves vṛttis. VM says this of doubt and of the confusion of philosophies or *viparyaya.* It appears, however, that any of the *antarāyas* consisting of a mental state are vṛttis. For this purpose they do not have to have been named in Sūtras I.5 and I.6 because it was clarified there that the list was not exclusive; there are not only five vṛttis, but rather innumerable vṛttis divided fivefold.

Whether or not an *antarāya* is a vṛtti in itself, other vṛttis always accompany it. In fact these *antarāyas* produce vṛttis, and no vṛttis are produced without them (NBB). Vṛttis cease to interrupt the practice of samādhi as soon as the *antarāyas* are mastered. Then and only then the mind-field progresses from *vikṣhipta* to *ekāgra.* A few comments on each *antarāya* need to be included here.

Illness (*vyādhi*) is the imbalance of *dhātus, rasas* and *karaṇas.* The *dhātus* are the constituents of the body such as blood, flesh, bones and so forth. The three humours, namely, air, bile and phlegm, are also called *dhātus.* The *rasas* are the fluid essences such as hormones, gastric juices and so forth. *Karaṇas* are the active and cognitive senses, as well as the mind. Their imbalance is an obstacle in the practice of yoga because the mind reacts to an illness, and an unbalanced or sick body disturbs meditation in many ways. It is possible through the practice of *japa* for the mind to cease to react to physical illness and not be depressed or otherwise emotionally troubled by it. Disciplines of diet and regularity of life habits as well as the practices of *haṭha*-yoga help to purify the body and bring about restoration of its internal balances so that discomforts of the body may cease to distract the mind.

There is no single English word expressive of *styāna.* When the mind is habituated to restlessness and fickleness, it refuses to settle down to being applied in a constant manner. It procrastinates, postpones, finds excuses, does not become fixed on anything for long. Its capacity for concentration is limited. Even without an external cause it remains distracted and refuses to work for the purpose the *sādhaka* has set for himself.

Doubt (*saṁshāya*) can exert a strong, adverse effect on the efficacy of yoga (BR, NBB, BM) as taught by the tradition, the texts and the guru, as well as on one's own capacity and the possibility of one's success (NT). In doubt the mind keeps oscillating between two possibilities (VM, VB, BG, NB, RY, AD, SS) as to whether what has been taught is correct or incorrect, and whether one should undertake to apply it or not. Along with confusion of philosophies, it is the most difficult adversary in the endeavour to bring about the *nirodha* of vṛttis (VM).

Negligence (*pramāda*) is a failure in the practice of *bhāvana* (constantly impressing an experience on the mind through repeated observance). It can take the form of the arousal of passion, etc. (NTC) or the failure to gather the sixfold wealth of *śhama, dama, uparati, titikṣhā, śhraddhā* and *samādhāna* (NB) (see p. 67). One fails to pay attention to the observance (VM, BG, AD), remains disinterested (BR) and especially fails to practise the *aṅgas* of yoga (NTB, RY) such as non-violence and truth (SS) or any other means of samādhi (NBB, BR, BM).

Sloth (*ālasya*) is failure at the endeavour owing to heaviness of the body because of fat, phlegmatic tendencies, etc., and heaviness of mind because of tamas (VM et al).

Non-abstention (*a-virati*) is a craving for sense objects. This is all that the commentators say. In our view this is the opposite of *uparati* (see p. 67), which is the first stage of *vairāgya.* The strong pull of the senses prevents one from concentrating on the path.

Confusion of philosophies (*bhrānti-darśhana*) is identified by Vyāsa with *viparyaya* and should be studied in Sūtra I.8. In this *antarāya* one views a fact as a non-fact (BM), sees what is not there in any entity (SS), and decides against what has been taught by the gurus and so forth (VB, NB, NBB, BG). Here there is no oscillation as with doubt; instead the mind has become settled on the issue, has taken a side that is in error (NT). In doubt a possibility was allowed that the fact might be accepted as fact; here it has been totally rejected. Together with doubt, this is the most difficult adversary of the *nirodha* of vṛttis.

A-labdha-bhūmikatva, failure to gain a ground, refers to the condition in which in spite of much observance one has not yet reached the plateau of confirmed achievement of a state of consciousness. It may be because the conditions of Sūtra I.14 have not yet been fully and effectively fulfilled or because one is in the category of a person of little momentum and lower capacity (per Sūtras I.21-22). In any case, the progressively higher grounds (*bhūmis*), the *madhumatī,* etc., listed on p. 78, are referred to by all commentators. Unless one has overcome all the previous *antarāyas,* the higher ground is simply not gained.

The same reasons apply to the next *antarāya,* instability (*anavasthitatva*), wherein one gains the higher ground but falls from it. Unless the anterior ground becomes firm the posterior one remains weak (NT): one reaches the higher state but keeps slipping from it. It is not enough that one should practise any kind of samādhi once or twice or a few times and be satisfied by that experience. The endeavour should continue until *asamprajñāta* becomes the normal state, from which one no longer falls.

Once again it should be remembered that this and the next sūtra occur in the context of *īśhvara-praṇidhāna.* It is through the practice of the presence of God in *japa* that all the *antarāyas* are gradually overcome by the grace of God.

Sūtra I.31 दुःखदौर्मनस्याङ्गमेजयत्वश्वासप्रश्वासा विक्षेपसहभुवः।

duḥkha-daurmanasyāṅgamejayatva-śhvāsa-praśhvāsā vikṣhepa-saha-bhuvaḥ

duḥkha-: pain
daur-manasya-: frustration, anguish, bad mood, ill-mindedness
aṅgam-ejayatva-: unsteadiness, movement of limbs
śhvāsa-: inhalation (and)
pra-śhvāsāḥ: exhalation (these are)
vikṣhepa-: of *vikṣhepas,* of distractions
saha-bhuvaḥ: natural accompaniments, correlates

Pain, frustration, unsteadiness of limbs, involuntary inhalation and exhalation—these are the natural accompaniments of distractions.

Vyāsa's Commentary

Pain (*duḥkha*) is (of three kinds):

ādhyātmika: within oneself
ādhibhautika: caused by other beings
ādhidaivika: caused by deities or natural forces

Pain is that afflicted by which beings endeavour to ward it off.

Ill-mindedness (*daur-manasya*) is the mind's agitation and anguish (*kṣhobha*) when a desire is frustrated.

Unsteadiness (*aṅgam-ejayatva*) is the movement of limbs.

Inhalation (*śhvāsa*) is the *prāṇa* breathing in external air. Exhalation (*pra-śhvāsa*) is (the *prāṇa*) breathing out visceral air.

These natural accompaniments or correlates of distractions (*vikṣhepas*) appear with them and accrue to one whose mind-field is in the distracted (*vikṣhipta*) state. They do not happen to one whose mind is harmonized in samādhi.

Discussion

This sūtra requires only a few comments.

Duḥkha is any kind of pain, grief, sorrow or suffering. It is that which all beings seek to avoid. It is the first of the fourfold noble truths of the Buddhist doctrine and the first concern of the Sāṅkhya-yoga philosophy. *Sāṅkhya-kārikā,* the most important Sāṅkhya text, begins with the statement:

> Because one intends to prevent the three kinds of pain, there arises inquiry as to the means of that prevention.

The same sorrow is spoken of in *YS* II.16, and *YS* II.15-26 are devoted to understanding pain, the cause of pain, the removal of pain, and the means of removing pain. Whereas the sūtras in Chapter 2 deal with the totality of the universal problem of pain, the connotation of *duḥkha* in this sūtra is somewhat limited to the personal experience of pain. Both universal and personal pain are experienced from three sources:

1. *Ādhyātmika:* internal to oneself—physical (such as illness) and mental (such as passions and desires)
2. *Ādhibhautika:* caused by other beings (such as beasts of prey or one's enemies)
3. *Ādhidaivika:* caused by planetary influences (NT, RY) and other natural forces (such as heat, cold, etc.)

Even though all pain is experienced mentally, one attributes it to various external forces; it is only in this sense that the above three classifications are made (VB). All of this pain is actually the mind's rajasic mutation (BR, AD) and always impedes the practice of yoga. When it is realized that all pain actually originates and is experienced in the mind as a correlate of the previous nine obstacles and the vṛttis, then one is in a position to control it mentally. In spite of the presence of pain, one may elect to suffer it less and may prevent it from becoming a barrier on the path of yoga.

If the mind in daily life is filled with *duḥkha,* pain of desires, the mind in meditation remains disturbed (*vikṣhipta*) and sattva fails to overcome rajas. More about *duḥkha* will be discussed in Chapter 2.

Daurmanasya, literally "bad-mindedness" (from *dur* 'bad' + *manas* 'mind'), is the antonym of a widely used Sanskrit word, *saumanasya,* "good-mindedness" (from *su* 'good, happy, harmonized' + *manas* 'mind'). Since mental pain (*duḥkha*) is desire, its product is *daurmanasya,* frustration, anguish, despair, bad moods, emotional disturbances and instability. All of these are expressed together in *daurmanasya,* ill-mindedness, all the way to psychopathic situations.

If the mind in daily life is filled with *daurmanasya,* meditation also remains disturbed (*vikṣhipta*).

Aṅgamejayatva, shaking of body and twitching of limbs in meditation, is part of the same rajasic tendencies which keep a person restless and listless in daily life and is caused by emotional instability. Without mental stability there can be no stabilisation of the body in meditation. Unless sattva helps settle one down, this inability to sit still is not brought under control and the posture does not fulfil the requirements (*YS* II.46) of steadiness and comfort.

Śhvāsa and *pra-śhvāsa,* involuntary inhalation and exhalation, are the well-known symptoms of mental and emotional disturbance. They are the opposite of the total control of *prāṇāyāma* described in *YS* II.49-53. Involuntary inhalation is the opposite of *pūraka,* the *prāṇāyāma* of controlled inhalation. Involuntary exhalation is the opposite of *rechaka,* the *prāṇāyāma* of controlled exhalation. Without this control the ultimate natural *prāṇāyāmas* of *YS* II.50-51 cannot be accomplished. In daily life this symptom of a disturbed mind is seen in gasping, sighing and such. The same mental conditions cause the breath to flow unevenly and in jerks during meditation. Until the breath flows smoothly and evenly without jerks or pauses during meditation, it should be understood that desire and frustrations (*duḥkha* and *daurmanasya*) are present.

All five symptoms are correlates of the nine obstacles (*antarāyas*) and should be seen as five aspects of a single condition, that of a personality disturbed both in life and in meditation. These five aspects have to be cured altogether. Only then does *vikṣhipta* progress to *ekāgra* (Sūtra I.1). Vyāsa states clearly that these symptoms accrue to one whose mind-field is in the distracted (*vikṣhipta*) state; they do not happen to one whose mind is harmonized in samādhi.

The word *samāhita* means "harmonized; that in which conditions of conflict have been resolved, as though previously broken pieces have been set and fused together" (from *sam* + *ā* + *dhā* 'to set together, join together' [as of broken bones]); and "that which is in samādhi." The two, again, are actually one condition. From *sam* + *ā* + *dhā,* "samādhi" is the abstract noun and *samāhita* is the perfect participle expressing the fact that this harmonizing, resolving, of the conditions of conflict has been accomplished by reaching samādhi. Only then are the nine impediments and their five correlates overcome.

Sūtra I.32 तत्प्रतिषेधार्थमेकतत्त्वाभ्यासः।

tat-pratiṣhedhārtham eka-tattvābhyāsaḥ

tat-: those
pratiṣhedha-: prevention, opposing, prohibiting, negating, voiding, nullifying
artham: for the purpose of
} For the purpose of negating those (*antarāyas* and their companions)
eka-: one
tattva-: principle, factor, reality, real element
abhyāsaḥ: practice

To prevent and negate those impediments, the distractions and their correlates, the practice of a single reality, one principle, is enjoined, prescribed.

Vyāsa's Commentary

Now, these distractions, being the adversaries of samādhi, should be brought under control by the same practice and dispassion (*abhyāsa* and *vairāgya*) (which have been explained). Of those, to sum up the topic of practice (*abhyāsa*), he (Patañjali) says

> [*Sūtra:*] To prevent and negate those impediments, the distractions and their correlates, the practice of a single reality, one principle, is enjoined, prescribed.

For preventing and negating the distractions (*vikṣhepas*) one should make a practice of the mind-field's resorting to a single reality or one principle alone.

For someone who holds the opinion that chitta is distinct and limited only to each experienced factor, comprises only a single cognition and is momentary, then that entire chitta is already one-pointed (*ekāgra*) and is never and not at all distracted (*vikṣhipta*). If, however, it is gathered together from all over, withdrawn from there and placed into samādhi on a single matter (*artha*) and thereby becomes one-pointed (*ekāgra*), then it is not, cannot be considered to be, limited only to a given object.

If someone believes that the mind is one-pointed when it is flowing along similar cognitions and that this one-pointedness is an attribute of the flowing mind-stream, then at the same time there could be no such mind-stream, the chitta being momentary in this view. If, however, it is an attribute of that single cognition which is a part of the flowing stream, the mind being confined to a single experienced factor, it will be one-pointed all the same whether flowing along similar cognitions or dissimilar ones. Then it would be inappropriate to postulate a distracted mind. Therefore we must conclude that there is only one mind conditioned towards many factors of experience, changing in condition according to each of the many purposes.

Furthermore, if the cognitions arise that are by nature distinct and not associated with a single mind-field, how is it possible that one should remember a cognition experienced by some other? And, how is it possible that one cognition should experience (the results of) the domain of karmas gathered by some other? No matter how one tries to reconcile this, still the analogy of the cow dung and the milk pudding applies. Not only this, but if we adhere to the separateness of chittas, one's own experience has to be disowned. How? "I am touching what I saw"; "I am seeing the same thing that I touched"—such cognition is present as the non-distinction of the cognizer when all the cognitions are separate and distinct. If all the chittas were completely distinct, how could this idea, the subject of a single cognition, persist and substrate in one common cognizer as "I am a nondistinct, undivided self"? And this cognition that "I am a nondistinct, undivided self" is grasped and proved by one's own experience. Nor can the power of direct experience (*pratyakṣha*) be overwhelmed by any other proof. Any other proof, however, becomes effective only on the strength of direct perception.

Therefore, we conclude, the mind-field is one and conditioned to many factors of experience, constant, yet changing its condition to serve many purposes with regard to many objects.

Discussion

Are these distractions overcome only by the practice of the presence of God as has been stated in Sūtra I.29? The answer appears to be that *īśhvara-praṇidhāna* precludes the arising of distractions. One who practises the presence of God is naturally free of these distractions (NB). But one who cannot fully succeed in *praṇidhāna* requires the aid of another practice (NB). Once the distractions do arise, the only resort is the practice (VB).

There still appears to be a contradiction between Sūtra I.29 and this one. Some commentators (VM, RY, SS, BM) resolve it by saying that, in Vyāsa's phrase,

> a practice of the mind-field's resorting to a single reality or one principle alone

means, again, *īśhvara-praṇidhāna.* God (īśhvara) is that reality, that principle whose presence is practised. Others (VB, NBB) are of the opinion that it refers to the gross elements, etc. that are progressively the objects of concentration in the various samādhis discussed in Sūtra I.17. Yet others (BR, NTB) say that one may practise concentration on any object of one's choice (*abhimata*) (BG, NB). But this last interpretation of the sūtra would render Sūtra I.39 redundant.

The correct interpretation of the sūtra would reconcile the various views. If one could successfully maintain the practice of the presence of God, the *vikṣhepas* would not arise. It was stated in the previous sūtra that these *vikṣhepas* occur to one whose mind-field is distracted (*vikṣhipta*) and not to one whose mind is harmonized in samādhi. However, it is not possible for a large majority to maintain this presence fully and all the time. To arrive at the practice of the presence of God, most seekers require going through other practices, starting from concentration on gross elements in *sa-vitarka* samādhi. Even when one comes to *īśhvara-praṇidhāna,* this itself requires continuously directing the mind towards God until one maintains himself in the great presence. Furthermore (HA), in the beginning of *īśhvara-praṇidhāna* the mind wanders to all the different notions concerning the attributes of God: His omnipresence, kindness, love, etc. Here, again, the mind must be withdrawn from all these notions and trained to maintain only the awareness of a single reality, the One Principle, God alone.

In this context it must be made clear that only until one actually reaches the presence of God are there various notions to which followers of different credos try to remain loyal and about which others merely speculate. When God is experienced, however, it is found that none of these notions is accurate. God is not at all as He is thought to be; the experience of the One Reality (*eka-tattva*) is entirely apart from all ideas which were held before.

Vyāsa says:

> Now, these distractions, being the adversaries of samādhi, should be brought under control by the same practice and dispassion (*abhyāsa* and *vairāgya*) (which have been explained). Of those, to sum up the topic of practice (*abhyāsa*) [this sūtra is taught].

In other words the topic of *abhyāsa* that was begun in Sūtra I.12 is now summed up and concluded here. Since Sūtra I.12 had made *abhyāsa* and *vairāgya* associates (*saha-kārin*), Vyāsa includes *vairāgya* here in his comment even though it is not found in the sūtra itself (VM). *Vairāgya* is not out of place here, as that topic still continues through all these sūtras and is concluded in Sūtra I.40. In everything stated from Sūtra I.12 up to here, *abhyāsa* and *vairāgya* remain the necessary accompaniment and condition, an aid to everything, a precondition for all realizations. Furthermore, just as *abhyāsa* is accompanied with *vairāgya* in this sūtra without the latter's being mentioned specifically, *abhyāsa* will continue to accompany *vairāgya* up to Sūtra I.40 even though the topic of *abhyāsa* as a primary factor is being brought to conclusion here. Such are always the implications in the way the sūtras are organized.

Here Vyāsa challenges the Buddhist view of mind. In this, especially in *vijñāna-vada,* the theory of "ideation only," no external objects exist. Only idea (*vijñāna*) arises as an error from within. A corollary to this view is *kṣhaṇika-vāda,* the theory of momentariness. All ideas exist for a moment only. Any continuity that appears is merely a string of independent ideas arising one after another and subsisting for a moment only. Consequently, there does not exist an entity called the mind. The ideation at each moment brings into existence the mind (chitta) of that moment, which immediately upon the expiration of that moment, ceases. Thus nothing is permanent, nothing lasts more than a moment. Vyāsa challenges this view, constructing his argument on the basis that the Buddhist also believes that the mind is distracted, and needs to be brought to one-pointedness. Vyāsa's argument may be paraphrased briefly as follows. If the mind is momentary and exists only for the duration of a single, momentary ideation or cognition thereof, then obviously for that moment the mind remains one-pointed on that idea or cognition. Immediately after that moment the said cognition, idea and the mind vanish and some other cognition, idea and the mind arise. This next momentary mind also is one-pointed with reference to that cognition and idea in relation to which it has come into being. Where then is there any distraction from which the Buddhist wishes to lead the mind into one-pointedness?

The Buddhist might defend himself by saying that his definition of one-pointedness is that at each moment in each successive momentary mind a similar ideation and the cognition thereof should occur. This is based on the notion of *pravāha*-chitta, a flowing mind, the mind-stream in which each successive wave causes the appearance of continuity even though there is no stream by itself, only the succession of waves. When the waves arising in each successive moment are dissimilar, the mind-stream is considered distracted and when they are similar, it is one-pointed. Vyāsa challenges this definition. Whether the successive cognitions and ideas arising with each momentary mind are similar or dissimilar is irrelevant since the Buddhists do not believe that there is a single continuous mind at all. This brings us back to the implication that each momentary mind is already concentrated on its relevant idea and cognition. There is no distraction at all, and that being so, what other samādhi can there be for the Buddhist?

Vyāsa, therefore, refutes the entire notion of the succession of momentary minds. If there is no single, continuous mind-field, and each cognition and each successive mind is distinct and separate, how is it possible that we remember anything at all? Only a single, continuous mind can be a repository of memories. If one Chaitra memorizes the scriptures, it is not someone named Maitra who remembers them! How can one momentary mind remember something that transpired in and expired with another momentary mind, a million moments—or even a single, contiguous moment—ago? Also, without a single, continuous entity can there be any kind of effectiveness in the world? Can the mere idea of a momentary fire warm our hands? Again, if the idea of momentary minds were taken seriously, the entire doctrine of karma and its fruition would fall into dire straits. Since in this view there is no continuous mind and no continuous personality, who gathers the karmas and who deposits them in the *karmāśhaya,* the repository or domain of the karmas? Yet again, how can one independent, momentary mind be responsible for, suffer or enjoy the karmas gathered by a million other momentary minds? It sounds like the analogy of the milk pudding and the cow dung, which goes as follows:

> All that a cow produces is milk.
> Milk pudding is produced from the (milk of a) cow.
> Cow dung is produced from a cow.
> Therefore, milk pudding and cow dung are one and the same!

That is to say, in the Buddhist view there appears to be no cause and effect relationship between the successive, momentary minds nor between the karma of a preceding one and the pain-pleasure fruition thereof in a subsequent one. Yet, both are in a single substratum, in a single personality. What exactly is that personality? Merely the process of unbroken succession? A process such as succession by itself is nothing concrete, not a substance nor an entity. How can the succession by itself perform karma, gather it and enjoy or suffer its consequence? The whole argument is even more fallacious than the analogy of milk pudding and cow dung (VM). The Buddhist thinks that the cow named "Succession" produces both karmas and their results!

The Buddhist view, says Vyāsa, contradicts all personal experience. By experience we know, for example, "I am touching exactly the object I previously saw," or "What I touched is what I am seeing now." We see that the cognitions "object," "touching," and "seeing" are each separate and distinct, but they unite in the single cognizer. By this experience we know "I am an undifferentiated, continuous, single entity." How could this experience occur if there were only distinct, momentary minds?

Experience is the supreme arbiter, the highest proof. The validity of all other proofs is derived from that of direct experience (*pratyakṣha*) which alone renders them effective. On the basis of our experience we know that the mind-field is a single, continuous entity, constant through the changing cognitions, yet undergoing a variety of conditions to serve many purposes with regard to many objects.

Vyāsa's word *ava-sthitam* is loaded with meaning. On one hand it means "constant, stable." On the other, it is derived from *ava* + *sthā,* "to go through a process or condition." The mind is a single constant but passes through many conditions, *aṇeka-artham,* "to serve many purposes (*arthas*) with regard to many objects (*arthas*)." This mind is to be brought under control, freed from obstacles and their correlates, through the practice of concentration on a single principle alone.

Sūtra I.33

मैत्रीकरुणामुदितोपेक्षाणां सुखदुःख-
पुण्यापुण्यविषयाणां भावनातश्चित्तप्रसादनम्।

maitrī-karuṇā-muditopekṣhāṇāṁ sukha-duḥkha-puṇyāpuṇya-viṣhayāṇāṁ bhāvanātaśh chitta-prasādanam

maitrī-: (of) amity, love
karuṇā-: compassion
muditā-: joyfulness, gladness, and
upekṣhāṇām: of indifference, equanimity
suhka-: (of) pleasure, comfort; those comfortable
duḥkha-: pain, sorrow, suffering; those suffering
puṇya-: virtue, merit, virtuousness, meritoriousness; the virtuous and meritorious (and)
a-puṇya-: vice, nonvirtue, nonvirtuousness, nonmeritoriousness; the nonvirtuous and nonmeritorious
viṣhayāṇāṁ: in relation with, with regard to
bhāvanātaḥ: through cultivating, by impressing into (upon) oneself
chitta-: (of) mind-field
pra-sādanam: purifying, rendering clear, making happy, making serene, pleasing, making pleasant

By cultivating and impressing into oneself the sentiments of amity and love, compassion, gladness, and indifference with regard to those comfortable, those suffering, the virtuous and the non-virtuous (respectively), the mind is purified and made pleasant.

Vyāsa's Commentary

That mind-field the purification (*parikarman*) of which is advised by the Scripture—how is that?

[*Sūtra:*] By cultivating and impressing into oneself the sentiments of amity and love, compassion, gladness, and indifference with regard to those comfortable, those suffering, the virtuous and the nonvirtuous (respectively), the mind is purified and made pleasant.

Of these, one should cultivate amity towards all living beings who are endowed with comfort and pleasures, compassion towards those who are suffering, gladness towards those of virtuous nature and indifference towards (those of) nonvirtuous disposition. As one cultivates himself thus, his white nature increases, grows. Then the mind is purified and becomes pleasant. Purified and pleasant, it attains the state of one-pointed stability.

Discussion

Sūtra I.20 enumerated the various methods (*upāyas*) for perfecting yoga. The topic of their practice (*abhyāsa*) was brought to summation in the last sūtra. The subject of the highest kind of lower dispassion (*apara-vairāgya*), called *vaśhīkāra,* was introduced in Sūtra I.15 and will be brought to conclusion in Sūtra I.40. Both *abhyāsa* and *vairāgya,* however, are interdependent, and since the consideration in the sūtras is never confined to either one exclusively, the two topics weave in and out of the discussion.

It is understood that the mind-field must become one-pointed (*ekāgra*) to experience samādhi. The five methods of faith and the other four *upāyas* stated in Sūtra I.20 are the prerequisite means for attaining one-pointedness (VB) and *samprajñāta* samādhi (SS), but success in the practice of these is blocked and the mind cannot reach one-pointedness if it is filled with undesirable sentiments such as intolerance and jealousy (*asūyā*) (VM, RY). For this reason one seeks to purify the mind and to make it pleasant. This can be done only by warding off the blocks of negative emotions by establishing the controls of *vaśhīkāra* (Sūtras I.15, I.40). Otherwise the sentiments of jealousy and so forth continue to destabilise the mind no matter how much the five *upāyas* are practised. The practices described in Sūtras I.33-39 provide a way to attain final control (*vaśhīkāra*). Sūtra I.35 uses the term *sthiti-nibandhana,* which means not merely "stabilising" but "rendering (that stability) permanent, unshakable; making (it) binding and fastening (it)." That term is synonymous with *chitta-prasādana* 'purifying the mind and making it pleasant', as it occurs here (BG, NB, NBB). Let us summarize the above approach as follows:

- Samādhi being synonymous with yoga, its lower stage, known as *samprajñāta,* can be attained only when the mind is made one-pointed (*ekāgra*).
- Through practice of the five *upāyas* stated in Sūtra I.20 the mind is made *ekāgra*. This practice (*abhyāsa*) (*YS* I.12) must be undertaken together with dispassion (*vairāgya*), the highest level of which is the final control (*vaśhīkāra*) (*YS* I.15).
- Though *abhyāsa* is defined (I.13) as the endeavour to make the mind stable, one fails to maintain such stability because the undesirable sentiments such as jealousy and intolerance keep intervening.
- Sūtras I.33-39 explain the ways to make that stability permanent (I.35), which is the same as purifying the mind and making it pleasant (*chitta-prasādana*) in the current sūtra.

The way to purify the mind, to make it pleasant and permanently stable, so that one-pointedness of *samprajñāta* may become the yogi's natural state, is to impede and counteract the force of the undesirable and destructive sentiments by cultivating, imprinting upon the mind, developing, the *bhāvanā* of the positive sentiments described in this sūtra. The practices spoken of in Sūtras I.33-39 are in general called *pari-karman* or *pari-karma* (ways of adorning, polishing, preparing, training the mind). The primary four *parikarmas* are stated in this sūtra. The Buddhist tradition also refers to them as *parikarmas* or *brahma-vihāra* (frolicking in Brahman). *Parikarman* is actually a supportive act in any science (BR). It is also like polishing, seasoning, giving a final protective or enhancing touch that prevents deterioration.

This purification of mind means abolishing the dark stains and taints (BG, NB) such as attachments and aversions (*rāga* and *dveṣha*) (BG, BN); transgressions, evil acts, sin (*pāpa*) (BG, NB, SS); meritorious acts, virtue (*puṇya*) (SS); jealousy (*īrṣhyā*) (NB); malice (*asūyā*) (NB); and intolerance (*amarṣha*) (NB).

The dichotomies of attachments and aversions, virtue and sin, stain the mind (SS). Attachments and aversions are the primary agents of sullying the mind (BR). If these two can be eradicated, then the mind becomes pleasant and consequently one-pointed (BR). The antidotes to these sullying sentiments are the four right attitudes described in this sūtra.

The sūtra provides therapeutic prescriptions, antidotes, for the poisons of negative sentiments. In following these prescriptions one learns to replace rajasic and tamasic vṛttis with sattvic ones, starting with *maitrī,* known in Buddhism as *mettā* in the Pāli language. *Maitrī* is *sauhārda* (VM, VB, BR, NB, AD, NT, BM), *eucardia* or goodheartedness, amity, friendship. It is not affection, because affection binds (BM) instead of freeing an individual. This becomes clear when one understands jealousy (*īrṣhyā*) (VM, HA, BR, NT, NBB, BM) and other sentiments such as the inability to acknowledge others' good qualities (*asūyā*) (i.e., being fault-finding) and small-mindedness in general (*mātsarya*). These various maladies have been included by different commentators. Jealousy (*īrṣhyā*) is closely coupled with attachment (*rāga*). *Rāga* is not merely an attachment to something specific but a certain general tendency of the mind which gives rise to specific attachments. One broods upon pleasures one has experienced in dreams or has heard of or seen elsewhere. But when the tangible or the intangible means of fulfilling the desire for the objects of attachment are not available, this rajasic vṛtti or *rāga* darkens the mind (SS). To ward off this vṛtti one cultivates the sentiment of friendship even towards malevolent beings who are enjoying comfort and happiness. Let one be happy at their happiness as though they were all one's friends (HA). Let one think that all these beings and people are one's own (SS). As their happiness thus becomes one's own the darkness of *rāga* vanishes (SS), and all the other attendant weaknesses listed above also drop off.

Karuṇā, compassion, is the desire to remove the pain of others as if it were one's own (VM, BM), with the constant thought as to how their pain may be reduced or removed (BR, BM). This must be an unconditional sentiment (VB, BG, NB, NBB) towards friend or foe (HA). This prevents the desire to hurt others (BM) and the pride that develops at seeing oneself comfortable while others are in suffering (SS). When fully cultivated, this virtue of compassion wards off hatred (*dveṣha*) (SS).

One should cultivate joyfulness at seeing others virtuous, consenting to and rejoicing at their virtue (BM). Whether they are one's equals or unequals in virtue, one should always be happy at seeing, hearing or remembering the good deeds performed by them (HA) and not belittle their goodness (BR). Beings often incline towards evil and away from good. Then this conflict of good and evil causes *paśhchāt-tāpa. Paśhchāt-tāpa* is a very common term in Indian teachings of ethics. Literally, it means "afterwards (*paśhchāt*) burning (*tāpa*)." This "burning" within oneself "after" the fact of an evil deed is very desirable if it leads to a redemption in the future. It is a defeatist guilt feeling if it does not lead to the vow of self-purification. When one rejoices at the good acts of others, the imprint created on the mind leads to purification and enhances one's own inclination towards virtue. This gladness saves one from tendencies to commit evil, and also serves as an antidote to the internal burning of *paśhchāt-tāpa.*

Towards the nonvirtuous, those who are not one's equals (HA), one cultivates *upekśhā* or indifference, that is, a sense of neutrality (*audāsīnya*) (VB, BR, BG, NB, NBB), which is the middle way (VB, RY, BM), so that one neither consents to their acts nor feels hatred or condemnation (BR, BM, HA). This serves as an antidote to intolerance (*amarṣha*) (VM, NT, BM). One cultivating indifference towards the nonvirtuous himself turns away from evil and, again, frees himself from burning in *paśhchāt-tāpa.*

Thus the sattvic vṛttis replace rajasic and tamasic ones. Without cultivating these four *parikarmas* of amity, compassion, gladness and indifference, the five *upāyas* mentioned in Sūtra I.20 do not stabilise (VM) and the practitioner continues to totter. Vyāsa says:

> As one cultivates himself thus, his white nature increases, grows. Then the mind is purified and becomes pleasant. Purified and pleasant, it attains the state of one-pointed stability.

Cultivating these attributes, one develops a fresh mental personality in which one's "white nature" has gathered strength, *upa-jan* 'increased, grown'. This sentence of Vyāsa's will be more clearly understood with reference to Sūtra IV.7:

> The action, karma, of a yogi is non-white and non-black; of others, however, it is of three kinds.

On that sūtra, Vyāsa explains:

> The species called karma is four-footed. (Karma may be) black, white and black, white, or neither white nor black. The black one is of the wicked. The white and black is effected through external means so that the domain of karma is strengthened by hurting and helping others. The white belongs to those who practise ascetic endeavour (*tapas*), *japa* and self-study (*svādhyāya*) and meditation (*dhyāna*). This extends in the mind alone and because it is not dependent on any externals, it is accomplished without hurting others. The neither white nor black belongs to the renunciates. . . .

A person who needs to cultivate the *parikarmas,* the attributes of amity and so forth, is not yet a full yogi or renunciate. There is yet in him a conflict between black and white. By cultivating these attitudes, he reduces the strength of the black sentiments which impede his progress and he strengthens the white characteristics of a meditator, the habits of *tapas, svādhyāya,* and *dhyāna.* He is yet at the seventh *aṅga* (See *YS* II.29) and has not reached yoga, that is, samādhi. By constant practice of the four *parikarmas* he becomes pleasant-minded so that ugly thoughts of jealousy, hatred, intolerance, etc. no longer arise in his life or in his meditation. This then leads to firming up, sealing, the stability of his mind. Only then does his mind cease to be distracted (*vikṣhipta*) and attain to one-pointedness (*ekāgra*) that abides undisturbed and uninterrupted. Such a one-pointed mind enters samādhi.

Sūtra III.23 gives the effects (*siddhis*) that accrue from the practice of these *brahmā-vihāras.* A distinction is made, however, between the first three that do lead to samādhi and the fourth one, indifference (*upekṣhā*), which is neutral with regard to attainment of samādhi since it is not a positive cultivation of any given concentration or attitude.

Sūtra I.34 प्रच्छर्दनविधारणाभ्यां वा प्राणस्य।

prachchhardana-vidhāraṇābhyāṁ vā prāṇasya

prachchhardana-: (by) explusion, exhalation
vidhāraṇābhyāṁ: and restraint, control
vā: or
prāṇasya: of *prāṇa*

Or, by exhalation and restraint of breath and *prāṇa* (mind's stability is established).

Vyāsa's Commentary

A careful expulsion of the visceral air through the nostrils is *prachchhardana. Vidhāraṇa* is the expansion of breath and *prāṇa* (*prāṇa* + *āyāma*). Also through these one should effect stability of the mind.

Discussion

Now that the mind has been purified, pacified and made pleasant, naturally the next step is to affirm its stability (RY). In most commentaries and translations the word *vā* is indicated to mean the optional "or," which would imply that the practice of breath control is an alternative to the four *parikarmas* prescribed in the last sūtra. The commentators are agreed that this would not be true to the intent of the sūtra. They are, therefore, of the opinion that this sūtra does not take the *anuvṛtti* of *chitta-prasādanam* from the preceding sūtra, and that this is a case of *anuvṛtti* in reverse, drawing here the words *sthiti-nibandhanī* from the next sūtra (VB, BM), so that this sūtra begins the topic of firming up the stability of the mind, with *vā* expressing an optional method for effecting the same. These methods are described in Sūtras 34-39. This is definitely Vyāsa's opinion. The option expressed by *vā,* therefore, is not meant as an alternative to the four *parikarmas;* they must be practised for the purification of mind as per Sūtra 33 (RY, BM) even as one embarks on effecting the mind's stability, as per Sūtras 34-39. It was explained in the last sūtra that without mental purity and pleasantness, *chitta-prasādana* (Sūtra I.33), it is not possible to effect stability of the mind, *sthiti-nibandhana* (Sūtras I.34-39), which alone leads to the one-pointed (*ekāgra*) state so that *samprajñāta* samādhi may ensue. VB, BG, and NB contradict Vyāsa in thinking that the *prāṇāyāma* prescribed here first leads to *prasādana* and then to *nibandhana.* However, these and other commentators agree in stating that *chitta-prasādana* is the essential prerequisite to any attempt at or method for *sthiti-nibandhana* (NB, RY, BM).

The next issue needing clarification is the subject of *prāṇāyāma* being introduced in this sūtra. Many commentators are confused as to why *prāṇāyāma* is prescribed here when it is also discussed in greater detail in Sūtras II.49-53. Since the sūtra system requires the utmost economy of words, it is not the custom of the sages to indulge in repetition. It is clear then that what is prescribed here will not be repeated in later sūtras describing *prāṇāyāma.*

In this context special attention needs to be paid to the unusual terms *prachchhardana* and *vidhāraṇa* used in this sūtra. These terms are not commonly found in the texts and passages on *prāṇāyāma* and are most probably expressive of some method not included in Sūtras II.49-53. The commentators who have failed to notice this (VB, BR, NT, BG, NB et al.) have interpreted *prachchhardana* as the familiar exhalation of visceral air. Similarly, *vidhāraṇa* is interpreted by them as the ordinary retention (*kumbhaka*). In other words they have tried to read in this sūtra the same *rechaka, pūraka* and *kumbhaka prāṇāyāmas* described elsewhere. Others (BR, NT) see in *prachchhardana* a measured breathing pattern, even to the ratio (SS) of 16:32:64, performing perhaps the *nāḍī-śhodhana prāṇāyāma* using one nostril at a time (VB, NT, SS), while others see *vidhāraṇa* as retention of exhaled breath outside (NT) or after inhalation (VB, BR, BG, NB, NBB). Clearly, these commentators are reading here the techniques they know of. Only two commentators (VM, BM) seem to have an idea of the simple and effective technique that is actually meant to be conveyed. VM (echoed by BM) says:

> *Prachchhardana* is explained: it is whereby the visceral air is slowly exhaled through the nostrils with a particular care, effort and method (*prayatna*) as taught in the yoga science (*yoga-śhāstra*). . . . *Vidhāraṇa* is stretching or expanding (*āyāma*) of the visceral air, that is, maintaining it outside, and not a quick or sudden (*sahasā*) intake.

The technique is similar to what is known among the Buddhists as *ānāpāna-sati,* or among the Himalayan yogis as breath awareness. It involves a slow exhalation and inhalation and training oneself not to allow a sudden, quick and jerky inhalation. The slow exhalation is *prachchhardana,* and the careful, slow inhalation is *vidhāraṇa.* The term *vidhāraṇa* not only means controlling the flow of breath but also suggests the sixth *aṅga* of yoga, called *dhāraṇā* (mental attention). The mind should be attentive to the flow of breath and observe it as is taught in the Himalayan tradition as well as throughout the Buddhist world. The verb root meaning of *vidhāraṇa,* "to hold or restrain," here does not indicate the well-known practice of retention of breath but refers to holding a steady flow, restraining it to prevent the sudden and jerky intake that often occurs. This practice is the antidote to *śhvāsa* and *praśhvāsa,* uncontrolled inhalation and exhaltion, which are two of the correlates of the *vikṣhepas* (*YS* I.31).[31] To anyone experienced in this type of practice the term "visceral air" (*kauṣhṭhya vāyu*) suggests the diaphragmatic breathing which is the fundamental method of breathing in all yoga practice.

The personality and the body (VM and BM) become lighter by such practice, and then the mind naturally gains steadiness and stability. In the entire yoga system there is no other breathing practice equal to this. All other practices are variations on this one. Only if this is mastered can the rest be undertaken. It may be done with *japa* of the mantra and with mind concentration directed to any one spot or a *chakra.*

31. It is worth observing that where the lack of breath control is described as a symptom of mental distraction (*vikṣhepa*) the words used for inhalation and exhalation are *śhvāsa* and *praśhvāsa,* expressive only of the physical aspects of breath. In this sūtra, where concentration and awareness are emphasized, the word used is *prāṇa.*

Since the entire tradition states that *prāṇāyāma* is the best way to burn dross from the mind and cleanse it of stains, strains, sin and evil (*pāpa*), it is consistent that with this practice the mind should become stabilised (NTB). The *Lawbook of Manu* (V.72) states:

> As the impurities of minerals are burnt off by being smelted,
> so the corruptions of the senses are burnt through
> control of breath and *prāṇa.*
> One should burn the impurities by the *prāṇāyāmas,*
> the sins by the practices of *dhāraṇā,*
> by *pratyāhāra* the attractions of senses, and
> by meditation the ungodly attributes.

NB quotes from an unknown source:

> The *prāṇas* are the force of the senses; by controlling them with effort the heaps of impurities of the senses that are the causes of distractions (*vikṣhepas*) are burnt.

All the operations of the senses are dependent on the operations of *prāṇa;* therefore the control of breath and *prāṇa* calms the senses.

Because the activities of the mind and *prāṇa* are intertwined, when the *prāṇa* is made lighter and subtler, the senses are controlled and finally the mind-field becomes one-pointed (BR). SS quotes the *Yoga-vāsiṣhṭha:*

> That which is the vibration of the *prāṇa* and air is the same as the vibration of the mind-field. Therefore a wise man should make great effort towards the diminution of the vibration of *prāṇa.*

"Diminution" here assuredly means making the *prāṇa* vibration subtler by refining the breath. This is the intent of the sūtra. The topic of effecting the mind's stability continues in the forthcoming sūtras.

Sūtra I.35 **विषयवती वा प्रवृत्तिरुत्पन्ना मनसः स्थिति-निबन्धनी।**

viṣhayavatī vā pravṛttir utpannā manasaḥ sthiti-nibandhanī

viṣhayavatī: having sense objects, having sense experiences
vā: or, also
pravṛttiḥ: inclination, manifestation, direct perception, apprehension
utpannā: born, appeared, occurred, become manifest, an advent having taken place
manasaḥ: mind's
sthiti-: (of) stability, steadiness
ni-bandhanī: that which binds, fastens, firmly establishes, seals

The advent of direct perception of the experiences of subtle or celestial sense objects is called *viṣhayavatī pravṛtti,* which also firmly establishes the stability of the mind.

Vyāsa's Commentary

The apprehension of celestial fragrance that occurs when one holds the mind at the front point of the nostrils is called the manifestation of smell, *gandha-pravṛtti.* The apprehension of taste occurs at the tip of the tongue, the apprehension of form at the palate, the apprehension of touch at the mid-tongue and the apprehension of sound at the root of the tongue. It is thus that the occurrence of these manifestations fastens the mind-field into stability, blows away doubt and becomes the gateway to the wisdom of samādhi. By these examples one should consider included the manifestation that occurs (through concentration) on the moon, the sun, planets, jewels, a candle, rays and so forth.

Even though it is true that the fact of the matter comprehended from the texts of particular sciences, inferential processes and the teachings of the *āchāryas* indeed becomes real because they expound the matter exactly as it is, yet, so long as at least some one part is not experienced directly with one's own instrumentation, everything is invisible and as though absent. That fails to produce a firm belief in the subtle facts such as the *summum bonum* (*apavarga*). Therefore, in order to reinforce (the conclusions drawn from) the Scripture, inference and the teachings of the *āchāryas,* it is necessary that something specific be experienced directly. In that, when a fact which is one part of the teachings of those has become the subject of direct experience, then the very subtle matter all the way up to the final liberation (*apavarga*) is easily accepted on faith.

It is for such purpose that this refining (*parikarman*) of the mind-field is directed, so that when there has occurred what is defined as total mastery (*vaśhīkāra*) with regard to the indeterminate fluctuations, vṛttis and their objects, the mind-field should become fit for and capable of the direct experience of the given matter.

And when this has happened for one, the faith (*śhraddhā*), vigour (*vīrya*), mindfulness (*smṛti*) and harmony (samādhi) will develop for him without an obstruction.

Discussion

Vyāsa's commentary on this sūtra is very clear and requires little elaboration. This sūtra explains that the experiences of (*a*) the individual subtle body and (*b*) its universal extension, the celestial world, consist of the realization of the subtle elements (*tan-mātrās*) well known to students of the Sāṅkhya-yoga philosophical system. Even though the detailed methods are to be taught in Chapter 3, a glimpse is given here. By way of an illustration, concentration on various parts helps gain entry into different powers of the subtle body and the celestial world, resulting in certain extrasensory perceptions. These may be listed as follows:

- where the center base, the septum, of the nose joins the upper lip: celestial smell
- at the tip of the tongue: celestial tastes
- in the palate: celestial forms and visions
- at the mid-point of the tongue: celestial touch
- at the root of the tongue: celestial sounds

Other experiences occur when one concentrates on the moon, the sun, planets, gems, a candle flame, rays and so on. Even though all translators translate *nāsāgra* as the tip of the nose, I follow the practical instructions given by my master and translate the phrase as the spot where the center of the nose just ends and the upper lip begins.

We concur with HA(E) concerning the rationale for these practices and quote him:

> The optic nerve is situated above the palate. On the tongue the sense of touch is most developed. The root of the tongue is closely related to the ear for purposes of articulation. Therefore, concentration on these points develops a finer power of perception of the sense organs.

Through these practices, which must be undertaken for a long period of time with perfect intensity, one becomes master of the specific elements within the subtle body (*viśheṣhas*), for which see Sūtra II.19.

The word *pravṛtti* has many meanings. Here it is used in the sense of *pra-vṛtti,* an intense vṛtti of the mind-field, one that remains in concentration, unlike those which appear and disappear fleetingly. The word *pravṛtti* also means "a natural urge, inclination or tendency." In the context of this sūtra and the next, when such a concentration is so fully mastered that the intense vṛtti and the attendant inner experience manifest effortlessly and become a natural inclination, then it is called a *pravṛtti.* Perfecting any such concentration finally changes the mind's habit of wandering, and then the mind can easily be applied to a higher and more worthwhile pursuit. In other words the experiences are only a by-product of the concentrations; the actual purpose is to train the mind, to habituate it to stability.

The use of the word *karaṇa* is significant. *Sva-karaṇa-saṁvedya* has been translated as

> experienced directly with one's own instrumentation.

Karaṇas are senses, including the *antaḥ-karaṇa* (the inner mental instrument). In practices of this nature it is the subtle senses and their subtle objects such as the internal faculty of smell, etc. that are brought under control of the mind. The instrumentation for the entire process of concentrations is meant here by the word *karaṇa.*

For the mind to be able to experience and withstand the explosion of power that occurs and to be able to direct and channel it after such experiences, it is essential that the mind be made *samartha* 'strong and capable', the term used by Vyāsa. This means that the mind's power of concentration must be intensified and its capacity increased. Its *sāmarthya,* increased capacity, shows itself in the yogi's daily life and acts, as well as in the duration, depth and intensity of concentration.

Vyāsa says that success in such concentrations, which shows itself by way of the extrasensory experiences, then

(1) fastens the mind-field into stability,
(2) blows away doubt, and
(3) becomes the gateway to the wisdom of samādhi.

The wisdom of samādhi is inherent in the term *prajñā* that occurs as part of the word *sam-prajñā-ta,* which was explained in Sūtra I.17. In other words, these experiences indicate the lower states of *samprajñāta* samādhi. The beginning of this wisdom is in the *upāyas* of Sūtra I.20 and the culmination is in the Truth-bearing wisdom of Sūtra I.48, which will be elucidated there.

Are these experiences not detrimental to spiritual awakening, as will be stated in *YS* III.37? Vyāsa implies that they could be detrimental if one had no higher goal. On the other hand, they can be supportive of the higher goal. When, from sources such as

(*a*) texts and scriptures,
(*b*) one's own rational analysis, and
(*c*) the teachings of the sages and teachers,

one has learned of that higher goal called *apavarga* 'deliverance, the Supreme Good', there nonetheless yet lingers a doubt about the reality of any existence subtler than that of the gross physical elements which are the objects of our daily, direct experience, *pratyakṣha.* That *pratyakṣha* proof, defined in Sūtra I.7, therefore needs to be extended and expanded to the *yogi-pratyakṣha,* the direct experience of the subtler world. This is only a small part of the teaching; but when one experiences this directly with one's own instrumentation, it reinforces the faith that what one has inferentially arrived at and what the texts and the teachers have propounded is indeed true. It strengthens one's resolve to proceed to the greater inner reality which one has not yet experienced.

As stated under Sūtras I.15, 16 and 17 and further insisted upon in Sūtra I.40, at each step of the subtle and yet subtler realizations one finds them to be short of the ultimate spirituality, full of the faults of impermanence and of a painful nature. So one develops dispassion (*vairāgya*) towards them until the fourth order of *vairāgya,* called the final mastery (*vaśhīkāra*), is reached. As this wisdom (*prajñā*) develops in the mind that has been made to work at its most intense capacity (*sāmarthya*), it removes obstacles from the way of the other four *upāyas* known as *śhraddhā, vīrya, smṛti* and samādhi, which were defined in detail in Sūtra I.20.

This sūtra has described the second method for effecting stability of that mind which has already been brought to *prasādana,* the pure and pleasant state explained in Sūtra I.33.

Sūtra I.36 विशोका वा ज्योतिष्मती।

viśhokā vā jyotiṣhmatī

viśhokā: free of grief or suffering
vā: or
jyotiṣhmatī: luminous, full of light (of sattva), lucid

Or, the natural mental state that becomes manifest as free of grief is called lucid and effects the stability of the mind.

Vyāsa's Commentary

This natural mental state (*pravṛtti*) having arisen, "effects the mind's stability"—this thought is brought forward from the preceding sūtra. As one practises concentration (*dhāraṇā*) in the heart lotus, the apprehension of buddhi there is such that the sattva of buddhi is luminous and clear like the sky. By mastering the steadiness there, the manifestations alternate as the appearances of the light of the sun, the moon, planets or gems.

Similarly, the mind-field that has reached accomplishment (*samāpatti*) in *asmitā* becomes pacific and infinite like a great ocean without any waves and is identified only as "I am." Concerning that, it is said, "Having found that self who is minute like an atom, one realizes himself only as 'I am.' "

This *viśhokā* (without grief) is twofold: one relating to objects (*viṣhayavatī*); and the other only as I-am-ness (*asmitā-mātrā*). This manifest, natural state (*pravṛtti*) is called the luminous one (*jyotiṣhmatī*), by which the yogi's mind reaches the state of stability.

Discussion

In the heart center there is an eight-petaled lotus turned downwards. Concentration on exhalation, when the *prāṇa* is made to flow through the *kundalinī* slowly, makes the lotus turn upwards. Then the state called *viśhoka jyotiṣhmatī* 'the one without grief, and luminous' manifests itself (VM, VB, BM, RY, SS, NTC, NTB). The advent of such a *pravṛtti* (as this word was defined in the previous sūtra) effects the stability of the mind. The thought "effects the stability of the mind" (*sthiti-nibandhanī*) is brought forward by way of an *anuvṛtti* from the last sūtra.

The *suṣhumnā* stream connects the heart center to the internal solar region and so forth, as well as to all the external lights such as the sun. Concentration (*dhāraṇā*) (as defined in *YS* III.1) practised in the heart center connects this center to the regions of inner lights (VB, VB, BM) whereby the yogi experiences his own faculty of intelligence and wisdom (buddhi) and grasps its sattva. It is the light of the sattva of buddhi that manifests itself within (BR, AD). This light of the sattva of buddhi shows itself in many alternative luminous forms, rays and radiances such as the sun, the moon, planets, gems and so forth. These luminosities shine brilliantly within the expansive space (*ākāśha*) of buddhi. That is, the buddhi is experienced like a clear, illuminated sky or space (VM, VB). It is not broken apart or cluttered by any other object nor surrounded by a delimiting horizon (HA); and it is within this clear expanse that the various radiant manifestations are experienced. This expansiveness of buddhi is experienced because here the individual buddhi has broken its barriers and the universal buddhi is realized as all-pervading (*vibhu*) (VB). Then all directions are unified and the buddhi cannot be divided into numerous parts (HA).

Even though the buddhi itself is being experienced as a single expanse of sattva, it still contains alternative radiances, luminosities, that appear and disappear. Hence this *pravṛtti* is called *viṣhayavatī*, "having objects of experience." This *viṣhayavatī* is not to be confused with the lower *viṣhayavatī* of the last sūtra, which operates within the realm of subtle senses, subtle elements and their corresponding or derivative objects. The *viṣhayavatī* of this sūtra has only the internal objects (*viṣhayas*), which are constituted of the light of sattva.

The next stage of this *pravṛtti* is called *asmitā-mātrā* 'only the awareness, "I am" '. Here the yogi experiences the inward face of buddhi and its universal counterpart, mahat, in which the reflection of puruṣha is seen (as explained in Sūtras I.8, I.17 and II.6). Here not even the diversity and manifoldness of the lights continue.

Because puruṣha is like an infinite, undisturbed ocean, the inward face of buddhi as *asmitā* receiving its reflection appears like an infinite ocean, calm and without waves. The experience of this reflection of puruṣha is both expansive like the ocean and minute like an atomic particle. (The expansive aspect will be discussed further in Sūtra II.19.) Here Vyāsa quotes from Āchārya Pañcha-śhikha:

> "Having found that self who is minute like an atom, one realizes himself only as 'I am.' "

There is no contradiction between the description of the self or of its reflection as both minute and expansive. It is repeatedly described as minute as, or in the Upaniṣhads more minute than, an atomic particle. (For example, *Kaṭha Upaniṣhad* II.8, *Maitrī Upaniṣhad* VI.20, VI.38, VII.7, *Muṇḍaka Upaniṣhad* II.2.2, III.1.9, and *BhG* VIII.9.) But it is also described as great, expansive (*mahān*), as in the *Bṛhadāraṇyaka Upaniṣhad* IV.4.20,22, *Kaṭha Upaniṣhad* II.22 and so forth. Both ends of the great, subtle force are brought together by stating that it is

> More minute than the atom, greater than the great.
>
> *Kaṭha Upaniṣhad* II.20

> The one more minute than whom there is none, nor is there one greater.
>
> *Śhvetāśhvatara Upaniṣhad* III.9

It is noteworthy that the descriptions of the experience of ātman or puruṣha and of its reflection in *asmitā*—the mahat ātman or *mahān ātmā*—are very similar. It is as though one person were to describe the sky and another speak of its reflection in a pond. This sūtra, however, is concerned with the experience of *asmitā* alone.

Briefly again, the *pravṛtti* called *viśhoka jyotiṣhmatī* 'the one without grief, and luminous' is experienced at two levels. First the yogi experiences it as *viṣhayavatī,* where the lights and radiances like the sun, etc. are seen shining and alternating as though in a clear sky. Thereafter comes *asmitā-mātrā,* wherein the reflection of puruṣha is subtler than the subtle and more vast than an ocean and yet without any waves, not even the alternation of lights appearing or disappearing but only a pacific, infinite span. The reason for its name, *jyotiṣhmatī* 'the luminous or lucid one', is obvious. It is called *viśhokā* because the mutation of rajas called *śhoka* (sorrow, grief, pain and suffering) ceases here (BR) as the process called restiveness (*chāñchalya*), by which rajas produces pain, stops (BG, NB). This causes sattva to become dominant, and the consequent, repeated pleasure in the mind-field (AD) and the illumination of wisdom that accompanies it (BR) cause the mind to become established in the habit of stability.

Sūtra I.37 वीतरागविषयं वा चित्तम्।

vīta-rāga-viṣhayaṁ vā chittam

vīta-: devoid of
rāga-: attraction, attachment
viṣhayam: sense objects
} those from whose mind the attraction towards sense objects is gone
vā: or
chittam: mind-field

Or, the mind-field having as its objects (of concentration) those (sages) who are free of attachments (becomes stabilised).

Vyāsa's Commentary

The yogi's mind-field, coloured by and reflecting as support (*ālambana*) the mind-fields of those from whom all attraction for and attachment to sense objects is gone, attains the state of stability.

Discussion

There is an apparent bringing together of two conflicting ideas in Vyāsa's phrase

vīta-rāga-chitta-ālambana-uparaktam.

Someone totally dispassionate and free of attractions and attachments is *vīta-rāga.* The word *rāga* is derived from the verb root *rañj,* meaning "to colour," as explained in Sūtra I.7. *Upa-raktam,* also from *rañj,* means "coloured by proximity." While on one hand one aspires to free oneself from all worldly *rāga,* it is advised here to let one's mind be drawn to those minds which have perfected *vairāgya* and to let the light of those minds reflect into one's own. One exposes one's mind to this process of becoming *upa-rakta* by the minds of the *vīta-rāga* saints because they will not permit an aspirant to become attached to them. Their love reflects into one's mind without forming a worldly kind of dependence and attachment.

Only one commentator (AD) has misunderstood this sūtra to

mean that a mind from which the attraction to sense objects has gone becomes calm. This is indeed not the intent of the sūtra. *Vīta-rāgas* are those sages whose mind-fields have perfected *vairāgya*. They are part of that guru lineage which begins with Hiraṇya-garbha. They are considered disembodied masters helping the aspirants. An aspirant practises the teachings of this sūtra in the following steps: (1) First he turns his mind to the lives, personalities and beings of these sages. (2) Then he concentrates on surrendering his mind to link up with theirs so that their *vīta-rāga* chittas, dispassionate mind-fields, become his *ālambanas,* supportive factors (see Sūtra I.17) or objects of concentration.

This is as far as the aspirant can go on his own. The guru then initiates the aspirant to link the aspirant's mind to his own and through himself to the mind-fields of the sages of the lineage. Then the minds of the sages descend into that of the aspirant, purify and still his mind, and he goes into involuntary meditation. All their knowledge descends into him and he slowly ascends to their higher consciousness. It is these sages of the lineage, such as Sanaka, Kṛṣhṇa Dvaipāyana Vyāsa and so forth—and all the past Buddhas in the Buddhist tradition—to whom homage is paid by the disciple.

The deeper meaning of this sūtra cannot be understood by those not initiated into this tradition of linkage with the lineage.

Sūtra I.38 स्वप्ननिद्राज्ञानालम्बनं वा।

svapna-nidrā-jñānālambanaṁ vā

svapna-: dream
nidrā-: sleep
jñāna-: knowledge, awareness, observation
ālambanaṁ: supportive factor, object of meditation
vā: and, or, also

Also, the mind-field whose object in meditation is the observation, awareness and knowledge of the dream or sleep state becomes stabilised.

Vyāsa's Commentary

The yogi's mind-field attains the state of stability when

- its object in meditation is the observation, awareness and knowledge of the dream state, or
- its object in meditation is the observation, awareness and knowledge of the sleep state,

and it is identified with the same.

Discussion

The words in the sūtra are not simply *svapna-nidrā-ālambanam,* "resorting to dream or sleep state"; rather, the word *jñāna,* "knowledge," is added. It is clear, therefore, that the mere experience of ordinary dream or sleep is not meant here. But the intent of the word *jñāna* needs to be understood. In the opinion of some (RY, BM, NTB, NTC), the word "knowledge" here means the objects of knowledge (*jñeya*). Since there can be no knowledge without an object of knowledge, both the knowledge and the object thereof are to be included (VM). Therefore the dream experience implies some of the dream objects which may be used as supportive factors or objects of meditation (*ālambanas*). Such an object should be attractive to the mind and approved by texts and traditions (SS).

In particular, if one sees the deity in a dream and then wakes up, he should immediately fix his mind on that image and meditate on it (RY, BM, NT). Vāchaspati puts it in accordance with the bhakti tradition of the Purāṇas:

> When one wakes—
> having in dream worshipped the image of the great Lord,
> so attractive that it drew the mind,
> adorned with garlands of the most fragrant jasmines,
> made of the most virtuous moonstone,
> as though sculpted from the moon itself,
> with all the limbs so gentle and tender
> as though imitating a lotus stalk,
> dwelling in the solitude of a pleasant grove—
> when one wakes up from such a dream with a pleasant mind,
> then contemplating the same image, his mind-field
> becomes totally absorbed in it,
> becomes one with it and attains the state of stability.

It is known that such dreams occur

- (in rare cases) when a devotee's mind projects an image it has longed for and makes it real in the dream, or
- (in even rarer cases) when the deity presents itself to the devotee
  - to draw him to worship, or
  - to respond to his prayers.

Such dreams may, of course, also be symptoms of a disturbed mind, but that is not a consideration here. The *Yoga-sūtras* deal only with minds which have embarked on the path to stillness and not those in the *kṣhipta* or *mūḍha* categories (*YS* I.1). Hence Vāchaspati clarifies:

> When one wakes up . . . with a pleasant mind (*prasanna-manāḥ*).

The word *prasanna* has a special sense in yoga,[32] which does not apply in psychopathological cases. Such dreams of one with a

32. See *prasāda*-guṇa (Sūtra I.2, p. 102), *prasāda* (Sūtra I.16, pp. 212 and 215) and *prasādana* (Sūtra I.33, p. 340).

pleasant mind are considered in all spiritual traditions to be either (*a*) the mind's genuine response to its own longing for God or (*b*) a vision conferred by God in response to the devotee's longing. It is, however, the consensus of all commentators that indiscriminate experience of all kinds of dreams is not meant here but only those whose images are conducive to the mind's stability.

As to concentration on sleep, it is suggested that one should fix the mind on the pleasure that occurs in sleep (RY, NTB, SS) and that, remembering, one should contemplate that pleasure (NTC). The sleep, however, must be that sattvic one waking from which one makes the observation, "I slept pleasantly," (VM, BM) as explained in Sūtra I.10. It is also a matter of experience that such a sleep is a good preparation for meditation by rendering the mind light and alert. The sattva of such a sleep lingers on in the mind when one wakes up and meditation after such a sleep is very refined and pure. One should let the mind become filled with the sattvic impression created by such dream or sleep (NTC); preferably one should contemplate it and get into meditation immediately after the experience of such dream or sleep.

The commentators (VB, BG, NB) who are more biased towards a Vedāntic interpretation of the *Yoga-sūtras* follow the themes provided in the *Māṇḍūkya-kārikās* and the *Yoga-vāsiṣhṭha.* According to this philosophy one views the ordinary wakeful world as the cosmic dream. The entire worldly existence is a sleep in which the pure self has forgotten itself. As one develops dispassion (*vairāgya*) towards it, the mind attains stability.

All of the above interpretations are accurate but incomplete without the special practices prescribed to the initiate in the experiential tradition. Here one learns to observe one's own dream and sleep states. First one learns to observe the dreams, then he learns to monitor, modulate and direct them. Finally as the unconscious mind, whose saṁskāras produce dreams, is purified, and a full understanding and mastery of the sleep state is established, the habit of dreaming is altogether eliminated. It is thus that the observation, awareness and knowledge of the dream state stabilises the mind.

Training for mastery of the sleep state also follows several steps. Philosophically, one views the experience of personal sleep as part of the cosmic sleep of tamas, which has befallen consciousness. Knowing, however, that the pure self is ever-awake (*nitya-buddha*) and that only a small part of the mind actually sleeps (Sūtra I.10), one learns to observe the sleep process by dwelling in the light of the pure self and by resorting to the higher mind, which observes the lower, sleeping mind. Thus one learns to enter *yoga-nidrā,* conscious sleep. When the mind becomes absorbed in this experience of consciousness, the true knowledge of sleep thus becomes the object of meditation. The mind then becomes established in stability.

Sūtra I.39 यथाभिमतध्यानाद् वा।

yathābhimata-dhyānād vā

yathā-: as
abhimata-: agreeable, desired, favourite, object of choice
dhyānāt: by meditation
vā: or, and, also

Also through meditation in whatever way or on whatever object agreeable the mind-field attains stability.

Vyāsa's Commentary

Let one meditate on whatever is agreeable. (The mind-field) attaining stability there becomes stabilised on whatever else, too.

Discussion

Different individuals have varying inclinations; likewise the yogi also feels reverent faith (*śhraddhā*) towards different entities. By meditating on these he may attain desired perfection (BR). These objects of one's meditation can be many—such as various deities and divine incarnations (VB, VM, BG, NB, BM, RY, SS, NT), or external objects (AD) such as the moon (BR), or internal ones such as the network of channels (*nāḍīs*) (BR) of nerves and the *kundalinī* flow. These objects should be those approved of in the texts and traditions (SS) and not something licentious like nude women, etc., (RS) such as some people imagine.

While all the other commentators are very brief on this sūtra, NTC fills many pages and provides an exhaustive list of the possible internal objects or points of meditation. Gradually the external objects must be replaced by the corresponding internal ones. For example, if one is inclined to make pilgrimages to sacred places, let him give way to that inclination; but then the practice should help him to discover that all sacred places of pilgrimage are within oneself. NTC has given a complete map of consciousness (such as the *chakras,* nerve channels and energy channels, which he identifies with various sacred rivers and holy cities and temples). *Yantras,* visual concentrations for each *chakra,* are given, following the norms of the tantric tradition. He also lists the points on which concentrations called *nyāsa* are performed; these concentrations require one-letter mantras contemplated into particular points of the body. The loci of various deities within the personality are indicated.

The correspondence of the *tattvas* (the five gross elements) with the states of breath is explained by NTC in accordance with the *svara* science. The secrets of the *haṁsa*-mantra (*soham*) are abridged from the *Haṁsa Upaniṣhad.* Various ways of contemplation and concentration on all these objects of meditation are also suggested. All these are not being elaborated here, because each individual needs to learn the method appropriate to his personality from a qualified guide only. The selection is made on two grounds:

1. On the basis of a person's natural inclinations, which are of two kinds:
   a. The ordinary objects of attraction and experience in life. If one is unable to practise restraint and turn the mind away from a particular object, let him enter into total one-pointed concentration on it. For example if one loves delicious foods, let him so concentrate on the experience of the taste buds that a minute amount of food produces great ecstasy. Gradually one will thereby establish mastery over the object of attraction and will no longer be enslaved by it.

   The habit of concentration thus formed can be applied to other meditations.

   b. The objects of one's faith (deities, incarnations and so forth). One may concentrate on these and the success in such concentration, again, can be applied to other meditations.
2. On the basis of the fact that a meditator's mind is often drawn towards certain points (such as the heart center) or certain sensations and experiences (such as of light). When the experience becomes persistent and consistent, one should respond to it and let the mind become absorbed in it.

Sūtras I.35-39 list the various ways of stabilising the mind on objects of meditation. In addition, Sūtras I.33-39 give the *chitta-parikarmas,* the ways of adorning, refining, purifying, preparing, the mind through diligent practice (*abhyāsa*). By so doing, the mind may reach the perfection of stability and of *vairāgya* (to be defined in the next sūtra) so as to be readied for the attainments of samādhi (to be explained in Sūtra I.41).

Sūtra I.40 परमाणुपरममहत्त्वान्तोऽस्य वशीकारः।

paramāṇu-parama-mahattvānto'sya vaśhīkāraḥ

parama-aṇu-: (from) minutest atom
parama-: (up to) ultimate
mahattva-: greatness, magnitude
antaḥ: ending in, extending up to
asya: of this one
vaśhīkāraḥ: power, mastery, control

This yogi's mastery and control is established over (the subtlest, starting from) the minutest atom and extending up to the ultimate magnitude.

Vyāsa's Commentary

As he enters into the subtle, his mind-field attains the state of stability at every level, all the way up to the minutest atom. As he enters into the large, the mind-field's level of stability reaches the ultimate greatness. Thus, his remaining unhindered as he pursues both ends is what is called the highest mastery (*vaśhīkāra*). The yogi's mind-field, brought to all-round perfection through such mastery, no longer requires the preparation (*parikarma*) that is produced through practice (*abhyāsa*).

Discussion

The preparations and purifications of the mind-field (*chitta-parikarmas*) through various practices (*abhyāsas*) have been described in the previous sūtras. This sūtra states their final result, the total mastery and control (*vaśhīkāra*), which we shall explain below.

There are two kinds of concentrations in yoga: those on the subtle and those on the expansive. Concentrations on subtle objects lead to the experience of the minutest entity. For example, if one concentrates on a flame or a white circle, gradually the area of concentration should be narrowed until only the minutest spark remains in the mind. Conversely, to expand the mind one may send the thought as though the mind is spreading out to touch all the possible dimensions, up to infinite space. On all these paths the mind encounters many obstacles, and consequently it wavers. Gradually the *parikarmas* help it to settle down, until all obstacles are overcome. The mind-field grasps the ultimate in the subtle and the minute as well as in the most expansive, not one or the other at a time (*ekatara koṭi*) but *ubhayāṁ koṭim* (both simultaneously), or at any level of the yogi's choice in either direction. When the mind becomes thus settled, it no longer encounters even physical obstructions such as hunger and thirst (NTC) as interruptions of samādhi. Wherever the yogi chooses, his mind remains settled indefinitely. This *vaśhīkāra* is not to be confused with the highest of the four states of *apara vairāgya,* explained in Sūtra I.15. This is no mere dispassion but, in Vyāsa's words, *para vaśhīkāra,* "supreme mastery." As this mastery is established over the mind, the objects of concentration also come under the yogi's total control.

There are disagreements among commentators as to the intent of the word *mahattva,* which in ordinary Sanskrit simply means "greatness." Contrasted with the subtlest and the minutest, it becomes "the largest" or "the most expansive." In the view of some commentators, this "most expansive" is twofold: the internal and the external. The internal is the endless universal *asmitā,* and the external is the cosmos (HA).

In the view of others (BR, RY, AD), the expansive objects are those such as space (*ākāśha*). Whether one is speaking of the cosmic physical space or the internal space of consciousness (*chid-ākāśha*) is not specified. To BM the word *mahattva* has suggested *mahat-tattva* or mahat. Mahat, the first evolute of prakṛti, is indeed the most expansive of the material modes and is the substratum of *asmitā* in the samādhi experience. In the opinion of VB, NB, BG, and NTC the phrase *parama-mahattva* in this sūtra refers to the great beings of high accomplishment, puruṣhas, the great spirits in the universe whom NTC calls the *virāṭ*-puruṣhas, or "shining space-persons"—in other words the beings of deific attainments. All these meanings seem acceptable, each being the ultimate in its own dimension. The expansive objects may be divided into the following categories:

- Among the five physical elements, *tattvas,* the greatest is space (*ākāśha*).
- Among the evolutes of matter, mahat is the first and the most expansive.
- Among the objects of *samprajñāta* samādhi, *asmitā,* whose substratum is mahat, is the highest.
- In the entire inward journey one continues to gain greater access into the inner space of consciousness (*chid-ākāśha*) and finally rests in it.
- Those who are the greatest among the accomplished ones are the deific beings with whom one establishes contact, which finally becomes unhindered and permanent.

All of these are within the yogi's reach as his mind stabilises and reaches total mastery.

Sūtra I.41 क्षीणवृत्तेरभिजातस्येव मणेर्ग्रहीतृग्रहणग्राह्येषु तत्स्थतदञ्जनता समापत्तिः।

kṣhīṇa-vṛtter abhijātasyeva maṇer grahītṛ-grahaṇa-grāhyeṣhu tat-stha-tad-añjanatā samāpattiḥ

kṣhīṇa-vṛtteḥ: of one whose vṛttis have subsided
abhijātasya: of pure-born
iva: like
maṇeḥ: of gem, crystal
grahītṛ-: in, towards, the apprehender
grahaṇa-: process of apprehension, instrument of apprehension
grāhyeṣhu: apprehended objects
tat-stha-: becoming stable on them
tad-añjanatā: coalescence with them
samāpattiḥ: encounter, transmutation, coalescence, attainment of a state of consciousness, proficiency

When one's modifications (vṛttis) have subsided, his (mind's) stability on and coalescence with the apprehender (*grahītṛ*), the process and instrumentation of apprehension (*grahaṇa*) and the objects of apprehension (*grāhya*), like pure crystal (which takes on the reflection and colour of proximate objects), is called *samāpatti.*

Vyāsa's Commentary

Now that one's mind-field has attained stability, what is the nature and the field of his proficiency, attainment and transmutation? It is explained:

[*Sūtra:*] When one's modifications (vṛttis) have subsided, his (mind's) stability on and coalescence with the apprehender (*grahītṛ*), the process and instrumentation of apprehension (*grahaṇa*) and the objects of apprehension (*grāhya*), like pure crystal (which takes on the reflection and colour of proximate objects), is called *samāpatti.*

"When one's modifications (vṛttis) have subsided" means "when one whose causal cognition (*pratyaya*) has set." "Like pure crystal" proffers an analogy. As a crystal depending on a particular proximate object (*upāśhraya*) becomes affected by its colour and appears to take on the form of that proximate object, so also the mind-field coloured by that object of apprehension (*grāhya*), which is its supportive factor (*ālambana*) in meditation, and transmuted into that very object, appears to take on the form of that *grāhya.* Similarly, when coloured by the subtle aspect of elements, it appears as the subtle element. Again, coloured by the gross *ālambana,* transmuted into that gross *ālambana,* it appears as the gross *ālambana.* Yet again, coloured by the diversities of the universe, and transmuted into those diversities, it appears in their form.

The same should be applied in the case of the senses, which are the instruments of apprehension (*grahaṇas*). The mind-field, coloured by the *grahaṇas,* which are its *ālambana,* appears in their form. Similarly, when coloured by that puruṣha who is the agent of apprehension (*grahītṛ*) and its *ālambana,* the mind becomes transmuted into such a *grahītṛ* (puruṣha) and appears to take on the nature of the same. Again, when it is coloured by the liberated puruṣha who is its *ālambana,* transmuted into that liberated puruṣha, it appears in the nature of that liberated puruṣha.

The mind is like a pure-born crystal. The puruṣha, the senses and the elements are respectively the agent, the instruments and the objects of apprehension (*grahītṛ, grahaṇa* and *grāhya*). The mind-field's "stability on and coalescence with" them means that it remains concentrated on them and takes on their form. This is called proficiency, transmutation, coalescence and attainment of the given state of consciousness (*samāpatti*).

Discussion

The methods for stabilising the mind have been presented (VM, BM, RY, SS), starting with *abhyāsa* and *vairāgya* (Sūtra I.12) and continuing through the *chitta-parikarmas* (Sūtras I.33-39). *Vaśhīkāra,* the indication of a stabilised mind (VM, BM, RY), also has been explained. The two levels of yoga, *samprajñāta* and *asamprajñāta* samādhis, have been discussed in general (VB); now their principal end-result will occupy the rest of Chapter 1 (BG). First to be explained are the field (*viṣhaya*) and nature of *samprajñāta* (VM) samādhi, the samādhi with seed (*sa-bīja*) (VB, SS). When the mind-field has reached the one-pointed ground (*ekāgra bhūmi*), what is its nature and its field (HA)? Vyāsa says:

> "When one's modifications (vṛttis) have subsided" means "when one whose causal cognition (*pratyaya*) has set."

The term "set" was explained in Sūtra I.18 as, "(All the vṛttis) have set like the sun into the very source from which they have arisen." But that description referred to *asamprajñāta* samādhi, hence *all* the vṛttis. It was explained in Sūtra I.2 that that sūtra does not read "Yoga is the control of all vṛttis" because *all* vṛttis are controlled only in *asamprajñāta,* whereas *samprajñāta* is meant to be included in yoga. Since the current sūtra (I.41) deals with *samprajñāta,* Vyāsa here omits the word "all." In other words, the clauses "modifications have subsided" and "causal cognition (*pratyaya*) has set" mean that vṛttis other than those of the object of concentration (*dhyeya*) have been brought under control (VB, BG, NB), because the *samāpatti* defined in this sūtra is also a vṛtti (NBB). The subsiding of vṛttis in this context is limited to the rajasic and tamasic ones such as valid proofs (*pramāṇas*) (VM, RY, BD). For an explanation of *pratyaya* the reader is referred to Sūtra I.10.

Even though the mind-field has the full capacity to realize all matters, it fails to do so because of the intervention of other objects of thought (*viṣhayas*); only when such interruption is totally prevented through concentration does the full realization (*sākṣhātkāra*) of the objects of concentration (*dhyeya*) occur naturally (VB, NB, NBB). This is the true direct perception (*pratyakṣha*). Such a state of the mind-field occurs only in *samprajñāta* and not in the lower concentrations, where the totality of the object of concentration (*ālambana*) cannot be fully grasped (VB). *Samāpatti,* the proficiency, attainment and transmutation of the mind, is the wisdom (*prajñā*) thus gained as derived from *samprajñāta* (VB) and is technically defined in Sūtra I.17.

This is elaborated by way of an example. Vyāsa says:

> "Like pure crystal" proffers an analogy. As a crystal depending on a particular proximate object (*upāśhraya*) becomes affected by its colour and appears to take on the form of that proximate object, so also the mind-field. . . .

An *upāśhraya,* a proximate object, is an external condition (*upādhi*). For example, when a red flower is placed near a crystal, the crystal is affected, overshadowed by it (VM). This is possible only because the crystal is pure by nature. It receives the reflection of a nearby object only when external blemishes, such as dust, are cleansed off (VB, BG, NB, BD). The way it is affected by the colour of the proximate objects is a subduing of its true nature (RY, SS).

When *abhyāsa* and *vairāgya* have cleansed off the external impurities of the mind-field, the objects of concentration (*ālambanas*) can clearly and fully reflect in it (BD, RY), and a coalescence occurs like that of milk in a marble cup (RS).

The objects of concentration (*dhyeyas* or *ālambanas*), which were clearly defined in Sūtra I.17, are classified differently here. Their order in Patañjali's sūtra is

1. *grahītṛ:* the agent of apprehension, the one who grasps or experiences or cognizes
2. *grahaṇa:* the process and the instruments of apprehension, with which one grasps, experiences or cognizes
3. *grāhya:* the objects of apprehension, the ones that are grasped, experienced or cognized

The order in Vyāsa's commentary is the opposite: object, instrument and agent (*grāhya, grahaṇa, grahītṛ*). This discrepancy has been taken note of by VM, VB, BR and RY. VM states that the order in the sūtra is contrary to the sequence of attainments and should simply be ignored. VB and BR favour and justify Vyāsa's order on the ground that it follows the sequence of one's development in samādhi (VB), that is, the plateaus (*bhūmis*) that the yogi gains (BR). No commentator has explained the reason for Patañjali's order. An explanation is attempted here.

In Sūtra I.17 the progression was shown from the outward to the inward, from the gross to the subtle, from the objects perceived to the inner perceiver. This order is followed also in *YS* I.42-44. Patañjali's intent in the current sūtra might be to draw attention to the true sequence in any cognition, apprehension or perception. It is the perceiver whose will initiates the experience, who utilises the instruments of cognition which thereupon grasp the external objects. The sūtra does not state explicitly what it suggests implicitly: One whose mind is trained through *abhyāsa,* purified through *vairāgya* and brought to stability through *chitta-parikarmas* now begins to view not the objects as the principal constituent of a cognition but rather the cognizer as the principal constituent; hence the order is reversed, and the innermost one now predominates. Patañjali's order emphasizes that the *grahītṛ-samāpatti* is the principal attainment (NTC). Vyāsa only appears to be mute concerning the reason for his apparent contradiction of Patañjali. In fact, upon looking at his commentary closely, it becomes clear that even though he explains *grāhyas,* etc. in an order opposite to that of Patañjali (perhaps to help the non-proficient), in the last paragraph of his commentary he reverts to Patañjali's order:

> The puruṣha, the senses and the elements are respectively the agent, the instruments and the objects of apprehension (*grahītṛ, grahaṇa* and *grāhya*).

It is also noteworthy that in subdividing *grāhyas* he reverses himself and takes the subtler to the grosser progression! To quote Vyāsa:

> The mind-field coloured by that object of apprehension (*grāhya*), which is its supportive factor (*ālambana*) in meditation, and transmuted into that very object, appears to take on the form of that *grāhya.* Similarly, when coloured by the subtle aspect of elements, it appears as the subtle element. Again, coloured by the gross *ālambana,* transmuted into that gross *ālambana,* it appears as the gross *ālambana.* Yet again, coloured by the diversities of the universe, transmuted into those diversities, it appears in their form.

The agent, instrument and object are subdivided and explained here as follows:

I. *Grāhya*

Grāhyas are divided into three categories:

1. The subtleties of the elements (*bhūta-sūkṣhma*)
2. The gross objects of concentration (*sthūla-ālambanas*)
3. The diversities of the universe (*viśhva-bhedas*)

This threefold division is explained in two ways:

A. (VB, HA, NBB)
- The subtleties of the elements include all existence from the subtle elements (*tan-mātrās*) up to and including prakṛti.
- The gross objects of concentration are the five gross elements.
- The diversities of the universe (included in the gross objects by HA), are the conscious and unconscious entities and objects (such as (VM) cows and jars, respectively).

B. BG and NB hold that the *grāhyas* are divided into:
gross: the five elements and presumably their modifications, namely the diverse external objects
subtle: the five subtle elements (*tan-mātrās*)
subtlest: prakṛti

VM's opinion appears more consistent with *YS* I.17 and *YS* I.42-45, wherein *grāhyas* are the objects of concentration only in *sa-vitarka* and *sa-vichāra* samādhis, as shown in the chart on p. 247.

II. *Grahaṇa*

Concerning the *grahaṇas,* Vyāsa says:

> The same should be applied in the case of the senses, which are the instruments of apprehension (*grahaṇas*). The mind-field, coloured by the *grahaṇas,* which are its *ālambana,* appears in their form.

Grahaṇas are similarly subdivided into three (VB, NBB):

1. The diversities in the universe, that is, the physical senses of various beings
2. The gross senses (the perceiver's own)
3. The subtle senses, namely, ahaṁkāra and buddhi

In HA's opinion, the physical senses having been included in the gross elements, only the inner powers of senses (*indriya-śhaktis*) are to be understood as *grahaṇas*.

III. *Grahītṛ*

Vyāsa's commentary on *grahītṛ* is:

> Similarly, when coloured by that puruṣha who is the agent of apprehension (*grahītṛ*) and its *ālambana,* the mind becomes transmuted into such a *grahītṛ* (puruṣha) and appears to take on the nature of the same. Again, when it is coloured by the liberated puruṣha who is its *ālambana,* transmuted into that liberated puruṣha, it appears in the nature of that liberated puruṣha.

Grahītṛ, the agent, cannot be subdivided between gross and subtle, and no such attempt is made by the commentators. Vyāsa, however, differentiates between (*a*) *grahītṛ* puruṣhas, spiritual selves that appear to be agents, and (*b*) *mukta* puruṣhas, the liberated ones. Vyāsa not only says *"grahītṛ,"* the agent, but adds "puruṣha" so as to preclude buddhi alone (VB) but to include the puruṣha reflected in *asmitā* (VM, BR, RY) or in chitta (NBB), totally identified with it as *mahān ātma* (HA) (to be defined in Sūtra II.19).

The question arises: Are there indeed two kinds of puruṣhas? Certainly not. There is no difference between puruṣhas dwelling in a bound (*baddha*) personality and puruṣhas which are liberated. Puruṣha is ever-free by nature (*nitya-mukta-svabhāva*). The subject of the sūtra, however, is not the nature of puruṣha but the stages in the samādhi of wisdom (*samprajñāta*). The final stages may be divided into three levels:

1. The realization and mastery of buddhi and the mahat principle. There is not yet a realization of puruṣha.
2. Realizing the reflection of puruṣha in *asmitā* as the principal constituent, the agent, *grahītṛ*.
3. Realizing that the reflection is not *the* puruṣha. Puruṣha is ever-free (*mukta*); puruṣha is the conscious principle whose reflection is seen in *asmitā*.

Vyāsa, therefore, differentiates between the proficiencies of samādhi (*samāpattis*) between 2 and 3 above.

Another explanation of "*mukta* puruṣha" is that the term refers to the great liberated, historical figures like Śhukadeva (who was Vyāsa's son) (VM,VB). If such were the case, this type of meditation should be placed under the category of *sa-vitarka* samādhi, in which such external personages can be an object of concentration. But Vyāsa places *mukta* puruṣhas after and beyond the puruṣha reflected in *asmitā*. In fact, Vyāsa's statement and VM's and VB's subtle suggestion point to the greatest mystery in yoga. "*Mukta* puruṣha" does not refer to the bodies or physical appearances of historical personages, but to the puruṣhas themselves, the liberated spiritual selves. These disembodied masters do guide the aspirants who become linked to them in samādhi. These liberated puruṣhas, spiritual selves, may reflect into the chitta or *asmitā* of the aspirant in samādhi, thus imparting their purity to such a mind. This is the mode of the guru's guidance all the way to Hiraṇya-garbha and beyond.

And beyond the greatest *mukta* puruṣha is God (īśhvara), who, thereafter, begins to reflect in such a mind (NBB).

Vyāsa concludes his commentary thus:

> The mind is like a pure-born crystal. The puruṣha, the senses and the elements are respectively the agent, the instruments and the objects of apprehension (*grahītṛ, grahaṇa* and *grāhya*). The mind-field's "stability on and coalescence with" them means that it remains concentrated on them and takes on their form. This is called proficiency, transmutation, coalescence and attainment of the given state of consciousness (*samāpatti*).

At each of the stages of attainment of concentration on the various subdivisions of *grahītṛ, grahaṇa* and *grāhya* (namely: puruṣhas, senses, and elements), *samāpatti* is to be defined as the mind-field (*a*) dwelling on the object, becoming stable thereupon (*tat-stha*), and (*b*) achieving coalescence (*tad-añjanatā*) therewith (like milk in a marble cup), so that the mind takes the nature and form of that object and is identified with it. The relationship of the three—*grāhya-samāpatti, grahaṇa-samāpatti,* and *grahītṛ-samāpatti*—with the four levels of *samprajñāta* samādhi has been shown in the chart on p. 247 and should be studied there.

Sūtras I.17, 19, 20, 41, and 42-50 constitute the explanation of *samprajñāta,* and therefore the current sūtra should be studied within that context.

Sūtra I.42 **तत्र शब्दार्थज्ञानविकल्पैः सङ्कीर्णा सवितर्का समापत्तिः।**

tatra śhabdārtha-jñāna-vikalpaiḥ saṅkīrṇā sa-vitarkā samāpattiḥ

tatra: there, among them
śhabda-: (with) word
artha-: meaning, object denoted or signified
jñāna-: knowledge
vikalpaiḥ: with options (RP, BB), alternations, imaginary cognitions
saṅkīrṇā: mixed, mingled, commingled, alloyed
sa-vitarkā: *vitarka*-accompanied, accompanied with gross thought
samāpattiḥ: encounter, transmutation, coalescence, attainment of a state of consciousness, proficiency

Among them, the one commingled with alternations and imaginary cognitions[33] of word, the object signified as meaning and knowledge is called the *vitarka*-accompanied *samāpatti.*

Vyāsa's Commentary

Thus, for example: "cow"; this is a word. The cow is the object denoted as the meaning (*artha*). "Cow" is the knowledge (*jñāna*). Even though they (that is, the word, the object, and the knowledge) are all distinct (*vi-bhakta*), it is seen that they are apprehended as not divided by distinction (*a-vibhāga*). When divided and separated (*vi-bhajyamāna*), the characteristics of the word are different, the characteristics of the object—which is the meaning—are some other, and the characteristics of the knowledge yet other. Thus their paths are divided and separated (*vi-bhakta*). When the yogi has reached *samāpanna,* (an accomplishment) of coalescence (*samāpatti*) with regard to them (*tatra*), (an awareness of) the object meant[34] (*artha*) by "cow" and such imposes itself upon his samādhi-wisdom

33. *Vikalpa,* as explained in Sūtra I.9, also includes linguistic misconception.

34. This translation of the word *artha* is taken from HA(E).

(*samādhi-prajñā*). If it (this awareness) revolves[35] as intertwined (*anu-viddha*) with the alternating (sequences) of the word, the object meant and the knowledge (derived therefrom) and (the attendant) imaginary cognition, such a commingled *samāpatti* is called "the one accompanied with gross thought" (*sa-vitarka*).

Discussion

The last sūtra provided a general definition of *samāpatti.* Now specific *samāpattis* are being explained.

Of the four samādhis of wisdom (*samprajñāta*) which were explained in Sūtra I.17, the first two are further subdivided into two levels each. *Sa-vitarka* samādhi is thus divided into *sa-vitarka samāpatti* and *nir-vitarka samāpatti.* This sūtra explains *sa-vitarka samāpatti.* The field of both of these levels and the objects of concentration therein are the same as explained in Sūtra I.17, but the attainments are different.

Before a better understanding of these levels and of Vyāsa's commentary can be gained, one needs to fathom the meaning of the term *vikalpa. Vikalpa* was defined in Sūtra I.9 and translated as (1) "imaginary cognition," which also included linguistic misconception, all explained in that sūtra. This is the technical application of the word to yoga; however, more commonly the word also means (2) an option or alternative, (3) an alternation of occurrences between two or more factors (for example, there is a *vikalpa* of positive and negative currents), and (4) (in psychology) an alternative negative thought in opposition to and alternating with a positive thought or resolution (*saṅkalpa*). For example, "If I look at it this way it seems right, and I shall/should do it" is a *saṅkalpa;* but, "If I look at it from a different perspective it seems wrong, and I shall/should not do it," is a *vikalpa.*

All these contents of the term seem to be intended in the use of the word *vikalpa* in this sūtra. More specifically:

1. The word, the object denoted, and the knowledge or idea (RP, HA(E), BB) produced are distinct and separate, but a speaker or

35. That is, takes turns or appears in turns.

listener commingles the three as though they were one. This is an imaginary cognition or linguistic misconception, the *vikalpa* defined in Sūtra I.9.

2. However, there remains an option open to a clearer thinker as to which of these three (word, object or idea) he wishes to cognize or concentrate on at any given moment.
3. Thereafter these three or any two may alternate between moments.
4. As a consequence the sequence of *saṅkalpa-vikalpa* may continue on however subtle a basis.

All these *vikalpas* are present when the yogi is concentrating on any one word-object-idea complex in *sa-vitarka samāpatti* of the *sa-vitarka* samādhi. The word *tarka* designates any thought accompanied by words. *Vi-tarka* is a variation denoting that only particular objects are to be considered. Concentration in *sa-vitarka samāpatti* is invariably accompanied by the names of the objects of concentration; hence the discussion in this sūtra centres upon the words, the objects denoted thereby, and the knowledge which is the relationship between the words and objects grasped by the mind.

Because the primary objects of concentration in *sa-vitarka* are the five gross elements and the eleven senses themselves, as gross a combination of them as a cow would rarely be an *ālambana*. Vyāsa says:

> Thus, for example: "cow";[36] this is a word. The cow is the object denoted as the meaning (*artha*). "Cow" is the knowledge (*jñāna*). Even though they are all distinct (*vi-bhakta*), it is seen that they are apprehended as not divided by distinction (*a-vibhāga*). When divided and separated (*vi-bhajyamāna*), the characteristics of the word are different, the characteristics of the object—which is the meaning—are some other, and the characteristics of the knowledge yet other. Thus their paths are divided and separated (*vi-bhakta*).

36. Vyāsa might have used words like "jar" or "cloth" (RY), but the word "cow" was chosen to illustrate this point, following the tradition of exposition used by grammarians of the schools allied with yoga. In discussing secular words, "cow" was almost always the first one chosen, perhaps because cows were the mainstay of an ashram's subsistence, and the disciples were almost always tending to "the guru's cows" when not attending to their studies.

(VM) When there is a word (in this instance, "cow"), there arises the misconception (*vikalpa*) that the object denoted (the cow itself) and the mental ideation (of the cow) are not distinct from the word. That is, when the cow is an object, there arises the *vikalpa* that the word and the ideation are not apart from the object. Similarly, when the mental idea of the cow appears, the *vikalpa* is that the word "cow" and the external object perceived as cow (which was denoted by the word) are both indistinct from the mental idea (VM, RY, BD). But (VB) when the learned experts apply the affirmative and negative methods of logic—somewhat similar to induction and deduction—and examine the three carefully, it is found that these components of the word-object-ideation complex named "cow" are all distinct, each with its own characteristics (VM, VB).

What, then, are the distinct characteristics of the word, the object meant, and the mental ideation? What attributes or qualifications divide, separate and distinguish them from each other? These can only be illustrated as examples rather than listed completely.

A. The word is of two kinds (BR), one a unitary revelation (*sphoṭa*)[37] and the other the sound qualified, for example, by high and low notes (VM, VB, NB, NBB). It is grasped with the sense of hearing (BR, HA) and dwells in the sense of speech. It is not the cow in the pasture that has high or low notes or is uttered or heard as the sound, nor is it the understanding, "cow."

B. The object denoted has genus, species, etc. (BR, AD). Furthermore, it has qualities like form (*mūrti*) or non-sentience (*jaḍatva*) (VM, VB, NB, NBB) (although the attribute of non-sentience is not applicable to a cow, the example in question).

C. The object is experienced with the senses of touch and sight, and dwells in the cow-pen (HA). It is not the word "cow" that

37. To explain the concept of *sphoṭa* in this present work would add great volume. The reader is enouraged to see the author's book *Mantra and Meditation* (Honesdale, Pa.: Himalayan International Institute of Yoga Science and Philosophy, 1981). There are also numerous academic studies on this subject in the field of Indian linguistics which do not relate the topic to the origin, practice and experience of the mantra.

is seen nor does that cow from the cow-pen migrate into the mind as the idea so that it is no longer seen in the cow-pen or pasture!

D. Knowledge or ideation (*jñāna*) is the predominantly sattvic vṛtti of buddhi (BR). It has the attributes of elucidation and formlessness (VM, VB, NB, NBB). It dwells in the mind-field (HA).

The word is formed of syllables or letters of the alphabet; the object has hardness, etc.; the idea is devoid of dimension and parts, and so forth (HA). In *vikalpa* the error of non-distinction (*abheda-bhrama*) among these appears (VB, NB, NBB, BG, NTC), causing them to be identified with each other (SS). But each takes its own path, its own development in causation, and undergoes independent mutation. Each has its own way of presenting its nature (VM, VB, HA).

Let us read Vyāsa further:

> When the yogi has reached *samāpanna,* (an accomplishment) of coalescence (*samāpatti*) with regard to them (*tatra*), (an awareness of) the object meant (*artha*) by "cow" and such imposes itself upon his samādhi-wisdom (*samādhi-prajñā*). If it (this awareness) revolves as intertwined (*anu-viddha*) with the alternating (sequences) of the word, the object meant and the knowledge (derived therefrom) and (the attendant) imaginary cognition, such a commingled *samāpatti* is called "the one accompanied with gross thought" (*sa-vitarka*).

In *sa-vitarka samāpatti* the word, the object and the ideation are commingled, causing the samādhi to be alloyed, mixed, with the notions and ideations whose constituents are unanalysed and consequently are several. Having these many constituents as the *ālambana,* as though they were one, superimposed (*adhyāsa*) on each other (BR), prevents the true one-pointedness from developing in its fulness. Hence this samādhi is the lowest, the most impure. The processes of this commingling occur in such patterns as the following.

The yogi experiencing the presence of a single word-object-ideation complex such as "cow" does not distinguish among these three constituents. Therefore it is uncertain which one of these three constituents is being realized or mastered. The mastery is, therefore, incomplete.

Also the coalescence of the object of concentration (*ālambana*) with the mind-field is incomplete. There remains a separation between the observing mind and the *ālambana* of concentration so that (VB) there may appear such observations as

- "This is a cow I am concentrating on."
- "This is a vision of God (Nārāyaṇa)" (VB).
- "This is space, this is light or fire (*tejas*) that I am experiencing; it all consists of material elements and should be avoided with the help of *vairāgya*" (HA).

Of these the first is a translation of the expression *gaur-ayam bhāsate* (VB, NBB), literally, "Here this cow shines forth, appears, is being experienced." In this experience the occurrence of the thought "cow" comprises the superimposition (*vikalpa*) of the word and the object. In the occurrence of the thoughts "appears, is being experienced," it is the object and the ideation that are commingled (NBB).

Since these superimpositions of word, object and idea upon each other (causing the appearance of an imagined unity in a manifold reality) only present what, in effect, is unreal, all such superimpositions come under the category of *vikalpa*. Such a superimposition does not aid the yogi to realize fully or master the reality of any of its constituents (RY), just as water and milk mixed together cannot be classified separately either as one or the other (RS).

Furthermore, where there are many constituents to an idea, there are many ideas. They cannot occur simultaneously. Therefore, just as in ordinary consciousness, where thoughts come and go one after another—and are called *sa-vikalpa* (NB)—so also on the subtle level of *sa-vitarka* samādhi this *vikalpa* occurs. Also, as explained earlier, the mind is divided into three thoughts or vṛttis, and the constituents of this threefold complex revolve, occur in turns, producing alternations of *saṅkalpa* and *vikalpa* (BG).

The same applies to all objects of concentration, among which the mantra must be mentioned here. Since a mantra in its utterable, audible form is a physical sound, in the Sāṅkhya scheme it would be a product of the subtle element of sound (*śhabda-tanmātrā*). Space (*ākāśha*) is the gross element produced from *śhabda-tanmātrā,* and the audible sound is described both as an attribute of space and as having space as its locus. Thus concentrations on an articulate, audible mantra, until such time as it is refined into and experienced as a subtler vibration, may be considered as coming within the realm of concentration on space, one of the five gross elements which serve as *ālambanas* of *sa-vitarka* samādhi. So long as any of the following (or similar) observations remain in the mind, full coalescence has not occurred and the meditation is still alloyed and impure:

- "The mantra is a sequence of syllables."
- "The mantra has such-and-such particular meaning associated with it."
- "I am practising the mantra."
- "The mantra is becoming refined."

Because the gross thought is a *vikalpa* by definition, the *sa-vitarka* samādhi is also called *sa-vikalpa,* that is, accompanied by *vikalpa* (NBB). Because it is still touched by ignorance (*avidyā*), it constitutes a lower category of direct perception (*apara pratyakṣha*) (NBB), as against the transcendental direct perception (*para pratyakṣha*) to be explained in the next sūtra.

Sūtra I.43 स्मृतिपरिशुद्धौ स्वरूपशून्येवार्थमात्रनिर्भासा निर्वितर्का।

smṛti-pariśhuddhau svarūpa-shūnyevārtha-mātra-nirbhāsā nir-vitarkā

smṛti-: (of) memory
pari-śhuddhau: upon purification all-round, upon complete purification
svarūpa-śhūnyā: devoid of its own form
iva: as it were, as though
artha-mātra-: (of) only the object meant
nir-bhāsā: illuminative
nir-vitarkā: without a gross thought

When there has occurred complete and all-round purification of memory and (the mind-field) is, as it were, devoid of its own form and illuminative of only the object signified, it is called the samādhi without a gross thought (*nir-vitarka*).

Vyāsa's Commentary

When, however, there has occurred all-round and complete purification of the memory of the conventional usage and meaning (*saṅketa*) of the word, then the object signified remains only in its own form in the samādhi-wisdom (*samādhi-prajñā*), which has become devoid of the imaginary cognition and linguistic misconceptions (*vikalpa*) of the knowledge which results from teaching (*śhruta*) and inference (*anumāna*).

(The object of concentration then) excludes all else and remains distinctly in the form of its own nature. That is the *nir-vitarka* coalescence (*samāpatti*). That is the transcendental (*para*) direct perception (*pratyakṣha*). That is the seed of the teaching (*śhruta*) and of the inferential process (*anumāna*).

Teaching and inferential knowledge (*anumāna*) originate from that. That perception and realization (*darśhana*), however, is not an accompaniment of the teaching and of the inference. Therefore (it is to be concluded that) the yogi's realization (*darśhana*) arising from *nir-vitarka* samādhi is not intermingled with and confused by other valid proofs (*pramāṇa*). That's it.

This sūtra elucidates the definition of *nir-vitarka samāpatti:*

> [*Sūtra:*] When there has occurred complete and all-round purification of memory and (the mind-field) is, as it were, devoid of its own form and illuminative of only the object signified, it is called the samādhi without a gross thought (*nir-vitarka*).

When the all-round and complete purification of the memory of the imaginary cognition and linguistic misconceptions (*vikalpas*) of the knowledge that originates from the teaching and inferential processes has occurred,

- wisdom (*prajñā*) then becomes coloured by the object apprehended (*grāhya*) because of its proximity (*upa*),
- it (wisdom) abandons, as it were, its own nature and form as the instrument of apprehension (*grahaṇa*), and
- it takes on the nature and form of the object (*padārtha*) itself alone, transformed, as it were, into the nature and form of the object apprehended (*grāhya*),

that is called the *nir-vitarka samāpatti.* It is also explained as follows: Its world, introduced by a unitary intelligence, consists of the self-nature of the real object (*artha*-ātman), such that it is a particular (*viśheṣha*) collection of atoms—the "cow" and so forth, or the "jar" and so forth.

And that particular configuration (*saṁsthāna*) consists of a common characteristic (*dharma*) of the subtle (origins of) elements having taken on a self-nature. It is inferred by the results manifested. It manifests itself as representing that which has revealed it, given it appearance. It disappears when another characteristic (*dharma*) rises. This characteristic (*dharma*) is called the whole (*avayavin*) constituted of separable parts (*avayavas*). It is that, the one, the large or the minute, the tangible; it has processes, activity, practicability, motion and efficacious execution (*kriyā*) as its attribute. It is non-eternal. It is with such a whole consisting of parts (*avayavin*) that practical transactions (*vyavahāra*) are conducted.

But to one in whose opinion "That particular collection (of atoms) is insubstantial, and the subtle cause is not to be apprehended," when he is free of *vikalpa,* there being no whole consisting of parts, it (the concept of a whole) is false knowledge not based in the nature or form of the respective object. Then (for him) mostly everything incurs (the possibility of) false knowledge. Also, if there is no object, then what can even be true knowledge?

Since whatever is apprehended is found to be a whole constituted of parts, therefore there definitely exists a whole constituted of parts that, coming into empirical attributes such as largeness, becomes the object (*viṣhaya*) of *nir-vitarka samāpatti.*

Discussion

Some editions[38] consider Vyāsa's introduction to the sūtra to be part of his commentary on the last sūtra and thus place the passage from the beginning ("When, however, there has occurred. . .") up to the end of the third paragraph (". . . That's it.") at the end of Sūtra I.42. We, however, concur with the majority. The word "however" at the beginning of the commentary contrasts the *sa-vitarka* with the *nir-vitarka,* and the rest of the paragraph introduces *nir-vitarka.* This samādhi is also called *nir-vikalpa* because it is free of that *vikalpa* which is the superimposition of word, object and idea upon each other (VM). This superimposition is otherwise called *saṅketa,* an indication, denotation (VM, VB, NBB, BG, BM) or conventional usage and meaning of the word. There is no other relationship between words and ideas except such imagination (*vikalpa*), which is then held in memory and which in turn helps one to infer that a word spoken, representing an idea, refers to a given object (BG, SS, NTC, NTB). Vyāsa says:

> When, however, there has occurred all-round and complete purification of the memory of the conventional usage and meaning (*saṅketa*) of the word, then the object signified remains only in its own form in the samādhi-wisdom (*samādhi-prajñā*) which has

38. (1) NBB, ed. Vasudev Shastri Abhyankar, Bombay Sanskrit and Prakrit Series no. 46 (Bombay: Government Central Press, 1917) and (2) RP.

> become devoid of the imaginary cognition and linguistic misconceptions (*vikalpa*) of the knowledge which results from teaching (*śhruta*) and inference (*anumāna*).

In the tradition of ashram education one attains knowledge through

> *śhravaṇa:* listening from a teacher,
> *manana:* contemplating, and
> *nididhyāsana:* meditation (NB, BG), which leads to
> *sākṣhātkāra:* realization.

Among the valid proofs, *āgama* (knowledge derived from inspired texts, from the tradition, or from a realized teacher) and *anumāna* (inference) are both based on remembering what is indicated (*saṅketita*) by the word (VM, VB, BM). For example (VB, NBB), the Vedic texts (*śhrutis*) state:

> It is indeed the immanent and transcendental Brahman that is *OM*.
>
> *Praśhna Upaniṣhad* V.2

The books of the Law (*smṛtis*) state (VB):

> *a, u, m*—these are Brahmā, Viṣhṇu and Śhiva.[39]

Similarly, lexicons (as, for instance, *Amara-koṣha*) (VB) state synonyms and meanings.

Learning from these statements is called listening (*śhravaṇa*), which is the same as receiving knowledge from *āgama pramāṇa*. Thus *āgama* is based on remembering words and their indications and denotations (VB, NB, BG, NBB). The remembrance or memory (*smṛti*) comes from the power (*śhakti*) inherent in words to help grasp the meaning[40] (NB, RY).

The logical processes of inference (*anumāna*) are derived from

39. Source unknown.

40. This doctrine of the power (*śhakti*) of words is one of the fundamental principles in Indian linguistics but cannot be discussed here in detail.

such verbal knowledge. Thus contemplation (*manana*) of what one has learnt through *śhravaṇa* is also based on words (VB, BM, NB). The word *anumāna* 'inference' also includes all that is inferred, all conclusions (VM). All these *vikalpas* do not lead to pure knowledge. Therefore the first samādhi (*nididhyāsana*) based on the *vikalpa* of words and their relationships is *sa-vitarka* and does not lead to perfect realization (*sākṣhātkāra*) (VM, VB, NBB, RY). Hence Vyāsa later states the requirement that there should occur an

> all-round and complete purification of the memory of the conventional usage and meaning (*saṅketa*).

The word is not merely "purification" (*śhuddhi*) but *pari-śhuddhi* 'all-round and complete purification'. It has been translated as denoting the abandonment and eradication of such memory altogether (VM, VB, NB, NBB, BG, RY, NTC). This means the dissolution (*pra-laya* or *pra-vi-laya*) of such memory (BR, AD, SS). The memory being a vṛtti, its dissolution into its very causes is its *nirodha*. This does not mean, however, that the yogi suffers a loss of the memory of words and meanings in ordinary life; rather, it means that he does not carry the memory into samādhi. He does not use these as *ālambanas* (supports for the mind) or as objects of concentration when he is past the *sa-vitarka* and beginning entry into *nir-vitarka*.

At this stage, the practice of meditation becomes free of names (of objects) and sentences (of contemplation); the object of meditation is dissociated from speech and language. This is total purification (HA). Now not only does the yogi not resort to the memory of words and their denotations, but he leaves behind the entire process which was caused by the presence of words and indications (VB, VM, NB, NBB, BG, RY)—of *śhravaṇa* (that is, *āgama pramāṇa*) and *manana* (that is, *anumāna pramāṇa*), as well as the first *nididhyāsana* (that is, *sa-vikalpa* samādhi), with its lesser degree of *sākṣhātkāra* (that is, lower realization), which was described in the last sūtra as impure and alloyed.

This also implies that the method of contemplation (*vichāra*) as taught among the followers of Vedānta, when an initiate is given a profound statement (*mahā-vākya*) to contemplate, must also be refined until the contemplation merges into meditation and becomes a realization. The words as well as the verbal processes of contemplation also come under the category of *vikalpa*. Even though the original realization of a *ṛṣhi* in samādhi is conveyed in words, the practising initiate is bound to a *vikalpa* until the words are abandoned and he has the same non-verbal realization which the original *ṛṣhi* had.

Again, we read from Vyāsa:

> (The object of concentration then) excludes all else and remains distinctly in the form of its own nature. That is the *nir-vitarka* coalescence (*samāpatti*). That is the transcendental (*para*) direct perception (*pratyakṣha*). That is the seed of the teaching (*śhruta*) and of the inferential process (*anumāna*).
>
> Teaching and inferential knowledge (*anumāna*) originate from that. That perception and realization (*darśhana*), however, is not an accompaniment of the teaching and of the inference. Therefore (it is to be concluded that) the yogi's realization (*darśhana*) arising from *nir-vitarka* samādhi is not intermingled with and confused by other valid proofs (*pramāṇa*). That's it.

At this stage the instrument of apprehension (*grahaṇa*), the mind with all its faculties, forgets itself, as it were. There is not even the cognizance that "I perceive" or "I concentrate." The mind is possessed, taken over (*āveśha*), by the object of concentration (*dhyeya*) (BG), diving deep into the reality of the object of concentration (*dhyeya-artha*) (NB, BG). Its attention is focused only on that reality, as though that reality is superimposed upon the mind, as though the wisdom in samādhi causes it to abandon any claims to being an agent of apprehension or concentration (RY). It is as though the internal process (*bhāvanā*) of samādhi is devoid of "being a process" (*bhāvanātva*) (SS).

There is now not the slightest superimposition of the unreal (VM, VB, NBB); the real and the unreal are fully differentiated (NB, BG). Nothing unreal enters into the real (HA). The reality (*artha*) does not take on fictitious (*vikalpita*) impositions (BM, SS) of words and so forth. The commentators reiterate that because there is not the slightest touch of confusion and ignorance (*avidyā*) in this samādhi, it is indeed the transcendental direct perception (*para pratyakṣha*) of the yogis (VM, NB, NBB, BG, RY).

The reality of the object of apprehension and concentration rises clearly and shows its own form. The union and coalescence is such that the mind's own nature in the process of ideation becomes subordinated (*nyag-bhūta*) to that of the reality being realized (BR). It is thus that the phrase

> *svarūpa-śhūnyā iva* 'as though devoid of its own form'

with reference to the mind and to the *samāpatti* becomes meaningful. "As though" expresses the fact that the yogi does not become mindless, that only the self-awareness of the mind and the cognizance that "I know the object" are lost in the awareness of the object of samādhi (NTC, HA).

Here an argument ensues (VM): The yogis receive the transcendental knowledge in this higher perception and realization. Then they convey that knowledge through *āgama* and *anumāna,* which are not the subject of that realization. Because *āgama* and *anumāna* are fictitious, the yogi's knowledge must therefore also be fictitious. This is answered by Vyāsa:

> That is the seed of the teaching (*śhruta*) and of the inferential process (*anumāna*). . . .
>
> That perception and realization (*darśhana*), however, is not an accompaniment of the teaching and of the inference. Therefore (it is to be concluded that) the yogi's realization (*darśhana*) arising from *nir-vitarka* samādhi is not intermingled with and confused by other valid proofs (*pramāṇa*). That's it.

It is not that wherever there is teaching (*āgama*) and inference (*anumāna*) true realization exists, nor is it necessary that all realization be expressed in teaching and inferential processes. Thus realization is not dependent upon these *pramāṇas,* although it is their source or origin. The word *darśhana* means "seeing, gaining insight" into that realization which occurs in samādhi. *Darśhana* is the Sanskrit word for philosophy because all philosophy, with its logical processes, is derived from such realization alone.

An origin is not dependent on its effects. Even though perception of smoke leads to the inference that there is fire, the fire itself is not dependent on smoke. So it is clear that the yogis receive their knowledge through non-imaginary, non-fictitious (*a-vikalpita*) samādhi and use the fiction (*vikalpa*) of *āgama* and *anumāna* to convey the true knowledge (VM). This knowledge is the seed from which they are brought forth into being (*pra-bhū*). Even though this knowledge is taught in the revealed texts (*śhruti*) and inspired lawbooks (*smṛti*) or by a guru, it is impossible to experience it without the experience of samādhi, just as one cannot experience the sweetness of sugarcane or rice pudding by description alone. Nor can a guru give guidance in the matter without that full realization in which no room for doubt is left and no realities are reversed. Hence, once again, the valid proofs of *āgama* and *anumāna* are dependent on it, and not vice versa. No valid proofs (*pramāṇas*) sully the realization in *nir-vikalpa* samādhi (VB, NBB, HA).

The argument of the sūtra up to here is summarized by Vyāsa as follows:

> This sūtra elucidates the definition of *nir-vitarka samāpatti:*
>
> > *[Sūtra:]* When there has occurred complete and all-round purification of memory and (the mind-field) is, as it were, devoid of its own form and illuminative of only the object signified, it is called the samādhi without a gross thought (*nir-vitarka*).
>
> When the all-round and complete purification of the memory of the imaginary cognition and linguistic misconceptions (*vikalpas*) of the knowledge that originates from the teaching and inferential process has occurred,
>
> - wisdom (*prajñā*) then becomes coloured by the object apprehended (*grāhya*) because of its proximity (*upa*),
> - it (wisdom) abandons, as it were, its own nature and form as the instrument of apprehension (*grahaṇa*), and

- it takes on the nature and form of the object (*padārtha*) itself alone, transformed, as it were, into the nature and form of the object apprehended (*grāhya*),

that is called the *nir-vitarka samāpatti.*

All this has been explained so far.

Now the question arises as to the nature of that reality of the object of concentration which is realized in this samādhi. The *ālambanas* in this samādhi are still the sixteen *viśheṣhas* and their products. One important aspect of their nature is stated by Vyāsa which refutes views held by certain opponents and reasserts the Sāṅkhya view.

Taking, for instance, an object such as a jar, the Buddhists of the Sautrāntika and Vaibhāṣhika schools hold that it is simply a combination of uncountable numbers of atoms, not their transmuted product, and that there are not cause and effect relationships between the atoms and the jar. This is known as the aggregation doctrine (*saṅghāta-vāda*).

The Buddhists of the Vijñāna-vāda school hold that all the objects exist merely as ideas, within a universal idea (*ālaya-vijñāna*), and have no objective existence.

Followers of the Nyāya-Vaiśheṣhika schools hold either to *asat-kārya-vāda*—the doctrine that qualities of effects do not exist in their causes, but that fresh qualities are produced—or to *ārambha-vāda*—another name for the same doctrine based on the view that these qualities begin (*ārambha*) fresh in the effects which are produced when atoms of various elements combine, and that their *prāg-abhāva* (prior absence) in the anterior (the cause) is evident, that is, that it is known that those qualities were not there previous to their appearances in fresh objects.

The Sāṅkhya view, of course, is *sat-kārya-vāda:* that the qualities of objects pre-exist in their causes and that the guṇas are constantly transmuted in the evolutes and do not remain the same even for a moment.

Although the commentators have summarized some of the arguments of the various schools and their refutation by others pertaining to these doctrines, space does not permit an adequate discussion of them here. Those interested in the topic may explore it in the formal systems of Indian philosophy. Only Vyāsa's view needs to be explained here. He says:

> Its world, introduced by a unitary intelligence, consists of the self-nature of the real object (*artha*-ātman), such that it is a particular (*viśheṣha*) collection of atoms—the "cow" and so forth, or the "jar" and so forth.

The world (*loka*) of the yogi in samādhi is described. The word *loka* means "that which shines." Whatever shines forth in samādhi, that alone is the yogi's world. The object of realization that becomes his whole world, says Vyāsa, is

> *eka-buddhi-upa-krama* 'introduced by a unitary intelligence (buddhi)'.

The intelligence is unitary because it is not divided up among many ideas. It is also unitary because it sees the object as a complete whole, one, not merely as many parts, such as atoms, put together. The object is *artha*-ātman, that is, it has a real self-nature. It is neither a non-self (*an*-ātman or Pali *anattā*), nor a mere idea. It may be agreed that it is *anu-prachaya-viśheṣha-ātmā* 'a particular collection of atoms', whereby it becomes, for example, a cow or a jar—that is, a sentient or an insentient being or an object—but what exactly does this mean? Vyāsa goes further:

> And that particular configuration (*saṁsthāna*) consists of a common characteristic (*dharma*) of the subtle (origins of) elements having taken on a self-nature. It is inferred by the results manifested. It manifests itself as representing that which has revealed it, given it appearance. It disappears when another characteristic (*dharma*) rises. This characteristic (*dharma*) is called the whole (*avayavin*) constituted of separable parts (*avayavas*). It is that, the one, the large or the minute, the tangible; it has processes, activity, practicability, motion and efficacious execution (*kriyā*) as its attribute. It is non-eternal. It is with such a whole consisting of parts (*avayavin*) that practical transactions (*vyavahāra*) are conducted.

An effect is neither totally different from nor totally identical with its cause. The particular configuration (*saṁsthāna*) of an object—that substratum in which the qualities (*dharma*) of an object reside, because of which it is *that* object, without which it would become transmuted into some other evolute—partakes of certain characteristics (*dharma*) of the subtler evolutes from which it is produced. Thereby it takes on a self-nature (*ātma-bhūta*); that is, it becomes itself. The presence of these characteristics is not a passive, non-productive idea alone. It is efficacious (*artha-kriyā-kārin*), producing certain results by which the observer infers its characteristics. In other words, it is anointed (*añjana*) by the attributes of its cause, and it represents that cause which has revealed it, has given it its appearance as an effect. When another characteristic from among those hidden in the very cause manifests itself, the configuration changes again. This will be explained further in Sūtras IV.12-15. The object in question, however, is the one whole (*avayavin*) to which all its separable parts (*avayavas*) belong. This one object is (*a*) one, whether large or minute, and (*b*) tangible. It has *kriyā,* that is,

> processes, activities, practicability, motion, and efficacious execution.

Because it is ever-changing, it is non-eternal. It is such an object with which practical transactions are conducted. Furthermore, Vyāsa challenges those opposed to this realism by saying:

> But to one in whose opinion "That particular collection (of atoms) is insubstantial, and the subtle cause is not to be apprehended," when he is free of *vikalpa,* there being no whole consisting of parts, it (the concept of a whole) is false knowledge not based in the nature or form of the respective object. Then (for him) mostly everything incurs (the possibility of) false knowledge. Also, if there is no object, then what can even be true knowledge?

Briefly, if everything experienced were insubstantial, unreal and false, then all knowledge would be false. Not only is this obvious, but all objects would then be inefficacious, useless, producing no results whatsoever. Furthermore there could be no objects of concentration if there were no objects. Vyāsa says:

> Since whatever is apprehended is found to be a whole constituted of parts, therefore there definitely exists a whole constituted of parts that, coming into empirical attributes such as largeness, becomes the object (*viśhaya*) of *nir-vitarka samāpatti.*

The real objects of the practical and empirical world are indeed the objects of concentration in meditation; they are not merely the idea or their atoms, but rather the complete whole. That their true nature is realized internally in samādhi does not mean that their objective, external nature is denied. Since their full nature is realized internally, this realization includes the fact of their external reality, which is also thereby mastered.

Sūtra I.44 एतयैव सविचारा निर्विचारा च सूक्ष्मविषया व्याख्याता।

etayaiva savichārā nirvichārā cha sūkṣhma-viṣhayā vyākhyātā

etayā: by this
eva: just, alone, very one
sa-vichārā: accompanied by subtle thought, *vichāra*-accompanied
nir-vichārā: devoid of subtle thought
cha: also
sūkṣhma-viṣhayā: having subtle objects as domain
vyākhyātā: is explained, defined

In the same way, the samādhi accompanied by subtle thought (*sa-vichāra*) and the one devoid of subtle thought (*nir-vichāra*) are explained.

Vyāsa's Commentary

Between these, that coalescence (*samāpatti*) is called *vichāra*-accompanied which occurs with regard to the subtle aspects of the elements which are delimited by the experience of space, time and causes and have manifest characteristics.

In that samādhi the subtle aspect of the elements is present as the supportive factor (*ālambana*) in the samādhi-wisdom (*samādhi-prajñā*) qualified by the ascendant characteristics. This also is to be grasped by the unitary intelligence alone.

That coalescence, however, is called devoid of subtle thought (*nir-vichāra*) which occurs with regard to the subtle aspects of elements when all their characteristics are non-sequential, their self-nature comprises all the characteristics, and they are completely undelimited in every mode by their submerged, ascendant or as-yet-unrepresented attributes.

That subtle aspect of the element in this very form only, and becoming a supportive factor by this form alone (*eva*) and by no other (*eva*), colours the samādhi-wisdom by its proximity (*upa-rañj*). And when the wisdom (*prajñā*) becomes as though devoid of its own form, merely the object remaining, then it is called "devoid of subtle thought" (*nir-vichāra*).

Of these, *sa-vitarka* and *nir-vitarka* have gross objects and realities (*vastu*) as their domain (*viṣhaya*), and *sa-vichāra* and *nir-vichāra* have the subtle objects and realities (*vastu*) as their domain.

Thus, by explaining *nir-vitarka,* the absence of *vikalpa* in the case of both of these has been explained.

Discussion

In the *sa-vitarka* and *nir-vitarka samāpattis* the gross elements in various tangible forms grasped with the external senses are the objects of concentration and realization. In *sa-vichāra* and *nir-vichāra* samādhis the five subtle elements (*tan-mātrās*) and the subtle senses are the objects of concentration and realization.

Nyāya-Vaiśheṣhika philosophers, who emphasize investigation of the physical realities of nature, propound that four gross elements—earth, water, fire, and air (but not space)—exist at two levels of reality: tangible impermanent forms, and intangible permanent atoms. The atoms are, obviously, the subtler aspects of the gross elements. The combining of atomic particles produces the tangible forms of the elements.

The Sāṅkhya philosopher does not engage in a discussion of the atomic nature of elements. His primary interest is in realities as perceived by the personality. In Sāṅkhya philosophy, therefore, it is the subtle elements (*tan-mātrās*) that mutate to become the evolutes called the five gross elements. The more syncretic philosophers, who are not careful to distinguish between the formal technicalities of the separate philosophical systems, are tempted to equate the Sāṅkhya concept of *tan-mātrās* with the Vaiśheṣhika concept of atoms. This has led to a confusion among *Yoga-sūtras* commentators (VM, VB, NB, NBB, RY, BM) as to the precise relationship between (*a*) the tangible gross elements and the forms produced by them, (*b*) their intangible atoms, and (*c*) the five subtle elements (*tan-mātrās*). Most of them (VM, VB, NB, NBB, RY) are agreed that atoms come within the subtle realities realized in *sa-vichāra* and *nir-vichāra samāpattis*.

It is just possible that Vyāsa has used the term

> *bhūta-sūkṣhma* 'subtle (aspects) of elements',

and not *sūkṣhma-bhūta* 'subtle elements' (*tan-mātrās*), in order to imply inclusion of the intangible atomic reality of the elements. Even though there is no other ground to support this view, it appears best here to respect the various commentators who quite correctly have found a place for the atomic reality among the various levels of reality to be realized in respective *samāpattis*.

Even though Vyāsa in explaining the last sūtra does state that a tangible object is a particular collection of atoms (*anu-prachaya-viśheṣha*), it was made clear that in the *nir-vitarka* samādhi the entire whole (*ayayavin*), and not such parts (*avayavas*) as atomic particles, are realized. It seems obvious, therefore, that both the subtle atomic aspect of the gross elements and the five subtle elements themselves are realized in the *sa-vichāra* and *nir-vichāra* samādhis. But these two subtle realities should not be misidentified with each other.

Now to Vyāsa's statement:

> Between these, that coalescence (*samāpatti*) is called *vichāra*-accompanied which occurs with regard to the subtle aspects of the elements which are delimited by the experience of space, time and causes and have manifest characteristics.

The distinction between *sa-vitarka* and *nir-vitarka* was stated to be that in *sa-vitarka* the *vikalpa* of word, object and idea is present, whereas in *nir-vitarka* it is absent. In *sa-vichāra* the object of concentration is experienced with reference to space, time and causation. Even though the minutest particles occupy no space, a relationship in space is attributed to them, the detailed mechanism of which is a specialized field for Vaiśheṣhika philosophers (and modern physicists). The same applies to time, which will be further discussed in Sūtras IV.12-15. Causation here refers to the fact of the subtle, atomic realities of the gross elements being products of the respective *tan-mātrās* (VM, NB, NBB, RY, HA). VB, on the other hand, holds that causation (*nimitta*) here refers to the relationship of the elements with the conscious purusha, the efficient cause whose purpose the elements serve. This seems farfetched, because such causation is not limited to the subtle aspects of the elements alone. Even though the word *nimitta* normally refers to an efficient cause, here it has to be taken in the broader sense of any causative factor. Even the subtle elements' process of producing respective effects may be included (RY). Briefly, again, the objects of concentration in *sa-vichāra* samādhi are perceived as delimited in relation to space, time and causation and, says Vyāsa, have manifest characteristics, which he clarifies as follows:

> In that samādhi the subtle aspect of the elements is present as the supportive factor (*ālambana*) in the samādhi-wisdom (*samādhi-prajñā*) qualified by the ascendant characteristics.

This statement may be understood better in the light of the three states of characteristics listed in Vyāsa's next paragraph. There it is stated that the characteristics of an evolute may be (*a*) submerged, (*b*) ascendant, or (*c*) as yet unrepresented. An object has many attributes which become manifested from time to time while others become dormant or await being brought into manifestation from the dormant state. When certain attributes have already made an appearance, after a while they become submerged and are called the past. Those that now become ascendant are in the present. Those yet to be manifested are in the object's future.

In *sa-vichāra* samādhi concentration on and realization of the nature of the object is limited only to those characteristics which are manifest, ascendant, in the present. The wisdom (*prajñā*) thus received is delimited. However, Vyāsa says:

> This also is to be grasped by the unitary intelligence alone.

To summarize the rest of Vyāsa's commentary on this sūtra, it is clear that in contrast to *sa-vichāra,* the awakening wisdom (*prajñā*) in *nir-vichāra* comprises the entirety of the object of concentration. The object here is not delimited by space, time or causation, nor limited to those attributes which are apparent only in its present time. All of its possibilities and potentials are realized as being one with an undivided and unitary intelligence (buddhi). Vyāsa is very emphatic in stating that the objects here are

sarva-dharma-anu-pātin: such that they relate to all their characteristics (and)
sarva-dharma-ātmaka: such that their self-nature comprises all their characteristics
sarvathā: in every possible way
sarvataḥ: from whichever possible mode.

In the next sentence Vyāsa uses "the very one" or "the only one" (*hi*) once, and "only" or "alone" (*eva*) twice. He says:

> That subtle aspect of the element in this very form only (*hi*), and becoming a supportive factor by this form alone (*eva*) and by no other (*eva*), colours the samādhi-wisdom by its proximity (*upa-rañj*).

The discussion in Sūtra I.17 has already explained what is meant by the mind ("wisdom" in Vyāsa's commentary) being as though devoid of its own form, with merely the object remaining. There are, however, disagreements among commentators on two points. In the opinion of some (VM, BR, BG, SS, NTC, BM), the *sa-vichāra* and *sa-vitarka* samādhis share the state of *vikalpa* of the divisions of the word-object-idea triad, and *nir-vichāra,* like *nir-vitarka,* is free of such *vikalpa.* Others (VB, NB, NBB, HA) disagree and state clearly that since such *vikalpa* has already been abandoned in *nir-vitarka,* which is a lower samādhi, how can it continue to be pursued in the next higher stage, which is *sa-vichāra*? This seems to be more in accord with Vyāsa, who says:

> Thus, by explaining *nir-vitarka,* the absence of *vikalpa* in the case of both of these has been explained.

Sūtra I.45 सूक्ष्मविषयत्वं चालिङ्गपर्यवसानम्।

sūkṣhma-viṣhayatvaṁ chāliṅga-paryavasānam

sūkṣhma-: subtle
viṣhayatvaṁ: the state of having as objects } the state of having subtle objects
cha: and
a-liṅga-: without marks, unmodified prakṛti
pary-avasānaṁ: extending up to, ending at

And "having subtle objects" extends up to unmodified prakṛti.

Vyāsa's Commentary

The subtle realm of an object related to the atoms of the earth element is the odour *tan-mātrā;* of the water element is the flavour *tan-mātrā;* of the light or fire element is the visibility (or form) *tan-mātrā;* of the gaseous element is the tangibility *tan-mātrā;* of the space element is the sound *tan-mātrā.*

The (subtle realm) of these *tan-mātrās* is ego (ahaṁkāra). The subtle realm of even this ahaṁkāra is *liṅga-mātra* (mahat). The *a-liṅga* (prakṛti) is the subtle domain of even the *liṅga-mātra.* There is nothing subtler beyond *a-liṅga* (prakṛti).

Now, puruṣha also is subtle, is that not so? True. But the subtlety of puruṣha is not in the same category as that of *a-liṅga* beyond the *liṅga.* Furthermore, puruṣha is not the material cause of *liṅga* but an efficient cause. Thus the unexcelled subtlety as it is in prakṛti has been explained.

Discussion

The relationships among the various evolutes of prakṛti were somewhat explained in the overview of Sāṅkhya-yoga (Part 2 of the General Introduction to this volume) and in the paraphrase of the *Tattva-samāsa-sūtras* (Part 3 of the General Introduction). These will be further studied in Sūtra II.19. Two charts from the overview of Sāṅkhya-yoga (on pp. 34 and 35) are repeated here to help clarify this scheme.

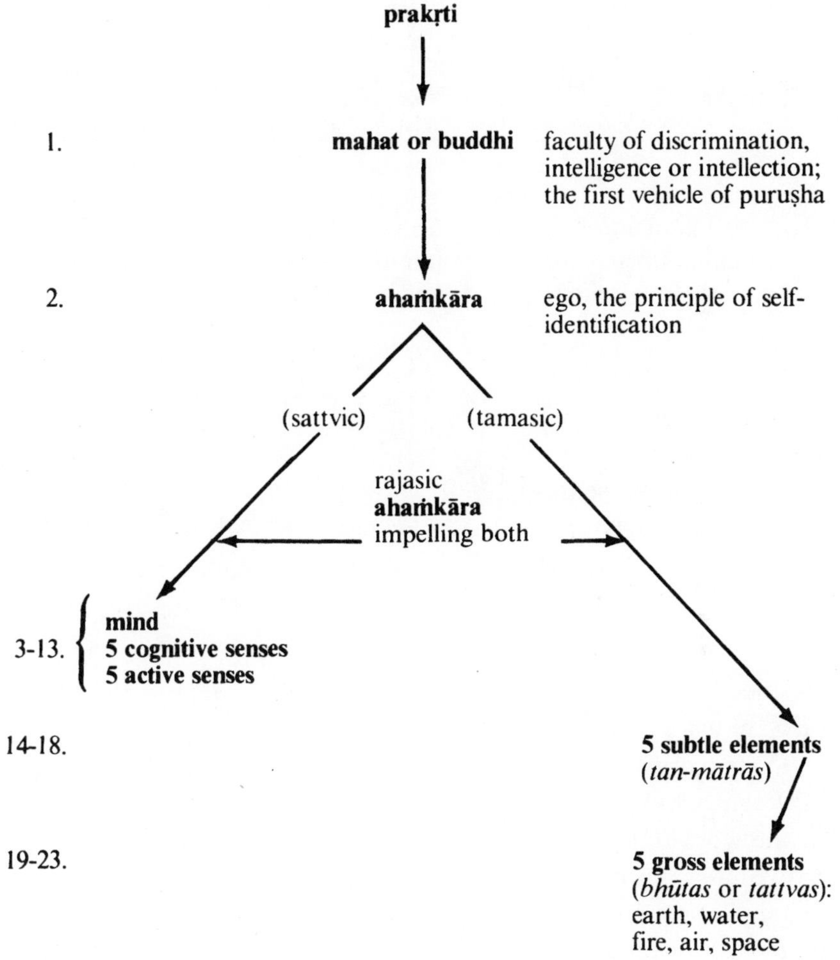
prakṛti
1.
mahat or buddhi
faculty of discrimination, intelligence or intellection; the first vehicle of puruṣha
2.
ahaṁkāra
ego, the principle of self-identification
(sattvic)
(tamasic)
rajasic
ahaṁkāra
impelling both
3-13.
mind
5 cognitive senses
5 active senses
14-18.
5 subtle elements
(tan-mātrās)
19-23.
5 gross elements
(bhūtas or tattvas):
earth, water,
fire, air, space

Yoga-sūtra II.19 gives alternative explanatory titles as follows:

prakṛti	*a-liṅga,* without a distinguishing mark
	↓
1. mahat	*liṅga-mātra,* merely a mark but with no distinguishing features
	↓
2-7. ahaṁkāra and 5 *tan-mātrās* (subtle elements)	6 *a-viśheṣhas;* general, non-specific, intermediate links between mahat and the final 16 products
	↓
8-23. mind and 5 cognitive senses 5 active senses 5 *bhūtas* (gross elements)	*viśheṣhas,* specific, final 16 products

Further explanatory details of these may be studied in the works on Sāṅkhya philosophy.

Three words used by Vyāsa should be well understood: (1) *liṅga,* (2) *liṅga-mātra,* and (3) *a-liṅga.* The conventional (*rūḍhi*) meaning of the word *liṅga* is "a mark" or "a sign." Because a subtle energy or evolute cannot by itself be observed, its grosser evolutes serve as its manifestations, the marks or signs of its presence. The derivative (*yaugika*) meaning of the word *liṅga* is "that which dissolves, vanishes, dis-appears," from the verb root *lī.* The products, effects, evolutes, alter or cease their appearance in the evolute mode as they vanish and dissolve back into their subtler causes, as a jar dissolves into clay in the process of *prati-sañchara* (*TSS* 7) or *prati-prasava* (*YS* IV.34). For this reason all the twenty-three evolutes (*TSS* 2, 3) are called *liṅga.*

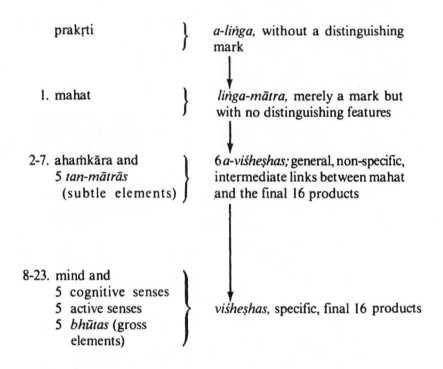

Mahat, however, is called *liṅga-mātra,* "a mere sign." It has no other special distinguishing marks. Because of its sattvic nature, it has no form but merely the capacity to receive puruṣha's reflection, as explained in defining *asmitā* (*YS* I.8,17,36; II.6,19).

Prakṛti, the equilibrium of guṇas, dissolves into nothing further; therefore, it is non-*liṅga* (*a-liṅga*).

As explained in Sūtras I.17 and I.42-44, after concentration on the five gross elements has perfected the *sa-vitarka* and *nir-vitarka samāpattis,* meditation progresses to the realization of the subtler principles, such as the corresponding *tan-mātrās,* into which a person's consciousness of the gross elements is dissolved.

Vyāsa takes pains to emphasize that the reference to the subtle objects of concentration (*sūkṣhma-viṣhaya*) in the last sūtra does not mean that only atoms (*paramāṇus* or *aṇus*) and the subtle elements (*tan-mātrās*) constitute the limit of the subtle realm. Such a mistake could be made because objects of concentration in the *vichāra*-accompanied samādhi are the subtle elements and the subtle senses, and Sūtra I.44 speaks of the *savichāra* and *nir-vichāra samāpattis* as being realizations of the subtle realm. The subtle realm does not end there but extends all the way up to the higher *samprajñātas,* where ahaṁkāra and *liṅga-mātra* (mahat) are realized. Thereafter *a-liṅga,* the nonquantitative principal matter, prakṛti, is understood.

Another important point needs to be made here: Even though the formal Sāṅkhya system considers prakṛti to be beyond any cognition at all—too shy a maiden to show her face to puruṣha's consciousness—she *is* mastered by *prakṛti-layas,* as Patañjali and Vyāsa have pointed out in Sūtra I.19. Thus the yogi's subtle realm extends all the way up to prakṛti. But, as Vyāsa says,

> There is nothing subtler beyond *a-liṅga* (prakṛti).

Vyāsa now answers another question:

> Now, puruṣha also is subtle, is that not so? True. But the subtlety of puruṣha is not in the same category as that of *a-liṅga* beyond the *liṅga.* Furthermore, puruṣha is not the material cause

of *liṅga* but an efficient cause. Thus the unexcelled subtlety as it is in prakṛti has been explained.

Puruṣha is not an object of concentration. He is subtle but in an entirely different category from prakṛti and its evolutes. Whereas the grades of subtlety in prakṛti's evolutes are comparative, puruṣha's subtlety is not relative but absolute. Unlike prakṛti, puruṣha has no products as its effects. He is an indirect cause of the awareness *asmi*, "I am," that makes its appearance in the composite sentience (*asmitā*) when puruṣha's presence passively reflects in *liṅga-mātra*. That is the entire extent of his involvement.

Since the topic of these sūtras is *samprajñāta* samādhi, and it is not till the *asamprajñāta* that puruṣha's isolation occurs, the degrees of subtleness mentioned here lead only up to prakṛti.

A question arises: Bearing in mind that Sūtras I.47-50 extol the perfection of *nir-vichāra* samādhi and that Sūtra I.51 explains *asamprajñāta* samādhi, what happened to the *ānanda*-accompanied and *asmitā*-accompanied samādhis which were included in Sūtra I.17? Though this has not been answered by Vyāsa or any of the commentators, it appears that the term *nir-vichāra* is not limited to being a variation of the *vichāra*-accompanied samādhi alone. The term has to be taken in a broader sense to include the other two samādhis, which appear to have been left out here. There are two reasons why this is so:

1. The higher two samādhis also are in this sense *nir-vichāra samāpattis* because the accompaniment of subtle thought has ceased. The experience in *ānanda*-accompanied samādhi is "I am in rapture," and in *asmitā*-accompanied samādhi it is simply "I am." These are neither discursive thoughts associated with *vitarka*-accompanied samādhi nor subtle thoughts of *vichāra*-accompanied samādhi, but rather experiences in *nir-vichāra samāpatti.*
2. The subtle realm of samādhi extending up to prakṛti implies recognition of the other two *samprajñātas.*

Since there are such significant differences of opinion or interpretation among the commentators on this sūtra, no reference has been made to them.

Sūtra I.46 ता एव सबीजः समाधिः।

tā eva sa-bījaḥ samādhiḥ

tāḥ: those
eva: very ones
sa-bījaḥ: with seed, seeded
samādhiḥ: samādhi

Those very ones are the samādhi with seed.

Vyāsa's Commentary

Those four *samāpattis* have exterior realities as their seeds; thus samādhi, too, is with seed (*sa-bīja*). Of these, *sa-vitarka* and *nir-vitarka* are (concentrations on) the gross object and *sa-vichāra* and *nir-vichāra* are on the subtle object. Thus is samādhi counted to be fourfold.

Discussion

Most commentators (VM, VB, NB, NBB, BG, NTB, RY, BM) have struggled with this sūtra, trying to resolve the apparent contradiction in the number of samādhis. Ignoring Vyāsa's clear statement, these commentators have said that there are eight (VM, NTB, RY, BM) or six (VB, NBB) kinds of samādhi and have tried to determine the exact position of the *ānanda*-accompanied and the *asmitā*-accompanied samādhis with reference to the four *samāpattis*. It is unimportant to present their enumerations, classifications and differing arguments. Suffice it to say that Vyāsa has *not* stated that there are four kinds of samādhi but rather that they are *chaturdhā,* "divided fourfold." As explained in the last sūtra, the division is as follows:

sa-vitarka samāpatti = *sa-vitarka* samādhi
nir-vitarka samāpatti = *nir-vitarka* samādhi
sa-vichāra samāpatti = *sa-vichāra* samādhi

nir-vichāra samāpatti = { *nir-vichāra* samādhi; *ānanda*-accompanied samādhi; *asmitā*-accompanied samādhi }

All of these, being concentrations on and realizations of supportive factors (*ālambanas*), are samādhis with seed (BR, BM). Some commentators (NB, BG) say that they cause saṁskāras which serve as the seed of the elimination of sorrow and hence they are *sa-bīja;* this is obviously incorrect—otherwise how would this category of samādhi be contrasted with the seedless (*nir-bīja*), which is the final freedom from sorrow? Others (NBB, RY, NTB, NTC, SS) say accurately that it is *sa-bīja* because it yet contains the seed of bondage. Since the yogi has still not reached the discriminating wisdom (*viveka-khyāti*), his concentrations are on realities that are within the composite person and exterior to puruṣha.

Sūtra I.47 निर्विचारवैशारद्येऽध्यात्मप्रसादः।

nirvichāra-vaiśhāradye'dhyātma-prasādaḥ

nir-vichāra-vaiśhāradye: upon purification and proficiency of *nir-vichāra*
adhyātma-: spiritual, in regard to ātman
prasādaḥ: pleasant clearness

Upon reaching the purity and proficiency of *nir-vichāra,* the yogi gains spiritual clearness.

Vyāsa's Commentary

Luminosity is the self-nature of the sattva of buddhi. "Proficiency and purity" (*vaiśhāradya*) means that the maculateness (*mala*) of the veil of impurity is removed from it and its stable flow, unsubjugated by rajas and tamas, is clear.

When the proficiency (*vaiśhāradya*) of *nir-vichāra* samādhi has occurred, then there ensues the yogi's spiritual clarity (*prasāda*), which is the illumination of wisdom (*prajñā*) revealed (*sphuṭa*) with regard to the realm of matters as they are, and without being obstructed by sequence.

As it is said:

Having risen to the clarity (*prasāda*) of wisdom (*prajñā*),
the wise man, no more to be grieved for,
looks upon grieving people
as one on a mountaintop (views) those on the ground (below).

Discussion

This sūtra describes the lucid beauty of the *nir-vichāra* state (VM) as follows:

Impurity means the accumulation of rajas and tamas (VM, MB) as well as the vice, etc. which cause their growth (VB, NBB). The same is the taint, macula, maculateness (*mala*), that becomes a veil (VM, VB, NBB) consisting of instability and dullness (HA). Even though the sattva of buddhi is naturally luminous, luminosity being its very self-nature (*prakāśha*-ātman), it loses its immaculate nature when it becomes subdued by such a stain. When it is no longer tainted, purification and spiritual proficiency (*vaiśhāradya*) occurs. This means that the mind-field becomes free of afflictions (*kleśha*) and the resultant propensities (*vāsanās*) and is thereby capable of a stable flow (BR). *Vaiśhāradya* is further defined as that stream of concentration (*ekāgratā-dhārā*), synonymous with stable flow, which receives and reflects back the clearly reflected image of the entire whole as well as the particular aspects of the object of meditation (*dhyeya*) (VB, NB, NBB, BG, RY). Briefly, this proficiency means the mind's firmness in its stability (BR, AD). Consequently it also means that because of the expertise in advanced practice (*abhyāsa*) (BR, SS), the material aspects all the way to prakṛti are subordinated and the power of consciousness (*chiti-śhakti*) is ascendant (SS).

A question arises as to the use of the word *adhyātma* 'spiritual'. Since the field of *samprajñāta* samādhi consists yet of objects exterior to puruṣha, how can there already occur an awareness of the spiritual self (*adhi*-ātman)? This can be answered in two ways. First, the word *ātman* does not always mean the spiritual self. This word is frequently used in the reflexive sense of "oneself." *Adhyātma* here means the development of oneself inward, towards one's spiritual nature and the faculties controlled by the self (*TSS* 8). Here its field is limited to buddhi (VB, NB, NBB, BG, HA), although some commentaries mistaking this sūtra as referring to *asamprajñāta* (SS) erroneously include puruṣha (NBB) or the spiritual self (RY). One should not argue too much against this because the final result of *samprajñāta* is discriminating wisdom whereby the force of the power of consciousness (*chiti-śhakti*) is realized (SS) as the origin of all one's awareness.

But Vyāsa clarifies that the primary intent of the words "spiritual clarity" (*adhyātma-prasāda*) here is that

> there ensues the yogi's spiritual clarity (*prasāda*), which is the illumination of wisdom (*prajñā*) revealed (*sphuṭa*) with regard to the realm of matters as they are, and without being obstructed by sequence.

The wording here is very suggestive. It reminds one of Vyāsa's passage on Sūtra I.1:

> That, however, is called samādhi of wisdom (*samprajñāta* yoga), which in a one-pointed mind-field
>
> - fully illuminates an actual state or object that has become real, has been realized,
> - diminishes the afflictions and impurities (*kleśhas*),
> - loosens the bonds of karma, and
> - brings about the possibility of control (*nirodha*) face to face, as it were.

All these promises of samādhi are being fulfilled in this sūtra. Not only does the pleasant clarity (*prasāda*) as explained in Sūtra I.16 occur, but also the same *prasādana* promised through the mind-purifications (*pari-karmas*) in I.33 and the following sūtras is gained. The light of wisdom shines, illuminates, the objects of concentration without reference to sequence of moments or states; it sheds light simultaneously upon their entirety without being hindered in any way.

In the verse from the *Mahābhārata* which Vyāsa quotes, the word *prasāda* also suggests *prāsāda* 'a palace'. The yogi has climbed upon the palace of purity, from where, as a sovereign, he observes those below, but not in pride. *Anu-paśhyati* suggests that he looks after and cares for them in compassion. "No more to be grieved for, (he observes the) grieving people" also carries this message: So long as a human being remains in such a pitiable, ignorant condition that others should sympathize with and grieve for him, he considers others to be happier than himself, and thinks that he alone has fallen into sorrows; but the yogi is now happy and sees those below him as sorrowful (VB, NBB), suffering the three kinds of pain (VM) as defined in *TSS* 23.

Sūtra I.48 ऋतम्भरा तत्र प्रज्ञा।

ṛtambharā tatra prajñā

ṛtam-bharā: Truth-bearer, Truth-bearing, bearer of Supreme Truth
tatra: there
prajñā: wisdom

Therein occurs that wisdom which bears the Supreme Truth (*ṛta*).

Vyāsa's Commentary

The wisdom (*prajñā*) that accrues when the mind-field has reached samādhi in that (*nir-vichāra samāpatti*) has the appellation "bearer of Supreme Truth" (*ṛtam-bharā*). The meaning befits its name because it bears Truth alone. Nor is there even a modicum of falsified knowledge. As is said,

> By authority (*āgama*), and by logic (*anumāna*),
> And by enjoyment of the practice (*abhyāsa*)
> of meditation (*dhyāna*),
> Cultivating wisdom in three ways
> One gains the highest yoga.

Discussion

The ancientmost word for the Supreme Truth of universal and divine laws is *ṛta,* extolled in many hymns of the *Ṛg-veda.* The Vedic sages (*ṛṣhis*) constantly sought, strived for and prayed for that wisdom in which the knowledge of *ṛta* is revealed.[41] According to the tradition (VB, VM, BG), *ṛtam-bharā* (the bearer of Truth) is the technical term (*tāntrikī paribhāṣhā*) used within the circle of yogis for the realization that occurs in the *nir-vichāra* samādhis. It does not occur in *sa-vitarka* and *nir-vitarka* samādhis because they are alloyed with imaginary cognitions (*vikalpa*), as explained in Sūtra I.42. This *ṛtam-bharā* is never veiled by perversive cognition (*viparyaya*) (BR, AD), for it bears unalterable (*a-vikalpita*) Truth

41. For further study of this concept in the Vedas see Raimundo Panikkar, *The Vedic Experience: Mantra-manjari* (Berkeley and Los Angeles: University of California Press, 1977).

(RY). Commentators mistaking this sūtra to refer to *asamprajñāta* also say that it bears, brings forth, the knowledge of the absolute puruṣha (NB, BG, NTC, SS) and is synonymous with *dharma-megha* (SS). But that is inaccurate, as others (VB) point out that the word "therein" (*tatra*) refers to *sa-bīja* samādhi, spoken of in Sūtra I.46, and even there, only to the highest of the *sa-bīja,* namely, *asmitā*-accompanied samādhi (NBB).

The source of the verse quoted by Vyāsa is unknown and is probably from some lost text. The three ways of cultivating wisdom, namely authority (*āgama*), logic or inference (*anumāna*) and the practice of meditation (*dhyāna-abhyāsa*), are again equated, respectively, with *śhravaṇa* (hearing the teaching), *manana* (contemplating) and *nididhyāsana* (meditating). These are common to all traditions and have been referred to earlier in Sūtra I.43. The efficacy of the first two, *āgama* and *anumāna,* will be emphatically denied in the next sūtra; and here they are given perhaps only to introduce their forthcoming dismissal.

The phrase

dhyāna-abhyāsa-rasa

is quite meaningful, as it points out that mere practice of *dhyāna* is inefficient without *rasa,* which means "due respect" (*ādara*) (VM, VB), as was explained in Sūtra I.14. Furthermore, the word *rasa* also means "essence," "flavour" and "enjoyment." One seeking to receive Truth-bearing wisdom should take pleasure in and enjoy the flavourful essence of the practice of meditation.

Sūtra I.49 श्रुतानुमानप्रज्ञाभ्यामन्यविषया विशेषार्थत्वात्।

śhrutānumāna-prajñābhyām anya-viṣhayā viśheṣhārthatvāt

śhruta-: (from) tradition, learning, hearing
anumāna-: (from) logical processes, logic, inference
prajñābhyām: (from two kinds of) wisdom
anya-: (having) different, other
viṣhayā: scope, field, object, domain, realm
viśheṣha-arthatvāt: because of having special purpose, aim, significance

(Truth-bearing wisdom) is different in scope from the wisdom gained by learning or from processes of logic because it has a special aim, that of dealing with particulars.

Vyāsa's Commentary

Now, that

[*Sūtra:*] (Truth-bearing wisdom) is different in scope from the wisdom gained by learning or from processes of logic because it has a special aim, that of dealing with particulars.

Scriptural authority and the teaching received orally (*śhruta*) is the same as the knowledge conveyed within the *āgama* proof category. The field is generalities. The *āgama* cannot communicate the particular. Why (not)? Because a word is not established in its signification with reference to the particular. Also, the field of inference is already the general. It is said that wherever there is arrival or attainment (*prāpti*), there is locomotion or endeavour (*gati*). Furthermore, inference leads to a conclusion (only) through a generality. Therefore no *particular* (*viśheṣha*) is the field of teaching (*śhruta*) and inference (*anumāna*).

Nor can this subtle, concealed and distant reality (*vastu*) be grasped with direct mundane perception (*loka-pratyakṣha*). Nor (should it be thought that) because there is no proof for the particular, it is non-existent. It can be grasped only through samādhi-wisdom, whether it occurs in the subtle aspects of the elements (*bhūta-sūkṣhma*) or in the spiritual self (puruṣha). Therefore, that wisdom is different in scope from the wisdom gained by learning or from the processes of logic, because it has a special aim, that of dealing with particulars.

Discussion

It was stated in the last sūtra that one receives wisdom from authoritative teaching (*śhruta* and *āgama*) and from the processes of logic, that is, inference (*anumāna*). Concentration on realities which have been understood through these means leads a yogi to *nir-vichāra samāpatti*. That being the case, *nir-vichāra* would succeed in helping to realize the subjects of *śhruta* and *anumāna* only because a mental impression (saṁskāra) created from observation of one object is incapable of producing knowledge of a different object. Following the same line of thought further, it would then appear that if *nir-vichāra* produces Truth-bearing wisdom, *śhruta* and *anumāna* should also be able to produce the same (VM). Then what purpose is served by yoga (VB, NB, NBB, BG)? The response to this objection is as follows: The nature of the sattva of buddhi is illumination. It is capable of observing all matters, but since buddhi is covered and obscured by tamas, it is only when rajas opens a way that the sattva of buddhi grasps any reality. However, when the maculation of both rajas and tamas is washed off through practice (*abhyāsa*) and dispassion (*vairāgya*), then buddhi's clarity shines forth and all boundaries and limitations imposed by external proofs burst through. There is only endless light. What then can be left unilluminated (VM, RY)?

The field of *śhruta* and *anumāna* is indeed apart from that of *nir-vichāra* samādhi. Words are incapable of producing knowledge of particulars. The word "cow," for example, cannot refer to each individual cow separately because there are simply an endless number and variety (HA) of them, nor can they all be present simultaneously as a singularity. Furthermore, one can be confused with another (VM, VB, NB, NBB, BG, RY). As to the efficacy of inference (*anumāna*) to reveal particulars, its failure was already pointed out in Sūtras I.7 and I.43. For instance, a statement of concomitance, such as "Wherever something is seen to have arrived, it must have moved," is based on generalities or commonalities, and all conclusions drawn are based on connecting the common attributes. Only direct perception gives knowledge of anything particular; but the direct perception of Truth-bearing wisdom is entirely different in scope from that of the direct perception with senses in the ordinary world (*loka-pratyakṣha*). In the Truth-bearing wisdom even those subtle, concealed or distant realities, which are closed to direct perception, become known to the yogis with respect both to their subtle, material aspects and to their spiritual aspects (VM, HA). All aspects of such realities are realized in their entirety all at once (BM).

The things which the senses are incapable of grasping are what is grasped in *nir-vichāra* samādhi. And that particular nature of the subtle evolutes and atoms on one hand and of the spiritual realities on the other is what is validated by the yogi's direct perception (*yogi-pratyakṣha*) (VM).

It may be asked that since direct perception in the philosophy of logic requires close contact between a perceiver's senses and the object perceived (Gotama's *Nyāya-sūtra* 1), how can a yogi perceive the subtle, the hidden or the distant which is beyond such contact? The answer is that the internal sense (*antaḥ-karaṇa*) is undivided and all-pervading. It is in close contact with all realities at all times. Once again, when rajas and tamas are washed off, it perceives without hindrance those realities which are too subtle, hidden or distant for the occluded external senses (VB). This direct experience also replaces the need for any external physical proof of the existence of such higher reality.

One might ask how the inner sense, an evolute of prakṛti, can grasp the reality of the particular spiritual self (puruṣha). The answer is that since the present discussion is about the Truth-bearing wisdom of *nir-vichāra* and the realization of puruṣha occurs only in *asamprajñāta,* it is only the spiritual reality of puruṣha's reflected presence in *asmitā* that is intended here by Vyāsa (HA). Furthermore, the discussion on the inefficacy of *śhruta* and *anumāna* with regard to the experience of *asamprajñāta* applies equally to the final realization of the spiritual self.

Sūtra I.50 तज्जः संस्कारोऽन्यसंस्कारप्रतिबन्धी ।

taj-jaḥ saṁskāro'nya-saṁskāra-pratibandhī

tat-jaḥ: arising from that, produced from that
saṁskāraḥ: saṁskāra, impression, imprint in the subtle domain (*karmāśhaya*)
anya-: (of) other
saṁskāra-: saṁskāras
prati-bandhī: that which impedes, hinders, resists, opposes, checks, inhibits, blocks, prevents, annuls

The imprint (saṁskāra) produced from that (samādhi-wisdom) opposes and annuls other saṁskāras.

Vyāsa's Commentary

Upon attainment of samādhi-wisdom, the yogi's saṁskāra produced by that wisdom is continuously renewed, being repeatedly strengthened afresh.

[*Sūtra:*] The imprint (saṁskāra) produced from that (samādhi-wisdom) opposes and annuls other saṁskāras.

The imprint (saṁskāra) produced by the samādhi-wisdom impedes (*bādh*) the domain (*āśhaya*) of the saṁskāras of worldly disturbance (*vyutthāna*). Once the *vyutthāna*-saṁskāras are overpowered, the cognitions (*pratyayas*) arising from them no longer occur. Upon control and cessation (*nirodha*) of the cognitions (*pratyayas*), samādhi presents itself. Thence the wisdom (*prajñā*) born of samādhi; thence the saṁskāras created from the wisdom; thus accumulation (*āśhaya*) of (such) saṁskāras repeated anew. Thence wisdom; thence (again) the saṁskāras—thus.

How is it possible that this accumulation of saṁskāras in their domain will not give power (*adhikāra*) to the mind-field? The saṁskāras created by wisdom (*prajñā*), being the means (*hetu*) of the reduction (*kṣhaya*) of afflictions (*kleśhas*), do not cause the mind-field to become possessed (*vi-śhiṣhṭa*) of such power (*adhikāra*).

They, in fact, cause the mind-field to exhaust and turn away from its act (*kārya*). Indeed, the mind-field's endeavour terminates at discriminating wisdom (*khyāti*).

Discussion

The reader should bear in mind that the word "wisdom" (*prajñā*) conveys the same sense as was explained in Sūtra I.17: the realization attained in *sam-**prajñāta*** samādhi. The word *vyutthāna* is the antonym of *samādhi* and means "worldly involvement," as used in Sūtras I.3 and I.14. The saṁskāras accumulating in their domain in the subtle body form the *saṁskāra-āśhaya,* as explained in Sūtra I.24.

As the saṁskāras of samādhi gather force and are constantly renewed, the *vyutthāna*-saṁskāras weaken. The old *āśhaya* is replaced with continuously replenished new saṁskāras of samādhi, which produces the wisdom of realizations, which again reinforces the saṁskāras of samādhi. Thus the cycle of vṛttis and worldly saṁskāras described in Sūtra I.5 is broken. Because these saṁskāras of the wisdom of samādhi are of the unafflicted (*a-klishṭa*) kind, they do not add to that power (*adhikāra*) of the mind-field which draws one's awareness into the external world. The mind-field's power to serve as the vehicle of ignorance (*avidyā*) and I-am-ness (*asmitā*) is therefore weakened. Upon attainment of discriminating wisdom its function ceases except as an instrument totally under the yogi's command. (The continuity of this residue of saṁskāras was explained in Sūtra I.18.)

This sūtra indicates the fruit and result of the Truth-bearing wisdom (*ṛtambharā prajñā*) of the last two sūtras (BR). A question arises, however, as to the ability of the newly acquired samādhi saṁskāras to overcome the *vyutthāna* saṁskāras. Some commentators argue that it may be that *samprajñāta* practised with the proper methods (*upāyas*) leads to higher realizations (VM), but it is actually as powerless before the beginningless (see Sūtra I.4) worldly saṁskāras as a tiny candle flame before a stormy wind (VM, NBB); also the saṁskāras of past enjoyments (*bhoga*) of the senses are too powerful to let it become stable (RY). The present sūtra answers this argument. The word "that" (*tat*) in the sūtra refers to the *nir-vichāra samāpatti* (VM). It is the nature of buddhi to be attracted towards reality (*bhūta-artha*) (see Sūtras I.1 and I.47). It wanders confused only until it finds the true nature (*tattva*). Having found the true nature of things, buddhi becomes established towards it (VM, NBB). Saṁskāras of this stability produce a like buddhi, and thus the new cycle breaks the former beginningless cycle of ignorance of *tattva* and the like buddhi (VM). This samādhi produces saṁskāras of a real nature (*tattva*) which impede opposing, or non-that-ness (*a-tattva*), saṁskāras (BR, RY). This bias of buddhi towards reality is accepted even in other philosophical systems (as, for example Kumārila's *Pramāṇa-vārttika* III.222) (VM, NBB).

What is the meaning of *prati-bandh* in the sūtra? That the wisdom impedes (*bādh*) the other saṁskāras. That is, it prevents their effects (VB), namely the vṛttis (NB) or their memory (*smṛti*) (BG). It renders them inefficacious, incapable of functioning (BR). This refers only to the saṁskāras that are dormant in their domain. The word *āśhaya* (from *ā* + *śhī*) means "that which sleeps" (VB, NBB). The reference, then, is not to those saṁskāras which have already become awakened as vṛttis or as results and fruits of past actions, but to those which yet lie dormant (VB, NBB). It also opposes the saṁskāras produced from the distracted (*vikṣhipta*) ground (HA), one of the five grounds (*bhūmis*) of the mind-field (see Sūtra I.1). The growth of the wisdom-saṁskāra is the same as the diminution of the *vikṣhepa-saṁskāras;* the two are simultaneous (HA). However, only the unbroken flow of the stream of one-pointedness (*ekāgratā-dhārā*) is effective (NB).

Now, when a certain realization (*prajñā*) has occurred in *samprajñāta* samādhi, does that then suffice to overcome the power of the worldly saṁskāras (VB, NBB)? In addition, when a yogi has once accomplished *samprajñāta,* why must he then keep practising it repeatedly (VB, NB, BG)? Repeated experience of *samprajñāta* confirms and strengthens its saṁskāras, without which the worldly *vyutthāna*-saṁskāras will keep arising. A single experience alone does not thwart them, but the opposing saṁskāras of repeated practice gradually attentuate them, thin them down (*tanū-karaṇa*)

(*YS* II.2,4,10). Thus a cycle of samādhi-wisdom-saṁskāra-samādhi ensues, and the cycle of saṁskāras and vṛttis diminishes in power. When the final realization (*prajñā*) occurs, the power of the *vyutthāna*-saṁskāras ceases. In other words the Vedānta view that knowledge (*jñāna*) alone leads to liberation is accurate only with reference to the ultimate wisdom, but first the attenuation (*tanū-karaṇa*) of the worldly saṁskāras by cultivating the samādhi-saṁskāras must occur and reach its perfection (VB, NBB). The statement that the realization of this wisdom diminishes and abolishes *kleśhas* and past saṁskāras has led commentators to ask a further question (VB, BG) about the state and status of karma in the yogi who has reached this far. As the texts (such as *Viṣhṇu-purāṇa* VI.7.35 and *BhG* IV.37) state, the fire of yoga burns away all karmas, and yoga abolishes all accumulated sin (*pāpa*). There are many levels at which the strength of karmas is reduced. There are many expiatory observances of prayer, ritual and right acts that reduce the power of existing karmas and their saṁskāras by adding to the *karmāśhaya,* the internal domain of karma, the force of these thoughts and acts. But this does not free one from the totality of karma, because that which has been planted must bear fruit, and the inclination towards involvement in further acts still remains. Thus, diluting past accumulations of evil saṁskāras by the addition of fresh and benevolent acts is not in the same category as burning them by the power of yoga, that is, samādhi.

The statements about yoga burning the karmas apply only to the extent that yoga eliminates those evil accumulations which impede the realization of true knowledge. When knowledge has arisen, all karmas and their saṁskāras are abolished *except* the *prārabdha* saṁskāras, the sum total gathered from past lives which had initially determined the yogi's birth in the given species, life span in that particular life, and pleasures and pains (such as physical illness) that ensue in that lifetime. *Prārabdha* saṁskāras thus keep the momentum going for the yogi's continued existence in the present life. But there is no additional fresh accumulation of worldly saṁskāras (VB, BG).

There is, however, a great difference between cultivating the saṁskāras of *samprajñāta* and the awakening of final wisdom. The samādhi-saṁskāras reduce the pain-causing power of the *vyutthāna*-saṁskāras, but one still needs to say "Enough!" to this wisdom. The desire for *siddhis* has yet to be conquered. The trap of desiring to become a *videha* or *prakṛti-laya* still has to be avoided. When even these saṁskāras vanish with the mind-field's dissolution into its cause, only then and not before will the saṁskāra of ignorance (*avidyā*) be overcome as the *dharma-megha* samādhi ensues. When all these saṁskāras are vanquished, then the cycle of the fruition of karma in reincarnation ceases. The single knowledge, beyond this process, which leads to liberation is the one beyond discriminating wisdom (*viveka-khyāti*). Of that higher stage the next sūtra will speak (VB, NB, NBB, BG).

Another question may be raised: It is known throughout the *Yoga-sūtras'* teaching that saṁskāras give power to the mind to become active so that vṛttis are produced; even though the saṁskāras of samādhi subdue the worldly saṁskāras, do not the samādhi-saṁskāras produce their own kind of activity in the mind and enhance its continuation as an involver (*pra-varttaka*)? Would not this then produce further afflictions (*kleśhas*)? The answer is that the vṛttis and saṁskāras of samādhi are unafflicted ones (*a-kliṣhṭa*); therefore they produce no more afflictions. Furthermore, prakṛti, including its evolute the mind, has only two purposes:

- to present experiences (*bhoga*) to puruṣha, and
- to aid him in attaining liberation (*mokṣha*).

At the perfection of *samprajñāta* samādhi and attainment of *viveka-khyāti* the mind has fulfilled its purpose and can proceed no further; its *adhikāra,* that is, its assignment, duty, and the power to carry them out, is now exhausted. The mind is henceforth dismissed, dissolved into equilibrium.

Sūtra I.51 तस्यापि निरोधे सर्वनिरोधान्निर्बीजः समाधिः।

tasyāpi nirodhe sarva-nirodhān nir-bījaḥ samādhiḥ

tasya: of that
api: even
nirodhe: upon control, cessation, dissolution
sarva-: (of) all
nirodhāt: through *nirodha,* dissolution
nir-bījaḥ: seedless
samādhiḥ: samādhi

When the control, cessation and dissolution (*nirodha*) of even that saṁskāra occurs, the *nirodha* of all else ensues and, thereby, seedless (*nir-bīja*) samādhi (is attained).

Vyāsa's Commentary

And what else happens to him?

[*Sūtra:*] When the control, cessation and dissolution (*nirodha*) of even that saṁskāra occurs, the *nirodha* of all else ensues and, thereby, seedless (*nir-bīja*) samādhi (is attained).

This samādhi not only opposes the samādhi-wisdom (*prajñā*) but impedes even the saṁskāras produced by samādhi-wisdom. Wherefore? Because the saṁskāra produced by control (*nirodha*) counteracts (*bādh*) the saṁskāra generated by samādhi.

The existence of saṁskāras created by the mind-field in the state of *nirodha* (*nirodha*-chitta) is inferred on the basis of the experience of the sequences of time (that elapse) during the state of the stability of *nirodha.* The mind-field dissolves into its own causal nature (prakṛti), which (ever) remains in that inactive condition. It does so together with those saṁskāras which have been produced by the samādhi that constitutes worldly involvement (*vyutthāna*)[42] and

42. Here *vyutthāna* means *samprajñāta* samādhi, which is a worldly involvement in contrast to *a-samprajñāta,* which is the topic of this sūtra.

cessation (*nirodha*). Thus, those saṁskāras are opponents of the empowerment (*adhikāra*) of the mind-field, not causes of its (continued) maintenance (*sthiti*).

Since that mind-field whose empowerment (*adhikāra*) has been terminated withdraws (*vi-ni-vṛt*) together with the saṁskāras that are conducive to isolation, upon its thus turning off (*ni-vṛt*), the spiritual self (puruṣha) is established in his own self-nature (*sva-rūpa*) and is therefore called pure, one alone in isolation (*kevala*), and free or liberated (*mukta*).

Here in Patañjali's Sāṅkhya-pravachana, *and in Vyāsa's Commentary, ends the first, the chapter on samādhi, within the Science and Discipline of Yoga.*

Discussion

It has been explained that the purpose of creating the saṁskāras of samādhi-wisdom in *samprajñāta* is to eliminate the mind-field's empowerment (*adhikāra*) to provide experience of the material world (*bhoga*) to puruṣha (VM). However, this accumulated wisdom from *samprajñāta* is not sufficient to free one from reincarnation (VB).[43] How can a mind-field filled with and perpetuating the saṁskāras of samādhi-wisdom reach seedless samādhi (RY)? To answer this question, the sūtra now states the result of *asamprajñāta*. The saṁskāras of *samprajñāta* still maintain the mind-field's other assignment, which is to lead one to isolation (*kaivalya*). This assignment, too, must be fulfilled so that the final termination of this *adhikāra* may occur (VM). VB says that at the lower levels of *asamprajñāta* each succeeding level brings under control and dissolves the realization of the preceding one, at the same time attenuating their saṁskāras. Only with the final *asamprajñāta* does the total elimination of the lower wisdoms, the realizations that occur at lower *samprajñātas,* occur. Since Patañjali and Vyāsa, however, do not divide *asamprajñāta* into these levels, VB's statement is more appropriately applicable to the differentiation into levels of

43. NB, NBB, and BG for the most part repeat VB on this sūtra, and BM echoes VM. Where any have an original opinion, it is indicated.

samprajñāta. As one progresses in *samprajñāta,* the wisdom-vṛtti at each level is dissolved into its own cause; as each vṛtti arises from a saṁskāra, the yogi observes "not this, not this" (*neti, neti*), and thus denying them any worth and continuing to pursue reality, he finally reaches the seedless, *asamprajñāta,* samādhi (BR, AD). This view is more in harmony with what has been discussed in Sūtra I.17 and echoes the teaching of the Upaniṣhads (e.g., *Bṛhadāraṇyaka Upaniṣhad* II.3.6; III.9.26; IV.2.4; IV.4.22; IV.5.15).

Asamprajñāta not only eliminates the lower wisdoms of *samprajñāta* but also overcomes their saṁskāras. This is the transcendent dispassion (*para-vairāgya*) explained in Sūtra I.16, and is synonymous with *nirodha* (VM). The question arises (VM): Granted that the realization arising from such dispassion may counteract the *samprajñāta*-wisdoms which are a form of ideation (*vijñāna*); but how can it also overcome these saṁskāras, since they are not in the category of ideation? Would they not have to remain the way the memory of a dream object remains during wakeful experience? Vyāsa says (VM) that while *nirodha* itself eliminates the wisdom of *samprajñāta,* the saṁskāras of the *nirodha* counteract the saṁskāras of that wisdom. Again, it is not that a single realization of *asamprajñāta* accomplishes all this, but rather that when continuous and uninterrupted practice, observed for a long time and with due respect (see Sūtra I.14), is constantly strengthened, it causes an unbroken flow of *asamprajñāta,* and these final results accrue.

Some commentators, however, have asked, How can we know that there exist saṁskāras of *nirodha*? There can be no direct perception of it to serve as proof, since such proof is a vṛtti and this *nirodha* is the elimination of all vṛttis. Nor can such a non-vṛtti leave a memory. Being above the chain of causation, its existence cannot be inferred by seeing some effect. How can one establish the proof of such a nonentity and of any possible saṁskāras being created by it (VM, VB)? Vyāsa answers that the transcendent dispassion grows in stages. When the yogi comes out of *asamprajñāta* he observes the time that has elapsed and thereby infers that *nirodha* has indeed occurred. (VM) It is the accumulated force of such frequent *nirodhas* that creates an imprint (saṁskāra), till it grows to the utmost possible degree; if this were not so, the growth in intensity and length of *asamprajñāta* would not occur. Thus one infers that both *nirodha* and its saṁskāras do occur.

The argument is constructed slightly differently by HA: How vṛttis produce saṁskāras is obvious. That saṁskāras in turn produce vṛttis is also known. They do so by first generating *pratyayas,* cognitions, presented to the mind. As saṁskāras arise to the surface, a cognition (*pratyaya*) is formed and presented to the mind-field, just as vṛttis introduced externally present cognitions (*pratyayas*) to the mind-field, creating further saṁskāras. Saṁskāras have only one function, and that is to generate *pratyayas.* When such *pratyayas* arise no more, it may be assumed either that the saṁskāras were not formed or that they have been exhausted or, finally, that *nirodha* has occurred. However, the question remains as to the nature of the saṁskāras of *nirodha.* Since *nirodha,* not being a vṛtti, cannot produce a cognition (*pratyaya*), how can a *nirodha*-saṁskāra form? The answer is that the flow of *pratyayas* exists before *nirodha* and continues after it. The break in that flow is recognized by the mind, and this recognition constitutes the *nirodha*-saṁskāra. As these breaks occur more frequently and become prolonged, the tendency to *nirodha* grows. Again, if *nirodha* formed no saṁskāras at all, how would its growth, which is clearly noticed, occur? Finally the flow of *pratyayas* totally ceases and samādhi becomes permanent (HA). Activity alone constitutes a reason for the continuity of the mind. That reason having been abolished, the mind is dissolved and puruṣha dwells in his own nature.

A further objection is suggested by VM and VB: It is well that the saṁskāras of the samādhi-wisdom are eliminated; but, then, how may the saṁskāras of *nirodha* be overpowered? Or do they remain? But if so, the mind-field thus keeps its empowerment to act. For could not these saṁskāras again be revived into activity through the will of a yogi or of īśhvara, in the same way that a seed which looks burnt sometimes sprouts? This question is resolved by a better understanding of Vyāsa's position (VM, VB): Up to the mastery of *samprajñāta,* the word *vyutthāna* served as an antonym to *samādhi* and denoted worldly involvement of the mind. In contrast to *asamprajñāta* now, *samprajñāta* also is *vyutthāna,* a lower-level awareness. The innermost part (*antar-aṅga*) of yoga is *asamprajñāta,* in comparison to which *samprajñāta* is an exterior part (*bahir-aṅga*) (SS). What for an ordinary person is opening the eyes from *samprajñāta* into the world, for a yogi is coming down into *samprajñāta* from *asamprajñāta*. Those saṁskāras of *samprajñāta* which are conducive to isolation (*kaivalya*) have helped the mind-field to fulfil its final assignments. Now, when the saṁskāras of *nirodha* form, they do not produce further vṛttis, thus rendering the mind inactive. Having fulfilled its assignment and having no further purpose to accomplish, the mind-field now dissolves into its cause (RY). As to the case of *videhas* and *prakṛti-layas,* let it not be said that the mind's empowerment continues because of *nirodha*-saṁskāras; these yogis, not having reached *asamprajñāta,* do not have any *nirodha*-saṁskāras. The power (*adhikāra*) of their chittas continues because of the propensities (*vāsanās*) produced by the afflictions (*kleśhas*).

An argument is presented by NB and BG: Knowledge gained in *samprajñāta* burns all the past karmas except *prārabdha.*[44] *Prārabdha* is spent and exhausted as it comes to fruition in the form of karma-produced pains and pleasures. Thus, through *samprajñāta*-wisdom all other karmas are exhausted and the *prārabdha* takes care of itself and eventually becomes exhausted. Naturally liberation (*mokṣha*) will follow. Why, then, is there need for *asamprajñāta*? BG says that *asamprajñāta* only hastens the liberation so that the yogi does not have to wait for the *prārabdha* to be exhausted. NBB, however, has a better answer: The saṁskāras produced by *samprajñāta* are saṁskāras of a vṛtti from the exterior world. Until these saṁskāras are somehow burnt, there can be no final *nirodha* and consequently no liberation. *Asamprajñāta* alone is capable of burning the *prajñā*-saṁskāras and is thus absolutely essential for liberation. In fact, propensities (*vāsanās*) of *prārabdha* cannot find

44. See Sūtra I.1 (p. 90) for an explanation of *prārabdha.*

a substratum when the very *karmāśhaya,* the domain and realm of karmas and saṁskāras, has been purified or burnt and the mind-field itself has been dissolved. That being the case, even *prārabdha* may not come to fruition and is burnt out because its coefficients (*saha-kārin*) have been eliminated.

There being no objects of concentration (*ālambanas*) in *asamprajñāta* (in contradistinction to *samprajñāta*), it is called seedless (*nir-bīja*) samādhi. Then one no longer rises from samādhi. This must not be misconstrued to mean that the yogi remains physically sitting in meditation; rather, it means that his awareness remains pure. This state is free of those seeds, such as saṁskāras, that produce sorrows (VB); it is also free of the saṁskāras of *samprajñāta*-wisdom, which otherwise might bind the yogi again (NBB). All these seeds being absent, this samādhi is called seedless (*nir-bīja*). *Asamprajñāta* is also called the "great sleep" (*mahā-nidrā*) of the mind-field (NBB, BG).

It is not that puruṣha had become sullied and is now pure (*śhuddha*), but rather that pains, etc. are no longer attributed to it. It is not that it had become involved and is now isolated (*kevala*), but rather that it cannot be considered to be involved. It is not that it was bound and has now been liberated (*mukta*), but rather that the bondages of buddhi can no longer be said to have been transferred to it. Hence, says Vyāsa:

> The spiritual self (puruṣha) is established in his own self-nature (*sva-rūpa*) and is therefore called pure, one alone in isolation (*kevala*), and free or liberated (*mukta*).

In other words, upon the attainment of *nir-bīja* samādhi the mind-field can no longer arise into *vyutthāna,* and so it vanishes; then the consciousness-potentia or the consciousness-force (*chiti-śhakti*), which is absolutely eternal (*kūṭastha-nitya*), infinite and pure, dwells in her own glory, without obstruction and forever, and this is very beautiful (SS).

This chapter (VM) has stated:

- *uddeśha:* the name and title (Sūtra 1)
- *nirdeśha:* the definition (Sūtras 2-4) (and, in that context, all the following:)
- the definition of *vṛtti* (Sūtras 5-11)
- the methods for accomplishing yoga (Sūtras 12-16, 20-24)
- the divisions or classifications of yoga (Sūtras 17-19, 41-51)

This may be expanded (BR) as follows:

- stating the commencement of yoga (Sūtra 1)
- the definition of yoga (Sūtras 2-4)
- explanation of the words *chitta-vṛtti* and *nirodha* (Sūtras 5-11)
- the two means, *abhyāsa* and *vairāgya,* and their definition (Sūtras 12-16)
- the primary (*asamprajñāta*) and secondary (*samprajñāta*) yogas (Sūtras 17-19)
- briefly, the methods (*upāyas*) of yoga (Sūtras 20-22)
- an easy method (*īśhvara-praṇidhāna*)
  and the relevant explanation
  and statement of its results (Sūtras 23-29)
- (in the context of the results of *īśhvara-praṇidhāna*)
  the nine obstacles (*vikṣhepas*)
  and their correlates (Sūtras 30-32)
- the methods for overcoming the obstacles
  and their correlates (Sūtras 32-40)
- (as these obtacles are overcome)
  further explanations of samādhis
  and their accomplishments (*samāpattis*)—
  first the seeded (*sa-bīja*)
  and then the seedless (*nir-bīja*) samādhi (Sūtras 41-51)

Bibliography

Primary Sources

Patañjali, *Yoga-sūtras*

- with *Yoga-pradīpikā* by Baladeva Miśhra. Edited by Dhundhiraja Shastri. Varanasi: Chowkhambā, 1931.
- with the commentaries *Rāja-mārttaṇḍa* by Bhojarāja, *Pradīpikā* by Bhāvāgaṇeśha, *Vṛtti* by Nāgojī Bhaṭṭa, *Maṇi-prabhā* by Rāmānanda Yati, *Pada-chandrikā* by Ananta-deva Pandit, and *Yoga-sudhākara* by Sadāśhivendra Sarasvatī. Edited by Dhundhiraja Shastri. Varanasi: Chowkhambā, 1930.
- with the commentaries *Yoga-siddhānta-chandrikā* and *Sūtrārtha-bodhinī* by Nārāyaṇa Tīrtha. Edited by Ratna Gopāla Bhaṭṭa. Varanasi: Chowkhambā, 1911.
- with the commentary *Bhāṣhya-vivaraṇa* of Śhaṅkara-bhagavat-pāda. Edited with an introduction by Polakam Sri Rama Sastri and S. R. Krishnamurthi Sastri. Madras Government Oriental Manuscripts Library Series, no. 94. Madras, 1952.
- with the commentaries *Tattva-vaiśhāradī* of Vāchaspati Miśhra and *Yoga-vārttika* of Vijñāna-bhikṣhu. Edited by Narayana Mishra. Varanasi: Chowkhambā, 1971.
- with the commentaries *Tattva-vaiśhāradī* of Vāchaspati Miśhra edited by Rajaram Bodas and *Vṛtti (Bṛhatī)* of Nāgojī Bhaṭṭa edited by Vasudev Shastri Abhyankar. Bombay Sanskrit and Prakrit Series, no. 46. Bombay: Government Central Press, 1917.

• with the scholium of Vyāsa and the commentaries of *Tattva-vaiśhāradī, Pātañjala-rahasya, Yoga-vārttika* and *Bhāsvati* of Vāchaspati Miśhra, Rāghavānanda Sarasvatī, Vijñāna-bhikṣhu, and Hariharānanda Āraṇya. Edited by Gosvāmī Dāmodara Shāstrī. Varanasi: Chowkhambā, 1935.

Bhāgavata-purāṇa. Gorakhpur, India: Gita Press, 1968.

Bṛhad-yogi-yājñavalkya-smṛti. Edited and translated into Hindi by Swami Kuvalayananda and Pandit Raghunatha Shastri Kokaje. Lonavla, India: Kaivalyadhama, 1951.

Dīkṣhita, Rāma-bhadra. "Ṣhaḍ-darśhana-siddhānta-saṅgraha." Sarasvatī-bhavan Library, Tanjore.

Krishna-vallabhāchārya. *Kiraṇa.* Edited by Shveta-vaikuntha Shastri and Narayana Sharana Shastri. Banaras, 1939.

Mādhava. *Sarva-darśhana-saṅgraha.* Edited by Uma Shankar Sharma. Varanasi: Chowkhambā, 1964.

Mahābhārata, with Nīlakaṇṭha's Commentary. Pune: Chitrashala Press, 1968.

Mārkaṇḍeya-purāṇa. Edited by Śhrīram Sharma Acharya. Bareli, India: published by the editor, 1978.

Udāsīna, Balarāma. *Commentary on the Yoga-sūtras.* Edited by K. B. R. Sinha. Bankipore, 1867, 1897.

Upaniṣhad-brahma-yogin. *Bhagavad-gītārtha-prakāśhikā* [a Sanskrit commentary on the *Bhagavad-gītā*]. Edited by the pandits of the Adyar Library. Adyar, India: Adyar Library, 1941.

Vijñāna-bhikṣhu. *Yoga-sāra-saṅgraha.* Edited by Swami Sanatana Deva. Delhi: Motilal Banarsidass, 1956.

Viṣhṇu-purāṇa. Gorakhpur, India: Gita Press, 1932.

Other primary texts consulted and cited such as the Upaniṣhads, Purāṇas and *Bhagavad-gītā* are not included in this bibliography. Well-known editions of these texts are readily available to scholars. Numerous translations of the *Yoga-sūtras* in several Indian languages have been reviewed but are not useful to the average reader. A detailed bibliography of primary and secondary sources on Patañjali is to be found on pp. 58-65 in Karl Potter's *Bibliography of Indian Philosophies,* vol. 1 of *The Encyclopedia of Indian Philosophies,* citing 126 titles. It does not include some of the titles consulted by us.

Translations of the *Yoga-sūtras* of Patañjali

Āraṇya, Swami Hariharānanda. *Yoga Philosophy of Patañjali.* Calcutta: University of Calcutta, 1977.

Ballantyne, James Robert. *The Aphorisms of the Yoga Philosophy of Patanjali, with illustrative extracts from the Commentary by Bhoja Raja.* Allahabad: Presbyterian Mission Press, 1852-53.

Bangali Baba. *Patanjala Yoga Sutra.* Delhi: Motilal Banarsidass, 1976.

Boissenain, J. W. *Yoga-Soetra's door Patanjali: Leerspreuken der Eenheidsstreving.* Haarlem, Netherlands: J. W. Boissenain and Co., 1918.

Dvivedi, Manilal Nabhubhai, ed. and trans. *The Yoga-Sūtras of Patañjali.* Adyar, India: Theosophical Publishing House, 1934.

Feuerstein, Georg. *The Yoga-Sūtra of Patañjali: A New Translation and Commentary.* Folkestone, England: Dawson, 1979.

Isbert, Otto Albrecht. *Raja Joga, der königliche Weg der Selbstmeisterung in Westlicher Sicht und Praxis.* Gelnhausen, West Germany: Verlags-Union Bündingen-Haingründau, 1955.

Johnston, Charles. *The Yoga Sutras of Patañjali.* London: John M. Watkins, 1964.

Judge, William Q. *The Yoga Aphorisms of Patanjali.* Los Angeles: United Lodge of Theosophists, 1920.

Leggett, Trevor. *Śaṅkara on the Yoga-sūtra-s: The Vivaraṇa sub-commentary to Vyāsa-bhaṣya on the Yoga-sūtra-s of Patañjali.* Vol. 1, *Samādhi;* Vol. 2, *Means.* London: Routledge and Kegan Paul, 1981, 1983.

Mangoldt, Ursula von. *So Spricht das Yoga-Sutra des Patanjali.* Munich: O. W. Barth, 1957.

Mitra, Rājendralāla. *Yoga Aphorisms of Patañjali, with the Commentary of Bhoja Rāja.* Bibliotheca Indica Series, no. 93. Calcutta: Asiatic Society of Bengal, 1881-83.

Prabhavananda, Swami, and Christopher Isherwood. *How to Know God: The Yoga Aphorisms of Patanjali.* London: Allen and Unwin, 1953.

Rāma Prasāda, trans. *The Yoga-sūtras of Patañjali with the Commentary of Vyāsa and the Gloss of Vāchaspati Miśhra.* Vol. 4 of *The Sacred Books of the Hindus, Translated by Various Sanskrit Scholars.* Edited by Major B. D. Basu. 1912. Reprint. New York: AMS Press, 1974.

Shree Purohit, Swami. *Aphorisms of Yoga by Bhagawan Shree Patanjali.* London: Faber and Faber, 1938.

Stephen, Daniel R., trans. *Patanjali for Western Readers.* London: Theosophical Publishing House, 1919.

Taimni, I. K. *The Science of Yoga.* Madras, India, and Wheaton, Ill.: Theosophical Publishing House, 1961.

Tīrtha, Swami Omananda. *Pātañjala-yoga-pradīpa* (in Hindi). Gorakhpur, India: Gita Press, 1960.

Woods, James Haughton, trans. *The Yoga System of Patañjali.* Harvard Oriental Series, vol. 17. Cambridge: Harvard University Press, 1914. Reprint. Delhi: Motilal Banarsidass, 1927.

Woods, James Haughton. "The Yoga Sūtras of Patañjali as Illustrated by the Commentary entitled 'The Jewel's Lustre,' or Maṇiprabhā." *Journal of the American Oriental Society* 34 (1915): 1-114.

Translations of Other Source Material

Mādhavāchārya. *The Sarva-darśana samgraha; or, Review of the Different Systems of Hindu Philosophy.* Translated by Edward Byles Cowell and Archibald Edward Gough. London: Trübner and Co., 1882.

Mahadeva Sastri, Alladi, ed. *Yoga Upanishads, with the Commentary of Śrī Brahma-Yogīn.* Madras: Adyar Library and Research Centre, 1968.

Vijñāna-bhikṣhu. *Yoga-Sāra-Saṅgraha.* Translated by Ganganatha Jha. Rev. ed. Theosophical Publishing House Oriental Series, no. 10. Madras, India: Theosophical Publishing House, 1933.

Secondary and Reference Literature

Apte, V. S. *Sanskrit-English Dictionary.* Delhi: Motilal Banarsidass, 1970.

Arya, Usharbudh. *God.* Honesdale, Pa.: Himalayan International Institute, 1979.

———. *Mantra and Meditation.* Honesdale, Pa.: Himalayan International Institute, 1983.

Bahm, Archie J. *Yoga: Union with the Ultimate.* New York: Unger, 1967.

Bedekar, V. M. "The Dhyānayoga in the Mahābhārata (XII.188)." *Munshi Indological Felicitation Volume, Bharatīya Vidyā* 20:115-25, 21:1960-61.

Catalina, Francis Victor. *A Study of the Self Concept of Sankhya-Yoga Philosophy.* Delhi: Munshiram Manoharlal, 1968.

Dani, Ahmad Hasan. *Alberuni's Indica.* Islamabad, Pakistan: University of Islamabad Press, 1973.

Dasgupta, Surendra Nath. *A History of Indian Philosophy.* Vols. 1 and 2. Cambridge: Harvard University Press, 1963, 1965.

———. *A Study of Patañjali.* Calcutta: University of Calcutta, 1920.

———. *Yoga as Philosophy and Religion.* Calcutta: University of Calcutta, 1924.

———. *Yoga Philosophy in Relation to Other Systems of Indian Thought.* Calcutta: University of Calcutta, 1930.

Deussen, Paul. *Allgemeine Geschichte der Philosophie.* Vol. 1, pt. 3. Leipzig: F. A. Brockhaus, 1920.

Edgerton, Franklin. "The Meaning of Sāṇkhya and Yoga." *American Journal of Philosophy* 45 (1924): 1-46.

Eliade, Mircea. *Yoga: Immortality and Freedom.* Translated by Willard R. Trask. 2d ed. Bollingen Series, no. 61. Princeton: Princeton University Press, 1969.

———. *Patañjali and Yoga.* Translated by Charles L. Markmann. New York: Schocken Books, 1975.

Feuerstein, Georg. *The Essence of Yoga: A Contribution to the Psychohistory of Indian Civilization.* London: Rider, 1974.

———. *The Philosophy of Classical Yoga.* New York: St. Martin's Press, 1980; Manchester: Manchester University Press, 1980.

———. "Some notes on the final stages of yoga according to Patañjali." *Bharatiya Vidya Bhavan* (Bombay: Rajendra Prasad College of Mass Communication and Media) 37 (1971): 1-12.

———. *The Yoga-Sūtra of Patañjali: An Exercise in the Methodology of Textual Analysis.* New Delhi: Arnold-Heinemann, 1979.

Feuerstein, Georg, and Jeanine Miller. *Yoga and Beyond: Essays in Indian Philosophy.* New York: Schocken Books, 1972.

Frauwallner, Erich. *Geschichte der indischen Philosophie.* Vol 1. Salzburg: O. Muller, 1953.

Garbe, Richard von. *Sāmkhya und Yoga.* Strassburg: K. J. Trubner, 1894.

Gonda, Jan. *Die Religionen Indiens.* Vol 1. Stuttgart: W. Kohlhammer Verlag, 1960.

Hauer, Jakob Wilhelm. "Das IV Buch des Yogasūtra." *Studia Indo-Iranica: Ehrengabe für Wilhelm Geiger,* edited by Walther Wüst. Leipzig: Otto Harrassowitz, 1931.

———. *Der Yoga, ein indischer Weg zum Selbst.* Stuttgart: W. Kohlhammer, 1958.

———. *Die Anfange der Yogapraxis im Alten Indien.* Stuttgart: W. Kohlhammer, 1922.

Hopkins, E. Washburn. "Yoga Technique in the Great Epic." *American Oriental Society Journal* 22 (1901): 333-79.

Hultzsch, E. "Sāmkhya und Yoga im Śiśupālavadha." *Aus Indiens Kultur: Festgabe für Richard von Garbe,* edited by Julius von Negelein. Erlangen: Palm and Enke, 1927.

Isbert, Otto Albrecht. *Raja-Joga, der königliche Weg der Selbstmeisterung in Westlicher Sicht und Praxis.* Gelnhausen, West Germany: Verlags-Union Bündinger-Haingründau, 1955.

Jacob, George Adolphus. *A Concordance to the Principal Upanishads and Bhagavadgita.* Bombay: Government Central Book Depot, 1891.

Jacobi, Hermann. "Uber das Ursprüngliche Yoga System." *Sitzungsberichte der Preusischen Akademie der Wissenschaften.* Berlin: Akademie Verlag, 1929.

Janāček, Adolf. "The Meaning of Pratyaya in Patañjali's Yoga-Sūtras." *Archiv Orientalni* 25 (1957): 201-60.

———. "The Methodological Principle in Yoga according to Patañjali's Yoga-Sūtras." *Archiv Orientalni* 19 (1951): 514-67.

———. "Two Texts of Patañjali and a Statistical Comparison of their Vocabularies." *Archiv Orientalni* 26 (1958): 88-101.

———. "The 'Voluntaristic' Type of Yoga in Patañjali's Yoga-Sūtras." *Archiv Orientalni* 22 (1954): 69-87.

Johnston, Charles. *The Yoga-Sūtras of Patañjali: The Book of the Spiritual Man.* New York: Quarterly Book Dept., 1912.

Joshi, K. S. "On the Meaning of Yoga." *Philosophy East and West* 15, no. 1 (1965): 53-64.

Karṇāṭak, Vimla. *A Critical Study of the Patanjala-Yoga-Sūtra in the Light of its Commentators* (in Hindi). Banaras Hindu University Sanskrit Series, no. 10. Varanasi: Chowkhambā, 1974.

Koelman, Gaspar M. *Pātañjala Yoga: From Related Ego to Absolute Self.* Poona, India: Papal Athenaeum, 1970.

Larson, Gerald James. *Classical Sāmkhya: An Interpretation of its History and Meaning.* Delhi: Motilal Banarsidass, 1969.

LaVallee Poussin, Louis de. "Le Bouddhisme et le Yoga de Patanjali." *Milanges Chinois et Bouddhiques* 5 (1937): 223-42.

Müller, M. *The Six Systems of Indian Philosophy.* London: Longmans, 1916.

Oberhammer, Gerhard. "Gott, Urbild der Emanzipierten Existenz im Yoga des Patañjali." *Zeitschrift für Katholische Theologie* (Vienna) 1964: 197-207.

———. *Strukturen Yogischer Meditation. Veröffentlichungen der Kommission für Sprachen und Südasiens, Heft 13.* Vienna: Verlag der Osterreichischen Akademie der Wissenschaften, 1977.

Panikkar, Raimundo. *The Vedic Experience: Mantra-manjari.* Berkeley and Los Angeles: University of California Press, 1977.

Pensa, Corrado. "On the Purification Concept in Indian Tradition, with Special Regard to Yoga." *East and West* n.s. 19 (1969): 194-228.

Pines, Shlomo, and Tuvia Gelblum. "Al-Bīrūnī's Arabic Version of Patañjali's Yogasūtra." *Bulletin of the School of Oriental and African Studies* 29 (1966): 302-25 and 40 (1977): 522-49.

Potter, Karl H., comp. *Bibliography of Indian Philosophies.* Rev. ed. Vol. 1 of *The Encyclopedia of Indian Philosophies.* American Institute of Indian Studies. Delhi: Motilal Banarsidass, 1979.

Rama, Swami. *Choosing a Path.* Honesdale, Pa.: Himalayan International Institute, 1982.

———. *Inspired Thoughts of Swami Rama.* Honesdale, Pa.: Himalayan International Institute, 1983.

Rama, Swami, Rudolph Ballentine, M.D., and Swami Ajaya. *Yoga and Psychotherapy.* Honesdale, Pa.: Himalayan International Institute, 1976.

Sahay, Mahajot. "Pātañjala-Yogasūtras and the Vyāsa-Bhāṣya: An Examination." *Vishveshvaranand Indological Journal* 2 (1964): 254-60.

Śhaṅkarāchārya. *Bhāṣhya* on *Śhvetāśhvatara Upaniṣhad.* In *Ten Principal Upanishads with Śāṅkarabhāṣya.* Delhi: Motilal Banarsidass, 1964, 1978.

Shukla, Nalini. *Pātañjala-yoga-sūtra kā vivechanātmak evaṁ tulanātmak adhyayan* (A critical and comparative study of Pātañjala-yoga-sūtra; in Hindi). Kanpur: Shakti-yogāśhram and Nalini Shukla, 1975.

Takagi, S. Shingen. "On 'Kriyā-yoga' in the Yoga Sutra." *Journal of Indian and Buddhist Studies* 15, no. 1 (1966): 451ff.

Weldon, Ellwood Austin. "The Sāṁkhya Term, Liṅga." *American Journal of Philology* 31 (1910): 445-59.

———. "The Sāṁkhya Teachings in the Māitrī Upanishad." *American Journal of Philology* 35 (1914): 32-51.

Winternitz, Moriz. *Geschichte die indischen Litteratur.* 3 vols. Leipzig: Amelang, 1905-22.

Zigmund-Cerbu, Anton. "The Ṣaḍaṅgayoga." *History of Religions* 3 (1963): 128-34.

Zimmer, Heinrich Robert. *Kunstform und Yoga in indischen Kultbild.* 1926. Reprint. New York: Garland, 1981.

Glossary/Index

The Glossary/Index lists in English alphabetical order the most significant Sanskrit and occasional Pāli words used in the text. Information given with each word includes a brief definition and selected locations in which the word appears. No effort has been made to cite every place in which a given word may be found.

a-bhāva Negation; a negative; absence; non-being; a state of non-being; non-production; non-appearance; absence of *vṛttis* of waking and dream states; absence of all other *vṛttis* mentioned in the *Yoga-sūtras.* 176, 178, 179, 249, 254, 320

abhāva-pratyaya Causal principle; cognition principle of negation. 178

abhāva-yoga Yoga of absence or negation of all transient feelings and states. 120

abheda-bhrama Error or illusion of non-distinction. 384

abhi-buddhi An activity of intelligence, e.g., "I must do this." 43

abhi-dheya *Significatum* (the signified). 315

abhi-dhyāna Directing one's thought, will or concentration towards (God). 277

abhijāta Pure-born. 371

abhimāna An activity of intelligence, e.g., "*I* do this"; assumption of a false identity attributed to the spiritual self. 43, 127

abhimata Agreeable, desired, or favourite object of choice; any object of one's choice. 335, 365

abhiniveśha Fear of death; "May I not cease to be"; "I fear my death, the death of this body that I am." *Abhiniveśha* is a *kleśha* whose real name is blind nocturnal (*andha-tāmisra,* q.v.) 44, 162, 169, 170

abhi-vyakti Manifestation. 120

ābhoga (The mind-field's gross) expansion; the awakening of a wisdom (*prajñā*) in which a realization of the true nature of an object of concentration has occurred. 218, 226

ābhyantara Internal. 98

abhyāsa Practice; the endeavour (*yatna*) to make the mind stable; the endeavour with regard to, for the purpose of, stilling the mind. (See also *abhyāsa*'s correlate, *vairāgya.*) 106, 193, 195-97, 198, 248, 336, 342

abhyāsa-pāṭava Expert or skillful practice. 146

abhyudaya Worldly success in the present life. 36

āchārya A teacher who has himself experienced self-realization; a scholar-savant and commentator. 6, 27, 110, 214

ādara Respect. 415

a-dharma Unrighteousness; vice. 85, 93, 285

adhi-ātman The spiritual self. 412

ādhibhautika Caused by other beings such as beasts of prey, enemies, etc. One of the three kinds of pain (*duḥkha*). 47, 329, 330

adhi-bhūta Pertaining to the attributes of the five gross elements and other beings. 42, 43

ādhidaivika Caused by deities, planetary influences and other natural forces such as heat, cold and conscious powers of the subtler worlds. One of the three kinds of pain (*duḥkha*). 47, 329, 330

adhi-deva (adhidaiva) Pertaining to celestial and subtle worlds, conscious powers of nature, angelic beings, planetary deities, etc. 42, 43

adhigama Attainment; realization. 320

adhikāra Purpose; topic; beginning of subject matter; prerogative; empowerment; teacher's authority, a student's qualification, and the statement of a commencement; assignment; assignment or duty and the power to carry it out. 19, 66-67, 141, 419, 423, 425, 428

adhikāra-sūtra A *sūtra* that states the purpose or subject matter of a text or a portion thereof. 21, 61

adhikārin Qualified; one who is qualified for a study. 280

adhimātra Extreme; ultimate. 258, 275

adhiṣhṭhātṛ Ruling power. 306

adhiṣhṭhātṛtva Command over the dominion (one of the ten immutables in the Lord). 301

adhyāropa Superimposition. 127

adhyāsa Superimposition. 311, 384

adhyātma Spiritual; pertaining to *ātman;* development of oneself inward, towards one's spiritual nature and the mental and physical faculties controlled by the self. 42, 411, 412

adhyātma-prasāda Spiritual clarity. 412

adhyātma-vidyā Pursuit of proficiency, knowledge, of a spiritual science. 200

ādhyātmika Within oneself; internal to oneself. One of the three kinds of pain (*duḥkha*). It is twofold: mental, such as desire, passion, jealousy, greed, fear, depression; and physical, such as caused by the imbalance of humours. 47, 329, 330

adhyāya Study in the formal sense of study of the Vedas, requiring recitation, adhering to strict principles of enunciation and accentuation, memorizing each word accurately, etc. 318

a-dvaita Non-dual. 67n

advaita-yoga Yoga of non-duality. 91

āgama Revealed authority (one of the valid proofs [*pramāṇas*]); textual, scriptural or inspired-revealed authority; authoritative textual tradition; knowledge derived from an inspired text, one's tradition or a realized teacher; (one's accepted) tradition and scriptural authority. A matter seen or inferred by an accomplished person is transferred in the form of words *into* another person: the *vṛtti(s)* from that word, together with its matter and meaning as the object, is the listener's acquisition (*āgama*). Literally, "that which comes." 143, 149, 161, 214, 266, 295, 390

āgamin One who is versed in the *āgama,* the textual authority as well as the tradition of the yoga lineage. 312

aham I. 237

ahaṁkāra Ego; ego process; the identifying principle by which the composite sentience (*asmitā*) begins to identify itself as such-and-such a being, e.g., "I am this body." 94, 225, 245

aiśhvarya Sovereignty and spiritual freedom; lordship (one of the ten immutables in the Lord); worldly success; power, luxury and affluence. An abstract noun formed from *īśhvara* (the Lord). 93, 101, 205, 206, 301

a-jñāna Ignorance, e.g., false perception and sleep. 93, 105

ākāṅkṣhā Aim; intent. 115, 137

ākāśha Space. 356, 369, 370

a-khyāti Non-apprehension; non-perception. 166-67

a-kliṣhṭa Not painful; not afflicted; pure; not imbued with *kleśhas*. A proof (*pramāṇa*) or a *vṛtti* leading one to rise beyond attraction or aversion is *a-kliṣhṭa*. 135, 138

a-kuśhala Not well; ill. 282, 285

alabdha-bhūmikatva Failing (despite observances) to reach the plateau of confirmed achievement of a state of consciousness (failing to gain a ground). 324, 327-28

a-lakṣhya Unworthy of a detailed definition. 83

alam! Enough! 213

ālambana Resorting to; supported by; leaning on; dependent on; having as a base; object of concentration or meditation as support. A supportive factor (for *samprajñāta*) may be any of the following: the twenty-three evolutes of matter; primary matter (*prakṛti*); the individual self; an aspect or incarnation of God. (See also *dhyeya.*) 120, 178, 220, 361, 372, 374, 429

ālasya Laziness; languor; sloth; (because of) heaviness of body owing to fat, phlegmatic tendencies or heaviness of a *tamasic* mind. 324, 327

alāta-chakra Circle of fire (as) when a torch is whirled rapidly. 137

ālaya-vijñāna Universal idea. (See also *vijñāna-vāda.*) 395

a-liṅga Unmanifest; without mark; non-quantitative; without characteristics; unmanifest, unmodified *prakṛti* in the state of complete equilibrium of the three *guṇas* (*sattva, rajas* and *tamas*). 35, 225, 404, 407

a-liṅga-paryavasāna Extending up to unmodified matter (*prakṛti*). 404

a-lupta-śhakti Power, potentia (*śhakti*) that never suffers a loss or a reduction. 301

a-marṣha Intolerance. 342

anādhi-bodha Beginningless wisdom (enlightenment). 301

an-aiśhvarya Loss of sovereignty. (See also *aiśhvarya.*) 93

an-ākula Free of disturbance. 269

ānanda Ecstasy; rapture. 218

ānandamaya koṣha Sheath of bliss (in which the self is mistaken to be happy, unhappy, suffering pain or enjoying pleasure). 245

ānanda-anugata A *samādhi* accompanied by ecstasy, rapture (*ānanda*). (See also *sānanda*.) 224

ānantarya Transition in a sequence. 66

ananta-śhakti Infinite power; potentia (*śhakti*). 301

ānāpāna-sati Pāli for mindfulness of inhalation and exhalation—the paramount Buddhist meditation practice; breath awareness entailing slow, controlled exhalation (*prachchhardana*) and slow, controlled inhalation (*vidhāraṇa*); measured breathing. 268, 348

an-ātman Non-self. 396

anattā Pāli for *an-ātman* (non-self). 396

an-avachchheda Absence of delimitation, break or division. 305

an-avasthitatva Instability, inability to maintain a ground or level; having gained a higher ground, one falls from it. 324, 328

andha-tāmisra Blind nocturnal (the real name of *abhiniveśha*, q.v.); blind night (period of dissolution in a single cycle). 168, 169

aṅga Limb; part; support; means; complement. 37, 75, 76, 85, 96, 200, 301

aṅgam-ejayatva Unsteadiness or shaking of the body; movement and twitching of the limbs in meditation. 329, 331

aṅgāṅgi-bhāva A convention of Indian logic whereby when a statement is made concerning a complete entity (*aṅgin*, one who owns *aṅgas* or parts), each one of its parts (*aṅgas*) is already presumed to be included. 75

aṅgin A whole constituted of parts (*aṅgas*). 75, 85, 96

aṇimā Power to become minute (a *siddhi*). 168

añjana That which anoints. 397

annamaya koṣha Sheath made of food (in which the mortal personality passing through various physical states is mistakenly identified as the self). 245, 246

antaḥ Ending in; extending up to. 368

antaḥ-karaṇa Inner mental instrument; the eleventh sense; psyche; the fourfold inner sense or instrument consisting of *manas, buddhi, ahaṁkāra* and *chitta*. 94-95, 352

antaḥ-prajña Inwardly conscious (as with the sleep state). This term is used in verses 4 and 7 of the *Maṇḍūkya Upaniṣhad*. 180

antaḥ-sañjña Inwardly conscious (as with a sleeping person). 180

antar-aṅga Innermost part. 428

antarāya Obstacle; impediment; obstruction. (See also *chitta-vikṣhepa.*) 320, 324

antarāya-abhāva Absence of obstacle, impediment or obstruction. 320

antar-yāmin Indweller; the dweller within; pervading within all things and beings. 300, 306

anu Prefix meaning "within, subsequent, following" (as *anu-śhāsana,* "within" a tradition). 62, 71, 72

aṇu Atom; minute. 368, 407

anubandha Binding reason. 60

anu-bhūta That which has been experienced. 185, 186

anu-gama Accompaniment. 218

anugata Accompanied by. 224

anu-graha Grace; grace given; benefit conferred; benevolence; kindness. 295

anugraha-sarga (Fivefold) compassionate creation, which includes the five subtle elements (*tan-mātrās*) as well as appearances of divine, incarnate sages. 46

anumāna Inference (a valid proof [*pramāṇa*]); a rational, logical, inferential process leading to a conclusion. *Anumāna* (primarily) determines the general rather than the specific since its object is the inferable conforming to the homogeneous and excluding the non-homogeneous. 143, 149, 150, 159, 214, 266, 387, 390, 414, 416

anumāna-prajñā Wisdom gained from inference or logical processes. 416

anu-paśhya To look after; to care for. 413

anupātī (anu-pātin) Following; dependent upon. 171

anu-śhāsana Instruction; discipline; teaching that follows within (*anu*) a tradition. *Anu-śhāsana* connotes (*a*) that the yogic discipline is imparted only after a disciple has demonstrated purity of observances in self-discipline and has prepared the ground for the seed to be sown, and (*b*) that what is being taught has been taught before, that it is within an existing tradition with no claim that anything new has been created. 62, 69, 71-73

ānuśhravika Heard of in a tradition, scripture or in any other authoritative source. 169, 205

anu-smṛti Repeated awareness. 268

anussati Pāli for *anu-smṛti:* cultivating repeated awareness (as with *ānāpāna-sati*). 268

anu-viddha Intertwined. 381

anu-vṛtti Implicit succession, i.e., a word in one *sūtra* is implied in one or more subsequent *sūtras* until it is no longer needed. 178-79, 315 n. 30

anu-vyavasāya The awareness *buddhi* has that it cognizes, apprehends, or experiences. 189

anvaya Induction (as in logic). 152

anya Another; the other; different. 248, 258, 416, 419

anya-saṁskāra-pratibandhin That which blocks, counters or prevents other impressions. 419

anyathā-khyāti Misapprehension. 166

anya-vishayā Different in scope. 416

apāna *See prāṇa(s).*

a-para Not transcending. 209

a-parā-mṛṣhta Unsmeared. 282

apara pratyakṣha A lower category of direct perception as opposed to transcendental, direct perception (*para pratyakṣha*). 386

apara-vairāgya The lower dispassion (which is an attempt at dispassion for *all* attraction whatsoever), which falls within *samprajñāta samādhi* only. *Apara-vairāgya* relates to worldly objects, unlike *para-vairāgya* (q.v.), which relates to the *guṇas* and to knowledge. It is divided into four steps or stages: *yatamāna* (initial effort), *vyatireka* (ascertainment), *ekendriya* (pertaining to the single sense, mind, only), and *vaśhīkāra* (control and mastery). 209-11

apariṇāmin Immutable. 126

āpātataḥ Incidentally. 145

apavarga Liberation; final liberation; deliverance; the Supreme Good. 145, 351, 353

āpta An accomplished person; one who has attained; a noble teacher; authority; one who combines (*a*) *tattva-darśhana*—realization of reality; (*b*) *kāruṇya*—motivation to remove the suffering of others (compassion); and (*c*) *karaṇa-pāṭava*—strength of senses and body and expertise in the use thereof. 160

āpti Attainment. 160

a-puṇya Vice; nonvirtue; nonvirtuousness; nonmeritoriousness. 340

āpyāyita Filled and expanded. 214

ārambha-vāda *See a-sat-kārya-vāda.*

artha A matter; meaning; reality; an actual substance; actual state or object that is realized; a purpose; aim; object of pursuit; object denoted, signified or meant; object of concentration. 62, 84, 153, 173, 187, 315, 333, 380, 392

artha-ātman Self-nature of a real object; that which has a real self-nature. (See also *ātman.*) 388, 396

artha-bhāvana Cultivating or absorbing the real meaning (in meditation). 315

artha-kriyā-kārin Efficacious, i.e., anything producing certain results by which the observer infers its characteristics. It is anointed *(añjana)* by the attributes of its causes; it represents that cause which has revealed it, which has given it the appearance of an effect. 397

artha-mātra Only the object meant. 387

artha-mātra-nirbhāsā That in which only the object meant shines forth. 387

artha-śhūnya Devoid of interests; without interest or purpose; without a substance. 248n, 255

asamprajñāta samādhi Acognitive *samādhi; nirodha-samādhi* (the *samādhi* of total control and final cessation of *vṛttis*); *nir-bīja samādhi* (seedless *samādhi* requiring no *ālambanas*), wherein *saṁskāras* can no longer produce *kleśhas,* karmas and their fruition; the great sleep (*mahā-nidrā*) of the mind-field; the state in which the self dwells in the self. 63, 146-47, 186, 220, 248, 251

a-sampramoṣhaḥ Non-theft; not being stolen; not being lost. (From the verb root *muṣh* 'to steal'.) 185, 186

āsannaḥ Near; very close; impending; imminent. 271, 277n

āsannatara Closer; imminent. 277, 280

a-sat-kārya-vāda A doctrine of the Nyāya-Vaiśheṣhika schools, viz.: Qualities of effects *do not* exist in their causes, but fresh qualities are produced and their prior absence (*prāg-abhāva*) in the cause is evident. We know they were not there when we see them appear in fresh objects. (This view is also known as *ārambha-vāda.*) 395

ā-sevita Pursued; thoroughly served; maintained in assiduous and complete observance; assiduously undertaken for a long time and without interruption. 202

a-śhakti (Twenty-eight kinds of) incapacity of mind and intelligence. 44

āśhaya Propensity; accumulation; domain; storehouse; the domain wherein something lies dormant; that which lies dormant; that which sleeps. (From *ā* + *śhī.*) 188, 282, 286-87, 419-21

ashram (āśhrama) Hermitage; retreat; center for religious or spiritual study and practice. 7, 71-72

aśhvattha A tree; metaphor for the universe, "with its roots above, branches below." 299

āsīta Let one establish the posture, sitting (in yoga). 318

asmi I am. 408

asmitā I-am-ness (synonymous with *svatva* ([possession]); *liṅga-mātra;* composite sentience. *Asmitā* is produced when *liṅga-mātra* (*mahat* or *buddhi*) receives and reflects consciousness from *puruṣha,* thus creating the composite (reflected spirit plus matter, i.e., reflected *puruṣha* plus *prakṛti*) sentience. It is *asmitā* and not *puruṣha* that is the agent of apprehension (*grahitṛ*), the one who apprehends. *Asmitā* is a *kleśha* whose real name is stupor (*moha*). 38-39, 44, 128, 139, 162, 167, 168-69, 218, 225, 226, 239, 244, 245, 246, 247, 357, 408

asmitā-anugata A *samādhi* accompanied by I-am-ness (*asmitā*). (See also *samprajñāta samādhi.*) 224

asmitā-mātrā Only the awareness of "I am"; I-am-ness alone. One of the two *viśhokā samāpattis,* the manifestation of I-am-ness. 355, 356, 357

a-sphuṭa Indistinct. 181

āstika-buddhi An attitude of affirmation that there is a God, karma and life after death. 266

asūyā Jealousy; intolerance; malice; the inability to acknowledge others' good qualities, i.e., being petty or faultfinding. 341, 342, 343

Āsuri A disciple of Kapila and second in line among the founders of Sāṅkhya. 41, 129, 296, 304

a-tad-rūpa-pratiṣhṭha Established in a nature or form *not* of that (object). 163

a-tattva Opposite to a reality or to the self-nature of any object or entity; non-that-ness. 421

atha Now, at an auspicious moment of transition; expressing: transition in a sequence (*ānantarya*), a teacher's authority, a student's fulfilment of a qualification, and/or the statement of commencement. The word *atha* (together with *OM*) came from the Creator's throat in the beginning of the creation; hence both words are auspicious. *Atha* is a particle (*avyaya*) word, i.e., invariant in all syntactical situations and capable of expressing states that are themselves immutable. 62, 63-71

atideśha-sūtra A *sūtra* that presents an analogy. 20

atikrānta-bhāvanīya Yogis on the last of four levels of yogic attainment; those who have transcended all processes and no longer have anything remaining to be cultivated. 78

atīndriya Supersensual; (knowledge) gained by means other than the senses, such as knowledge of objects beyond the range of the senses, e.g., too small or too large. 99, 296

ātivāhika śharīra The subtle body as the vehicle of migration in which *saṁskāras* continue to be maintained. 261

ātma-bhūta Having become a self; having a self-nature. *Ātma-bhūta* expresses the self-nature of any object or entity (not to be confused with the spiritual self). 397

ātma-jñāna Self-knowledge. 214

ātma-kalpena Standing on its own, i.e., the mind dwelling in itself, by itself; identifying with the self (*ātman*); imagining itself to be the self. 145-46

ātman (*1*) The self; spiritual self; oneself. (See also *Brahman*.) 29, 121, 154, 245, 412 (*2*) The self-nature, essence, real self-nature, of any object or entity. 388, 396, 397, 412 The student must be alert to the two definitions of *ātman* so as not to confuse the two in a given context.

ātma-sambodha Self-awareness; self-realization (one of the ten immutables in the Lord). 301

ātmīya Belonging to (the self); akin to (a kin to); belonging to or related to (some realm or other). 168, 186

ātyantika Total and permanent. 119, 146

audāsīnya Sense of neutrality; the middle way. 344

aupādhika A condition by reason of proximity and not an innate quality; a temporary condition of appearance. 90, 118

autsukya Interest. 210

ava-dhāraṇa A determinant process (whereby general, shared properties are eliminated by the mind so as to enable it to focus on the specific, e.g., cows→the brown cow); to maintain continuously in the mind. 150, 228

a-vairāgya Lack of dispassion. 93

ava-sthāna Stability; settling; remaining; being in a given state. 114

avasthā-pariṇāma Mutations of condition (like a candle flame), of which there are two kinds: internal (*ābhyantara*) and external (*bāhya*). 98

ava-sthita Constant; stable. *Ava-sthita* derives from *ava* + *sthā* 'to go through a process or condition' and therefore connotes something (e.g., the mind) which remains constant or stable while passing through many conditions. 339

a-vastu Insubstantial; not a real object. 127

avatāra Incarnation of the deity. 301

avayava Separable; part; component. 388

avayavin A whole; having parts or components. 388

āveśha Process or state of being possessed or taken over. 392

a-vibhāga Not being divided or distinguished; non-division; non-distinction; non-separation. 380, 382

a-vidvān Ignorant. 292

avidyā Ignorance; nescience; mistaking the self to be non-self. *Avidyā* is a *kleśha* whose real name is darkness (*tamas*). It is both its own cause and the cause of the other *kleśhas*. 44, 85, 139, 162, 167, 168, 170, 292

a-vikalpita Non-fictitious; non-imaginary; unalterable; not alternating. 394, 415

a-vinā-bhāva Sine qua non (without which not); something absolutely essential. 298

a-virati Failing to turn away from the world and the senses; non-abstention; craving for sense objects. (Antonym: *uparati.*) 324, 327

a-vi-saṁ-vādin That which is consistent and cannot be challenged. 151

a-viśheṣhas Non-specific, intermediate links between *mahat* and the final sixteen products of *prakṛti,* the *viśheṣhas.* Thus the *a-viśheṣhas* are the causes of the *viśheṣhas,* viz.: five gross elements, five active senses, five cognitive senses, and the mind. There are six *a-viśheṣhas,* consisting of the five subtle elements (*tan-mātrās*) and the ego (*ahaṁkāra*). 35, 225, 247

a-viśhiṣhṭa Undistinguished (as when the mind sees itself as undistinguished from *puruṣha*). 156

a-viveka Absence of correct knowledge; indiscrimination. 167, 193

a-vividiṣhā The tendency that blocks desire for knowledge; absence of the desire to know. 43

a-vyakta Unmanifest *prakṛti* and its evolutes. 168

avyaya Particle. 64

avyayatā Immutability. 300

āyāma Expansion. 348

āyur-veda Medical science.. The *Ayur-veda* is the Veda treating of the science of medicine. 4

āyus Life span. 286

baddha Bound, i.e., not free. 377

bādh Impede; counteract. 419, 424

bahir-aṅga Exterior part. 428

bāhya External. 98

bandha Bondage. 46, 289-90

bhakti Devotion, of which a specific form taught in the *Yoga-sūtras* is practising the presence of God. 277, 280

bhakti-viśheṣha A specific form of devotion. 277, 279

bhakti-yoga The yoga of devotion and surrender to a personal God. 91

bhāṣhya A disciple's detailed commentary on a master's *sūtras,* including background and experiential information presenting connections among *sūtras,* amplification, etc., to render the *sūtras* comprehensible. 6

bhāva State; being; worldly continuity; delimited material existence subject to rebirth. 176, 258, 259-60

bhāvana, bhāvanā Cultivated concentration; cultivating and absorbing a meaning; an internal process of impressing an object of concentration (*bhāvya*) repeatedly onto the mind. 220, 228, 242, 279-80, 315, 316, 340, 392

bhāvanātva Being a process. 392

bhava-pratyaya A *samādhi* whose causal cognition develops into the continuity of worldly being (*saṁsāra*) at (re)birth. This *samādhi* accrues to *videhas* and *prakṛti-layas* and is the experience of bodiless shining gods (*videha devas*). 256-60

bhāvya Object of concentration. 220

bheda A division or category. 60, 94

bhoga Experience; enjoyment; the material world as the object of experience; experience presented to the spiritual self; pleasant or painful experience during one's life span as the result of karma (a *vipāka,* q.v.). 145, 282, 286, 288, 420, 425

bhoktṛ Experiencer; one who partakes of experience (*bhoga*). 288

bhrānti-darśhana Wrong views; confusion of philosophies. (See also *viparyaya.*) 324, 327

bhūmi Ground, level or plateau at which the yogi arrives, then leaves behind on the way to the highest *samādhi.* Four different levels of attainment (*bhūmis*) are associated with the yogi en route to *kaivalya.* 77-78, 82

bhūmikā Step; stage. (See also *bhūmi.*) 209

bhūta Gross element. There are five *bhūtas:* space, air, fire, water, earth. (See also *tattvas.*) 34, 42

bhūta-artha Reality; a real object; true nature. 421

bhūtādi Beings with *tamasic* ego who perform acts of stupefaction: *sānumāna* (performing good acts of stupefaction), and *niranumāna* (performing evil acts of stupefaction). 44

bhūta-sūkṣhma Subtleties or subtle aspects of the elements. Not to be confused with *sūkṣhma-bhūta.* 376, 401, 417

bīja Seed; *liṅga;* sign; indicator; root; root of all knowledge. 295, 299

bodha Spiritual awakening; a teaching; direction given. (From the verb root *budh* 'to awaken, to get to know'.) 87

bodhi A Buddha's enlightenment. (From the verb root *budh* 'to awaken, to get to know'.) 87

Brahmā The Progenitor; the Creator who takes the universe as His body. Brahmā is a masculine word, not to be confused with the neuter word Brahman. (See also *Hiraṇya-garbha.*) 29, 70, 301

brahmacharya Celibacy; maintaining control over sexual passion. 202, 203

Brahman The One Principle; the Single Transcendental Reality which is Existence (*sat*), Consciousness (*chit*) and Bliss (*ānanda*); the Self of all that is; the Expansive One. (From the verb root *bṛh* 'to expand, to be expansive'.) 28, 300

brāhmaṇa Philosopher; child of Brahman; the highest Hindu caste. 72

brahma-vihāra Frolicking in Brahman. (See also *parikarma(n).*) 342

brahma-yoga The yoga of Brahman. 91

buddhi The faculty of intelligence, intuitive wisdom, intellection and discrimination in a sentient being; *sattva* of the mind-field. *Buddhi*'s twofold faculty of discrimination is:

1. The outward-looking face of *buddhi* (towards the conscious mind), called the faculty of intelligence. The twofold faculty of intelligence includes (*a*) the outward face (intellect) and (*b*) the inward face (intuitive wisdom).
2. The inward-looking face of *buddhi* (towards the spiritual self, i.e., *puruṣha*), called the faculty of intuition.

An inherent relationship existing between self and matter is an eternal attribute of *prakṛti,* the cause of *mahat* and *buddhi.* 33, 34, 77, 81, 94, 133, 163, 356, 403

buddhi-bodha-ātmā *Puruṣha* as ordinarily identified with the apprehensions of *buddhi.* 116

budh To awaken; to get to know. 87

chaitanya Consciousness (an attribute of the spiritual self alone). 130, 172

chakras Centers of *kundalinī* energies within the composite person. 11

chāñchalya Restiveness (by means of which *rajas* produces pain). 358

charyā-yoga The yoga of denominational ritual devotions. 91

cheṣhṭā-moha Confusion of the physical posture, gait, movement or effort as though one's limbs are not under one's own observation or moved by one's own will. 192

chetanā Consciousness. (See also *chaitanya.*) 320, 321, 322

chetayitṛ Source and cause of awareness, i.e., *puruṣha.* 288

chid-ākāśha (The inner) space of consciousness. 369, 370

chit, chiti Consciousness; pure consciousness; consciousness of the spiritual self; seer; *puruṣha.* (See also *chiti-śhakti.*) 80, 94, 106, 109, 114, 120, 151, 200

chiti-śhakti Consciousness-power (consciousness-potentia); consciousness principle; pure consciousness; energy; the spiritual self; absolute and eternal power called consciousness. 94, 106, 108-10, 113, 114, 115, 120, 155

chitta (*1*) The mind-field whose universal attribute is *samādhi.* (*2*) The entire mind-field (*antaḥ-karaṇa*), including *manas*—active mind; *buddhi*—intellect and intuitive wisdom; *ahaṁkāra*—ego; and *chitta*—the mind-field per se, including the universal unconscious (as well as *manas, buddhi* and *ahaṁkāra*). The five levels or grounds of *chitta* (mind-field) are: disturbed (*kṣhipta*); somnolent or stupefied (*mūḍha*); distracted (*vikṣhipta*); one-pointed (*ekāgra*); and controlled (*niruddha*). Only the latter two are considered to be states of yoga. 62, 76, 93, 94-95, 96, 98, 106, 110, 114, 124

chitta-nadī River of the mind-field. 196

chitta-parikarmas Ways of adorning, refining, purifying and preparing the mind (through diligent practice). 367, 368

chitta-prasādana Purifying the mind and making it pleasant. 341, 342, 346

chitta-sattva *Sattva* of the mind-field (*buddhi*); illumination, *sattva,* that has taken the form of the mind-field. 93, 100-1

chitta-vikṣhepa Distraction, impediment, obstacle or disturbance of the mind-field. There are nine such *chitta-vikṣhepas* (*YS* I.30), together with their five correlates or companions (*YS* I.31). (See also *vikṣhepa.*) 324

chitta-vṛtti-nirodha Control and dissolution of the *vṛttis* of the mind-field. 93

daitya Demonic being. 104

dākṣhiṇā bandha (dākṣhiṇika bandha) Bondage by which worldly people remain involved with desires and hope for liberation through ritual practices. Included are renunciates who become dependent on the offerings of basic necessities received from householders. 46, 290

dama Restraint (one of the six treasures of Vedānta). 67

dānava Demonic being. 104

darśhana Derived from the verb root *dṛśh* 'to see', *darśhana* is a many-faceted word, including: perception; school of philosophy; philosophical view; philosophy of life; vision; insight; realization; a yogi's realization; seeing or gaining insight into that realization which occurs in *samādhi. Darśhana* is the Sanskrit word for philosophy because all philosophy, together with its logical processes, derives only from such (*samādhi*) realization. 130, 160, 193, 195, 212, 214, 387, 393-94

daur-manasya Frustration; anguish; despair; bad mood; ill-mindedness; emotional disturbance; instability. Literally, "bad-mindedness" (from *dur* [bad] and *manas* [mind]). (Antonym: *saumanasya.*) 329, 331

devas Celestial beings; shining ones; celestial, shining ones; angelic beings without physical bodies. 104, 207, 261

dhairya Steadfastness and patience. 200

dhamma Pāli for conditions (*dharma*). 268

dhāraṇa Concentration; mental attention. 348, 355, 356

dharma Virtue; righteousness; attribute; characteristic; quality; condition. 85, 93, 101, 175, 285, 287, 303, 388, 397

dharma-megha samādhi The *samādhi* of the raincloud of virtue and of the knowledge of the nature of all things (in which the mind dwells in itself by itself, then identifies with the spiritual self); the final state of *samprajñāta samādhi;* the higher stage of the *asmitā*-accompanied *samādhi* and the initial stage of the acognitive *asamprajñāta samādhi. Dharma-megha* is endless; the yogi perceives worldly objects as unmentionables (having abandoned them) and dwells only in his own essential nature. 94, 107, 113, 145, 147, 216-17, 253

dhātu A constituent of the body, e.g., blood, flesh, bones, the three humours (air, bile, phlegm), etc. 326

dhṛti Fortitude; resolution of mind, speech and action (one of the ten immutables in the Lord). 43, 301

dhyāna Meditation. 303, 345

dhyāna-abhyāsa The practice of meditation. 415

dhyāna-abhyāsa-rasa Enjoyment of the flavour and essence of the practice of meditation. 415

dhyāna-yoga The yoga of meditation. 92

dhyeya Object of concentration; object of meditation. (See also *ālambana.*) 373, 392, 412

dhyeya-artha The reality of the object of concentration. 392

dik (diśh) Dimension. 36

doṣha Fault; blemish; defect. 211

draṣhṭṛ Seer; *chiti-śhakti* (consciousness-potentia). 114

dravya Substance. 36

dṛḍha-bhūmi Firm of ground. 202

dṛk-śhakti Power of the seer; seer-potentia. 120, 322

dṛśhi Sight; seeing. 120

dṛśhi-śhakti Seeing-potentia; seeing power. 120

dṛṣhṭa Seen; tangible; perceived with the physical senses; insight (realization within); realized or seen in the state of *samādhi.* 160, 169, 205

dṛṣhṭānta Exemplification (a term in the Indian five-member syllogism). 159

dṛśhya Something that is perceptible; a perceptible. 131-32

duḥkha Pain; an attribute of the *rajas guṇa;* pain produced by *vṛttis* taking the form of objects experienced; any kind of pain, grief, sorrow, suffering; pain of desires; those suffering; first of the fourfold noble truths of the Buddhist doctrine; the first concern of Sāṅkhya-yoga philosophy, which identifies three kinds of suffering: *ādhyātmika, ādhibhautika, ādhidaivika.* 139, 184, 329-31, 340

dveṣha Aversion; hatred. *Dveṣha* is a *kleśha* whose real name is nocturnal (*tāmisra*) 44, 137, 162, 167, 169, 170, 343

dyotayati Illuminates. 84

eka One; only one, e.g., *ātman,* the self. 240

eka-ātmikā saṁvit The perception of a unified self. 240

eka-buddhi-upa-krama Introduced by a unitary intelligence (*buddhi*). 396

ekāgra One-pointed; concentrated. One of the five grounds or states of the mind-field. 62, 78, 84, 157, 242, 333

ekāgra bhūmi One-pointed ground. 373

ekāgratā One-pointedness. 200, 252

ekāgratā-dhārā Stream of one-pointedness or concentration. 412, 421

eka-tānatā Being an unbroken stream. 214

ekatara koṭi One (or the other) of two categories at a time. 369

eka-tattva The One Reality (God), one principle, factor or reality; real element; a single matter. 333, 336

ekendriya Pertaining to the single sense, the mind, alone. (See also *ekendriya dispassion.*) 209, 210

ekendriya dispassion The third stage on the path to *apara-vairāgya.* The mental attraction is reduced while one yet continues to experience the objects with one's external senses. Effort is directed towards attaining dispassion towards mental attractions (since mind is the only remaining barrier to *vaśhīkara*). 210

gandha-pravṛtti Manifestation of smell (such as apprehension of a celestial fragrance) from concentration on the point between the two nostrils where the base of the nose joins the upper lip. 350

gati Gait; goal; locomotion; endeavour. *Gati* conveys a sense of movement and revelation. (From the verb root *gam* 'to know, to move, to reach, to go, to grasp'.) 307, 416

Gauḍapāda Guru of Śhankarāchārya's guru, Govinda. Gauḍapāda authored the *Māṇḍūkya-kārikās,* the most complete ancient statement on the Vedānta philosophy. 67n, 180

gaurava Cumbersomeness. 129

ghora Ferocity attribute (a major personality disposition, which *buddhi* assumes in association with *rajas*). 118, 126

grahaṇa Instruments of grasping (mind and senses); instrument; process and fact of experience; process and means of apprehension with which one grasps, experiences or cognizes. 188, 225, 226, 234, 235, 247, 277, 290, 296, 371, 372, 374, 375, 376-77

grahaṇa-samāpatti Having instruments of grasping as the field of coalescence and command. 247, 378

grahītṛ That which grasps (I-am-ness, the reflection of the pure self in the *buddhi*); the one who apprehends; the agent of apprehension; the one who grasps or experiences or cognizes. 225, 226, 235, 247, 277, 371, 372, 374, 375, 377-78

grahītṛ puruṣhas Spiritual selves that appear to be agents of action and to be grasping the objects of experience. 377

grahītṛ-samāpatti Having the apprehender as the field of coalescence or command. 241, 247, 378

grāhya Object of apprehension; objects grasped, experienced or cognized, i.e., gross and subtle elements, etc. 188, 225, 234, 235, 247, 277, 371, 374, 375, 376

grāhya-samāpatti Having *grāhyas* as the field of coalescence or command. 228, 247, 378

grāhya-uparakta Associated with and coloured by the object of an apprehension. 187-88

guṇas The three attributes of unmanifest *prakṛti,* which are in equilibrium before the creation of evolutes and whose disequilibrium constitutes the process of creation. All material entities (evolutes) including the mind are composites of the three *guṇas:* purity and illumination (*sattva*); activity (*rajas*); and inertia (*tamas*). They are the seats of pleasure, pain and delusion. 29, 30, 31, 42, 77, 93, 126, 212

guṇa-vaitṛṣhṇya The state of being free of all craving for the *guṇas* (free of worldly desires). 212

haṁsa-mantra The word *soham* used with exhalation and inhalation to enter into meditation. 366

haṭha-yoga Physical yoga within the context of interior, subtle forces. 92

hetu Cause; purpose; effect; means (a term in the Indian five-member syllogism). 139, 159, 419

Hiraṇya-garbha The Golden Womb; the first guru; the universal being; the first wise one; the teaching spirit of the universe; the original teacher of yoga; Prajāpati (the Progenitor); Brahmā. The first human being is said to have been an incarnation of the Golden Womb. All revelation is of the grace that flows from Hiraṇya-garbha. 39, 69-71, 105, 281, 289, 297

hlāda Rapture. 235

ichchhā Desire; will. 43, 273

iḍā The subtle energy channel (*nāḍī*) that flows on the left side of *suṣhumnā* and controls the parasympathetic branch of the autonomic nervous system. 65

indriyas (*1*) The eleven senses: mind; five cognitive senses; and five active senses. 42 (*2*) In Buddhism the word *indriyas* refers to the "five strengths." 268

indriya-śhakti (Inner) power of the senses. 377

īrṣhyā Jealousy. 342

īśhitva Physical, mental and vocal lordship unimpeded by any (a *siddhi*). 169

īśhvara *Parama-ātman. Īśhvara* is forever and always free. Wherever the lordship (*aiśhvarya*) reaches its extremity, that is God (*īśhvara*). He is neither *prakṛti* nor what is referred to as *puruṣha;* hence *īśhvara* is a special *puruṣha.* He is the special Conscious Being (*puruṣha-viśheṣha*). *Īśhvara* is that special *puruṣha* not smeared by afflictions, actions and their fruitions, and by the domains of their accumulated propensities. *Īśhvara* also has temporal meanings such as: a lord; a lordship; commanding presence, etc. (From the verb root *īśh* 'to have power or control over; to be able to [create, control, direct]; to govern; to impart grace'.) 101, 154, 277-304

īśhvara-praṇidhāna Practising the presence of God; to dwell near and close to God; to place oneself down (in all humility and egolessness) in the proximity of God; to surrender and place oneself at the disposal of God. Such devotion should be mental, vocal and physical. In the context of *YS* I.23 *īśhvara-praṇidhāna* means that the grace of God, when invoked by a true devotee, leads to *samādhi* (as qualified in the commentary). This approach to *samādhi* is referred to as the easy path. 277-81, 309, 315-23, 335, 430

jaḍa Unconscious; dull. 151

jaḍa-samādhi *Samādhi* of the unconscious. 262

jaḍatā Dullness; stupefaction. 181

jaḍatva Non-sentience. 383

japa Concentration on a mantra. Chant, recitation, contemplation, etc., when faith and devotion are present, are all parts of the complete *japa* process. The word *japa* has essentially been left untranslated in the text for want of an appropriate English rendering. 242, 315

japā A kind of red flower. 127

jāti Species (in which one is reborn). 286

jijñāsā Desire for knowledge; desire to know. 61, 68

jijñāsu One who has desire for knowledge; a seeker. 61, 103

jīva Individual soul. Sāṅkhya holds that *puruṣhas* becomes *jīvas,* souls, when they assume a connection with *prakṛti.* 29, 302

jīva-ātman The individual self as soul of a body. 279

jīvan-mukta One who is liberated while yet in a body, still maintaining the body. *Pralaya* (dissolution) cannot occur in a *jīvan-mukta* even though the mind comes very close to *pralaya.* 86, 146

jīvan-mukti State of liberation while yet incarnate. 146

jñā To know. 219

jñāna Knowledge; awareness; observation; ideation; wisdom that arises

jñāna (*continued*)
from yoga (one of the ten immutables in the Lord). 68, 87-88, 101, 186, 301, 303, 361, 384

jñāna-prasāda Clarity of knowledge at its purest. 214

jñāna-yoga Yoga of knowledge. Vedānta is regarded as the path of knowledge (*jñāna*), and Vedāntic texts teach that liberation occurs through knowledge. 87, 92

jñeya Object of knowledge. 361

jyotiṣhmatī Luminous; full of light (of *sattva*); lucid; luminous one. 355

kaivalin One who attains *kaivalya,* q.v. 289

kaivalya Isolation; self-realization; final isolation of the self from matter, when the self dwells in its own nature; absoluteness; liberation; synonymous with *asamprajñāta samādhi,* which follows *dharma-megha samādhi.* 39, 60, 73, 79, 114, 119, 146, 194, 216

kāla Time. 36, 305

kalpa A cycle of creation and dissolution. 169, 303

kalyāṇa All that is beautiful, benevolent, propitious, desirable; a noble way; way of beatitude; *mokṣha;* liberation. 194

kāma Desire. 141

kāmāvasāyitā Whatever one says or intends with the mind comes true (whereas in the case of others it conflicts and is not fulfilled). A *siddhi.* 169

Kapila It is said that Kapila was the first *ṛṣhi,* to whom the knowledge of Sāṅkhya-yoga was given. He is thus the legendary founder of the Sāṅkhya-yoga system of philosophy. Pañchaśhikha stated that Hiraṇya-garbha created a great mind into which he incarnated, becoming the sage Kapila. The lineage thus began with Hiraṇya-garbha→Kapila→Āsuri→Pañchaśhikha. 4, 39, 41, 297, 303, 304

karaṇa Instrument; instrumentation; sense. There are eleven *karaṇas* in the Sāṅkhya system: five active senses, five cognitive senses, and mind (*antaḥ-karaṇa*), the inner instrument. The compound expression *sva-karaṇa-saṁvedya* means "experienced directly with one's own instrumentation." Thus collectively the *karaṇas* may be looked upon as the instrumentation for the entire concentration process. 326, 352-53

karaṇa-pāṭava Expertise in the use of strength of senses and body (one of the qualifications of a realized teacher). 160

kāraṇa śharīra Causal body; *liṅga śharīra.* 246

karma (karman) Action. 102, 135, 136, 140, 141, 144, 282-87, 334, 338

karma-devas Shining ones bound to action, as the *videhas* and *prakṛti-layas*. 263

karmāśhaya Repository or domain of karmas; storehouse of *saṁskāras;* that subtle domain of the mind-field where are left all impressions of the objective world without and *vṛttis* from the mental world within; karmic force. (See also *āśhaya.*) 91, 110, 135, 136, 140, 287, 338, 419, 429

karma-yoga Yoga of action. 92

kartavyatā An activity of intelligence: indulgence of the cognitive senses into that which needs to be done or acted upon. 43

kartṛ Doer; agent of an action. 176

karuṇā (kāruṇya) Compassion; motivation to eradicate the suffering of others (one of the qualifications of a realized teacher). Fully developed, *kāruṇya* wards off *dveṣha* (aversion). 160, 340, 343

kārya An act. 420

kaṣhāya Despoiler; emotion such as attraction (*rāga*). 204, 209

kauśhala Skillfulness. 286

kauṣhṭhya vāyu Visceral air. The practice of controlled exhalation of visceral air subsumes diaphragmatic breathing, which is the fundamental breathing method in all yoga practice. (See also *ānāpāna-sati.*). 348

kāya Body. 268

kevala One who has attained *kaivalya* (isolation of self from matter); one alone; isolated; exclusive; pure; joyful; absolute. 117, 282n, 320, 429

kevalin Absolute entity. *Kevalin* is a Jaina term and should not be confused with the *Yoga-sūtras'* term *kaivalin,* meaning one who attains *kaivalya.* 289

khyāti Discriminating wisdom; discernment; knowledge; clarity of wisdom (*prajñā-prasāda*); reflective cognition; illumination. 102, 122, 129-34, 141, 166, 212, 217, 420

kleśha Affliction; impurity. There are five *kleśhas* (afflictions); *avidyā* (ignorance), *asmitā* (I-am-ness), *rāga* (attraction), *dveṣha* (aversion), and *abhiniveśha* (fear of death). These *kleśhas* not only effect *vṛttis* but can also be the effects of *vṛttis.* (From the verb root *kliṣh* 'to suffer'.) 44, 62, 83, 110, 135-41, 162, 167-70, 285

kleśha-hetukā Caused by the *kleśhas;* cause of the *kleśhas.* 139

kliṣhṭa Afflicted; painful; impure; imbued with *kleśhas*. A proof leading one to favour an attraction (*rāga*) is considered *kliṣhṭa*. 135-42

koṣha A sheath. There are five *koṣhas: ānandamaya koṣha* (sheath of bliss), *vijñānamaya koṣha* (sheath of knowledge), *manomaya koṣha* (sheath of mind), *prāṇamaya koṣha* (sheath of *prāṇa*), and *annamaya koṣha* (sheath of food). 245, 246

kriyā Activity; process; operations of the active senses; motion; efficacious execution; practicability. 43, 302, 388

kriyā-śhakti The power of action; creativity by which the world comes into existence and is maintained within the Law. 291

kriyā-yoga Yoga of ascetic practices. 93

kṣhamā Forgiveness (one of the ten immutables in the Lord). 301

kṣhaṇika-vāda A Buddhist theory of momentariness, viz.: An idea exists for a moment only, and (rather like a kinetoscope) a stream of such moments gives the illusion of continuity. In such a context there need be no single, continuous *chitta*. 336

kṣhaya Reduction. 419

kṣhetra Field. 65

kṣhīṇa-vṛtti One whose *vṛttis* have subsided. 371

kṣhipta Disturbed; agitated state; simple agitation of an ordinary worldly mind; totally unsteady; dominated by *rajas;* always flung about from one object to another (the wakeful state of a "normal" person in the world). One of the five grounds or states of the mind-field. 62, 78, 82-83, 100, 103-4

kṣhobha Anguish, as when a desire is frustrated. 329

kumbhaka The *prāṇāyāma* of controlled breath retention. 347

kundalinī The snake of eternity, the residue that remains after material consciousness is dissolved. 59, 60

kuśhala Well; wellness; free of all physical, mental or situational ill condition (resulting from one's acts). Skillful, expert, proficient, e.g., one who is "expert at surgery" is *śhalya-kriyā-kuśhala*. 282, 285-86

kūṭastha The unmodifiable, immutable, unchangeble; a statement of the nature of Brahman. 39

kūṭastha-nitya Eternal as an Absolute; immutable and never modified; absolutely eternal. 313, 429

laghimā The power to become light (a *siddhi*). 168

lakṣhaṇa Definition. 60, 249

lakṣhaṇa-sūtra A *sūtra* that defines. 96, 195, 284

lakṣhya The state to be aimed for; whatever is defined. 249

lakṣhya-yoga Yoga of practising concentration on a target. 92

laya Dissolution (of effects into their causes—of the gross into the subtle, etc.); dissolution of the universe and its phenomena. (See also *nirodha.*) 38, 95, 196, 223

laya-yoga Yoga of dissolution. 93

līlā Play. 302

liṅga Sign; indicator; mark; *bīja* (seed); *liṅga* body (constituted of the *mahat* evolute alone). The conventional (*rūḍhi*) meaning of *liṅga* is a sign or a mark. All twenty-three evolutes of *prakṛti* are *liṅga* (with mark). The derivative (*yaugika*) meaning is "that which dissolves, vanishes, disappears." (From the verb root *lī.*) (See also *a-liṅga.*) 207-8, 299, 406

liṅga-mātra Merely a mark or sign with no distinguishing features; the subtlest evolute, *mahat* (the universal and individual *buddhi*), the barest sign of the presence of matter; *mahat,* the first evolute, the faintest presence, the first sign that *prakṛti* gives of its presence. 35, 225, 238, 406, 407

liṅga śharīra Causal body consisting of *mahat* alone; also called *kāraṅa śharīra.* 246, 262

loka The world; that which shines; that which "looks" (people are *lokas*); and that which is "looked at" (the worlds, locations [cognate to locus, loci]). (From the verb root *lok,* meaning [and cognate to] "to look.") 396

loka-pratyakṣha Direct perception with the senses in the ordinary world; direct (secular) perception; worldly perception. 416, 418

madhu-bhūmi The honeyed ground. The second of the four levels of yogic attainment. 77

madhu-bhūmika A yogi experiencing the honeyed ground. 108

madhumatī Honeyed; filled with sweetness. 78

madhu-pratīkā Where the honey of the first ground (*madhumatī*) has become as though it had been only symbolic of this second level. 78

madhya Medium, as in "medium methods" (*madhya-upāya*) or "medium progress" (*madhya-saṁvega*). 271, 275

madhya-saṁvega Those of medium progress. 271

madhya-upāya Those of medium methods. 271

mahā-moha Great stupor (of which there are ten types) associated with the nescience (*avidyā*) of attachment (*rāga*). 168, 169

mahān Great; expansive. 357

mahān ātmā Great, expanded, or expansive self. 377

mahā-nidrā The great sleep of the mind-field when it is dissolved at liberation. 429

mahā-pralaya Total dissolution of the universe after one thousand cycles. 303

mahat The universal *buddhi,* a small spark of which is the individual *buddhi;* liṅga-mātra; the most *sattvic,* finest and purest product of *prakṛti;* the first disequilibrium of the *guṇas;* the first evolute of *prakṛti;* "the great," "the *Magnum.*" An inherent relationship between self and matter is an eternal attribute of *prakṛti,* the cause of *mahat* and *buddhi.* 32-33, 34, 35, 133, 233, 235, 236, 238

māhātmya Exaltation; glory; power. 173

mahat-sevā Service to the great. 200

mahattva Greatness; magnitude. Contrasted with the subtlest and the minutest, mahattva becomes the largest or the most expansive, which is twofold: internal (*asmitā*) and external (the cosmos). 368, 369

mahā-vākya Great sentence; a profound statement. There are four such *mahā-vākyas* (taken from the Upaniṣhads) in the Vedānta philosophy, which form the basic statements of that philosophy for contemplation and realization. 392

mahā-yoga The great yoga; yoga of absence or negation of all transient feelings and states. There are no objects of concentration as supports (*ālambanas*) and there remains only the manifestation of one's own nature. 120-21

mahimā The power to become large (a *siddhi*). 169

maitrī Amity; love; *sauhārda* (goodheartedness; *eucardia,* friendship). 340, 343

mala Impurity; blemish; defilement; maculateness; taint; *macula.* 163, 217, 411

malina Defiled; impure; unclean. 179

manana Contemplating; contemplation. The second of the four stages of gaining knowledge. 91, 390, 391, 415

manas The active or lower mind that receives sensations and emits reactions to them. 94, 225

manasa Mind; mental. 350

mānasa-putra Mental offspring. 304

maṇi Gem; crystal. 371

manomaya koṣha The sheath of mind (wherein the process of mentation is attributed to the self). 245, 246

mantra-yoga Yoga of the practice of mantras. 92

mātra No other but; only; merely. 215

mātrā A measure. 104

mātsarya Small-mindedness. 343

māyā Brahman's potency (*śhakti*), with the twofold power to veil and unveil (reveal). 28

mettā Pāli equivalent of the Sanskrit word *maitrī* (amity, love, friendship). 343

mithyā-jñāna False knowledge. 162, 163

moha Delusion; somnolence; stupor. The attributes of the *tamas guṇa* are of three kinds: *vichāra-moha, cheṣhṭā-moha,* and *vedanā-moha. Moha* is eightfold and is associated with the nescience (*avidyā*) of I-am-ness (*asmitā*). 168, 184, 192

mokṣha Liberation; release; isolation; total and final liberation (the spiritual self dwelling in its own nature). (Antonym: *saṁsāra.*) 47, 61, 91, 97, 194

mṛdu Slow, mild, as in "mild methods" (*mṛdu-upāya*) or "mild progress" (*mṛdu-saṁvega*). 271, 275

mṛdu-saṁvega Those of mild progress. 271

mṛdu-upāya Those of mild methods. 271

mūḍha Stupefied or somnolent (one of the five grounds or states of the mind-field); unable to distinguish between right or wrong acts; dominated by the *tamas guṇa* (when *mūḍha* represents the state of sleep and other forms of stupor, such as being comatose, inebriated, drug afflicted, or otherwise generally not alert). *Mūḍha* also means stupefaction or somnolence as an attribute or major personality disposition which *buddhi* assumes in association with *tamas*. 62, 78, 82-83, 104, 105, 118

muditā Joyfulness; gladness. One of the *brahma-vihāras*. 340

mukta Free; liberated; one having attained *mokṣha*. 283, 377, 425

mukta puruṣhas Liberated ones; *puruṣhas* themselves; disembodied masters; spiritual selves; great liberated historical figures. In this latter context the term refers not to the bodies or physical appearances of historical personages but to the *puruṣhas* themselves, the liberated spiritual selves. 377-78

mukti Liberation. 146

mūlika-arthas The ten fundamental tenets of Sāṅkhya philosophy. 46

mumukṣhā Desire or determination for liberation. 61

mumukṣhu One who has the desire or determination for liberation. 61, 265

mūrti Form; image. 383

nāḍī(s) Subtle energy fields or channels which control movements and configurations of sentient beings. 65n

nāḍī-śhodhana *Prāṇāyāma* (the practice of physical breath control) using one nostril at a time. 347

nairantarya Without interval; without interruption. 202

Nārāyaṇa One of Viṣhṇu's names. 385

nāsāgra Tip of the nose; the point between the two nostrils where the base of the nose joins the upper lip. (See also *gandha-pravṛtti*). 352

neti, neti Not this, not this. 250

ni-bandhana (ni-bandhanī) That which binds, fastens, firmly establishes, seals. (See also *sthiti-nibandhana.*) 350

nididhyāsana Meditating (meditation). *Nididhyāsana* is based on words (i.e., not direct experience), hence is *sa-vitarka* and does not lead to perfect realization. It is also *sa-vikalpa.* In Vedānta, however, it is all higher meditation. The third of the four stages of gaining knowledge. 91, 390, 391, 415

nidrā Sleep; the sleep *vṛtti* itself: that modification of mind which causes the sleep state to ensue or to continue. 82, 102n, 148, 361

nigamana Conclusion (a term in the Indian five-member syllogism). 159

nigraha Conscious control. 96

niḥ-śhreyasa Spiritual success; the higher goal in this and the next life; the *summum bonum.* 36

nimitta Purpose; proof; causation; efficient cause; any causative factor. 283, 402

nir-ālambana Supportless; without an object of concentration in meditation. 253

nir-añjana Unanointed. 121

nir-anumāna Performing evil acts of stupefaction. 44

nir-atiśhaya Ultimate; not exceeded (by any other); unexcelled. 295

nir-bhāsa Manifest; shining forth; illuminating; illuminative. 185, 188, 387

nir-bīja samādhi Seedless *samādhi; samādhi* without objects of concentration (*ālambanas*); *asamprajñāta samādhi; samādhi* wherein the *saṁskāras* can no longer produce *kleśhas,* karma and their fruits. 94, 146, 242, 257, 429

nirdeśha Definition. 430

nirdeśha-sūtra A *sūtra* that defines. (See also *lakṣhaṇa-sūtra.*). 94

nirmāṇa-chitta Incarnation into an individual mind (not a physical incarnation) via Hiraṇya-garbha; a mind-field specially created to serve as a vehicle of incarnation; a produced mind. 281, 288-89, 304

nirmāṇa-kāya An incarnate form (Buddhist term for the historical, physical body of the Incarnate One). 281

nirodha Control; dissolution; restraint or control of all *vṛttis* of the mind-field; dissolution of *vṛttis* into their source in the mind-field; *kaivalya;* rendering inoperative. Characteristics of *nirodha* include: no fresh impressions arise from the external world, its experiences, relationships or memories; the state of *samādhi* creates its own impressions on the soul's mental mantle; but impressions left in the mind-field from past experiences remain. *Nirodha* (total control of the *vṛttis* of the mind-field) is dependent upon *both* practice (*abhyāsa*) and dispassion (*vairāgya*). (See also *laya.*) 38, 63, 86, 93, 95-99, 115, 120, 144, 193, 195-97, 252, 426-27

nirodha-chitta The mind-field in the state of total control (*nirodha*); the mind-field in the state of *samādhi* (*samādhi-chitta*). (Antonym: *vyutthāna-chitta.*) 114n, 424

nirodha-samādhi *Samādhi* wherein *nirodha* (control) has occurred; *samādhi* of total control and final cessation of *vṛttis.* 77, 145, 257

nirodha-saṁskāras In acognitive *asamprajṇāta samādhi* the *vṛttis* have ceased; only inoperative *nirodha-saṁskāras* remain as residue, and even these "ashes" are under the yogi's total control to maintain life support if so desired. 87, 252, 427

niruddha Controlled; brought under control; that which has reached the state of *nirodha.* One of the five grounds or states of the mind-field. 62, 78, 218, 219

nir-vichāra A *samādhi* devoid of subtle thought; a *samāpatti,* which includes higher stages of *sa-vichāra samādhi,* and *ānanda*-accompanied and *asmitā*-accompanied *samādhis.* 231, 399-403, 408, 409, 411, 414, 417-18, 421

nir-vikalpa Non-discursive (awareness in the form of a *vṛtti* of *buddhi*

nir-vikalpa (*continued*)
fixed on the self's own nature [*sva-rūpa*]); free of superimposition of word, object and idea upon one another. *Nir-vikalpa* is synonymous with *nir-vitarka* and *nir-vichāra-samādhis.* 111, 389

nir-vitarka Without a gross thought; the higher stage of *vitarka*-accompanied *samādhi.* 381, 387-98, 403, 409

niṣhkriya Inactive. 175

niṣhṇāta Immersed. 7

nitya-ānanda Ever-blissful. 121

nitya-buddha The pure self who is ever awake. 364

nityam a-lupta-śhakti Power (*śhakti*) that never suffers a loss or reduction. 301

nitya-mukta-svabhāva One who is ever free by nature (i.e., *puruṣha*). 377

ni-vartaka Disinvolver; terminator; inhibitor; abstainer; abolisher; urging and prompting one away from X. (Antonym: *pra-vartaka.*) 138

ni-vṛt To turn off. 425

niyamas Austerities; stability; restraint; control; the second of the eight *aṅgas* of yoga, viz.: cleanliness and purity (*śhaucha*), contentment (*santoṣha*), ascetic practice (*tapas*), self-study (*svādhyāya*), and practice of the presence of God (*īśhvara-praṇidhāna*). 145, 197

niyama-sūtra A *sūtra* that restricts or enjoins against an act. 20

nyag-bhāva Becoming a subsidiary. 240

nyag-bhūta Subordinated. 393

nyāsa A special form of concentration on points of the body which are identified with deities, syllables, stars, etc. 366

Nyāya One of the classical Indian philosophical systems, devoting its attention primarily to the science of logic. The syllogism of the Nyāya system consists of five parts: *pratijñā* (proposition); *hetu* (cause), *dṛṣhṭānta* (exemplification), *upanaya* (recapitulation of cause), and *nigamana* (conclusion). 153, 159

OM The sound that is God's name and is identical with Him; God (īśhvara) is the signified meaning of *OM; a, u, m,* followed by the silent half mora. Brahmā, Viṣhṇu and Śhiva are signified parts of *OM.* 310, 313-14, 316, 317

padārtha (pada-artha) An object; the meaning of a word (*pada*) as denoted or signified by that word. 388

pañcha-parvā Having five segments. 167

Pañchaśhikha A disciple of Āsuri and the sage third in line among the founders of the Sāṅkhya school. He is reputed to be the author of *Ṣhaṣhṭi-tantra.* (See also *Kapila.*) 122, 123, 297, 303, 304

Pāṇini Probably history's foremost grammarian. He finalized the system of Sanskrit grammar in four thousand *sūtras* perhaps sometime between the 7th and 4th centuries B.C. 73, 74

paññā A Pāli word, similar to *prajñā* of Vedānta, meaning "wisdom" or "knowledge." One of the "three jewels" (along with *sīla* and *samādhi*) of Buddhism. Buddhists regard *samādhi* as a step to *paññā.* 88

pāpa Evil; evil way; evil result; evil act; sin; transgression. 195, 342, 349, 422

para Transcending; beyond; supreme; transcendent; of a higher kind; transcendental. 209, 212, 387

para-ātman The transcendental self. 200

parāk *See parāñch.*

parama Ultimate. 368

parama-aṇu Minutest atom. 368, 407

parama-ātman The Supreme Self; Brahman; Īśhvara. 99, 278, 300

parama-mahattva Ultimate greatness or magnitude. 368

paramārtha The highest good; ultimate nature; Brahman, the Transcendental. (From *parama + artha.*) 143, 163-64

paramārtha-satya The transcendental reality. 109

pāramārthika Relating to *paramārtha,* q.v. 163

parāñch (parāk) Turned away from (the inward self) towards distant objects (From *parā + añch.*) 322

para pratyakṣha Transcendental direct perception (of the yogis), which is the basis or seed of teaching and of the inferential process. 386, 387, 393

Parāśhara Vyāsa's father. 318

paratra Into another. In the context of *YS* I.7 *paratra* means that the teacher's *chitta-vṛttis* appear in the *chitta-vṛttis* of the student. 161

para-vairāgya The higher or transcendental dispassion; final freedom from attachments. This higher dispassion relates to the *guṇas,* to knowledge (*jñāna*) and to the means thereof. (See also *apara-vairāgya.*) 85, 108, 139, 213, 241

para vaśhīkāra Supreme mastery. 369

paribhāṣhā-sūtra A *sūtra* that gives rules for the application of other *sūtras.* 20

parikarma(n) Purification; refinement; a refining; way or act of adorning, polishing, preparing, purifying, training (the mind); seasoning, giving a final protective or enhancing touch that prevents deterioration; supportive act in any science. Cultivation of the four *parikarmas—maitrī* (amity), *karuṇā* (compassion), *muditā* (gladness), and *upekṣhā* (indifference)—enables one to stabilise the mind-field. 340, 342, 344, 351, 368-69

pariṇāma Temporary state; mutation; alteration; mutative mode. 80, 95, 100, 129, 265

pari-śhuddhi All-round and complete purification. 387, 391

parvan (parvas) Segment, section or joint, as of bamboo or any such multipart, single object. 167, 216

paryavasāna Extending up to; ending at; reaching its limit at; etc. 404

paryudāsa Negation by omission (logically not a very strong negation). 137

paśhchāt-tāpa Literally, "afterwards burning." The burning within oneself after an (evil) action; a guilt feeling; repentance. 344

pauruṣheya *Puruṣha*-originated; *puruṣha's* own. 156

phala The end result(s) obtained; fruit; goal; ultimate goal. 60, 155

phala-sūtra A *sūtra* that defines the end results, fruit, ultimate goal, etc. 115

piṅgalā The subtle energy channel (*nāḍī*) that flows on the right side of *suṣhumnā* and controls the sympathetic branch of the autonomic nervous system. 65

piśhāchas The lowest kind of demonic beings; ghoul-like beings. 104

prabandha Dam; dike. 194

pra-bhū To bring forth into being. 394

prachchhardana Expulsion; exhalation. The visceral air is slowly exhaled through the nostrils with particular care, effort and method. This is the antidote to *praśhvāsa*. (See also *ānāpāna-sati*.) 346-48

pradhāna Unmanifest *prakṛti;* principal matter. 132

pra-dyotayati Illuminates fully. 84-85

prāg-abhāva Prior absence. 395

prāg-bhāra A dam or dike (*prabandha*). Its derivative meanings include: bearing a weight or load tipping in favour of (as on a scale); carrying a momentum towards; predisposed towards. 194

Prajāpati The Progenitor, which equates to Brahmā. (See also *Hiraṇya-garbha*.) 70

prajñā Wisdom; completely realized; realization of the true nature of the objects of meditation; the process of the awakening of wisdom and the wisdom itself, as in *samprajñāta.* 219-20, 229, 264, 421-22

prajñā-jyotis Those whose light is wisdom. Yogis on the third of the four levels of yogic attainment. Along with the *madhu-bhūmika,* the *prajñā-jyotis* are yogis at the middle ground of yogic attainment. 78, 108

prajñā-prasāda Clarity of wisdom. 141

prajñā-viveka Discrimination from awakening wisdom. 264, 269

prākāmya Power by which all that one may wish can be fulfilled (a *siddhi*). 168, 283

prakarṣha Supremacy. (From *pra* [expressing "initiating" and "propelling"] plus *kṛṣh* 'to draw forth'.) 306

prakarṣha-gati Supremacy which initiates and propels the process of creation and revelation. 306-7

prakāśha Light; illumination. 109, 197

prakāśha-ātman Having illumination as its very self-nature. 412

pra-khyā Illumination (from *sattva*). 93, 102

prākṛta bandha *See prākṛtika bandha.*

prakṛti Principal, not yet evolved, primordial matter in the state of equilibrium of the three *guṇas* not yet manifest as the phenomena of the universe; *a-liṅga* (without mark or sign); the unmanifest, intangible, subtlest origin or tangible matter (nature); the existence principle without consciousness (syncretic definition); the unconscious material-energy principle (Sāṅkhya definition). In Sāṅkhya philosophy there are eight origins of evolutes, collectively called *prakṛtis: prakṛti, buddhi* (*mahat*), *ahaṁkāra* and the five *tan-mātrās* (the five subtle elements of sound, touch, form, flavour and smell). The three *guṇas* (*sattva, rajas* and *tamas*) represent *prakṛti*'s attributes, qualities, creative potential. In a state of equilibrium *prakṛti* is pure, unmanifest potential. Upon disequilibrium the *guṇas* combine in endless ways to create manifest nature. An inherent relationship between self and matter is an eternal attribute of *prakṛti.* Not to be confused with *Prakṛti* with a capital *P,* q.v. (See also *pradhāna.*) 28-30, 41, 81, 97, 105, 133, 225, 299

Prakṛti (when written with a capital *P,* as against *prakṛti*) Brahman's nature, the source of *māyā,* often identical with *māyā.* 28

prākṛtika bandha Bondage by which one identifies the self with *prakṛti* or with any of its evolutes. *Prakṛti-layas,* q.v., exemplify this bondage. 46, 289

prakṛti-layas *Prakṛti*-dissolved ones; those who are absorbed in *prakṛti* (unmanifest matter in equilibrium before creation), but have not yet reached *kaivalya.* They have mastery over pure *prakṛti* and so may create universes, etc. They are not free of the cycles of *saṁsāra,* however. 207-8, 256-58, 262-63

prakṛti-vikṛti Modifications of *prakṛti* that may be modified further. 31

pralaya Final dissolution of an effect into its cause; dissolution of the universe (the alternate of creation); partial dissolution of a universe. 133, 144, 146, 303, 391

pramā The process of proof, i.e., any valid experience; apprehension of a state, condition, fact, object or entity not heretofore obtained. The end result is mind and *vṛtti* becoming one. 151, 155, 156

pramāda Negligence; failure in the practice of *bhāvanā* (contemplation); failure to practise the six virtues (of Vedānta). 324, 327

pramāṇa Valid proof; instrument, means, method for reaching an apprehension (*pramā*) not heretofore attained. In Sāṅkhya-yoga valid proofs are *pratyakṣha* (direct perception), *anumāna* (inference), and *āgama* (revealed authority). 37, 47, 148, 149-51, 156, 373, 388, 390, 391-94

prāṇa(s) The vital energy in any living being, which is regulated by the fivefold *prāṇas,* each of which governs a particular energy flow: *prāṇa* regulates inhalation; *apāna* regulates exhalation and excretion; *samāna* regulates digestion and distribution of energy and nutrients; *udāna* regulates the upward movement of *prāṇa* (as in coughing, sneezing, and death); and *vyāna* monitors the entire nervous, muscular and skeletal systems and regulates blood flow. 43

prāṇamaya koṣha Sheath of *prāṇa* (in which the self is erroneously thought to be the agent of actions). 245, 246

praṇava The word *OM.* There are several possible derivations of the word *praṇava: pra* + the verb *nu; pra* + *ni* + *dhā* (as in *praṇidhāna*); *pra* + *ṇam; pra* + *ni* + *dha* and *av* (*praṇidhātṛs*); *pra* + *nir* + *vā,* etc. 309-10.

prāṇāyāma (*Prāṇa* + *āyāma.*) Breath and *prāṇa* control. Control types include such methods as *rechaka, pūraka, kumbhaka* and *nāḍī-shodhana prāṇāyāmas.* 331, 346-49

praṇidhāna Practising the presence; placing something near, in the proximity of, to put something down. (From *pra* + *ni* + the verb *dhā.*) (See also *bhāvana.*) 277, 279, 309, 316

pra-ṇi-dhātṛs Those who practise the presence of God. 310

pra-nir-vā To lead to *nirvāṇa.* 310

prāpti The power to reach or touch the most distant things (a *siddhi*); arrival; attainment. 168, 416

prārabdha Karma gathered from past lives, whose fruition includes: assuming of incarnation in a species; the life span destined to be in this incarnation; and the pain and pleasure ordained for the life span. 90

prasāda Clarity and pleasantness (of the mind); pleasant clearness; clarity; which suggests clear flowing water and indicates a state of happiness, joyfulness and intense pleasantness felt in the mind. 212, 215, 265-66, 411-13

prāsāda A palace. 413

prasāda-guṇa Pleasantness of character. 102

prasādana Purifying; rendering clear; making happy; making serene; pleasing; making pleasant. 340

prasajya-pratiṣhedha Negation by direct statement (against a possibility). 137

pra-saṅkhyāna Discrimination between self (*puruṣha*) and non-self (*prakṛti*); realization of the difference between matter and the spiritual self. A source of the name of the Sāṅkhya philosophy. (See also *vaśhīkāra.*) 32, 205, 210

prasanna Clear; still; suggesting the quality of clear and still water and a pleasantness of mind that results from such clarity. 183, 362

pra-śhvāsa Involuntary exhalation (the opposite of controlled exhalation [*rechaka*]); breathing out visceral air. 329, 331, 348

prāthama-kalpika Beginners at the first of the four levels of yogic attainment. 77

prati-bandhin (prati-bandhī) That which impedes, hinders, resists, opposes, checks, inhibits, blocks, prevents, annuls, etc. 419, 421

pratijñā Proposition (a term in the Indian five-member syllogism). 159

pratīpa Opposite. 322

prati-prasava Dissolution of evolutes in reverse order of their creation; effects dissolving into their causes and finally into *prakṛti;* return of the *guṇas* into equilibrium in their ultimate cause (unmanifest *prakṛti*). (See also *prati-sañchara.*) 38, 95, 146

prati-sañchara In Sāṇkhya philosophy, the principle of orderly dissolution of material evolutes into their causes in reverse order of their evolution and development (*sañchara*); dissolution of the universe and its phenomena. (See also *prati-prasava.*) 38, 42, 146

pratiṣhedha Preventing; opposing; prohibiting; negating; voiding; nullifying. 333

pratiṣhṭhā Establishing; foundation; basis. 162, 163

prati-tantra-siddhānta Principles peculiar to a given discipline of philosophy or science. 23

pratīti Cognition, as in *pratyaya.* 179

pratyabhijñā Re-cognition. 189

pratyāhāra Withdrawal of senses from their objects. 107

pratyak (pratyañch) Inward (From *prati* 'towards' and the verb root *añch* 'to be directed'; 'pointed or turned towards a certain direction'.) 320, 321-22

pratyak-chetanā-adhigama Attainment of inward consciousness; realization of the inwardly conscious (self). 320, 321

pratyakṣha Direct perception or experience (one of the valid proofs [*pramāṇas*]); it determines the specific where specific and general are present. This definition is a pointer for the implicit, complete idea of realization. True *pratyakṣha* occurs in *samprajñāta,* when a reflection of pure consciousness appears. (See also *yogi-pratyakṣha.*) 149-55, 334, 354

pratyañch *See pratyak.*

pratyastamaya The condition of *vṛttis* of the mind-field having set like the sun (submerged, ceased) into the very source from which they had arisen. 251

pratyaya An idea or experience being presented to *buddhi* so that a cognition may occur; cognition principle; causal principle of cognition; causal cognition; cognition (*pratīti*); cause; origin; that whence a cognition as an effect proceeds. 132, 178, 179, 372

pravāha Flow. 144

pravāha-anādi One who continues eternally through the cycles. 303

pravāha-chitta A flowing mind, i.e., a Buddhist concept of the mind-stream in which each successive wave gives the appearance of continuity even though there is no continuous mind but merely a succession of waves. 337

pravāha-nitya The modifiable eternal is manifested and unmanifested, appears and disappears with creations and dissolutions. 313

pra-vartaka, pra-varttaka Involver; engager; initiator; promoter; inducer; producer; instigator; urging and prompting one towards X. (Antonym: *ni-vartaka.*) 138, 423

pra-vi-laya Dissolution. (See also *pralaya.*) 391

pra-viveka Increased and strengthened discriminating wisdom. 214

pra-vṛtti Inclination; manifestation; direct perception; apprehension; a manifest natural state; a natural mental state arisen; an intense *vṛtti* of the mind-field, one that remains in concentration; a natural urge, inclination or tendency; initiative; worldly inclination; adventurousness. When a sustained concentration is such that the intense *vṛtti* and the attendant inner experience are effortless and become a natural mental inclination, that is *pra-vṛtti.* 93, 102, 197, 350, 352, 355, 356

prāyaśhaḥ As a common experience; commonly. 221

prayatna Method; effort. 200, 348

prayoga-śhāstra A text or science to teach a practical method (whereby the yogi may sunder *puruṣha*'s connection with *prakṛti*). 284

prayojana Purpose. 60

prema-bhakti-yoga Yoga of love and devotion. 92

prīti Feeling of love (with which one feels the desire "May I attain yoga" through the *āstika-buddhi*). 266

puṇya Virtue; merit; virtuousness; the virtuous and meritorious; meritoriousness; meritorious acts. 340, 342

pūraka *Prāṇāyāma* of controlled inhalation. (Antonym: *śhvāsa.*) 331

Purāṇas Ancient legends, stories, philosophies and histories; cosmological texts often couched in a mythological form. 26, 170

puruṣha The conscious principle, ever-pure, ever-wise, ever-free; the conscious being; the spiritual self; spiritual noumenon; the one in whom knowledge reaches its ultimate dimension; the omniscient one. The syncretic definition is "the Conscious Principle coupled with Existence." The Sāṇkhya definition is "the conscious spiritual-energy principle (theistic: incorporating God [Īśhvara] and souls [*jīvas*]; non-theistic: incorporating individual souls [*jīvas*])." 28-29, 42, 94, 106, 107, 109, 110, 111, 113, 212, 236, 295, 297-300

puruṣha-darśhana-abhyāsa The repeated practice of realizing and seeing the spiritual self. 214

puruṣhārtha The purpose of *puruṣha. Prakṛti* serves two purposes of *puruṣha:* involvement and disinvolvement. Having served these purposes of *puruṣha, prakṛti* withdraws. (From *puruṣha* + *artha.*) 255

puruṣha-khyāti Discernment or realization of *puruṣha.* 212

puruṣha-viśheṣha Īśhvara, the Lord; the special Conscious Being. 284

pūrva Anything past, former, anterior; preceding one; ancient; the very first one; preceding creation; predecessor gurus. 305-8

pūrva (pūrvaka) Preceded by; having as a prerequisite or precondition. 248, 264

rāga Attachment; colouration; pleasure; attraction. (From the verb root *rañj* 'to colour; to be drawn towards, to be attracted to', q.v.) *Rāga* is a *kleśha* whose real name is great stupor (*mahā-moha*). 44, 125, 137, 162, 169, 170, 191, 342

rajas A *guṇa* (attribute of *prakṛti*); activity; endeavour; energy; movement; producing pain; dust. *Rajas* impels and energizes, overcoming stagnation. (See also *prakṛti, guṇas.*) 29, 30, 42, 112, 215

rajasic jñāna Active knowledge; knowledge imbued with *rajas*. 24

rākṣhasas Demonic beings. 104

Rāma An incarnation of Viṣhṇu. 301

rañj To colour; to be drawn towards, to be attracted to. 152, 206, 359

rasa Body-fluid essence such as hormones, gastric juices, etc.; essence; juice; flavour; enjoyment. 68n, 326, 415

rasāyana(s) Derived from *rasa,* which refers to fluid esences of anything: in alchemy—mercury; in herbal medicine—juice; in the human body—all fluids. Hence *rasāyana* refers to cleansing and purification processes for rejuvenation or for spiritual objectives, etc. 68

rechaka The *prāṇāyāma* of controlled exhalation (the opposite of *praśhvāsa*). 331

ṛṣhi A sage who has reached the highest *samādhi* and who then promulgates a science, text or tradition; an enlightened sage. 3, 5

ṛta The oldest word used in the Vedas for the Supreme Truth of universal and divine laws. 414

ṛtambharā Truth-bearer; Truth-bearing; bearer of Supreme Truth. 414-15

ṛtambharā prajñā Intuitive wisdom; Truth-bearing, intuitive wisdom; bearer of Supreme Truth, Wisdom. 77, 85, 414-15, 420

rūḍhi Conventional (meaning of a word). 18

Rudra Śhiva as Dissolver. 302

rūpa Nature; form; appearance; feature. 162, 187, 218

sa-bīja samādhi Seeded *samādhi; samādhi* with seed, i.e., with objects of concentration (*ālambanas*), as with *samprajñāta samādhi,* q.v. 242, 373, 409-10

sad (sat) Existent; reality (accurately seen only by the inner self directly in concentration without the intervention of the senses, mind and *buddhi*)—this is direct perception [*yogi-pratyakṣha*]). 85

sad-bhūta Real. 84

sādhaka A spiritual aspirant. 12, 244

saha-bhū Natural accompaniment; correlate. 329

saha-kārin Associate in an act; coefficient. 336, 429

sāhasa Courage, such as embarking upon an endeavour without considering whether it can or cannot be accomplished. 200

sahasā Quickly; suddenly. 348

sākṣhāt-kāra Realization; perfect or full realization; coming face-to-face. The fourth and highest of the four stages of gaining knowledge. 154, 373, 390, 391

sālambana With supportive factors; *samprajñāta samādhi,* which needs an object of concentration; *sa-bīja,* q.v. (See also *ālambana.*) 242

sam-ā-dhā, samādhāna Resolution or harmonizing of all conflict (within and without); pacification; bringing together of all contrastive factors; resolving and reconciling. *Samādhāna* (freedom from all conflicts) is one of the six treasures of Vedānta. (From *sam* + *ā* + *dhā* 'to set together, join together [as of broken bones])'. 24, 67, 75, 251, 332

samādhi, samādhi-chitta *Nirodha;* harmony; meditation; absorption; *samādhāna;* mastery and control by the mind-field; also a Pāli word meaning "concentration" (one of the "three jewels" [along with *sīla* and *paññā*] of Buddhism). In effect the entire first chapter of the *Yoga-sūtras* of Patañjali constitutes a definition of the *samādhis* of yoga. (Antonyms: *vyutthāna, vyutthāna-chitta.*) 75-76, 82, 86-91, 108, 114n, 130, 134n, 218-47, 251, 264, 351

samādhi-prajñā *Samādhi*-wisdom. 387, 399, 402

samādhi-prārambha The beginnings of *samādhi,* as in *vikṣhipta* when *sattva* begins to gain ascendancy. 251-52

samādhi-saṁskāra Impressions of the *samādhi* being created on the mind. These impressions finally burn away even the past *saṁskāras.* 86

sam-ā-dhīyate Becomes harmonized and established in *samādhi;* the mind is free of polarities and conflicts. 269

samāhita Harmonized; conflicts resolved. (From *sam* + *ā* + *dhā.*) (See also *sam-ā-dhā.*) 332

samāna See *prāṇa(s).*

samanvaya Synthesis. 27

sāmānya General; generic; universal. (Antonym: *viśheṣha.*) 152

sāmānya-ava-dhāraṇa-pradhāna Primarily determining; chiefly the determinant of. 158

samāpanna Accomplished (as a *samāpatti*). 380, 384

samāpatti Field of command; field of coalescence; apprehension; accomplishment; encounter; transmutation; coalescence; attainment of a state of consciousness; proficiency of the mind; the mind-field dwelling on the object, becoming stable thereupon, and achieving coalescence therewith. This coalescence of the mind with the object, so that mind appears as though non-existent and only the object of concentration remains, is *samāpatti* proper. The four *samāpattis* and corresponding *samprajñāta samādhis* are:

sa-vitarka samāpatti = *sa-vitarka samādhi*
nir-vitarka samāpatti = *nir-vitarka samādhi*
sa-vichāra samāpatti = *sa-vichāra samādhi*

$$nir\text{-}vich\bar{a}ra\ \ sam\bar{a}patti\ = \begin{cases} nir\text{-}vich\bar{a}ra\ sam\bar{a}dhi \\ s\bar{a}nanda\ sam\bar{a}dhi \\ s\bar{a}smita\ sam\bar{a}dhi \end{cases}$$

(See also *samprajñāta samādhi*.) 355, 371, 373, 378, 380-81, 409

samāropa Superimposition. 127

samartha Capable; strong. 266, 353

sāmarthya Capability; intensified and increased capacity. 353, 354

samaṣhṭi-chitta Universal mind; collective mind. 299

samavāya-sambandha Inherent relationship. 288

sambandha Relationship; relationship or connection (rather than union with); the relationship of the subject matter (viṣhaya) of a text, its purpose (*prayojana*) and a student's qualification (*adhikārin*). 60, 132

sampadyate Succeeds; prospers; reaches the desired enrichment; a fulfilment in all directions; one comes to rest in the Supreme Self, becomes filled with the Supreme Self. 317

sampat Treasure. 67

sampatti Fulfilment; enrichment; perfection. 319

sam-pipādayiṣhā Desire, intent or will to achieve fulfilment. 200

samprajñāta samādhi The lower samādhi, also designated as *sa-bīja samādhi; samādhi* of wisdom; that *samādhi* in which wisdom comes to its most harmonized, perfect expansion. *Samprajñāta* requires supportive factors (*ālambanas, bījas*), objects of concentration. The nature of the *ālambanas* and the associated *vṛttis* becomes increasingly refined as the realization progresses through its four stages: *sa-vitarka* (with discursive, gross, thought), *sa-vichāra* (with subtle thought), *sānanda* (with ecstasy, rapture), and *sāsmita* (with I-am-ness). (See also *samāpatti*.) 63, 218-20, 224, 409-10

sam-prati-patti The perception of knowledge in consciousness (derivative, *yaugika,* meaning); the continuity of usage (conventional, *rūḍhi,* meaning). 313

saṁsāra Transmigration; continuous cycle of birth and death; transmigratory cycles of creation and dissolution; the worldly attractions from which the bondage of transmigration begins; worldly cycles. (Antonyms: *kaivalya, nirvāṇa, mokṣha.*) 89, 108, 167, 194, 216, 281

saṁśhaya Doubt; (the mind) oscillating between two alternatives. 164, 324, 325-26

saṁskāras Impressions; imprints. (See also *āśhaya, karmāśhaya, vāsanā.*) 99, 140, 185, 286-87

saṁskāra-śheṣha Residual *saṁskāras;* that in which *saṁskāras* alone remain as residue; where only the impressions of the past experiences and karmas remain as deposits and no fresh karma is formed. 78, 248, 250

saṁsthāna Configuration serving as foundation or substrate for attributes. 388, 396-97

samuchchhaya Combination. 303

saṁvega Vehemence; speed; velocity; force; momentum; progress. *Saṁvega* implies a strong *saṁskāra* from the past and a strong desire and will. 271, 273

samyak-jñāna Correct knowledge. 213

saṁyama Practice of the three internal limbs of yoga (*dhāraṇā, dhyāna* and samādhi) as one. 103

saṁyoga Union (a coming together of those that were separate). 132

sānanda *Ānanda*-accompanied; rapture-accompanied. (See also *samprajñāta samādhi.*) 224

sañchara Process of the development of evolutes from *prakṛti* to the gross elements. 42

sandhi A complex set of rules for euphonizing Sanskrit words, for example: *yoga* + *anuśhāsana* becomes *yogānuśhāsana.* 20

saṅghāta-vāda The aggregation doctrine of Buddhists of the Sautrāntika and Vaibhāṣhika schools. For example, according to *saṅghāta-vāda* an object such as a jar is simply a combination of uncountable numbers of atoms and not their transmuted product. There are no cause and effect relationships between the atoms and the jar. 395

sañjñā Term; definition; name. 20, 205

sañjñā-sūtra A *sūtra* that gives a definition, title, or topic. 20

saṅkalpa A positive thought or resolution. (Antonym: *vikalpa.*) 381

saṅketa Conventional usage and meaning; indication; denotation (as of a word). 387, 389

saṅketita Indicated; shown by or pointed to by a sign. 390

saṅkhyāna Permutation (a source of the name of Sāṅkhya philosophy). 32

Sāṅkhya-pravachana Enunciation of Sāṅkhya. 8

Sāṅkhya-trayī-pratipālaka "Guardian of the Threefold Sāṅkhya," a title accorded to the *śhankarāchāryas.* 39

saṅkīrṇa Mixed; mingled; commingled; alloyed. 380

saṅkrama Transitional. 212

sānnidhya Proximity. In the context of *YS* I.4 *sānnidhya* means compatibility of qualities and not time or space proximity. 132

sānumāna Performing good acts of stupefaction. 44

sārūpya Similarity; assimilation; appearance of; identification with the form of; identity. 122, 126, 128

sārva-bhauma Universal. The *samādhi* of the spiritual self remains unbroken. It is universal, *sārva-bhauma,* the common ground of all other operations of the compound personality (spirit and matter). Literally, "that which remains in all *bhūmis*" (grounds or levels of yogic achievement on the way to the highest *samādhi*). 77, 79

sarva-dharma-anu-pātin That which relates to all characteristics. 403

sarva-dharma-ātmaka That whose self-nature comprises all characteristics. 403

sarva-jña Omniscient; all-knowing. 295, 298

sarvajña-bījam Seed of the omniscient. 297-98

sarvajñatā Omniscience. 301

sārvajñya-bījam Seed of omniscience. 297-98

sarva-nirodha Cessation, dissolution or *nirodha* of all. 424

sarva-tantra-siddhānta Common principle(s) shared by all. 24

sāsmita With *asmitā; asmitā*-accompanied. (See also *samprajñāta samādhi.*) 224

sat Essence. 200

sati Pāli word for *smṛti,* q.v. The most important of the "five strengths" (*indriyas*) cultivated in the Buddhist tradition. (See also *sati-paṭṭhāna.*) 268

sati-paṭṭhāna Pāli expression for the presence of intentness and practice of mindfulness. Practice of mindfulness is perhaps the most central part of Buddhist meditation practice and includes mindfulness of body (*kāya*), emotions (*vedanā*), mind (*chitta*), and conditions (*dhamma*), as well as cultivating repeated awareness (*anussati* in Pāli), which in turn includes mindfulness of exhalation and inhalation (*ānāpāna-sati*). The practice of constant mindfulness is also taught by yogis of the Himalayas irrespective of their affiliations. 268-69

satkāra Respect; positive attitude; reverence; adoration; devotion. 202

sat-kārya-vāda A doctrine of Sāṅkhya schools stating that the qualities of objects pre-exist in their causes, that *guṇas* are constantly transmuted into their evolutes, and that a cause does not cease to be simply because it is transmuted into an effect. "That which is not, does not come into being; that which is, never ceases to be" (*BhG* II.16). (See also *a-sat-kārya-vāda.*) 29-30, 97, 133, 395

sattā-mātra Existence only (without any conditions, productions, evolutions or devolutions). 240

sattva (*1*) A *guṇa* (attribute of *prakṛti*). The *sattva guṇa* is characterized by purity, luminosity, lightness, harmony and the production of pleasure. It is the purest aspect of the three *guṇas*. (See also *prakṛti, guṇas*) 29, 30, 42, 112 (*2*) God's own essence and intelligence; the excellence of essence (being) and intelligence (knowing), the two being intertwined and the one not subsisting without the other. This *sattva* is not to be confused with the *guṇa sattva.* 283, 291

sattvic jñāna Pure, refined or luminous knowledge; knowledge imbued with the *sattva guṇa.* 24

satya Truth (one of the ten immutables in the Lord). 301

sauhārda Goodheartedness, amity, friendship. (See also *maitrī.*) 343

saumanasya Good-mindedness. (From *su* 'good, happy, harmonized' and *manas* 'mind'.) (Antonym: *daurmanasya.*) 331

sa-vichāra With *vichāra; vichāra*-accompanied *samādhi;* accompanied by subtle thought; a *samādhi* accompanied by subtle thought. (See also *samprajñāta samādhi, samāpatti.*) 224, 399

sa-vikalpa Accompanied by *vikalpa,* q.v., such as the coming and going of thoughts with resultant superimposition and lack of clarity. 386

sa-vitarka With *vitarka; vitarka*-accompanied *samādhi;* accompanied by gross thought; a *samādhi* accompanied by gross thought. Concentration in *sa-vitarka samāpatti* is invariably accompanied by the names of the objects of concentration. (See also *samprajñāta samādhi, samāpatti.*) 380, 382, 389

śhabda Word. 171, 380

śhabda-jñāna Verbal conception. 171

śhabda-jñāna-anupāti (-anu-pātin) Dependent upon a verbal knowledge (conception) only. 171, 173

śhabda pramāṇa Verbal proof; the same as *āgama*, q.v. 173

śhabda-tanmātrā Subtle element of sound, from which space (*ākāśha*) is created as the gross element. 386

śhabdena Through words; in the form of words; with the accompaniment of words. 160

ṣhaḍ-aṅgatā Constituting six complements. 300

śhakti Pure energy; potentia (potential); immutable potentia; power; force; potency; (inherent) power. 25, 109, 113, 120, 221, 301-2, 309

śhaktimān The omnipotent; he who has *śhakti;* the powerful one. 302, 317

śhama Quietude; pacification (one of the six treasures of Vedānta). 67, 69

śhānta Pacific; peaceful; calm; pacific attribute (a major personality disposition, which *buddhi* assumes in association with *sattva*). 118, 126, 199

śharīra(s) Body; the system of the three bodies: the causal body (*kāraṇa śharīra* or *liṅga śharīra*) consisting of *mahat* alone, the subtle body (*sūkśhma śharīra*), and the gross body (*sthūla śharīra*). 244, 246, 261, 262

śhās To impart a discipline or a teaching; to teach with a definite discipline. 71

Ṣhaṣhṭi-tantra *The Book of Sixty,* an ancient Sāṅkhya text now lost. 46

śhāśhvatika Perennial. 293

śhāstra Revealed teaching; scripture; "the Law"; a text taught within a tradition and with a discipline: hence the entire science of yoga is known as *yoga-śhāstra;* the eternal law which is synonymous with God's knowledge, the application of which is manifest in *kriyā-śhakti,* the power of action and creativity, by which the world comes into existence and is maintained within the Law; the revealed teaching, which is conveyed from the Lord to the individual *jīva* so that the latter may be raised and saved; the scripture itself in that verbal form which is conveyed by *jīva* to *jīva,* from teacher to disciple. 73, 283, 290, 291

ṣhaṭ-sampat The six treasures of Vedānta, constituting practices of pacification: quietude (*śhama*); restraint (*dama*); withdrawal from worldly interests (*uparati*); forbearance (*titikṣhā*); faith, humility, surrender (*śhraddhā*); and freedom from conflicts (*samādhāna*). 67

śhavāsana Corpse posture. 196

Śheṣha The curled-up snake of eternity, symbolizing *kundalinī,* upon which Viṣhṇu as Preserver sleeps at the end of an aeon. Patañjali is said to have been an incarnation of Śheṣha. 59, 60

śhiṣhya Disciple; one taught with and within a discipline. 71

Śhiva The Dissolver; Rudra, the Dissolver; the Benevolent One. 29, 300, 301-2

śhiva-yoga The yoga of Śhiva. 92

śhoka A mutation of *rajas,* e.g., sorrow, grief, pain, suffering. 358

śhraddhā One of the six treasures of Vedānta, connoting a gentle quality associated with humility, reverent faith and surrender; inclinations of faith such as generosity of mind, celibacy, charity, acts of prayer; devotion; full clarity and pleasantness of the mind-field; faith that *samādhi* is the only worthy goal and that one has chosen the way of self-realization. 43, 67, 202, 204, 265, 266, 351, 365

śhravaṇa Learning; listening to a teacher (the same as receiving knowledge from *āgama pramāṇa*); hearing the teaching. The first of the four stages of gaining knowledge. 91, 390, 391, 415

śhrotṛ Listener; student. 161

śhruta Teaching; tradition; learning; hearing; teaching received orally. 387, 416

śhruta-prajñā Wisdom received from learning or from authority. 416

śhruti Vedic texts; revealed texts; texts taught orally. 390, 394

śhuddha Pure. 429

śhuddhi Purification. 391

Śhukadeva Son of Vyāsa. 378

śhūnya Void; empty; devoid of. 121, 171

śhvāsa Involuntary inhalation; uncontrolled inhalation; *prāṇa* breathing in external air. (Antonym: *pūraka.*) 329, 331, 348

siddha One who is accomplished in the *siddhis* (yogic powers). 169

siddhis (*1*) Yogic accomplishments or so-called miraculous powers. 103, 168-69 (*2*) The eight accomplishments of Sāṅkhya philosophy (not to be confused with the yogic *siddhis*). 45

siddhi-yoga Yoga of *siddhis* (accomplishments of powers). 92

sīla Pāli word meaning "conduct"; one of the "three jewels" (along with *samādhi* and *paññā*) of Buddhism. 88

sīv To sew. 18

smṛti Memory; a *vṛtti* called memory; contemplation; meditation (*dhyāna*); awakening of *ekāgratā;* mindfulness; awareness; recollection; remembrance; intentness; presence of mind; inspired lawbooks. (From *smṛ* 'to remember'. 143, 148, 185, 264, 267-69, 351, 390, 394

smṛti-pariśhuddhi Purification of memory. 387

smṛti-upasthāna The presence of intentness (of the mind); the same as Buddhist *sati-paṭṭhāna.* 268

soham *See haṁsa-mantra.*

sopāna Rung (of a ladder). 27

sphoṭa Unitary revelation of knowledge becoming word. One of the fundamental doctrines in Indian philosophies of language, accepted by philosophers of yoga, Vedānta and grammar; disputed by the Mīmāṁsā school. 383

sphuṭa Revealed; clear. 411, 412

srashṭṛtva Creativity (one of the ten immutables in the Lord). 301

stambhana Stoppage. 144

sthiti Stasis; a product of *tamas;* stability; stagnation; veiling of the force of *saṁskāras;* heaviness; obscuration; dejection; feebleness; stillness; settling down, stabilising, coming to rest (of the mind-field); steadiness (of the mind-field); continued maintenance. 93, 102, 198-99, 350, 425

sthiti-nibandhana Stabilising and rendering the stability permanent and unshakable, making it binding and fastening it; that which effects stability of the mind; *chitta-prasādana.* 341, 347, 356

sthiti-nibandhanī The instrument of establishing, affirming, effecting, sealing, the mind's steadiness. 350

sthūla Gross. 226

sthūla-ālambana Gross object of concentration. 376

sthūla śharīra Gross body. 246

styāna Laziness; sloth; mental laziness; procrastination; mind's idleness. The mind refuses to settle down; it finds excuses, remains always distracted and refuses to work (for the *sādhaka*'s purposes). 183, 324, 326

sukha Pleasure (an inherent attribute of the *sattva guṇa*); comfort; those comfortable; acts undertaken with prayer or expectation of a comforting or pleasant result. 43, 184, 231, 340

sūkṣhma-bhūta Subtle elements (*tan-mātrās*). Not to be confused with *bhūta-sūkṣhma.* 401

sūkṣhma śharīra Subtle body. 246

sūkṣhma-viṣhaya(tva) Having subtle objects as the domain, field or object of concentration. 399, 404, 407

suṣhumnā The central subtle energy channel (*nāḍī*) that flows along the spinal column of the physical body. 65

suṣhupti The sleep state as different from or contrasted with wakefulness and dream. In references to sleep the student should determine whether *suṣhupti* as a state or *nidrā* as a *vṛtti* is intended. (See also *nidrā.*) 102n

sūtra A unifying thread; something to sew with; set of aphorisms or rules. 17, 115

sva Possession; one's own property. 122, 292

svādhyāya Study of scriptural sentences leading to liberation; the fourth discipline of the second *aṅga* of yoga (*niyamas*); silent recitation; self-study (*sva-adhyāya*) when the recitation is to oneself and not aloud; *japa* of purificatories like *OM;* the study of scriptures that lead to purification. 6, 229, 315, 318, 345

sva-karaṇa-saṁvedya Experienced directly with one's own instrumentation. 352

svāmin Proprietor; owner. 122, 292

svapna Dream. 361

svara science The science of breath rhythms. 366

sva-rūpa One's (the self's) own nature; own self-nature. 111, 114, 425

svarūpa-śhūnya Devoid of its own form, as mind appears to become in *nir-vichāra samādhi.* 387

svataḥ-pramāṇa Internally self-evident; self-authoritative. (Descriptive of texts or revelations in need of no proof external to themselves, but upon whose authority other statements may be proved.) 5

svatantratā Sovereignty. 301

svatva Possession (such as *asmitā* [I-am-ness]). 169

Svayam-bhū The "Self-Existent Being," teacher of Brahmā. 70

tad-añjanatā Achieving coalescence therewith. 371, 378

tādātmya Being identical, for example, the object in question is one that is both universal and particular, generic and specific. 153

tad-rūpa-a-pratiṣhṭham Not established in, having no basis in, the form of that (of a given object). 163

taijasa Beings with *rajasic* ego. 44

tamas One of the three *guṇas* (attributes of *prakṛti*). Its qualities are stability, stagnation, dullness, inertia, darkness, stasis, stupor. (See also *prakṛti, guṇas.*) 29, 30, 42, 112, 168

tamasic jñāna Darkened knowledge; knowledge imbued with *tamas*. 23

tāmisra Nocturnal (the real name of *dveṣha,* q.v.). 168, 169, 170

tamo-dravya The substance *tamas,* which is as real as any darkness. 179

tan-mātrās The five modifications (evolutes) of *tamasic ahaṁkāra;* the five subtle elements in the subtle body: sound, touch, form, flavour, odour. 33, 41, 168, 225, 230, 312

tantra The particular tradition or science. 296

tāntrikī paribhāṣhā A technical term within a given discipline, tradition or science. 230, 414

tanū-karaṇa Attenuation; thinning down. 421

tapas Ascetic observance, power or practice; austerity (one of the ten immutables in the Lord); reducing one's material and physical pleasures, luxuries, and the body's dependence on objects. 202, 203, 301, 345

tarka Any thought accompanied by words; logic. 382

tat-ja (taj-ja) Arising from that; produced from that. 419

tat-stha Stable on them. 371

tattva True reality; state; condition; fact; object; entity; principle; factor; reality; real element; true nature. Literally, "that-ness" (*tat-tva*); the essential nature of any object or entity. 34, 42, 103, 151, 333, 421

tattva-darśhana The realization of reality (one of the qualifications of a realized teacher). 160

tattva-jñāna Knowledge of reality. 102

tattvas The five gross elements; the final evolutes of *prakṛti;* space, air, fire, water, earth (evolved in that order). 34, 42, 366

tauṣhṭikas Those who have experienced *tuṣhṭi,* a feeling of complacency far short of the goal. 263

tejas Fire; light; illumination. 385

ṭīkā A gloss or commentary on a commentary (*bhāṣhya*) by subsequent scholars. 6

titikṣhā Forbearance (one of the six treasures of Vedānta). 67

tīvra Acute; fast; intense, as in "intense methods" (*tīvra-upāya*), and speedy, as in "speedy progress" (*tīvra-saṁvega*). 271

tīvra-saṁvega Those of speedy progress. 271

tīvra-upāya Those of intense methods. 271

tṛpti Satiety. 213, 301

tuṣhṭi Feeling of complacency; the nine complacencies (four spiritual and five external); philosophical complacency. 45, 258, 263

ubhaya koṭi Both of two possible categories simultaneously. For example, a pendulum touches only one *koṭi* at a time but a string is tied to both *koṭis* simultaneously. 369

udāna *See prāṇas.*

uddeśha Name and title. 430

uddeśha-sūtra A *sūtra* that states the subject of a text or portion thereof. 21, 61

upabhoga Enjoyment. 261

upadeśha The teaching of one's guru; a teaching. 266

upādhi A superimposed condition, not an inherent attribute or state; a temporary condition; a condition external to the intrinsic nature of an object or entity. 118, 374

upa-jana Increase or growth in strength. 344

upa-kāra Benefit (conventional, *rūḍhi,* meaning); service (derivative, *yaugika,* meaning). (From *upa* 'near' and *kāra* 'to do', connoting "to act in a certain way by mere presence.") 131

upa-karaṇas Instruments. 214

upalakṣhaṇa Example; pointer; indicator. 102, 154

upanaya Recapitulation of cause (a term in the Indian five-member syllogism). 159

upa-rāga Being drawn towards; being attracted to; the process of being coloured by, where colouring refers to *vṛttis* produced in the mind from external sources. (From *upa* 'near' and *rañj* 'to colour, to be attracted to'.) 149, 151, 152, 154

upa-rakta That which is drawn towards or coloured by. 187, 359

upa-rama To turn the *vṛttis* off. 250

upa-rañj To be coloured by something by reason of its proximity. (See also *upa-rāga.*) 187, 399

uparati Withdrawal from worldly interests (one of the six treasures of Vedānta). 67

upasarga Encumbrance. 323

upa-śhama Pacification; extinguishing; blowing out or snuffing out (as of a flame). 98

upāshraya Proximate object; serving as a support or source of conditioning through proximity. 372

upa-ṭīkā A supplemental gloss on a gloss; a subcommentary. 6

upāyas Means; instruments or methods of obtaining the desired ends (of a science). *Upāya* incorporates not merely the concepts of method and techniques but also attitudes of mind and a philosophy of life for one who desires liberation. (See also *upāya-pratyaya.*) 257, 265

upāya-pratyaya A *samādhi* whose causal cognition cultivated through method accrues to true yogis, yielding knowledge of exact reality (*yathārthaṁ vastu*). The methods (*upāyas*) may be mild, moderate or intense with respect to the following constituents: faith (*śhraddhā*), strength (*vīrya*), intentness (*smṛti*), mental harmony (*samādhi*), and discrimination from awakening wisdom (*prajñā-viveka*). 256-58, 260, 263, 265

upayoga Use. 261

upekṣhā Indifference; equanimity. 213, 340, 344

utpannā (utpanna) Born; appeared; occurred; became manifest; an advent having taken place. 350

utsāha Enthusiasm; perseverance; fortitude; firmness; exertion; vigourous pursuit; zeal. 200

vāchaka Signifier; signifying word or name; that which enunciates; that which signifies. 309, 317-18

vāchya That which is enunciated; that which is signified. 317-18

vaikārika Beings with *sattvic* ego. 44

vaikārika bandha Bondage by which one becomes attracted to the celestial pleasures (as the *videhas* do) or by which a renunciate may be drawn to the ordinary worldly attractions. 46, 290

vaikṛta bandha (vaikṛtika bandha) *See vaikārika bandha.*

vairāgya Dispassion and control over desires for worldly or other-worldly pleasures; state of being devoid of, free from, attraction (*rāga*) to objects reflecting into and colouring the mind; renunciation; disinterest in the world (one of the ten immutables in the Lord). *Vairāgya* (dispassion) and *abhyāsa* (practice) are the sine qua non of achievement on the yogic path. (See also *rāga.*) 45, 91, 101, 105, 193-97, 205, 206, 212, 301, 336

vaiśhāradya Proficiency and purity; the mind's firmness in its stability; that stream of concentration (stable flow) that receives and reflects the clearly reflected image of the entire whole as well as the particular aspects of the object of meditation. 411-12

vaitṛṣhṇya A state of being free of all craving; a pure state of self-knowledge. 212, 216

vārttika An aphoristic statement that takes into account stated, unstated-but-implied, and difficult-to-understand points of an original *sūtra.* 9

vāsanā Imprint of actions (*saṁskāras*) left in the mind (the inclinations that the strength of *saṁskāras* produce) and the inclinations or propensities towards like maturations (*vipāka*) that develop in the mind. *Vāsanās* lie dormant in the mind until maturity of karma. (See also *āśhaya.*) 133, 138, 216, 286-87

vāsanā-yoga The yoga of directing hidden propensities. 92

vaśha Control. 211

vaśhīkāra The fourth and highest order of *vairāgya;* the final stage of *apara-vairāgya,* characterized by total and supreme control or mastery. Herein one develops dispassion even towards the final attraction, however faint, which may accrue to the realization of the distinction between self and *prakṛti.* The *vaśhīkāra* dispassion indicates a wholly stabilised mind of total neutrality. 205, 206, 209, 210-11, 213, 341, 342, 351, 354, 368-70, 372

vaśhitva Control over all elements and beings; ability to create, rearrange or dissolve them (a *siddhi*). 169

vastu External substance; real object; a reality. 151, 171, 264, 400

vastu-śhūnya Devoid of substance, substantiality or a real object. 171

vāyu Air. The word *vayu* is sometimes used for the *prāṇas,* q.v. 43

vedanā Emotions (a Pāli word). 268

vedanā-moha Confusion of feelings and emotions, wherein one does not even know what is painful or pleasant to oneself. 192

vi-bhajyamāna Being divided and separated. 380

vi-bhakta Distinct; divided and separated. 380

vibhu All-pervading. 356

vichāra Rational thought; subtle thought; contemplation; movement of mind from gross objects to subtler objects of concentration (*vitarka* refined becomes *vichāra*). (From *vi* + *char:* 'progressive movement'.) (See also *sa-vichāra.*) 160, 218, 224, 229, 391

vichāra-anugata A *samādhi* accompanied by (*-anugata*) subtle thought (*vichāra*); *sa-vichāra,* q.v. 224

vichāra-moha Confusion of thought processes. 192

videha Bodiless even while dwelling in the body; the individual yogi who has attained dissolution of the mind-field into original *prakṛti* (a

videha (*continued*)
stage in the process of liberation). The *videha* state by itself is not the *Yoga-sūtras'* definition of *kaivalya* or *asamprajñāta*. Yogis who, after abandoning the physical body, continue to maintain the body constituted of *mahat, ahaṁkara* and mind are called *videhas*. Others say *videhas* maintain the *liṅga* body (*mahat*) only. 146, 207-9, 232, 257-61

videha devas Bodiless, shining gods; bodiless, shining ones. (See also *videha*.) 256, 259

videha-kaivalya The state of becoming bodiless even when dwelling in the body. *YS* I.19 clearly considers the *videha* state to be significantly lower than *kaivalya* (final isolation). (See also *videha*.) 146, 261

videha-mukti One who is liberated while yet dwelling in the body. (See also *videha*.) 146

vidhāraṇa Restraint; control; expansion; the stretching or expanding of the visceral air, maintaining it outside—not a quick or sudden intake. *Vidhāraṇa* is the antidote to *śhvāsa* (involuntary or uncontrolled inhalation). 346-48

vidhi Order; ordinance; system. 301

vidhi-sūtra A *sūtra* that enjoins an act. 20

vidyā Knowledge, proficiency in the tradition, texts, and particularly the systematic method of practice. 202, 203

vidyā-snātaka One who has graduated in a science, i.e., mastered a science. One of the three types of graduates (along with *vrata-snātaka* and *vidyā-vrata-snātaka*) in the ancient *āśhramas*. 72

vidyā-vrata-snātaka One who has proficiency in a field of learning and has demonstrated the mastery of personal disciplines. One of the three types of graduates (along with *vrata-snātaka* and *vidyā-snātaka* in the ancient *āśhramas*.) 72

vijñāna Ideation; idea. 336, 426

vijñānamaya koṣha Sheath of knowledge (wherein an assumption of delimited knowledge accrues). 245, 246

vijñāna-vāda A Buddhist theory of "ideation only," whereby no external objects exist except as they are ideas within a universal idea (*ālaya-vijñāna*). 336

vijñāna-vādin One holding the *vijñāna-vāda* view (*darśhana*), not accepting the independently real existence of perceptible objects in a phenomenal world. 158, 336

vikalpa Imaginary cognition; linguistic misconception; false cognition; option; alternation; alternative imaginary cognition; alternative negative thought; superimposition; fiction. 143, 148, 164, 171, 380-86, 394

vikalpita Imagined; fictitious; processed as a *vikalpa.* 171, 177, 392

vikāras Products; modifications; evolutes of *prakṛti;* categories of reality consisting of sixteen evolutes (the eleven *indriyas* and five *bhūtas* or *tattvas*). Also called *vikṛtis.* 29, 31, 41

vikṛtis *See vikāras.*

vikṣhepa Distraction of the *sattvic* mind by *rajas* and *tamas;* the nine impediments (*YS* I.30) and their five companions (*YS* I.31); obstacles. 83, 103, 204, 324-29

vikṣhepa-saha-bhū Correlates or accompaniments of *vikṣhepas.* 329

vikṣhipta Distracted; the distrcted state (one of the five grounds or states of the mind-field) wherein the mind is afflicted by *vikṣhepas* (distractions of the *sattvic* mind by *rajas* and *tamas*). Although it is a modification of and some improvement on the agitated *kṣhipta* state, a *vikṣhipta* mind-field is not fit to be included within the category of yoga since *samādhi* may occur only intermittently and in short bursts. (See also *chitta.*) 62, 78, 83, 105, 329-32

vi-laya Dissolution; dissolving. 96

vi-ni-vṛt To withdraw. 425

vipāka(s) Ripening (like a fruit), fruition of actions (derivative [*yaugika*] meaning). The *vipākas* are (*a*) the species (*jāti*) in which one is reborn, (*b*) one's life span (*āyus*), and (*c*) pleasant or painful experiences (*bhoga*) during the life span. 256, 282, 286

vipākāśhaya Domain or storehouse of *vipākas,* q.v. (From *vipāka* + *āśhaya.*) 287

viparyasta-pratyaya Inversion of awareness, i.e., turning the inward consciousness outward and not dwelling in the seer's own nature. 140

viparyaya Perversive cognition; false perception; false cognition; having no substance; false knowledge; misapprehension; perversive perception; confusion of philosophies; ignorance, which is of five kinds: *avidyā, asmitā, rāga, dveṣha, abhiniveśha.* 44, 105, 127, 143, 162-70, 190, 325

vīra A brave hero. 267

virakta Dispassionate; one who has reached *vairāgya.* 212, 213

virāma Cessation; absence of all *vṛttis;* causal awareness of the absence of all cognition. 248-50

virāma-pratyaya Awareness; the transcendent dispassion; that by means of which one attains the transcendent dispassion; that cognition (*pratyaya*) by which cessation of *vṛttis* occurs in *a-samprajñāta.* *Virāma-pratyaya* equates to *para-vairāgya.* 248-50

virāma-pratyaya-abhyāsa   Practice of the cognition of cessation of *vṛttis*. 248, 250

Virāṭ   Cosmic Immanent form of the godhead (an example of which may be seen in *BhG* IX, X, XI); the universe-form of God. 221, 227

virāṭ-puruṣha   Shining space-person; a being of godlike attainments. 369

vīrya   Virility; vigour; strength; energy; potency; the qualities of a hero; capacity to initiate; seminal strength of a celibate; endeavour with regard to the eight *aṅgas* of yoga. 199, 264, 266-68, 351

viṣhāda   Depression (the mind clouded with *tamas*). 82

viṣhaya   (*1*) Subject matter of a text. 60 (*2*) Subject or object of experience, e.g., the subject of a memory as the object of a past experience; domain; subjects; matters; objects of enjoyment; internal object; sense object; field or object of thought; worldly objects. (See also *viṣhayavatī*.) 185, 186, 194, 205, 213, 356, 359, 373, 389

-viṣhaya   In relation with; with regard to. 340

viṣhayavatī   Having sense objects; having sense experiences; having objects of experience. *Viṣhayavatī* are of two forms. The lower form operates within the realm of the subtle senses, elements, objects; and the higher form operates in the realm of internal objects (*viṣhayas*), which are constituted of the light of *sattva*. One of the two *viṣhokā samāpattis*, the manifestation of luminosities relative to objects in *buddhi*. (See also *viṣhaya*.) 350, 355-58

viṣhayavatī pravṛtti   Advent of direct perception of the experiences of subtle or celestial sense objects. 350

viśheṣha   Specific; particular; individual; distinction. (Antonym: *sāmānya*.) 153, 275, 388, 416

viśheṣhas   Elements within the subtle body. The *viśheṣhas* are distinct, specific forms of matter (the final sixteen products of *prakṛti*): five gross elements, five active senses, five cognitive senses and the mind (*antaḥ-karaṇa*). 35, 224-28, 352

viśheṣha-artha   Having a special purpose, aim or significance. 416

vi-śhiṣhṭa   To be possessed (of); to be distinguished by; to be qualified by. 419

Viṣhṇu   The Preserver. 301-2

viśhokā   Beyond grief; free of grief or suffering. 78, 355

viśhokā jyotiṣhmatī   The luminous or lucid one; the one without grief and luminous, experienced at two levels: (*1*) as *viṣhayavatī*, involving experiences of lights and radiances as in a clear sky; and (*2*) as *asmitā-mātrā*, involving reflection of *puruṣha* like an infinite, calm ocean (without the lights as in *viṣhayavatī*). 355-58

viśhva-bhedas Diversities of the universe, such as the forms of manifold objects. 376

vīta Devoid of. 359

vīta-rāga One who is devoid of attachment; one who is part of the guru lineage, starting from Hiraṇya-garbha, and whose mind has perfected *vairāgya* (highest dispassion); a saint; a disembodied master who helps aspirants. 359

vitarka Gross thought; thought accompanied by the names of the particular objects of concentration. (See also *sa-vitarka.*) 218, 382

vitarka-anugata A *samādhi* accompanied by *vitarka; vitarka*-accompanied; *sa-vitarka,* q.v. 224

vitṛṣhṇa One who has lost a craving, been turned away from a craving, or is free from a craving; one who is indifferent. 205, 206, 209

viveka Discernment; discrimination; discriminating wisdom; the spiritual self. 193, 195-96, 210, 214, 264

viveka-khyāti The separation of *buddhi* from *puruṣha;* discriminating wisdom; the discernment by the *buddhi* of the distinction between itself and the spiritual self (*puruṣha*). This discernment arises in the fourth stage of *samprajñāta* when the mind-field and *buddhi* are centered upon themselves. This is a quality, not an entity. 107-8, 135-36, 303

vividiṣhā The desire to know matters relating to spirituality, especially the conscious principle. 43

vi-yoga Separation. 75

vrata-snātaka One who has demonstrated mastery of personal disciplines. One of the three types of graduates (along with *vidyā-snātaka* and *vidyā-vrata-snātaka*) in the ancient *āśhramas.*72

vṛtti(s) (*1*) Operations, activities, fluctuations, waves, modifications (of the mind-field); mental state. *Vṛttis* are fivefold—*pramāṇa* (valid proof), *viparyaya* (perversive cognition), *vikalpa* (imaginary cognition), *nidrā* (sleep), and *smṛti* (memory)—and of two types—*kliṣhṭa* (painful [imbued with *kleśhas*]) and *akliṣhṭa* (not painful [not imbued with *kleśhas*]). A secondary meaning of *vṛtti* is "means of livelihood," as in "*vṛttis* are the mind-field's means of livelihood." 38, 63, 93, 98, 122, 135, 148, 178 (*2*) Commentary by a disciple that is a word-for-word explanation of (e.g.) a master's *sūtra.* 6

vṛtti-sārūpya Identification with the form and nature of *vṛttis.* 122

vyādhi Illness; the imbalance of body constituents (*dhātus*), body juices (*rasas*), and the eleven senses (*karaṇas*). 324, 326

vyākhyāta Defined; explained. 399

vyāna *See prāṇas.*

vyapadeśha Designation; predication; the relationship of qualification with the qualified. 174

vyatireka Deduction (logic); ascertainment. 152, 209-10

vyatireka dispassion The second *vairāgya,* i.e., ascertainment of where one stands and what yet remains to be done en route to *para-vairāgya.* 209-10

vyavahāra Usage; practical application; efficacy; practical transaction. 173, 388

vyavahāra-paramparā Continuity of usage. 313

vyutthāna To get up, as from meditation, and to be wandering about; the mind's wandering from meditation; getting up, being away from meditation; worldly disturbance; non-meditative; absence of concentration; worldly involvement (of the mind). (Antonym: *samādhi.*) 114, 117, 126, 202, 251-52, 419-20, 428

vyutthāna-chitta The mind-field involved with the ordinary world (in act or thought); absence of concentration, as in *kṣhipta* and *mūḍha.* (Antonyms: *nirodha-chitta, samādhi-chitta.*) 114

vyutthāna-saṁskāras *Saṁskāras* of worldly involvements. 202

Yājñavalkya, Yogi Famous metaphysician whose name appears frequently in the Upaniṣhads. 69

yamas Restraints; the first of the eight *aṅgas* of yoga: non-violence (*ahiṁsā*), non-lying (*satya*), non-stealing (*asteya*), control of passions, senses and mind (*brahmacharya*), and non-attachment (*aparigraha*). 145

yantra A visual (symbol or design) concentration for each *chakra* following tantric norms. 365

yatamāna The initial effort. 209

yatamāna dispassion The initial effort en route to *para-vairāgya:* learning what is of essence and what is not; uprooting the mind from attractions; understanding the nature of freedom from craving; inhibiting the senses from being drawn to worldly objects; and reducing desires. 209

yathā-abhimata As agreeable; as desired; as favoured; as object of choice. 365

yathārthaṁ vastu Exact reality. 264

yatna Endeavour; effort. 198

yatra-kāmāvasāyitā *See kāmāvasāyitā.*

yaugika Derivative (meaning of a word). 18

yoga Yoga is *samādhi* (and that *samādhi* is a universal attribute of the mind-field). Yoga is the control of the modifications (*vṛttis*) of the mind-field (*chitta*). Yoga is that *nirodha* which leads to the seer's remaining in his own nature totally and permanently. "Yoga is skillfulness (*kauśhala*) in actions (karmas)" (*BhG* II.50). The word *yoga* may be derived from the Sanskrit verb *yuj* (4th conjugation), meaning *samādhi*, or from *yujir* (6th conjugation), meaning *samādhi*, or from *yuj* (10th conjugation), meaning "to join, restrain, keep under control as in yoking." The primary meaning was probably *samādhi*, but there is much use of the sense of uniting, joining, yoking, in Vedic and Upaniṣhadic literature. For purposes of the *Yoga-sūtras* it is reasonable to accept Vyāsa's statement that the word *yoga* means *samādhi* and that *samādhi* is a universal attribute of the mind-field. 60-61, 73-92, 93, 119, 286

yoga-bhraṣhṭa One who has fallen from the path of yoga. 325

yoga-nidrā Yoga sleep (when the Lord rests after dissolution and before the next creation); conscious sleep. 293, 364

yoga-śhāstra The science of yoga. (See also *śhāstra, anu-śhāsana*.) 73, 348

yoga-yantrita Controlled by yoga. 254

yoga-yukta One who is joined to God in yoga. 99

yogi One who practises yoga, q.v.

yogi-pratyakṣha The supremely valid proof. During *samprajñāta* without externals there appears a reflection of the pure consciousness, *chiti-śhakti:* this is direct perception (*yogi-pratyakṣha*). Reality (*sad, sat*) is accurately seen only by the inner self directly in concentration without the intervention of the senses, mind and *buddhi:* this is the yogi's direct perception (*yogi-pratyakṣha*). (See also *pratyakṣha*.) 85, 154-55, 354, 418

yogyatā Compatibility. 132

yuj *Yuj* from *yujyate* means "practises *samādhi*"; *yuj* from *yunakti* also means "practises *samādhi*"; *yuj* from *yojayati* means "joins, restrains, keeps under control (as in yoking)." With the blending of oral tradition, philosophy, common parlance and other factors the fine distinctions of meaning have been blurred by time. The significant thing is, however, that irrespective of the verb of origin, Vyāsa has said that yoga is *samādhi*. (See also *yoga*.) 73-74

the Himalayan Institute

GLOBAL HEADQUARTERS (USA)

The main building of the Himalayan Institute headquarters near Honesdale, Pennsylvania, USA.

FOUNDED IN 1971 BY SWAMI RAMA, the Himalayan Institute has been dedicated to helping people grow physically, mentally, and spiritually by combining the best knowledge of both the East and the West.

Our international headquarters is located on a beautiful 400-acre campus in the rolling hills of the Pocono Mountains of northeastern Pennsylvania, USA. The atmosphere here is one to foster growth, increase inner awareness, and promote calm. Our grounds provide a wonderfully peaceful and healthy setting for our seminars and extended programs. Students from all over the world join us here to attend programs in such diverse areas as hatha yoga, meditation, stress reduction, ayurveda, nutrition, Eastern philosophy, psychology, and other subjects. Whether the programs are for weekend meditation retreats, week-long seminars on spirituality, months-long residential programs, or holistic health services, the attempt here is to provide an environment of gentle inner progress. We invite you to join with us in the ongoing process of personal growth and development.

Programs and Services *include:*

The Institute is a nonprofit organization. Your membership in the Institute helps to support its programs. Please call or write for information on becoming a member.

Programs and Services Include:

- Himalayan Institute Press
- Seminars and Workshops
- Meditation Retreats
- Yoga Teacher Training
- Self-Transformation Program™
- Residential Programs
- Pancha Karma
- Himalayan Institute Total Health Products and Services
- Spiritual Excursions
- Humanitarian Projects and Community Centers in Africa, India and Mexico
- YogaInternational.com

For further information about our programs, humanitarian projects, and products,

call: +1 800-822-4547

e-mail: info@HimalayanInstitute.org

write: The Himalayan Institute
952 Bethany Turnpike
Honesdale, PA 18431

or visit: www.HimalayanInstitute.org

HIMALAYAN
INSTITUTE®
INDIA

THE HIMALAYAN INSTITUTE INDIA is a beacon of practical wisdom and an indispensable guide for sincere spiritual seekers. Its main mission is to promote the wisdom of the Himalayan Tradition through publication of a wide range of titles on yoga, meditation, spirituality, and holistic health. Himalayan Institute India is headquartered in Allahabad (U.P.), at its 30-acre campus on the banks of the Ganga.

The Himalayan Institute Press has long been regarded as the resource for holistic living. We publish books that offer practical methods for living harmoniously and achieving inner balance. Our approach addresses the whole person—body, mind and spirit—integrating the latest scientific knowledge with ancient healing and self-development techniques. As such, we offer a wide array of titles on physical and psychological health and well-being, spiritual growth through meditation and other yogic practices, as well as translations of yogic scriptures.

Himalayan Institute Press Titles

Swami Rama

The Royal Path: Practical Lessons on Yoga .... ₹295
Wisdom of the Ancient Sages (Mundaka Upanishad) .... ₹295
Yoga and Psychotherapy .... ₹495

Pandit Rajmani Tigunait, PhD

From Death To Birth (Understanding Karma and Reincarnation) .... ₹295
Inner Quest: Yoga's Answers to Life's Questions .... ₹350
Lighting the Flame of Compassion .... ₹250
Sakti Sadhana (Tripura Rahasya) .... ₹350
Sakti: The Power in Tantra .... ₹350
Seven Systems of Indian Philosophy .... ₹350
Swami Rama of the Himalayas (Photobiography) .... ₹2500
Tantra Unveiled (Seducing the Forces of Matter and Spirit) .... ₹295
The Himalayan Masters: A Living Tradition .... ₹295
The Official Biography of Swami Rama of the Himalayas .... ₹395
The Power of Mantra & The Mystery of Initiation .... ₹295
The Pursuit of Power and Freedom: Katha Upanishad .... ₹295
The Secret of the Yoga Sutra: Samadhi Pada .... ₹695
Touched By Fire .... ₹395
Why We Fight .... ₹195

Books by Other Authors

Anatomy of Hatha Yoga, David Coulter PhD .... ₹695
Freedom From Stress, Phil Nuernberger, PhD .... ₹350
God, Swami Veda Bharati .... ₹295
Happiness: The Real Medicine, Blair Lewis .... ₹295
Healing the Whole Person, Swami Ajaya, PhD .... ₹295
Moving Inward: The Journey to Meditation, Rolf Sovik, PsyD .... ₹395
Philosophy of Hatha Yoga, Swami Veda Bharati .... ₹250
Spirit on the Move, Yoga International .... ₹295
The Muscle Book, Paul Blakey .... ₹250
The Practical Vedanta of Swami Rama Tirtha, Edited by Brandt Dayton .... ₹495
The Theory and Practice of Meditation, Rudolph Ballentine, M.D., Swami Rama .... ₹295
Yoga: Mastering the Basics (Photobook), Sandra Anderson & Rolf Sovik .... ₹995
Yoga Psychology (A Practical Guide to Meditation), Swami Ajaya, PhD .... ₹250
Yoga Sutras of Patanjali, Swami Veda Bharati .... ₹895

Hindi Titles

Anandmaya Jeevan Ka Utsav, Swami Rama .... ₹150
Himalaye ke Siddha Yogi: Sri Swami Rama (Shiksha aur Sadhana), Pandit Rajmani Tigunait .... ₹150
Himalaye ke Santo ke Sang Niwas, Swami Rama .... ₹295
Janam Mrithyu ka Rahasya (Kathopanishad), Swami Rama .... ₹125
Karam Bandhan se Mukti, Swami Rama .... ₹95